Risk Sharing, Risk Spreading and Efficient Regulation

T.V.S. Ramamohan Rao

Risk Sharing, Risk Spreading and Efficient Regulation

Springer

T.V.S. Ramamohan Rao
Indian Institute of Technology Kanpur
Kanpur, Uttar Pradesh, India

ISBN 978-81-322-2561-4 ISBN 978-81-322-2562-1 (eBook)
DOI 10.1007/978-81-322-2562-1

Library of Congress Control Number: 2015944074

Springer New Delhi Heidelberg New York Dordrecht London

Printed on acid-free paper

Springer (India) Pvt. Ltd. is part of Springer Science+Business Media (www.springer.com)

Dedicated to the generous presence of the Goddess Saraswati

Preface

A large proportion of economic exchange, even in predominantly market-oriented economies, utilizes contracts as the major institutional mechanism. Contracts are, in most cases, with independent agents outside the firm. There will be information issues, transaction cost considerations, risk sharing in several directions, issues related to control, and fixed cost considerations that define the nature of contracts. Almost invariably some fixed assets, such as technology and know-how, physical or financial capital, brand name and reputation, and/or the characteristics of information, underlie the specific contract under consideration. Coase initially identified transaction cost advantages. Spot contracts, or onetime exchanges, probably correspond to this closely.

Given the cost advantage of contracts over the market mode, there is always a possibility that contract execution will increase costs so long as the market does not supplant such contracts. Different agents may have different propensities to create inefficiency. But, given the market for the product of the contract, they tend to create significant variations in profits of the principal. Hence, diversification of production through contracts increases the variability of profits for the principal. Some efficient regulation by the principal may be conceptualized, but the variability will persist.

Over time, risk sharing emerged as an altogether different reason for any form of contracts. In essence there is an acknowledgment that some randomness is endogenous to all imperfect product markets. For instance, an automobile assembler may find the recovery, of fixed costs of full vertical integration, to be too risky once the assets are sunk. He may prefer subcontracts with outside agents who willingly make investments in such idiosyncratic assets. The agents, in their turn, may feel that the contracts reward their risk taking adequately. This is the essential precondition for contracts to materialize. Variability of demand may add to randomness in costs as a factor that prompts firms to enter into contracts with outside agents. Hence, two issues need careful analysis: Can the risk-sharing phenomenon preserve the transaction cost reduction that Coase emphasized? How can risk spreading be regulated?

Note that in case the transactions are conducted on the market, the necessity for information is low (because the price signal contains all the requisite information), and the participants provide all the requisite information completely and truthfully. For, competitors will prevail if they fail to do so. By way of contrast, self-interest-seeking outside agents may benefit from hiding information and/or not fulfilling the promises they make. This is more generally the case in spot contracts. However, it may persist even in long-term contracts. This suggests the possibility of adverse selection (choosing an agent who may not be the best choice) and/or moral hazard (the agent not delivering promises). For all practical purposes it may be claimed that depending on an agent results in agency costs, which are now internal to the contracting parties, in contrast to transaction costs as construed by Coase and Williamson. Many studies on contracts consider these as the major risks.

Once it is acknowledged that risks can be shared by contractual arrangements, it is axiomatic that both the principal and the agents will have the propensity to augment risks and engage in a larger volume of transactions not necessarily commensurate with the overall profitability of the enterprise. For all practical purposes their own self-interest-seeking behavior may overshadow the need for stability of the entire enterprise. Such shortsighted behavior and its long-term consequences may get to be acknowledged only when they reach catastrophic proportions. Anticipating such negative effects the agents may signal their suitability, their willingness and ability to comply with contract terms, and/or their understanding about sharing risks. Similarly, the firms (or principals) may devise mechanisms of monitoring, control, and incentives to ensure compliance. Both sides tend to make sure that risk sharing is along the lines stipulated in the contract.

Residual risk persists despite the best possible precaution on both sides. One of the sources may be the market (or any other) dimensions not under the control of the contracting parties. The most important example is that of agriculture tenancy where the output delivered by the tenant may be predominantly determined by weather conditions not under his control. Another context of this nature is related to health insurance. For, neither the insurance company nor the insured (the potential patient) has any control on the likely prescription of the physician when the insurer needs treatment. Similarly, both the firm and its franchisees may expect to succeed in a given location. But the market reaction may be quite the opposite even if the contacting parties operate at their maximum efficiency and in conformity with their agreement. The second source is the residual loss due to adverse selection and/or moral hazard. Such risks are internal to the design and execution of the contract.

Another aspect of behavior has come into prominence. Suppose markets are the predominant form of transactions. Given the efficient costs of operation, the nature of demand will place limits on output to maximize profits and/or assure positive profits. However, in their greed to surpass rivals, each firm tends to emphasize the market share and cross these limits. In their quest to augment market shares, firms may also produce goods of lower quality that tend to fail well before the durability stipulated. The market demand may be reduced once this behavior is discovered. They will not be able to repay their loans. A similar behavior on the part of financial institutions may induce them to subprime lending. This phenomenon leads to the kind of financial crisis experienced in recent times.

Will the switch to contracts reduce such risks? In the contract mode each of the participants may feel that their own losses, if any, are a small part of the loss to the firm. Basically the risk-sharing arrangements generate greater risks by spreading risks. This propensity to risk sharing in all markets, including the financial markets, has the origins of a financial crisis. In other words, risk sharing will emerge as another dimension of greed of the contracting parties.

Some studies suggest that a risk-averse agent tends to take action to modify his behavior. Similarly, the principal may create an atmosphere (monitoring) to suggest to the agent that his risks can be kept under control. Preventive maintenance of durables, deductible insurance, and sharing costs are examples of this nature. Risk reduction arrangements may be embedded into the analysis of risk sharing. This will have important implications for contract design and execution.

Efficient regulation, either by the participants in a contract or outside regulatory agencies, examines several means of ensuring the lowest possible cost of conducting transactions as well as enabling efficient risk sharing and minimizing the losses that arise due to risk spreading.

The principal agent models emphasize these fundamental dimensions of contracts. They tend to place a significant emphasis on the agent's participatory constraint (the conditions under which the agent can be drawn into the contract). In other words, these models postulate that both the agent and the principal can enforce their efficient choices on contract design. Several observed empirical contexts appear to suggest that contract design is dominated by the agent's choice rather than that of the principal. This is in contrast to the expectations of the transaction cost logic.

Several empirical studies have been designed to test the principal agent models in various practical contexts. Limitations of data haunt these studies. However, the more important difficulty is with respect to the appropriate econometric methods. One chapter of this book proposes a new technique to estimate all the parameters of principal agent models in various settings.

Three fundamental weaknesses of the principal agent models have come to light. First, the specification of agency costs lacks a proper theoretical justification. Many approximate, but useful, specifications persist. Second, the participatory constraints may be conditioned by the monopoly power of one participant. Such monopoly power may be simply a result of the contracting parties becoming specific to the transaction and increasing their mutual dependence once they are locked in. Third, there is an inadequate acknowledgment of the risk-spreading phenomenon and its control. In particular, much more attention is necessary to examine asset and/or cost sharing mechanisms in case of premature dissolution of a contract. Hence, some empirically observed contracts may not be efficient though the principal agent model postulates this.

Despite some limitations much progress has been made in the specification and implementation of principal agent problems in a variety of practical contracting contexts.

They offer very valuable insights into the contracting process. The chapters in this book are organized along the following lines: generation and transfer of scientific and technological knowledge, cost sharing and its control implications, regulating some aspects of quality by using warranties and insurance, examining the risk-spreading propensities of securitization and ratings, implications of the use of foreign institutional investors and other financial instruments, and the emergence and control of financial crisis. In the final analysis contracts may add to inefficiencies that they are expected to reduce when supplanting the market mode. That is, contracts give rise to many more sources of inefficiency though they are expected to improve market performance when they supplant it. Any verdict on the expected net effect appears quite premature. Though by no means exhaustive, this study offers a synthetic presentation of the various issues involved. My contention is that all the chapters in this book have new results not found elsewhere in the literature.

Almost all my earlier published work in this area reprinted here corresponds to the logical sequence of the implications of the principal agent models alluded to above. In Chap. 1 a detailed account of some significant variants of the principal agent models has been offered. It also highlights the consequences of individual greed in markets as well as its persistence in contracts. Regulatory policy, that is, perforce applicable to contracting individuals of various talents and predispositions, must be uniform for all parties. A brief outline of how this can be made to materialize is also presented. Chapters 2, 3, 4, 5, and 6 highlight various dimensions of knowledge transfer, risk sharing, and risk spreading. Chapter 2 emphasizes the empirically observed fact that conference presentations and research publications spread risks and mediocrity instead of efficiency. Chapter 3 highlights the emergence of risks in a patent regime and how contracts are necessary to provide intangible knowledge that patent specifications do not provide. Concerns of appropriability inhibit private organizations from undertaking certain types of otherwise socially desirable innovations. This chapter recounts how government-sponsored R&D offers a way out. The risks associated with the absorption of public scientific R&D in private firms will receive attention. Chapters 4, 5, and 6 then pursue the widespread phenomenon of technology transfer across international boundaries and financial arrangements that make it possible. This opens the issue of cost sharing and sharing fixed assets ex ante as well as post dissolution of contracts. These issues receive attention in Chap. 7. One dimension of risk spreading is the reduction of quality of products consequent on risk-sharing contracts and the adverse selection and moral hazard that they generate. Warranties and insurance are contract forms that attempt to contain such risk spreading. Chapters 8 and 9 outline several pertinent issues in these contexts. The pursuit of greed by private contracting parties will clearly be limited by market liquidity and availability of finances. The financial markets conceptualized and created many instruments, including securitization and derivatives, to increase the necessary liquidity. While this may improve cost reduction and efficiency, they also sow seeds of risk spreading. Foreign institutional investors, and the hot money that they provide, add to the risk spreading. Chapters 10 and 11 examine this aspect in detail and offer some results regarding efficient regulation. Financial crises, especially created by financing subprime assets resulting from enterprises taking undue risk, could not be avoided. Chapter 12 therefore describes such an extreme form of risk spreading and analyzes possible efficient regulation and the role of government-sponsored bailouts in such a context. Chapter 13 then takes up the issue of the empirical content of these models and their practical applications. It describes the difficulties in obtaining the necessary data and estimation procedures. A novel approach to estimation is also suggested.

Though these chapters cover a vast ground, many related issues did not receive the attention they deserve. Chapter 14 makes an attempt to put these issues in proper perspective. On the whole the studies presented here highlight the shifting emphasis in contracts from Coasian transaction cost saving to risk sharing, how it creates difficulties associated with risk spreading and offers a few, though inadequate, mechanisms of efficient regulation.

Many individuals contributed to my understanding of the principal agent models. Their observations on many chapters of this book have been very helpful. In particular, I appreciate the permission from Dr. Ruchi Sharma who consented to reprint three of our papers on international joint ventures. I also acknowledge the support of my wife, Krishnaveni, who made it a lot easier to sail through retired life. Further, I wish to record my appreciation and sincere thanks to all members of the editorial team of Springer India Pvt Ltd for their cooperation in the publication of this book. I encountered many occasions in which I had very little idea about how the issue I was confronting could be resolved. Invariably an idea occurred in a flash (call it intuition if you wish), and all my listeners/readers appreciated the innovative idea. I therefore dedicate this work to the gracious presence of the Goddess Saraswati.

Hyderabad, India
January 2015

T.V.S. Ramamohan Rao

Contents

About the Author

T.V.S. Ramamohan Rao has a PhD from the University of Southern California, Los Angeles. He was a professor at the Indian Institute of Technology, Kanpur, from 1978 until 2007. He also taught at the University of Southern California, California State University at Long Beach, and at the Kansas State University, Manhattan. He was a visiting professor at the University of Pennsylvania, Philadelphia, and the University of Alberta, Edmonton. Dr. Rao published extensively in the areas of microeconomic theory, industrial organization, and econometrics.

Chapter 1
Introduction

Abstract Initially contracts have been considered as a mechanism to save on transaction costs. However, over time they have come to be regarded a result of the need to share risks. Risks can be either exogenous to the contracting parties or generated by them (endogenous). In particular, information asymmetry creates adverse selection and exogenous randomness while endogenous randomness is due to moral hazard. The principal agent models essentially contain a formal characterization of risk sharing in contracts towards its efficiency. There is an acknowledgement that such sharing results in a propensity to take up more risky transactions and spread them to more individuals in various forms. Mature individuals are expected to regulate their activities and contain risks within acceptable bounds. Individual greed may however lead to systemic risks which are beyond their control. Efficient regulation must be conceptualized to move the system back to stability.

1.1 Contracts

Contracts are a major mechanism for conducting transactions.[1] They occur more often than market relations even in a predominantly market oriented economy. The basic justification for the choice of contracts to conduct transactions was set out in Coase (1937, 1960). In general, markets are imperfect and there is significant product differentiation. Hence, a consumer must incur search costs before making any purchase decision. The resulting price plus the transaction cost may exceed the cost at which the desired product can be obtained through a contractual relation. This may be generally valid even when all the costs implicit in contracts including those resulting from information asymmetry and asset specificity, are taken into account.

Specificity of the agent in repeated exchange over time facilitates reduction in transaction costs. The basic reasons may be the trust and compliance generated in repeated transactions, learning by doing, saving in capital costs, and so on. That is, repeated exchange over time reinforces this advantage. This is the crux of the transaction cost argument.

[1] The recent book by Bolton and Dewatripont (2005) contains details of contract design. However, they did not deal with the details of the principal agent models.

T.V.S.R. Rao, *Risk Sharing, Risk Spreading and Efficient Regulation*,
DOI 10.1007/978-81-322-2562-1_1

On the downside, every contract necessarily generates an agency relationship. Essentially, it implies that the two parties in the exchange are now specific to each other. Further, their talents and assets may have no value outside the contract. Information asymmetry is at the apex of this relationship. Some adverse selection and moral hazard are bound to occur. Agency cost notions capture the effect of this problem quite naturally.[2] The primary concern of contract theory[3] is in devising mechanisms to minimize this contractual hazard while preserving the advantages alluded to by Coase.

A different justification for contracts has aspects of randomness as the primary source. In particular, there may be exogenous randomness. For, due to contingencies external to the contracting parties, the desired level of output may not materialize (failure at the stage of regulatory approvals or field trials may add to this problem), market conditions may not enable the principals to achieve the expected revenue and so on. Similarly randomness may be endogenous or intrinsic to the operation of the contract. In particular, confronted with the choice among many agents the principal may make a wrong choice. This results in adverse selection and will have the effect of increasing costs and/or make the output achieved random. There is always a possibility that even efficiently chosen agents reneg and thereby render the output random.

Similarly, the competition for a greater share of the market may result in the principals producing more output than that can be sold. When all contracting parties indulge in such greed there is a possibility of crisis at a larger level. The agents may incur some costs to convince the principal of their bonding (fulfilling commitments efficiently) or the principal accepts certain costs of monitoring and control to make sure that the moral hazard is kept to a minimum. Irrespective of whether adverse selection and/or moral hazard are prevalent the output achieved in the contract will be random. The variance may be moderated by the actions of the principals and/or the agents. The achievement of cost reduction is relegated to the back stage when this aspect is emphasized in the design of mechanisms. In fact, it is obvious that the minimum possible cost of delivering the promised output is almost never realized. This signals possible inefficiency. Regulatory mechanisms, when put in place, try to achieve efficiency for almost all configurations of the variance. This has been a challenging task.

---

[2] Jensen and Meckling (1976) is the most influential specification of agency costs. On the other hand, Williamson (1988) contains a succinct exposition of the distinctions between transaction costs and agency costs.

[3] Note that vertical integration and circumventing the market lead to contracts within the firm. The labor market literature predominantly deals with this. Contracts with agents outside the firm, e.g., subcontractors, franchisees etc., is equally dominant. The first set of studies is closer to the transaction cost argument of Coase while the latter are more concerned about agency costs. They also differ with respect to the duration of contracts. The present study concentrates mostly on the second type of contracts.

The principal agent models essentially contain a formal characterization of this aspect[4] of randomness. Obviously, the objectives of the principals and the agents can vary with the contracting context. This is also true with respect to the instruments available to them. Consequently, a rather rich theoretical literature has been built under the rubric of principal agent models.

Seminal theoretical developments are at least 30 years old and can be traced to Mirrlees (1974) and Holmstrom (1979).[5] However, the work of Kawasaki and McMillan (1987) (KM hereafter) has influenced many recent studies. Each of the variety of applications developed in this framework, has its own distinct features. They enrich our experiences with the design and use of principal agent models.

Generally, as Datta and Radner (1994, p. 483) observed, "a notable feature of many real life principal agent contracts is that they specify simple compensation rules, i.e., they identify only a small set of contingencies on which a reward is conditioned." Basically, such a choice is a result of three types of costs of implementing contracts: costs of communicating with the agents, costs of obtaining information about output, profit etc., and the costs of computation (and the convenience of the principals) while implementing complex payment schemes stipulated in the contract. See, for instance, Ferrall and Shearer (1999). The most common contract in many practical contexts is a fixed upfront payment plus a share of output. Given this empirical reality, the linear quadratic models, of the KM type, provide the most satisfactory theoretical basis. The entire analysis in the following chapters utilizes this simplification.

Section 1.2 outlines the basic arguments involving risk sharing by the contracting parties. Several variations on the theme have been presented in Sect. 1.3. The nature and role of fixed assets will be the theme of Sect. 1.4. Such contracts involve risk spreading in addition to risk sharing. This has been highlighted in Sect. 1.5. Section 1.6 then outlines some pertinent aspects of the efficient regulation of such contracts.

1.2 Risk Sharing

Consider the context of a firm, e.g., an automobile assembly plant that subcontracts the production of various parts. Here, conventionally, the subcontractor is the agent and the automobile assembler is the principal.

---

[4]The literature on mechanisms design is rather extensive. Many useful concepts of efficient contract design are discernible. The principal agent model is one among the several alternatives. To the extent I am aware of it no formal comparisons, among the alternatives, has been attempted so far. The basic reason is that the econometric problems involved in such an enterprise are formidable. The reader may refer to Masten and Saussier (2002) for a review of econometric studies dealing with the choice of markets versus contracts.

[5]Though somewhat dated, the early exposition by Rees (1985a, b) contains very useful insights about the principal agent models.

The KM model may be structured in terms of the output that the assembler assigns to the agent. Assume that the contract is for an output y. For simplicity, it will be assumed that y is revenue as well. Let the assembler undertake the production on his own. Suppose he incurs a cost $y^2/2\varepsilon$. He will choose an output y to maximize

$$\pi_p = y - y^2/2\varepsilon$$

That is, the optimal choice of y is ε. The profit generated is $\varepsilon/2$.

Now suppose the principal assigns the job to the agent. The agent spends an amount $y^2/2\delta$ while planning production. In this formulation δ is the efficiency of the agent. Clearly, $\delta > \varepsilon$ is necessary for this arrangement to be efficient.[6] The actual output achieved, say y_a, depends on the agent's actions. Three possibilities, or some combination of these, must be acknowledged. First, purely due to external conditions beyond the control of the principal and the agent, it may not be possible to achieve y. Second, information asymmetry may result in adverse selection, i.e., choosing an agent who is not necessarily the most efficient. This may inhibit the expected y being achieved. Third, post contract the agent may reneg on the promises and involve the principal in lower output. Of course, favorable outcomes may not be ruled out either.

Hence, the principal agent model captures these three effects by postulating that the actual output y_a may be

$$y_a = y + u$$

where u is a random variable with expected value $E(u) = 0$ and variance[7] $V(u) = \sigma^2$.

The basic form of the contract is a payment $p(y + u)$ to the agent. That is, he is made to share the risk. A larger p provides him greater motivation to do better.[8] The profit of the agent is then written as

$$\pi_a = p(y + u) - y^2/2\delta$$

The fundamental assumption of the KM model is that the agent is generally risk averse. That is, his valuation of π_a will be

---

[6] Two aspects of this specification should be noted clearly. First, that the principal would spend more to achieve the same result. It is not possible to justify delegation to the agent otherwise. Second, the cost reduction y must exceed $y^2/2\delta$. For, otherwise, there is no point in entrusting the job to the agent.

[7] No specific effort, to categorize randomness as external to the contracting individuals or endogenous to their functions, has been discernible expect when some specific details have been incorporated.

[8] As the model implies σ^2 is a constant independent of p. Hence, it would be necessary to clarify the form that this improvement takes. An obvious approach is to make σ^2 a function of p.

$$v_a = py - y^2/2\delta - \lambda p^2\sigma^2$$

where λ is a measure of his degree of risk aversion.

The KM model then recognizes that the agent must make the investment $y^2/2\delta$ whatever may be the p that he will eventually receive. But, he is not sure about the y_a that can be achieved. Consequently, the agent's first priority is not about the fraction p that he can recover. Instead, the agent is more likely to choose y to maximize v_a.[9] Such a choice of y is clearly[10]

$$y = p\delta$$

Consider the return to the principal next. It is given by

$$\pi_p = (1-p)(y+u)$$

In the simplest version of the model it is assumed that the principal need not incur any costs. Further, the firm will be dealing with many such contracts. Hence, it can balance the losses in any one transaction against gains from another. It can be surmised that the firm will be risk neutral. Hence, the value to the principal is

$$v_p = (1-p)y$$

However, he is expected to take the following aspects into account.

For all practical purposes, $y^2/2\delta + \lambda p^2\sigma^2$ is the opportunity cost, to the principal, if he has to accept the burden of producing parts on his own. The principal reckons that the costs would be higher if he produces y on his own. It is this transaction cost argument that prompts him to assign the production to the agent in the first place.

That is, from the perspective of the firm, the net value of the contract is $N = va + v_p = y - y^2/2\delta - \lambda p^2\sigma^2$. Surely, the firm must take the incentive constraint

[9] Two aspects of this specification should be noted clearly. First, that the principal would spend more to achieve the same result. It is not possible to justify delegation to the agent otherwise. Second, the cost reduction y must exceed $y^2/2\delta$. For, otherwise, there is no point in entrusting the job to the agent.

[10] In this formulation u may be purely exogenous. In such a case, an agent who is made to share risk feels that he is being punished for something he did not do. There is then a possibility that he will reduce y if σ^2 increases. This was noted in Borenstein et al. (2007). Alternatively, Baker (2006) suggested the following. The agent may use more resources and incur greater costs, given his risk aversion, in order to be sure that he may deliver the promised output. This can also give rise to the possibility that y depends on λ and/or σ^2. However, note that in this formulation it is independent of σ^2 ex ante given p. Ex post p will depend on σ^2 and hence the observed y is not independent of σ^2. By way of contrast, based on some experimental evidence, Sloof and vanPragg (2008) noted that y does not depend on σ^2 even ex post. Some basic adaptations will be necessary to replicate this result in principal agent models of this vintage.

of the agent into account. That is, $y = p\delta$ must be acknowledged. Hence, it follows that

$$N = p\delta - p^2\delta/2 - \lambda p^2\sigma^2$$

Note that the output and revenue generated are beyond the control of the firm since it does not wish to interfere directly in the production activities of the agent. Consequently, the only choice available to it is p. Maximizing N with respect to p it follows that

$$p = \delta/\left(\delta + 2\lambda\sigma^2\right)$$

This is the basic structure of the KM model.[11]

1.3 Some Variants

The following alternative arrangement between the principal and the agent is quite plausible in many contracts.

(a) An automobile manufacturer may subcontract specialized parts. He may then specify the quantity he wants from the agent, the quality and technological standards that must be maintained, and consequently the cost that the agent should expect to incur.
(b) Consider a franchise contract. The franchiser has every reason to make efforts to preserve his brand name and reputation. For, this is the only thing that he is selling. Hence, from his point of view, it is necessary that the franchisee preserves the brand value. He then specifies the volume to be produced and the costs that the agent should expect.
(c) In the context of road building contracts the principal (say, a municipal authority) specifies the number of kilometers of the road to be built and the approximate cost that they are willing to accept. However, in general, the contractor is expected to bear the cost in the first instance.

The possibility that the agent may not generate the entire expected y is at the apex of the likely default that the firm envisages. It would therefore be logical to expect the principal to make the choice with respect to output y given a value of p. However, the agent must make an investment $y^2/2\delta$ prescribed by the principal. Hence, the agent would be more concerned about recovering his costs whatever the market conditions may be. This depends crucially on the choice of p.

[11] Clearly, delegation would be beneficial whenever

$$\varepsilon < \delta^2/\left(\delta + 2\lambda\sigma^2\right)$$

Clearly, these contexts imply that the agent chooses p and the principal defines y. For, now, the agent would like to have control over the recovery of his investment by choosing p. Reconsider the maximization of

$$v_a = py - y^2/2\delta - \lambda p^2\sigma^2$$

This results in

$$p = y/2\lambda\sigma^2$$

Similarly, the N can now be written as

$$\begin{aligned} N &= y - y^2/2\delta - \lambda p^2\sigma^2 \\ &= y - y^2/2\delta - y^2/4\lambda\sigma^2 \end{aligned}$$

Maximization with respect to y yields

$$y = 2\delta\lambda\sigma^2/\left(\delta + 2\lambda\sigma^2\right)$$

But, as before, the ex post p would still be

$$p = \delta/\left(\delta + 2\lambda\sigma^2\right)$$

This variant may be superior in such contracting contexts.

For the sake of completeness, note that some contracting contexts have a slightly different structure.

(a) Consider the context of an innovator who has a new patented idea that can be commercialized. However, it is generally impractical and expensive for him to pursue the innovation through the many stages of the commercialization process staring from scientific knowledge to the wealth generating end product. The innovator therefore transfers the innovation to a firm that specializes in translating knowledge to commercially viable technology and a marketable product. The innovator, however, acknowledges that his work may not result in the expected output post commercialization. The firm is subjected to some risk and hence the innovator agrees to share the realized output or revenue.

(b) In the context of land tenure contracts the principal bears the costs of cultivation and land reclamation for fear that the agent may not have the resources to do an efficient job. The landlord may also specify the nature of the crop and its volume that he expects the tenant to deliver.

(c) A firm employs several workers and managers. The firm, or its board of directors, specifies the output to be produced and also incur costs. The managers and workers get a compensation for their work.

(d) Firms generally employ advertising agents. The agents suggest the pattern of efficient advertising. The firm decides the nature and quantum of advertising and bears the costs.

Let the return to the innovator be

$$\pi_a = p(y+u)$$

As before, u may be a result of the firm's actions. The innovator exhibits risk aversion because he has the alternative of pursuing commercialization on his own. Hence, the value of π_a to him is

$$v_a = py - \lambda p^2\sigma^2$$

In a basic sense the risk aversion is a manifestation of the lack of resource base (inability) and/or unwillingness to bear the entire risk. When the innovator transfers the rights of use of his discovery to the firm he has no control on output y. Instead, he would be interested in making sure that he receives a proper share of the value generated from its use. That is, the author chooses p to maximize v_a. This optimization results in

$$p = y/2\lambda\sigma^2$$

In its turn, the firm receives a profit

$$\pi_p = (1-p)(y+u) - y^2 2\delta$$

It should also be noted that the principal is incurring all the costs in this variant of the KM model. The basic departure, in relation to the previous context, is that δ now represents the efficiency of the principal. However, as before, since the firm can diversify its risks by undertaking commercialization of many such innovations, it will be risk neutral. Hence, the net value to the firm is

$$v_p = (1-p)y - y^2/2\delta$$

The first priority of the firm is not about how much it wishes to pay the innovator. For, it should be in a position to realize y in the first instance. Hence, it can be expected that it would be more worried about the choice of y.

It can also be claimed that its entire profit generation is dependent on the existence of the innovator. Hence, it must take the value to the innovator into account in its decision process. Consequently, it can be expected that the firm maximizes

$$N = y - y^2/2\delta - \lambda p^2\sigma^2$$

keeping the incentive constraint of the innovator in perspective. This choice results in

$$y = 2\delta\lambda\sigma^2/\left(\delta + 2\lambda\sigma^2\right)$$

as one would expect.

Another variant of the principal agent model is relevant in practice. The basic characteristics of the variant can be detailed as follows.

(a) Consider the context of warranties and insurance. When the agent makes a claim it is the principal who bears the costs. However the realization of failure and the costs of providing the service depend on the actions of the agent. Hence, unlike the previous case, δ will be an efficiency parameter of the agent.
(b) A patient (a principal) approaches a doctor (an agent) for treatment. Usually the physician defines the nature of the treatment and the costs that the patient must incur. Such costs depend on the efficiency of the agent.
(c) A movie producer contracts with an actor. The actor may be in a position to bargain for payments that the producer must incur. However, note that the principal is never sure of the marketability of the movie produced.

Consider the gain to the agent given by

$$g_a = p(y+u)$$

The value he now assigns will be

$$v_a = py$$

Similarly, the gains to the principal are

$$g_p = (1-p)(y+u) - y^2/2\delta$$

and, being risk averse, he assigns a value

$$v_p = (1-p)y - y^2/2\delta - \lambda(1-p)^2\sigma^2$$

The principal defines y to maximize v_p. Consequently,

$$y = (1-p)\delta$$

The net value of the contract is

$$N = y - y^2/2\delta - \lambda(1-p)^2\sigma^2$$

So that the optimal choice of $(1-p)$ will be

$$(1-p) = \delta/(\delta + 2\lambda\sigma^2)$$

For all practical purposes this is the obverse of the cases considered earlier.[12]

[12] It would be reasonable to suggest that the labels principal and the agent are for analytical convenience only. Their functional roles determine the nature of the contract.

Note that the principal may just as well be interested in his share of y rather than y itself. For instance, the firm may choose the warranty offered rather than expect to control the extent of failure of the product necessitating repairs.

Conceptually, the parameter δ may be a characteristic of an outside agent like a credit rating agency or a regulator. Consider the context of a firm issuing bonds to raise finances. The ease with which it can raise finances, or the costs that it will incur, will depend on credit ratings. Similarly, when the quality of products sold on the market is strictly regulated the probability of failure and the costs incurred in restoring defective products will go down. The characterization of the principal agent model is invariant except for the interpretations noted here.

In general, it should be noted that there are several (a) sources of randomness, and (b) efficiency considerations and sources in defining the agency costs. A rich variety of principal agent models emerge.

Note that the entire argument so far assumed that the randomness is endogenous, i.e., it is in the nature of moral hazard. However, it was noted earlier that it may be purely exogenous and market related. The agent may be reluctant to share the risk. But his income will perhaps be reduced significantly if the principal must bear all the risk. Some sharing may then be efficient. The KM model may be modified as follows.

Let the market price per unit of y be $(p_y + v)$ where $E(v) = 0$, and $V(v) = \sigma_v^2$. We will assume that there is no moral hazard. That is, the output y is achieved with certainty. Hence, the gain to the agent is

$$g_a = p(p_y + v)y - y^2/2\delta$$

and hence his valuation will be

$$v_a = pp_y y - y^2/2\delta - \lambda p^2 y^2 \sigma_v{}^2$$

Assume that the agent chooses p. The choice is

$$p = p_y / 2\lambda \sigma_v^2 y$$

The net value of the contract is

$$N = p_y y - y^2/2\delta - \lambda p^2 y^2 \sigma_v^2$$

Hence, the optimal choice of y is

$$y = p_y \delta$$

Substitution in the expression for p results in

$$p = 1/2\delta\lambda\sigma_v^2$$

Unlike the previous case, a more efficient agent will receive a smaller share of revenue. For, the costs due to his risk aversion increase with δ. That is, the principal is made to bear greater risk.[13]

1.4 Fixed Payments

Many observed contracts involve fixed payments. On occasions they may be supplemented by sharing revenues. Pure sharing contracts are relatively rare. The following examples are representative.

(a) Low skilled workers, or those who do not have much risk bearing capacity because they have weak wealth positions, prefer to be paid fixed wages. Only at higher levels, like the managers and technical staff involved in innovative activity, tend to be paid a share of revenue or profits in addition to the fixed salary. Shareholders, on the other hand, get a share of profits alone in the form of dividends.

(b) Traditionally, artists, like actors in movies or TV serials and singers, ask for an upfront payment. Only in recent times, when the risks of their products failing on the market have gone up, we witness a shift to a fixed payment plus a share of collections at the box office.

(c) The owner of the premises of a commercial establishment generally claims a rent upfront rather than accept a share of revenue from the business conducted from his premises. One of the reasons for this may be the costs of monitoring and verification.

(d) On occasions the agent's performance may have to be judged on the basis of two or more interrelated aspects. For example, the quantity and quality of products may be important. For, a worker may reduce quality in a hurry to fulfill quantitative commitments. If the contracts cannot be made a function of both for whatever reason, firms prefer to make fixed payments. Contracts proportional to only one of these dimensions make the agents choose lower levels of the other.

In general, fixed payments may be a part of the contract whenever one or more of the following conditions hold.

(a) The agent, or the principal, requires a minimum income to allow his continuation in the contract. A share contract, based on the skill of the agent, may be inadequate.

(b) The agent may incur some fixed costs in the process of fulfilling contracts. Share contracts may be insufficient to recover these fixed costs.

---

[13] In the standard model a more efficient agent reduces the costs of production as in this case but the costs due to his risk aversion do not depend on y or δ *a priori*.

(c) The risks may be rather large. As in the KM model, a risk averse agent is generally paid a lower share of output. This, in itself, rather than his skill level may be the reason for a lower share and not having enough income to survive.
(d) The agent, like a subcontractor or a movie artist, contributes only a part of the final output and the revenue generated from their final output. He may be unwilling, or unable, to calibrate his own contribution to the total revenue that they are expected to share. This will induce him to ask for a fixed payment.
(e) When quality and quantity of output are both important it may be far more economical to make a fixed payment rather than incur disproportionate costs of monitoring quality.
(f) Random events, like the failure of a crop, may necessitate the landlord making a fixed payment to the tenant. In some cases, this is in the form of a loan instead of a fixed (and non-refundable) payment.

These, and related issues, can now be examined sequentially. Return to the efficient choice of p in the basic KM model. It is obvious that

$$p = \delta / \left(\delta + 2\lambda\sigma^2\right)$$

will be low if either δ is small and/or $\lambda\sigma^2$ is large. Under these circumstances the y and the agent's share may be insufficient for his maintenance if there is no other source of income or initial wealth.

Observe that

$$\begin{aligned} v_a &= py - y^2/2\delta - \lambda p^2\sigma^2 \\ &= p^2\delta/2 - \lambda p^2\sigma^2 \geq 0 \end{aligned}$$

if and only if $\delta \geq 2\lambda\sigma^2$. The value of δ can be modified if a minimum v_m is necessary. This suggests the following. Suppose $\delta < 2\lambda\sigma^2$. The agent would be compelled to seek a fixed wage w and accept $p = 0$. Similarly, for any given δ, if $2\lambda\sigma^2 > \delta$ the same problem arises. When $v_m > 0$ is postulated, three possibilities arise.

(a) $\delta < \delta_m$. The agent chooses $p = 0$ and an upfront payment v_m.
(b) $\delta_m < \delta < \delta_M$. The agent asks for some fixed payment to reach the value v_m.
(c) $\delta > \delta_M$. The share contract is efficient. Fixed payments are not necessary.

Consider the possibility that the agent claims a fixed payment W in addition to the share of output. The value, of the contract, to the principal will then be $v_p = p(1-p)\delta - W \geq 0$ if and only if

$$W \leq p(1-p)\delta$$

This defines the upper limit on the fixed wage payment that the principal will accept. From a practical standpoint this suggests that the agent may offer a fixed rent to the principal and will accept the entire risk if he is highly efficient and/or the risk is low.

The case where the agent incurs a fixed cost is analogous. For, suppose F represents such a fixed cost. Clearly, the value of v_a will now be

$$v_a = p^2\delta/2 - \lambda p^2\sigma^2 - F \geq 0$$

only for some combinations of δ and $\lambda\sigma^2$ given F. In general, values of δ_m and δ_M exist such that

(a) If $\delta < \delta_m$ the agent asks for an upfront payment.
(b) If $\delta_m < \delta < \delta_M$ the agent seeks an upfront payment in addition to a share in output.
(c) The share contract is sufficient to recover F if $\delta > \delta_M$

For all practical purposes, this argument is analogous to the minimum bills (or multi-part tariff) arguments in the context of market exchange.

Clearly, the efficient choice of contract parameters varies with the details of a situation. Many other variants will be presented in the sequel.

1.5 Spreading Risk

The specification of the principal agent models in the previous sections exclusively emphasized the risk generated in the process of delivering the output expected and did not explicitly consider the nature of the market demand and the randomness in specifying the costs of defining and execution of contracts. However, it should be quite clear that there will be risks in product markets. Coupled with the attitudes of the principals, perhaps prior to entering the contracts for production, the end result of the performance of the firm may be random. The first important issue for analysis is to identify the sources of risk spreading from the behavior of principals.

To reduce the analysis to the basics let both the demand and the cost of production be deterministic. Denote by y the level of output of the firm. Suppose it it is produced at a cost

$$C(y) = 16 + y^2$$

Let the price per unit sold be 10. Clearly, the profit for the firm is

$$\pi = 10y - y^2 - 16$$

The following results are obvious.

(a) The level of output y_c that can be produced most efficiently (i.e., at the lowest cost per unit of output) is 4.
(b) The minimum output at which $\pi = 0$ is $y_b = 2$.
(c) The profit maximizing level y_m is 5.

(d) The sustainable level, i.e., the highest value of y_s, for which $\pi = 0$, is 8.
(e) When $y > 10$ even the variable costs cannot be recovered and the firm is in deep financial crisis. Even the capital assets would have lost their market value.
(f) Any output beyond $y = 4$ implies a higher cost of production. Hence, it can be expected that the firm will increase the price per unit of y.

Clearly, restricting y to the sustainable level is one sure way to ensure that financial risks do not arise. Monitoring this is quite simple if the regulator obtains a profit and loss account of enterprises regularly. Alternatively, the financial institutions may be required to monitor. More pertinently, it should be clearly stated that enterprises, which exceed the sustainable level, will not be eligible for any sort of bailout or a government subsidy if a crisis were to occur even in circumstances beyond the control of firms. Such a policy eliminates both adverse selection and moral hazard.

It appears that enterprises have indeed targeted $y > 8$, may be even $y > 10$ purely due to their greed to improve their market share to gain an advantage over rival firms in the long run. The policy debates are converging on the opinion that financial bailout and credit policy should restore y to the pre-crisis level. This is entirely unwarranted. For, clearly, the crisis cannot be abated by pursuing this course since such greed is the primary reason for the occurrence of risk initially.

Is there any scope for designing efficient regulatory policy in this framework? First, fiscal action in the form of grants may be conceptualized to restore $y > 10$. This is highly undesirable since it has the seeds of the next financial crisis waiting to happen. Second, suppose the crisis is so deep that the production level is below 2. Enterprises are unable to cover parts of variable costs. A subsidy in the form of a fiscal incentive, i.e., at no cost to enterprises, will become essential to revive the firm. For, any form of credit expansion by the monetary authority will still be quite expensive for the enterprises to bear. Fiscal action must be withdrawn as soon as y is greater than 2. Regulatory policy should offer credit at a reasonable rate. This may continue until $y = 5$ or may be even until 8. However, when $y > 4$ the firm tends to increase prices. Note that $5 < y < 8$ corresponds to pushing sales to a level where some less than satisfactory sales is taking place. In common parlance there is an accumulation of non-performing assets. Regulatory policy should take this seriously.

It is therefore clear that the entire sustainable range is the domain of efficient regulatory policy. This reflects the choices that the consumer is willing to support. For the present it should be noted that the greed of the enterprise is the basic reason for the emergence of risks and randomness.

Consider the context where the risks are related to the delivery of the expected level of output. The simplest specification of σ^2 in Sect. 1.2 may be entirely due to such randomness. Note that the value of the contract to the agent is

$$V_a = \delta^2 \left(\delta - 2\lambda\sigma^2\right)/2\left(\delta + 2\lambda\sigma^2\right)^2$$

Consequently, an agent will agree to participate in the contract only if $\delta \geq 2\lambda\sigma^2$. Further, it can be readily verified that $\partial V_a/\partial\delta > 0$ when $\delta \geq 2\lambda\sigma^2$. That is, whenever the agent is more efficient, compared to the minimum $\delta = 2\lambda\sigma^2$, he will obtain positive profits. This suggests that the principal should set $p = ½$ in the absence of information about the efficiency of the agents. Such a mechanism enables agents to self-select so as to avoid adverse selection. They are also likely to avoid reneging once they enter the contract for fear of losing the value of V_a otherwise possible. However, note that $\partial V_a/\partial\lambda\sigma^2 \geq 0$ if and only if $3\delta \leq 2\lambda\sigma^2$. In other words, for any given δ, large values of $\lambda\sigma^2$ will render the agent worse off.

Consider the value of the contract to the principal

$$V_p = 2\delta^2\lambda\sigma^2/\left(\delta + 2\lambda\sigma^2\right)^2$$

It can be readily verified that $\partial V_p/\partial\delta \geq 0$ for all $\delta \geq 0$. Note, further that $\partial V_p/\partial\lambda\sigma^2 \geq 0$ for all values of $\delta \geq 2\lambda\sigma^2$. For all practical purposes for the entire operating range of the contract the principal prefers increasing σ^2. This signals risk spreading in the process of risk sharing. As noted above, this will not be beneficial to the agent.

As before define the net value of the contract as

$$N = V_a + V_p = \delta^2/2\left(\delta + 2\lambda\sigma^2\right)$$

so that

$$\partial N/\partial\lambda\sigma^2 = -\delta^2/\left(\delta + 2\lambda\sigma^2\right)^2 < 0$$

The dominant partner, viz., the principal, is likely to pursue his own self interest and increase risks. This results in greater volatility in the agent's gain as well as that of the contract. There will be greater chances of failure of the contract whenever he cannot sustain his role. Risk sharing results in the principal spreading the risks to others and contains seeds of a likely crisis.

The principal may agree to share a part of the costs. This will enable lower talented individuals to enter the contract but cannot reduce the risk spreading nature of the contract. This will be the case even if the principal reduces σ^2 by monitoring the market environment more efficiently.

1.6 Regulation

One dimension of practical detail needs emphasis. The market consists of a large number of agents that the principal can choose from. The principal also deals with many agents at any given point of time. Each of them will have a different δ and λ. To conceptualize separate values of p for each one of them will be expensive and impractical for the firm. Hence, the firm is more likely to choose a value of p apriori and allow agents to select themselves.

To appreciate this, rewrite the choice of p in the form

$$\delta(1-p) = 2p\lambda\sigma^2$$

That is, given a p and σ^2, there will be several combinations of δ, λ, and hence groups of agents who exhibit attributes that satisfy this equation. Only such agents will enter the contract. That is, the necessity to vary p for each agent is not as important as initially conceptualized.

Assume, now, that the firm chooses $p_1 > p$. Consider an agent who cannot (or who does not wish to) maintain the stipulated level of efficiency. That is, he exhibits a low δ. If he is also highly risk averse he will end up choosing a contract that offers a lower share. On the other hand, an agent who is less risk averse and more willing to maintain efficiency would be inclined to seek a higher share contract. Note, however, that the information contained in the model is inadequate to fix the share and output combinations that the firm should offer.

Sloff and vanPragg (2008) and Aggarwal (2007) pointed out that the choice of p need not depend on δ and/or $\lambda\sigma^2$. A similar argument can be found in Nichols (1983) and Svejnar and Smith (1984). The implications of such choices for franchise contracts have been explored in Lafontaine (1992) and Kaufman and Lafontaine (1994). We will now explore some variants of the KM model to identify the mechanisms that can justify such choices.

Note that to this point in the analysis it was assumed that δ and λ are independent characteristics of an agent. However, it would be realistic to expect that a highly risk averse agent would also pay a great deal of attention to maintaining the requisite level of efficiency to ensure that the expected net value from the contract materializes.[14] That is,

$$\mathrm{d}\delta/\mathrm{d}\lambda\sigma^2 > 0$$

It can be surmised that the agent makes this adjustment to achieve the maximum value of p that the principal can be induced to offer. Assume that η, the elasticity of δ with respect to $\lambda\sigma^2$, is positive. It can be readily verified that

$$\mathrm{d}p/\mathrm{d}\lambda\sigma^2 = 2\delta(\eta - 1)/\left(\delta + 2\lambda\sigma^2\right)^2$$

This expression will be zero if $\eta = 1$. This corresponds to the agent making a perfect correction in his efficiency for every change in $\lambda\sigma^2$. Suppose $\eta < 1$. That is, the agent is less than cautious while executing the contract. He cannot then demand an increase in p from the principal. Instead, he will accept a lower p thereby acknowledging that his negligence is a part of the reason for the lower level of output.

[14] Cooper and Ross (1985), Emons (1988), and Dybvig and Lutz (1993) acknowledged that the consumers can adjust the care with which they use the product. Thus, the consumers can exert some influence on the failure of the product depending on the way they use it. The issue is this. What determines the adjustments in δ? $\lambda\sigma^2$ is surely one of the determinants. Emons (1988) argued that p, viz., the warranty offered, may itself determine the choice of δ. Similarly, following the argument of Murty and Blischke (2000), it can be argued that even the firm makes adjustments in several characteristics of its product when it recognizes the pertinent dimensions of consumer risk aversion. This may include the warranty and the σ^2 itself. We will not consider these alternatives in detail here.

Analytically, the case where $\eta > 1$ is more illuminating. To be sure, the more careful agent recognizes that the contract failure, if it were to occur, cannot be a result of his negligence. He then demands a greater share from the firm. Thus, even under risk sharing arrangements, there will be an increase in p when $\lambda\sigma^2$ increases.[15] The ceteris paribus clause under the risk sharing formulation could not sustain this result.[16]

Observe that the maximum p that the firm would be willing to offer occurs when $\eta = 1$. That is,

$$\delta = C\lambda\sigma^2$$

where C is a constant, will be the combination that the agent chooses. Stated in broad general terms, C will be inversely related to the cost of making the adjustment. For, the greater the costs of adjustment the agent can be expected to be less willing to make adjustments. Corresponding to this

$$p = C/(C+2)$$

This is a monotonic increasing function of C and tends to 1 as C tends to ∞. In other words, an agent who exercises the utmost caution will demand $p = 1$. It should also be noted that this choice of p is independent of δ and $\lambda\sigma^2$ whatever may be the value of C. The advantage of this argument is that a specific value of p can be identified.

A different interpretation of the reaction of the agent to his efficiency appears equally plausible. Consider an increase in the efficiency of the agent. Since he is more confident of delivering a given output he may exhibit a greater willingness to take risk and thereby increase $\lambda\sigma^2$. He may, however, acknowledge that taking more risk would make it more difficult for him to deliver the promised output. The above argument, therefore, indicates that there exists a

$$\lambda\sigma^2 = \delta/C$$

where C is a constant. This interpretation also leads to an optimal

$$p = C/(C+2)$$

independent of δ and $\lambda\sigma^2$.

The choice of C is still not defined. In addition to inducing the principal to offer him the maximum share of output that the principal would be willing to concede the

---

[15] This argument holds only for a given $\lambda\sigma^2$. In such a case the resulting p is the minimum rather than a maximum. There will be a simultaneous choice of $\lambda\sigma^2$ that the agent would exhibit. This is entirely plausible if σ^2 is a result of the agent's action instead of its being fixed exogenously.

[16] Jullien et al. (1999) pointed out that the costs to the agent, of making such adjustments in his efficiency levels, will not be negligible. Hence, he must weigh the advantages due to an increase in p against such costs. This may be the primary reason why we do not expect $\eta > 1$ in practice. Secondly, there may be limits on the extent to which he would be willing to take increased risk. In the limit, even the maximum p may not be attainable.

agent may induce him to make $V_a \geq 0$. Continue to assume that one of his choices corresponds to $\delta = C\lambda\sigma^2$. For such values of $\lambda\sigma^2$ it can be shown that $V_a = E\lambda\sigma^2$, where $E = C^2(C-2)/(C+2)^2$. E will be the minimum for C satisfying the equation $C^2 + 6C - 8 = 0$. The $C^* > 1$ that satisfies this equation will still render $V_a < 0$. Hence, it would be more realistic if he prefers the choice of $C = 2$.[17] This can be assured if the agent insists on receiving a share $p = ½$. Only agents that satisfy the property that their efficiency $\delta = 2\lambda\sigma^2$ will enter the contract. Clearly, any deviation from this in the choice of δ, of the agent, will make $V_a < 0$. Note that the principal accepting these efficient regulatory constraints will be favorable to him as well.

The agents and the principals agreed to the efficient regulation as defined here. In the case of some other contracts it is entirely possible that a regulatory agency must interfere.

References

Agarwal RM (2007) Role of risk sharing and transaction costs in contract choice: theory and evidence from groundwater contracts. J Econ Behav Organ 63:475–496

Baker R (2006) Risk aversion in maintenance: overmaintenance and the principal agent problem. IMA J Manag Math 17:99–113

Bolton P, Dewatripont M (2005) Contract theory. MIT Press, Cambridge

Borenstein S, Busse M, Kellogg R (2007) Principal agent incentives, excess caution, and market inefficiency: evidence from utility regulation. NBER working paper 13679. Available at www.nber.org/papers/w13679

Coase RH (1937) The nature of the firm. Economica 4:386–405

Coase RH (1960) The problem of social cost. J Law Econ 3:1–44

Cooper R, Ross TW (1985) Product warranties and double moral hazard. Rand J Econ 16:103–113

Datta PK, Radner R (1994) Optimal principal agent contracts for a class of incentive schemes: a characterization and the rate of approach to efficiency. Econ Theory 4:483–503

Dybvig PH, Lutz NA (1993) Warranties, durability and maintenance: two-sided moral hazard in a continuous time model. Rev Econ Stud 60:575–597

Emons W (1988) Warranties, moral hazard and the lemons problem. J Econ Theory 46:16–33

Ferrall C, Shearer R (1999) Incentives and transaction costs within the firm: estimating an agency model using payroll records. Rev Econ Stud 66:309–338

Holmstrom B (1979) Moral hazard and observability. Bell J Econ 10:74–91

Jensen MC, Meckling WH (1976) Theory of the firm: managerial behavior, agency costs and ownership structure. J Financ Econ 3:305–360

Jullien B, Salanie B, Salanie F (1999) Should more risk averse agents exert more effort? Geneva Pap Risk Insur Theory 24:19–28

Kaufman PJ, Lafontaine F (1994) Costs of control: the sources of economic rents for McDonald's franchisees. J Law Econ 37:417–454

Kawasaki S, McMillan J (1987) The design of contracts: evidence from Japanese subcontracting. J Jpn Int Econ 1:327–349

[17] An increase in C beyond 2 will increase the value of the contract to the agent. However, it would be realistic to expect that the principal wishes to maintain as large a share of output as the agent will concede. Note that any $C \geq 2$ will be acceptable to both of them if both of them maximize their respective value and disregard the share of output.

Lafontaine F (1992) Agency theory and franchising: some empirical results. Rand J Econ 23:263–283
Masten SE, Saussier S (2002) Econometrics of contracts: an assessment of developments in the empirical literature on contracting. In: Brousseau E, Glachant JM (eds) The economics of contracts. Cambridge University Press, Cambridge
Mirrlees J (1974) Notes on welfare economics, information, and uncertainty. In: Balch M, McFadden D, Wu S (eds) Essays in economic behavior under uncertainty. North Holland, Amsterdam
Murty DNP, Blischke WR (2000) Strategic warranty management: a life-cycle approach. IEEE Trans Eng Manag 47:40–54
Nichiols S (1983) Agency contracts, institutional mode, and the transition to foreign direct investment by British manufacturing multinationals before 1939. J Econ Hist 43:675–686
Rees R (1985a) The theory of principal and agent: part 1. Bull Econ Res 37:3–26
Rees R (1985b) The theory of principal and agent: part 2. Bull Econ Res 37:75–95
Sloof R, vanPragg CM (2008) Performance measurement, expectancy, and agency theory: an experimental study. J Econ Behav Organ 67:794–809
Svejner J, Smith SC (1984) The economics of joint ventures in less developed countries. Q J Econ 99:149–167
Williamson OE (1988) Corporate finance and corporate governance. J Financ 43:567–591

Chapter 2
Conferences and Publications

Abstract Two broad trends are discernible in the context of the development of scientific R&D. First, there is a significant increase in conference culture and the tendency of many authors rushing the dissemination of their discoveries. Second, there is an increase in the willingness to accept and finance such activities. Clearly, both these features tend to be sustainable only because the parties involved in the transactions feel that they have something to gain commercially. The primary purpose of this study is to examine this nexus utilizing a modified principal agent model. The existence of these mechanisms renders the national wealth more volatile. Such volatility can be minimized only if firms, that undertake commercialization, are adequately skilled and/or highly volatile transactions can be screened out by making it more expensive to commercialize them. The least that can be done is to discourage proven losers over time if they fail to self-select.

2.1 The Theme

Innovations are the most important drivers of economic progress in every country. Generating new knowledge, disseminating it widely, and commercializing it efficiently constitute the crux of value addition and wealth creation. Hence, every society encourages and honors individuals who contribute to the augmentation of national wealth.

Conceptually, at any rate, an innovation deserves acknowledgement only after the value addition and wealth generation become a commercial reality. However, the expected wealth generation cannot be realized in time for the society to benefit from it unless scientific information is disseminated fast enough. As a result, diluted versions of output measures, like the number of patents, have been popular. It is by now well known that many patents are not, or cannot be, "worked" or translated into any tangible output and promised wealth generation. Individuals have shown a tendency to seek easy, and early, recognition instead of striving for the harder to achieve

Based on content from "Economics of Conference Presentations and Research Publications" first published in *Indian Economic Journal*, 56(3), 2008, pp. 1236–1242. Content reproduced here with permission from Indian Economic Association.

T.V.S.R. Rao, *Risk Sharing, Risk Spreading and Efficient Regulation*,
DOI 10.1007/978-81-322-2562-1_2

quality and greater value addition. In essence, the tendency to rush discoveries does not generate the expected wealth with any degree of certainty.

Pushed to an extreme, society has been granting recognition to research publications, conference presentations, and spending on R&D based on the same logic. The very fact that a citation index has become important, instead of the value addition and quality of output, is testimony to this degenerative process. It appears that this attempt to rationalize such surrogates as value drivers is inimical to the progress of meaningful innovation.

The clamor for recognition and rewards, the paucity of talent to produce really quality innovation, and the phenomenon of mutual praise and acceptance by peers as the only signal of high-value innovative work degenerated to a point where the conference culture has replaced all other forms of innovative work. It is a pity that presenting something, incoherent and incomprehensible, in a few minutes, to a largely disinterested and inattentive audience, has come to be designated as a signal of innovative contribution to the generation of national wealth.

From the viewpoint of economic theory, the advantage of accelerated knowledge diffusion cannot, by itself, explain this progression of events. Surely, there are many deeper economic and sociological factors contributing to this development in the scientific world. This study is an attempt to disentangle the underlying mechanisms. It will be shown that increased gains to the scientists, and other agents, in the process of commercialization and/or the expected risk-adjusted rate of return is at the apex of this progression.[1]

One of the consequences of the existence of these tendencies is to render the national wealth more volatile. This can be demonstrated using the framework developed in this study. Such volatility can be minimized only if the higher-level agents, that undertake commercialization, are adequately skilled and/or highly volatile transactions can be screened out by making it more expensive to commercialize them. The least that can be done is to discourage proven losers over time if they fail to self-select.

The rest of the study is organized as follows. The analytical framework is set out in Sect. 2.2 utilizing a modified version of the principal agent models. It will be shown that the lower the skill of the author in the process of commercialization, and/or the more risky the innovation, the greater will be the propensity to present the work in conferences, publish it in journals, and/or pass it on to other firms for development. Section 2.3 then reconsiders the result under the assumption that the author actively collaborates with the firm in the commercialization process. That is, he now bears some of the risks. It will be established once again that the commercial interests of both the authors and the firm tend to increase low-quality, high-risk innovations. Section 2.4 then develops a more general scenario in which the organizers of conferences, the publishers of journals,

[1] Consider the context of television programming. The potential viewers have to pay well before they can get a measure of the quality of programs that will be exhibited. Generally this results in substandard broadcasting. The low-quality and high-risk programming have been dominant despite the dynamic nature of television programs and viewers. Risks have been passed on effortlessly and to the commercial advantage of most of the parties involved. The losses, of poor quality programs, are mostly borne by the viewers. Perhaps there is a general feeling that even in the context of investments in the stock market and mutual funds, the intermediaries gain at the expense of investors who hold securities on a long-term basis. That is, the phenomenon exhibited in this study is very general over a wide spectrum of economic activities.

and firms tend to take up more than one innovation at a time. This process helps them to cushion risks and cross subsidize as and when necessary. Hence, this process should only aggravate the situation. It will be shown that under these conditions the number of innovations taken up will tend to increase. Further, it can be demonstrated that every author is likely to feel that his own interest is compromised when he joins the others. However, he is forced to accept it because there is a collective gain to all of them as a group. Similarly, firms find it worthwhile to increase the number of innovations they handle as well as the degree of risk implicit in each of them. Section 2.5 then offers a broad view of the results, some policy implications, and pointers for future work.

2.2 Basic Framework

An author of a scientific work, that has some valuable discovery, estimates, or believes, that his work will contribute an amount w to the wealth of the society. However, it is generally impractical and very expensive for him to pursue it through the many stages of the commercialization process, starting from scientific knowledge to the wealth-generating end product, to realize w.

The author is also often aware that not all scientific work culminates in the expected wealth. It is equally well understood that innovations vary widely with respect to their capacity to generate wealth. For analytical purposes, it may be postulated that the actual wealth generated is

$$w_\varepsilon = w + u$$

where u is a random variable with:

$E(u)$ = expected value of $u=0$.

$V(u)$ = variance of $u=\sigma^2$.

There is a possibility that σ^2 is indeed very large.[2]

The costs of commercialization, for the author acting on his own, may have three components. (a) He incurs a direct cost based on his skill. (b) There is also a cost equivalent to the business lost due to his inability to raise finances. (c) There is a loss to the society in the sense that the realization of w may get delayed, only partially achieved, or attained at a much greater cost than is otherwise possible. All these features can be subsumed under the specification of the cost as $w^2/2\varepsilon$ where ε is a generalized index of the skill of the author.

The society surely experiences a smaller variance, compared to σ^2, because only good-quality discoveries will survive and others are not "worked." Let the variance be $s^2 < \sigma^2$. The value to the society is

$$v_a = w - \lambda_a s^2 - w^2/2\varepsilon$$

[2] An alternative is to assume that a wide spectrum of innovations, with varying w, is available. The simplification adopted here is to assume variability around a given w. However, this w may still be a choice variable.

where λ_a = risk aversion of the author.

The author can be expected to commercialize only those innovations that maximize v_a. Accordingly, he will choose

$$w = \varepsilon$$

and the maximum value achieved is

$$v_a = \varepsilon/2 - \lambda_a s^2$$

The author has the alternative of using other avenues, such as conference presentations, publications in journals, or patent filing. In essence, he reckons that these other agencies – like an entrepreneur attending a conference where he presents his discovery, a reader of a scientific journal, or a firm specializing in translating knowledge to commercially viable technology (scaling up plants in industry parlance) – are better equipped to undertake commercialization and make w realizable. He therefore transfers it to such an agent. The return to the author may now take several forms. (a) He may be directly paid a share of the realizable wealth (a consideration) when the innovation is bought or licensed for further use. (b) Some institutions, for instance, the University of California at Berkeley, encourage scientists to undertake the progression to commercially viable products by collaboration with private industry. When the innovation is successful, private industry will be expected to share the wealth so generated through contributions to the pool of research funds. Several variants of this mechanism are discernible in practice. (c) Publication in a journal does not yield such returns. The return will be indirect, in the form of the scientist's institution or some other organization (but not the publisher of the journal) granting more research funds, provide job promotions, and the like. (d) The author's institution or some related organization usually encourages an author to present his discovery in a conference by paying the costs involved, counting the activities towards promotion, and so on. It may be expected that, in all these cases, the payments to the scientist will depend on w to a large extent. It appears as though the efforts that the author puts in, and perhaps the quality of the work, go down as we move from (a) to (d). To be sure, some exceptions can be found in practice.

In its turn, the firm, that acquired the knowledge, incurs some cost in the process of commercialization. It is conceivable that even the proportion pw paid to the scientist will be eventually borne by the firm. It will recover these costs while realizing w. Publications in journals are slightly different. The journals take copyright from the author and sell it to the firm (or readers that utilize it to further develop this knowledge) for its use. Perhaps the payments that the journal receives will also be a fraction of w.

To formalize the argument, note that the gains to the author under the alternative arrangement can be expressed as

$$g_a = pw + w^2/2\varepsilon$$

A more detailed justification can be offered. (a) Consider an author submitting and reading a paper in a conference. Usually his travel expenses and so on will be paid by the institution to which he belongs. The better the quality of the paper or the skill of the author in convincing the audience of the value addition of the paper, the fewer times he needs to present it before publication (for instance). On the other hand, lower-quality necessitates more repetition and greater expenditure. (b) In recent times, most of the journals have been collecting a submission fees from the authors. A similar argument holds in this context as well. It should also be acknowledged that the author is generally compensated by his institution without necessarily ascertaining the quality a priori.[3] Consequently, this is a gain to the author over and above the pw that he gets by way of compensation from the firm. Further, in the interest of continuing further research, the consideration *pw* will be paid to the author well before $(w+u)$ is realized. It is therefore deterministic.[4] The value of the discovery to the author therefore becomes

$$v_{\mathrm{a}} = g_{\mathrm{a}}$$

Note that the firm must finance the payment *pw* upfront. Large firms raise this sum from the capital market. In other words, the investor pays an amount *pw* In return, the investor gets a share of the value generated. The gains to the investor will then be

$$g_{\mathrm{i}} = q(w+u) - pw$$

where q is the fraction of the value generation that he recovers. In general, the investors are risk averse. Hence, the value of the transaction to them is

$$v_{\mathrm{i}} = (q-p)w - \lambda\sigma^2 q^2$$

The investors are not sure about the rate of return that they can expect and/or repayment of the money they invested. Hence, it would be natural for them to ask for, or at least monitor, the recovery of whatever investment they make rather than the volume of investment. They can be expected to choose q ceteris paribus. This choice results in

$$q = w/2\lambda\sigma^2$$

---

[3] Earlier, the quantity $w^2/2\varepsilon$ has been interpreted as the cost that the author has to incur if he undertakes commercialization on his own. Clearly, ε is a representation of his efficiency. The present specification of payments is also contingent on his efficiency. Hence, the use of $w^2/2\varepsilon$ is justifiable.

[4] The payment $w^2/2\varepsilon$ is essentially a result of the author licensing the innovation to the firm. In an alternative arrangement, where the author participates in the commercialization process, these payments will also be reflected in his share $p(w+u)$. Additional payments are unlikely, to be sure the optimal value of p will be different in these two contexts. This will be elucidated further in the next section.

Note that q increases with w and decreases with an increase in $\lambda\sigma^2$.

Usually the firm incurs a cost $w^2/2\delta$ in the process of commercialization. Since the firm is likely to be more efficient than the author with respect to this activity, it will be postulated that $\delta > \varepsilon$. The firm generally will not depend on its investors while financing these short-term operating costs. For analytical convenience, we will assume that the firm uses its own resources. The firm receives $(1-q)\,(w+u)$ as a compensation for its efforts. The firm's gain may then be denoted by

$$g_{\mathrm{f}} = (1-q)(w+u) - w^2/2\delta$$

In general, the firm is not paying pw to the author. Instead, it makes the investor pay for it. Hence, it is not necessarily sensitive to the risk of losing that investment. Further, the firm will be dealing with many such transactions. Hence, it can balance the residual losses in one transaction against gains from another. It can therefore be surmised that the firm will be risk neutral. The value of g_{f} to the firm may then be written as

$$v_{\mathrm{f}} = (1-q)w - w^2/2\delta$$

Note that, for all practical purposes, the firm is underwriting the investment pw, since it is required to pay pw to the author whether or not it can attract investors. Hence, from a pragmatic viewpoint, the firm should place a value on such effort as well. Such a valuation, for all practical purposes, will be v_{i}. For, in a way, that is the opportunity value to the firm if it has to accept the burden of underwriting that fails to attract investors. Hence, from the perspective of the firm, the net value of the contract is the sum of v_{i} and v_{f}. An efficient contract then requires that the firm maximize

$$\begin{aligned} N &= v_{\mathrm{i}} + v_{\mathrm{f}} \\ &= (1-p)w - w^2/2\delta - \lambda q^2\sigma^2 \end{aligned}$$

Two observations are in order. First, v_{a} is not included in N. For the author, by claiming a fixed consideration does not share the risk. Second, suppose the firm maximizes v_{f} only and eventually chooses a Nash equilibrium. This can be shown to be less efficient (lower optimized N) compared to the present approach.

Surely, the firm's first priority is not about how much it wishes to pay the investor. For the firm should be in a position to realize w in the first instance. Hence, it can be expected that the firm would be more worried about how much value it can recover. The possibility that the firm may not be in a position to recover the entire expected w is at the apex of the likely default that the investor envisages. It would therefore be logical to expect the firm to make the choice with respect to w, the wealth-generating capacity of an innovation.[5]

[5] Note one finer point of analytical detail. Suppose we assign the choice of w to the investor and that of q to the firm contrary to the argument in the text. It can be shown that such choices result in

In its choice of w, the firm should take the participation constraint, viz.,

$$q = w/2\lambda\sigma^2$$

into account. This choice results in

$$w = 2\delta(1-p)\lambda\sigma^2/(\delta + 2\lambda\sigma^2)$$

When an author transfers the rights of use of his discovery to the firm, he would be interested in making sure that he receives a proper share of the value generated from its use.[6] That is, the author chooses p to maximize v_a keeping the reactions of the firm and the investors in perspective. This optimization results in

$$p = (\varepsilon - 2\theta)/(\varepsilon - \theta) < 1$$

where

$$\theta = \delta\lambda\sigma^2/(\delta + 2\lambda\sigma^2)$$

The optimized value of N becomes

$$N = \delta(1-p)^2\lambda\sigma^2/(\delta + 2\lambda\sigma^2) > 0$$

It can be verified that $q > p$ whenever $\delta > \varepsilon$. This is in consonance with the expectation in contract theory that the more efficient party should receive a larger share.

Observe that $p < 1$ cannot be satisfied if $\varepsilon < \theta$. For, then, $p < 1$ if and only if

$$(\varepsilon - 2\theta) > 2(\varepsilon - \theta)$$

This inequality cannot hold since $\varepsilon > 0$. It must also be noted that even when $\varepsilon > \theta$, the inequality $\varepsilon > 2\theta$ will be satisfied if and only if $\lambda\sigma^2 < \delta\varepsilon/2(\delta - \varepsilon)$. That is, the analysis will hold only when $\lambda\sigma^2$ is sufficiently low. One reason for this is the fact that $0 < \theta < \delta$ for $0 < \lambda\sigma^2 < \infty$. Given this inequality, 2θ will exceed ε for sufficiently large values of $\lambda\sigma^2$. The second reason can be obtained from the definition of v_i. In particular, a ceteris paribus increase in $\lambda\sigma^2$ decreases the value of v_i. For high values of $\lambda\sigma^2$, the value of $v_i < 0$ and the investors will not accept the contract.

Is this alternative organizational arrangement superior to the author undertaking commercialization on his own? Note that, under the present arrangement,

---

a lower net value N. That is, such a contractual choice would be inefficient. This reinforces the practical aspects of the assumptions made in the text.

[6] Strictly speaking, every author can be expected to make efforts to recover an appropriate share of w created by every one of his discoveries. Hence, w is not a choice variable from his perspective

$$v_a = \varepsilon^2\theta/(\varepsilon-\theta)^2$$

Hence,

$$\varepsilon/2 - \lambda_a s^2 < \varepsilon^2\theta/(\varepsilon-\theta)^2$$

whenever ε is low and/or σ^2 is father away from s^2. That is, relatively low-skilled authors (especially with respect to their commercialization prowess) will pass on their innovations to other agents. Similarly, lower-quality discoveries tend to be passed on. In general, such discoveries will also tend to be passed on very quickly.

Observe that the author can be expected to have an incentive to increase v_a. Given that the contract already made optimal choices of p, w, and q, the only other choice available is σ^2. How does he choose σ^2? To appreciate this recall that

$$w = \varepsilon\theta/(\varepsilon-\theta), \text{ and}$$
$$v_a = \varepsilon^2\theta/(\varepsilon-\theta)^2$$

Further,

$$\partial\theta/\partial\lambda\sigma^2 = \delta^2/(\delta+2\lambda\sigma^2)^2 > 0$$

With this information in place, it can be readily verified that

$$\partial v_a/\partial\lambda\sigma^2 > 0$$

Therefore, the author gains by passing on more risky innovations.

From the foregoing analysis, it is also obvious that

$$\begin{aligned} v_i &= (q-p)w - \lambda\sigma^2 q^2 \\ &= \lambda\sigma^2 q^2 - 2\lambda\sigma^2 qp \end{aligned}$$

It can now be shown that

$$\partial p/\partial q = -\lambda\sigma^2/\varepsilon < 0$$
$$\partial v_i/\partial q > 0, \text{ and}$$
$$\partial q/\partial\lambda\sigma^2 > 0$$

Hence, it follows that

$$\partial v_i/\partial\lambda\sigma^2 > 0$$

In other words, the investors will stand to gain by increases in σ^2. They will not resist the author passing on lower quality and hence risky innovations to the firm.

Will the firm also gain by increasing σ^2? It can be shown that

$$\partial v_f / \partial \lambda \sigma^2 = \left(w^2/2\, \lambda^2 \sigma^4 \right) \left[3 - 2w\left(\delta + \lambda \sigma^2 \right) / \delta \lambda \sigma^2 \right] > 0 \text{ if}$$

$$3\delta\lambda\sigma^2 > 2w\left(\delta + \lambda\sigma^2\right)$$

This, in its turn, would hold whenever δ is sufficiently large relative to ε and/or $\lambda\sigma^2$ is not very large. Once again we have a proposition that the firm would gain by increasing σ^2 so long as it is within certain limits. The firm will not resist taking up relatively more risky innovations for commercialization.

However, note that increasing the value of v_f may not be the best goal for the firm. For it is risk neutral since it is handling many such innovations. Instead, it will seek out more business, represented by w, and expect to improve its position on an average.[7] It can actually be shown that

$$\partial w / \partial \lambda \sigma^2 > 0$$

In essence, if it maximizes w, the firm expects to increase its net return on all the transactions even if it gets a lower value on any one of them.

Note, incidentally, that

$$\partial \left(pw \right) / \partial \lambda \sigma^2 > 0$$

only when δ is sufficiently large relative to ε and/or $\lambda\sigma^2$ is not very large. In other words, the firm gains by passing on the risks to the investor only in a limited context. In other words, the inferences of the present section are not entirely dependent on the firm passing on the risks to the investors. This theme will be reconsidered in the next section.

Therefore, the author, the investors, and the firm gain by accepting more risky innovations, though within certain limits as elucidated above, for commercialization. This is one way of arguing that low-quality innovations predominate.

A related approach may also be elucidated. Consider the portfolio choice of the firm which decides to invest a total amount T in innovations. It will first seek the innovations that promise the highest risk-adjusted rate of return. If it is possible to invest the entire T in these innovations, the choice problem is solved. Suppose a smaller amount is all that is possible because there are only a few innovations that yield such a high risk-adjusted rate of return. The firm will then invest the maximum possible in that activity and turn to the next set of innovations that yield the second highest risk-adjusted rate of return. This lexicographic ordering suggests that the risk-adjusted rate of return is a superior measure when deciding the risk preferences of investors and the firm.[8]

---

[7] For all practical purposes, the contention here is that from a long-run perspective, an increase in market share is superior to short-term gains from the firm's viewpoint.

[8] The rate of return to the author cannot be defined meaningfully since the model did not acknowledge the costs incurred in his generating the innovation.

Consider the rate of return to the firm. It can be written as

$$\begin{aligned} r_{\mathrm{f}} &= v_{\mathrm{f}}/w \\ &= (1-q) - w/2\delta \\ &= 1 - [\theta\varepsilon/(\varepsilon-\theta)][1/\delta + 1/2\lambda\sigma^2] \end{aligned}$$

Consequently,

$$\partial r_{\mathrm{f}}/\partial\lambda\sigma^2 = \theta\varepsilon r_{\mathrm{f}}/(\varepsilon-\theta)\lambda^2\sigma^4 > 0$$

That is, the risk-adjusted rate of return to the firm increases with $\lambda\sigma^2$. Hence, the firm is prone to take on more risky innovations for commercialization.

Similarly,

$$\begin{aligned} r_i &= rate\ of\ return\ to\ the\ investor \\ &= v_{\mathrm{i}}/pr \\ &= q/rp - 1 \end{aligned}$$

Following a procedure similar to the one above, it can be shown that $\partial q/\partial\lambda\sigma^2 > 0$ and $\partial p/\partial\lambda\sigma^2 < 0$ given the assumptions made so far. Hence, it can be inferred that $\partial r_{\mathrm{i}}/\partial\lambda\sigma^2 > 0$. That is, if $\lambda\sigma^2$ is small enough, r_{i} will increase with $\lambda\sigma^2$.

For all practical purposes, it may be claimed that even with an increase in $\lambda\sigma^2$, the risk-adjusted rate of return may be favorable. This is the other inducement for the parties to create greater volatility in the production of innovations.

To sum up the argument of this section so far, note that lower the skill of the author, in the process of commercialization, and/or the more risky the innovation, the greater will be the probability that it will be presented in conferences, published in journals, and passed on to other firms.

One of the consequences of this tendency is that national wealth tends to be more volatile. This can be demonstrated as follows. To begin with, observe that

$$\begin{aligned} V(g_{\mathrm{i}}) &= q^2\sigma^2, \text{ and} \\ V(g_{\mathrm{f}}) &= (1-q)^2\sigma^2 \end{aligned}$$

where V is the variance.

Hence, the total variance generated in the process of commercial absorption of the innovation is

$$V = \left[q^2 + (1-q)^2\right]\sigma^2 < \sigma^2$$

since q is always less than 1. Hence, in general, sharing risks should be favorable in the stabilization of national wealth given σ^2. However, note that the basic argument of this section is that larger σ^2 tends to be preferred. It is therefore necessary to examine the changes in V as σ^2 increases.

Observe that

$$\partial V/\partial q = 2(2q-1)\sigma^2, \text{ and}$$
$$2q = \varepsilon\theta/\lambda\sigma^2(\varepsilon-\theta) > 1 \text{ whenever } \delta > 2\varepsilon$$

Hence, it follows that

$$\partial V/\partial q > 0$$

Similarly,

$$\partial q/\partial\lambda\sigma^2 > 0$$

Hence, $\partial V/\partial\lambda\sigma^2 > 0$

Consequently, any increase in $\lambda\sigma^2$ makes V larger. That is, there will be greater volatility of national wealth as $\lambda\sigma^2$ increases.

The inequality $\delta > 2\varepsilon$ indicates that the firm should be significantly more efficient to create greater volatility. An efficient firm, dealing with relatively low risk, can therefore be expected to prefer higher $\lambda\sigma^2$ and thereby create greater volatility. However, very high values of $\lambda\sigma^2$ will not support such a choice. As such, volatility increases only within certain limits.

2.3 A Modification

One of the fundamental assumptions of the analysis of the previous section is that the author of an innovative idea does not generally share the effort and expenses of its commercialization with the firm. This is quite generally valid. However, there are practical contexts in which this may be an exaggeration. (a) Recall that some institutions encourage their scholars to collaborate with private firms in the commercialization process. For instance, some German institutions have been granting a 3-year leave of absence. (b) Similarly, as in the case of the University of California at Berkeley, scientists are encouraged to collaborate with private firms in return for some royalties and research grants. (c) More recently, in the context of biotechnology, for instance, it is well known that scaling up of plants cannot be efficient unless the innovator participates in the process. It is generally acknowledged that transfer of informal knowledge along with the formal written down knowledge is essential. In short, many contexts are conceivable wherein the author actively participates in the commercialization process and shares the risks. It is therefore necessary to examine the propensity to pass on risky innovations under this dispensation. Intuitively, though, it will be expected that any degree of sharing risks will generate this tendency and the results of the previous section will remain intact.

The second assumption relates to the role of the investor. Once again this is a practical reality in the context of large firms. However, the conclusion, regarding the proliferation of risky innovations, gains strength if it can be shown that the result remains invariant even if the firm undertakes investment on its own. In other words, transferring risks through many layers is not a fundamental foundation on which the primary conclusions rest.

The basic purpose of the present section is to modify both these assumptions and demonstrate the validity of our basic contention. It will therefore be shown that even minimal possibilities of sharing risks creates a propensity to commercialize more risky innovations.

Assume that the author participates in downstream activities and receives a share of the wealth generated. In particular, he can no longer claim additional finances by way of research grants, promotions, and so on. Instead, he will be made to share the risk. That is, his gain now becomes

$$g_a = p(w+u)$$

It is still possible that he is providing resources, say, in the form of the scientific expertise, to the process of wealth creation. These costs can now be subsumed[9] under $w^2/2\delta$.

The value of the gains to the author can now be written as

$$v_a = pw - \lambda p^2 \sigma^2$$

where λ is the author's degree of risk aversion.

In a basic sense, the risk aversion is a manifestation of the lack of resource base (inability) and/or unwillingness to bear the entire risk. As in the previous section, it would be realistic to postulate that the author chooses p and would conceptualize working on all his innovations without any exception. The author's choice of p to maximize v_a will then be

$$p = w/2\lambda\sigma^2$$

The firm, on its part, incurs a cost $w^2/2\delta$ and receives a share $(1-p)$ $(w+u)$. Hence,

$$g_f = (1-p)(w+u) - w^2/2\delta$$

We once again assume that the firm is risk neutral. The value to the firm is

$$v_f = (1-p)w - w^2/2\delta$$

Clearly, the firm chooses w.

[9] If he does bear some costs, the p will be inflated to compensate him. Alternatively, the firm bears the costs and reduces p. We are choosing the latter specification for analytical convenience.

However, note that it will not be in a position to enlist the collaboration of the author if it acts selfishly. Consequently, it should be expected that it will (a) take the participation constraint of the author into account and (b) maximize the net gains to both of them. That is, it will maximize

$$N = v_f + v_a$$

Subject to

$$p = w/2\lambda\sigma^2$$

Writing

$$N = w - w^2/2\delta - w^2/4\lambda\sigma^2$$

and maximizing with respect to w yield

$$w = 2\delta\lambda\sigma^2/\left(\delta + 2\lambda\sigma^2\right)$$

The corresponding efficient choice of p will be

$$p = \delta/\left(\delta + 2\lambda\sigma^2\right)$$

We may now investigate the propensity of either one or both the parties encouraging commercialization of more risky innovations. Note that the optimized value of v_a is

$$v_a = \lambda\sigma^2\delta^2/\left(\delta + 2\lambda\sigma^2\right)^2$$

Hence, it can be verified that

$$\partial v_a/\partial\lambda\sigma^2 = \delta^2\left(\delta - 2\lambda\sigma^2\right)/\left(\delta + 2\lambda\sigma^2\right)^2 > 0$$

if and only if $\delta > 2\lambda\sigma^2$.

As in the previous section, it can be concluded that the author gains if $\lambda\sigma^2$ is relatively low and/or the firm is more efficient. In either case, it cannot be denied that the author has an incentive to commercialize more risky innovations.

How does the firm react? To begin with, note that

$$\partial w/\partial\lambda\sigma^2 = 2\delta^2/\left(\delta + 2\lambda\sigma^2\right)^2 > 0$$

Firms tend to choose high-risk innovations to increase their market share. Secondly, observe that

$$\partial v_f/\partial\lambda\sigma^2 = 4\delta^2\lambda\sigma^2/\left(\delta + 2\lambda\sigma^2\right)^3 > 0$$

The firm gains by increasing σ^2.

It may be concluded that the commercial interests of both the authors and the firm tend to increase low-quality, high-risk innovations to be paraded in conferences, journals, and so on. As the results of both these sections indicate, the firms tend to encourage this trend, and the authors accede to it wittingly or unwittingly.

2.4 Number of Innovations

A common feature of conferences, journals, and firms is that they pool many innovations together. The analysis so far has also acknowledged that the risk neutral attitude of the firms is a result of its handling many innovations simultaneously. However, the previous two sections considered the gains to the firm from one such innovation. The present section is an attempt to restructure the model of section 3 by incorporating this aspect of practical reality. Intuitively, it will be expected that risk pooling, by taking up many innovations, may simultaneously result in the firm putting together a large number of innovations and generating even lower-quality and higher volatility of national wealth.

By the very nature of their activities, the managers of these business units expect to derive some economies of scale by pooling activities. Though this is valid up to a certain number, there is a persistent impression that these activities are subject to diminishing returns when stretched to a limit. The emergence of diminishing returns can be justified along the following lines. Many prospective firms may fail to notice a successful innovation presented at a conference since sifting through many presentations may be too expensive. Similarly, as the volume of papers in a journal increases, the chance of a prospective developer missing an innovation increases. In an identical fashion, the difficulties in organizing production increase as the firm expands its operations. In general, such diseconomies may suggest that they discourage increases in the size of these business units. We will actually show that even in this most unfavorable situation, there are forces that increase the number of innovations that such business units pursue.

The point that we wish to elaborate in this section is that proliferation of low-quality innovations occurs purely due to the commercial interests of the authors and firms, while wealth generation per se becomes more volatile.

As before, we will assume that each innovation is expected to generate wealth w. Further, it will be expected that each author will come up with one innovation at a time. Hence, following the contours of the model in section 3, the gain to any one author will be

$$g_{\mathrm{a}} = p(w+u)$$

and its value to the author will be

$$v_{\mathrm{a}} = pw - \lambda\sigma^2 p^2$$

Consequently, he chooses

$$p = w/2\lambda\sigma^2$$

as before.

From the viewpoint of the firm, an increase in the number of innovations leads to increased costs. They can be represented by $(nw)^2/2\delta$ where n = number of innovations. The gain to the firm can, therefore, be represented by

$$g_f = n(1-p)(w+u) - n^2w^2/2\delta$$

Maintaining the assumption of risk neutrality, we have

$$v_f = n(1-p) - n^2w^2/2\delta$$

The net value to the parties is

$$N = nw - np^2\lambda\sigma^2 - n^2w^2/2\delta$$

Invoking the incentive constraint of the authors this becomes

$$N = nw - nw^2/4\lambda\sigma^2 - n^2w^2/2\delta$$

The firm now chooses w. Explicit optimization yields[10]

$$w = 2\delta\lambda\sigma^2/(\delta + 2n\lambda\sigma^2)$$

so that

$$p = \delta/(\delta + 2n\lambda\sigma^2)$$

To begin with observe that the gross wealth generated by the firm is

$$nw = 2n\delta\lambda\sigma^2/(\delta + 2n\lambda\sigma^2)$$

[10] It will be shown in the sequel that the firm and all the authors, together as a group, improve the respective value to themselves as n increases. Consequently, it is not possible to conceptualize an optimal value of n. Even otherwise, it is intuitively obvious that every author would like to promote his innovation instead of being left alone. There is no limit on n as a consequence. Journals do seem to limit n. This is true of any one journal. But in recent times, we have been witnessing a proliferation of journals to a point where every idea, irrespective of its quality, appears to find an outlet. A similar argument holds in the context of conference culture as well. Optimization with respect to n may just be a red herring.

From this, it follows that

$$\partial(nw)/\partial n = 2\delta^2\lambda\sigma^2/(\delta + 2n\lambda\sigma^2) > 0$$

That is, every increase in *n*, without any limit, increases the total business of the firm. Similarly,

$$\partial(nw)/\partial\lambda\sigma^2 = 2n\delta^2/(\delta + 2n\lambda\sigma^2)^2 > 0$$

From this, it can be inferred that firms have a propensity to accept lower quality of innovations to improve the volume of their business and hence their market share.

Consider the value to any one of the authors next. It will be

$$v_a = \lambda\delta^2\sigma^2/(\delta + 2n\lambda\sigma^2)^2$$

Clearly, $\partial v_a/\partial n < 0$. However, $\partial v_a/\partial\lambda\sigma^2 = \delta^3/(\delta + 2n\lambda\sigma^2)^3 > 0$

In other words, the authors lose when n increases. However, they will not resist the firm undertaking more risky innovations. For, note that for the entire group of authors the value is

$$nv_a = n\lambda\sigma^2\delta^2/(\delta + 2n\lambda\sigma^2)^2$$

It can be readily verified that

$$\partial(nv_a)/\partial n = n\lambda\sigma^2/(\delta + 2n\lambda\sigma^2) > 0$$

so that they gain collectively when n increases.

Similarly, it can be shown that

$$\partial(nv_a)/\partial\lambda\sigma^2 = n\delta^2(\delta - 2n\lambda\sigma^2)/(\delta + 2n\lambda\sigma^2)^3 > 0$$

if and only if $\delta > 2n\lambda\sigma^2$

As in the previous section, a more efficient firm would tend to commercialize more risky innovations.

These results correspond to the following economic intuition. When n increases, every author is likely to feel that his own interest is compromised by joining the crowd. But he has to accept it because there is a collective gain to all of them as a group. It is this feature that creates and perpetuates the conference culture.

Is there any advantage to the firm if *n* and/or $\lambda\sigma^2$ increases? To answer this question, note that

$$v_f = 2n^2\delta\lambda^2\sigma^4/(\delta + 2n\lambda\sigma^2)^2$$

so that

$$\partial v_{\mathrm{f}}/\partial n = 4n\delta\lambda^2\sigma^4\left(\delta+\lambda\sigma^2\right)/\left(\delta+2n\lambda\sigma^2\right)^3 > 0, \text{ and}$$

$$\partial v_{\mathrm{f}}/\partial\lambda\sigma^2 = 4n^2\delta^2\lambda\sigma^2/\left(\delta+2n\lambda\sigma^2\right)^3 > 0$$

That is, the firm has sufficient commercial motivation to undertake more and riskier innovations.

Consider the volatility of national wealth as a result of these choices. It can be readily verified that both $\partial V/\partial n$ and $\partial V/\partial\lambda\sigma^2$ are positive if and only if $\delta > 2\lambda\sigma^2$. From this, it can be inferred that firms with moderate efficiency tend to exhibit greater ambition to improve their lot. This group encourages low-quality innovations and contributes to greater volatility of national wealth.

2.5 Summary and Conclusion

Division of labor based on specialization and delegation has definite advantages of increasing efficiency and improving national wealth. However, it is by now very well documented that information asymmetry, that extreme forms of specialization entail, may provide avenues for one or more parties to take advantage of the others. This emphasis on commercialization may result in a greater volatility of national wealth while some parties gain disproportionately. The present study is essentially a reiteration of this general result. For, we have shown that the authors, firms, and investors derive commercial advantages to themselves, albeit somewhat conditionally, by propagating lower-quality and higher-risk innovations. The economy at large is the loser due to the lower-quality and riskier innovations and the greater volatility of national wealth. This is what we generally designated as the conference culture.

It is not obvious, despite this evidence, that these activities should be severely curtailed. For, the argument that encouraging diffusion of innovations as widely and as early as possible is basically sound. How, then, can quality be encouraged? This is a difficult question. The analysis of this study offers three possible pointers. (a) It is necessary to make it easier for the innovator to undertake commercialization. (b) Perhaps avenues can be identified to increase the cost to the firm of commercializing certain minor innovations while offering greater incentives to pursue major innovations. (c) It is possible to discourage authors of minor innovations until they develop them sufficiently to make their success transparent. At least we should discourage proven failures over time if they do not self-select.

Innovations and their development towards commercialization are dynamic processes. Hence, it is necessary to develop far deeper dynamic models to understand the stages at which the tendency to pass on lower-quality innovations predominate. It can be surmised that the authors have a greater propensity to pass on low-quality innovations as soon as possible. The present study suggests that the firms may have a greater commercial interest in encouraging this. One possibility is that a firm tends to be more attractive to a new innovator the more innovations he already captured or implemented successfully. The onset of diminishing returns as size increases is a complex phenomenon to disentangle.

Despite all the copyright and patent laws in place, we still have an ambiguity regarding the classification of useful innovations. The crass commercialization of today suggests that anything that sells is an innovation. The resulting volatility is a price we have to pay. Perhaps a detailed analysis of some failed innovations and their causes would be useful in obtaining deeper insights.

Chapter 3
Knowledge Intensity and Risk Sharing

Abstract It is often necessary to combine formal knowledge (written down, blueprints) with informal knowledge (rules of thumb and heuristic adaptations required to scale up technology) to "work a patent." Informal knowledge must be provided by the inventor through his participation. Adverse selection of partners and their personal interests (moral hazard) may create risks. These problems have been highlighted in the context of biotechnology in particular. An attempt has been made to model the sharing of knowledge, costs, and returns. R&D, that creates external effects, is generally entrusted to public scientific organizations and transferred to private firms for its adoption. The similarity of issues is highlighted. The advantages of risk sharing have been juxtaposed with dimensions of risk spreading that they involve.

3.1 Knowledge Transfer

Technological developments in traditional industries, like the mechanical and chemical activities, were a result of learning by doing and cumulative use. Much of the R&D was therefore a result of the efforts of workers within the firm Similarly, the fermentation process and related techniques enabled firms to undertake industrial production. It can therefore be inferred that the knowledge necessary to develop new technologies and products was easily available in most firms.

On the other hand, the novelty of biotechnology is the recognition that proteins are the key elements of all living cells. Developments in biotechnology therefore come from discoveries of the process by which living cells produce specific proteins and generate cell functions to create particular biological activity. These discoveries make it possible to use bacteria or other genetic manipulations to alter biological activity and in the end clone and produce specific organisms entirely in a laboratory or on an industrial scale. In other words, the utilization of chemical processes observed in nature replaces conventional chemical analysis.

In general, in the context of biotechnology discovery, the tasks are extensive, and each step of the discovery has been very difficult. Part of the reason is the constraint in using two-dimensional images obtained through X-ray crystallography and NMR (nuclear magnetic resonance) scans to identify the three-dimensional structure of protein molecules. Similarly, understanding a vast array of cell functions in the

T.V.S.R. Rao, *Risk Sharing, Risk Spreading and Efficient Regulation*,
DOI 10.1007/978-81-322-2562-1_3

human body or even in plants has been a challenging task. As a result, discoveries in biotechnology proceed in a fragmentary way. Only a few cell structures were recorded with difficulty. Examples of this nature are genetically modified cell lines that produce MAbs (monoclonal antibodies) for diagnosis of diseases and genome data bases that combine sequence data with protein structure. In general, such fragmentary knowledge must be accumulated and developed towards an ultimate product of use to society. For example, enriched vitamin A rice (popularly known as golden rice) is based on technology that spans 70 patents held by 31 different organizations.

The issue that had to be addressed is this: what are the most efficient institutional mechanisms to generate R&D, create extensive diffusion of knowledge, preserve the rights of intellectual property, and compensate the pioneers for their discoveries? The most commonly used institutional mechanism is patents. Article 7 of TRIPS agreement states the objective as "the protection and enforcement of intellectual property rights (with the objective of contributing) to the promotion of technological innovation and to transfer and (disseminate) technology, to the mutual advantage of producers and users of knowledge and in a manner conducive to social and economic welfare, and to balance rights and obligations." Thus, secrecy, confined to one research laboratory or a small network of related scientists, was the dominant organizational mechanism. Watson's book, *The Double Helix*, has a graphic description of this approach. The basic reason for this was that a great deal of this fundamental research could not be associated with any product from which the consumers derived value. Secrecy was the only protection for their proprietary knowledge because the patent laws at that time applied utility doctrine, i.e., usefulness of information to consumers of goods and services, as a precondition for the grant of a patent.

As a result, the developments in biotechnology were proceeding in a fragmented way. This rendered further progress towards a protein structure or a marketable product difficult and inefficient due to secrecy. Removal of findings (e.g., nucleotide sequences) from the public domain restricted development of derivative knowledge necessary to make the genetic information practically usable. Bottazi et al. (2001) noted a further complicating aspect of knowledge generation and transfer. As they pointed out, pharmaceutical inventions are such that imitative product development (reverse engineering, genetic drugs) is not very difficult and imitation costs are extremely low in comparison to the investor's costs. Knowledge erosion is relatively fast since new ideas are generated all the time. These features make advances in knowledge weakly appropriable from the viewpoint of the innovating firm. In particular, any mechanism that rewards only the final product discovery does not compensate the contribution of early innovators which is essential to achieve the latter stage developments. This is the crucial aspect of cost recovery in the context of biotechnology firms.

The only available means of recovering costs was patents. Hence, in the context of biotechnology, even intermediate stages of discovery needed patent protection. There was some precedence that pointed towards this alternative. First, as far back as 1911, the learned judge Hand upheld a patent on human adrenaline made by using a new process. The patent was not simply for the process but also the purified substance. Second, in 1975 Kohler and Milstein discovered that individual immune system cells, that generate antibodies to a specific antigen, can be fused with immortal cancer cells to create a small factory for producing antibodies. They did not patent it. Hybritech was the first to use monoclonal antibodies in diagnostic kits sold to doctors to identify the presence of diseases (e.g., AIDS) or elevated hormonal levels (pregnancy tests). It received a patent covering the whole family of diagnostic kits. Patents generally provide a 20-year exclusive market protection if the following conditions are satisfied, viz., novelty, non-obviousness, and full and complete disclosure so that any one knowledgeable about the trade can reproduce the production process. Such patents, once granted, assisted the progress of biotechnology but also became a hindrance.

In the context of biotechnology, scientific and/or specialized knowledge (for bioprocessing) is such that mere transfer of formal knowledge is inadequate. Instead, there is a necessity for more direct involvement of the scientist in explaining the use of scientific knowledge and making adaptations to it as the need arises. This is necessitated by the fact that scientific knowledge and technology cannot be formally codified and communicated in writing. Further, the corporate firm may not have the competence to absorb and implement such tacit knowledge. These issues have been highlighted in Liebeskind et al. (1996). Informal knowledge has to be obtained from outside since the knowledge available within the firm is incomplete and inadequate. It is generally understood that there is a need for implicit contracts based on the shared values and norms. The desired efficient behavior may be elicited through sharing royalty contracts, monitoring performance, and sharing of costs and investment financing to induce commitment.

To be more specific, there is a requirement of intangible knowledge in addition to the formal knowledge about the techniques and blueprints. Such knowledge consists of rules of thumb, heuristic adaptations to local production conditions, and other tricks of trade. The following example from the chemical industry is illustrative. As Arora (1996, p. 235) stated it, " transfer of chemical technology will typically involve training the licensee in a variety of issues such as how to handle and store chemicals, how to control the production process and return it to operation after (an) unscheduled breakdown caused by (an) accident or impurities in the feedstock." Assimilation of such intangible knowledge requires constant interaction with experts. To this extent, discoveries in biotechnology are knowledge intensive.

Note that contracting knowledge from outside eliminates the costs of developing and maintaining a large variety of talents in-house. The disadvantages of this approach relate to maintaining an information base and the risks associated with short-term contracts (e.g., frictions and delays in learning to work as a team). In general, the development of a commercially viable product entails basic research, bioprocess engineering and scaling up of laboratory technology, clinical testing (of medicines) and field trials (of crops) and obtaining government and/or regulatory approvals, and the production and marketing of the product. In other words, development of products of utility to the ultimate consumer involves cumulative knowledge. No single firm has all the necessary expertise. Instead, each successive stage of product development requires the expertise at the previous level. Hence, knowledge interface between the scientists and the NBFs (new biotechnology firms involved in bioprocessing) that scale up technology is significant.

The advantages of such contracts are the following. The more scientists are working on a crop, the more likely they are to find new research methods, new genes, new germ plasms, or new knowledge about the crop that will reduce the cost of an NBF developing a new variety. See, for instance, Schimmelpfenning et al. (2004). Similarly, as Decarolis and Deeds (1999) and Powell et al. (1999) pointed out, a large number of links means that the NBF learns to adapt to diverse management styles of the scientists. In other words, there is organizational learning over time. On the downside, scientists may agree to license only the least promising compounds and reserve more promising discoveries for in-house development. Conversely, NBFs may not take up even promising compounds if they are already handling a large number of diverse activities. Similarly, there may be organizational dissonance as the number of links increases. See, for example, Danzon et al. (2005). It is therefore necessary to have some formal agreement (contract) for sharing gains for achieving specific tasks.

Stated more explicitly, a specific contract between a star scientist and a NBF will be to cooperate and create the synergy necessary for the success of the project on hand and share the value generated through bioprocessing. In most cases there is an agreement, before the start of the collaboration, on the distribution of intellectual property, the property rights, and the resulting patents and the terms of license to other parties.

The rest of the chapter is organized as follows. Section 3.2 will outline the basic risk-sharing contract acknowledging the costs incurred by both the parties. Section 3.3 examines the implications of cost sharing. Section 3.4 considers the necessity for public scientific R&D in biotechnology and its implications for the functioning of private firms. Transfer of informal knowledge is explicitly considered. By way of conclusion, the last section will present the implications for risk spreading implied by these contracting arrangements.

3.2 Risk-Sharing Contract

Assume that the scientist offers his expertise and effort in scaling up technology. In its turn, the NBF provides its skills in bioprocessing, invests in the necessary capital, and incurs other expenditures. The NBF may expect a market value of its activity to be m. Note that there is no tangible marketable output at this stage of transformation. Hence, this is an imputation by the financial markets and/or the larger chemical firms who eventually utilize this to achieve marketable production.

This value is achieved through the cooperative effort of both parties. However, the expectations may not be fulfilled. First, there may be adverse selection of partners. Further, after the agreement is reached, either of the parties may decide to free ride on the effort of the other. This reduces the value of the outcome randomly.

Second, the pharmaceutical sector (in particular, the production of human healthcare products, including human diagnostic kits and products of therapeutic value, and associated delivery systems) is characterized by severe competition (from the established chemical firms). This uncertainty is compounded by appropriation problems (since not all aspects of scientific knowledge can be protected by patent rights), high degree of uncertainty of returns to R&D, and so on. Hence, NBFs cannot determine in advance the value that any particular R&D activity will generate. The realized net value may be $(m+u)$ where u is a random variable with $E(u)$ = expected value = 0 and $V(u)$ = variance of u[1] $=\sigma^2$.

Assume that the opportunity cost of the scientist's effort can be represented by $m^2/2\delta$ where δ represents the following. (a) The degree to which the scientist has to participate at the bioprocessing stage to guide the NBF. A low value of δ indicates that more informal knowledge transfer and involvement of the scientist are necessary. (b) It may also indicate the skills of the scientist and a possible cost reduction. (c) Greater organizational learning, if it materializes, necessitates lower involvement of the scientist in the operations of the NBF. That is, a larger value of δ may also signal greater organizational learning. The above specification posits diminishing returns to the effort of the scientist. Similarly, postulate that km^2 = investment of the NBF. Clearly, the magnitude of k reflects the fact that some technologies are more expensive than others.

The only way to compensate the scientist for his effort is to offer a fraction α of the realized market value. Clearly, a greater value of α acts as an incentive for efficient performance. The net return to the scientist can be represented by

$$\pi_s = \alpha(m+u) - m^2/2\delta$$

Note that the scientist is likely to be risk averse. That is, he will find it difficult to accept a large value of σ^2 given his opportunity cost. Hence, the net value of the contract to the scientist will be

$$V_s = \alpha m - m^2/2\delta - \lambda\alpha^2\sigma^2$$

where $\lambda > 0$ measures his degree of risk aversion. On the other hand, the gain to the NBF is

$$\pi_n = (1-\alpha)(m+u) - km^2$$

[1] In most theoretical models of this nature, the expectation of the expected output does not, or cannot, include all the relevant variables. These omitted variables are the primary source of randomness and variance. If some of them can be identified, but the expected value specification cannot incorporate them by utilizing appropriate economic theory, then their effect must be reflected in endogenous randomness. If they cannot be identified or measured suitably, then they will be the major source of exogenous randomness. Randomness is specified through variance even in situations where the direction of the effect of a variable cannot be predicted a priori.

By way of contrast, the NBF will be risk neutral, for he may be operating several ventures and can therefore diversify the risk. Hence, the net value for the NBF can be written as

$$V_n = (1-\alpha)m - km^2$$

The scientist will choose m for a given α. Maximizing V_s results in $m=\alpha\delta$. This is often designated as the incentive constraint of the scientist. Clearly, the scientist targets a higher *m* depending on his skill level and the share of value that he can recover.

One characterization of the behavior of the NBF is to examine the choice of α that maximizes the total net value given the incentive constraint of the scientist. For, in the ultimate analysis, the purpose of creating the NBF is to generate the maximum benefit for all the parties. Observe that the net value is

$$\begin{aligned} N &= V_s + V_n \\ &= m - m^2/2\delta - km^2 - \lambda\alpha^2\sigma^2 \end{aligned}$$

The value of α that maximizes N is[2]

$$\alpha = \delta / \left(\delta + 2k\delta^2 + 2\lambda\sigma^2\right)$$

The maximum net value turns out to be

$$N = \delta^2/2\left(\delta + 2k\delta^2 + 2\lambda\sigma^2\right)$$

This is an increasing function of δ.

Observe that as $\delta \to \infty$, the scientist need not incur any cost in his association with the NBF. That is, the knowledge transfer does not require the expertise of the scientist at any informal level. Instead, knowledge transfer is purely formal. Under these conditions, scientific knowledge can be procured by making a fixed payment. There will be no necessity to offer royalty payments proportional to the value generated. This is the implication of $\alpha \to 0$ as $\delta \to \infty$. Further, organizational learning can be represented by an increase in δ and/or a reduction in k. For, ultimately, one or both of the parties become more efficient if they learn about the knowledge requirements

[2] In most practical contexts, the royalty rates were shown to be independent of the skill level. For example, Kaufman and Lafontaine (1994, p. 314) observed that a franchise (such as McDonald's) keeps the sharing fraction constant. From a practical point of view, this enables them to attract only highly skilled franchisees and/or those with a low degree of risk aversion, for the constant royalty rate leaves greater ex ante rents with the franchisees. The existence of such ex ante rents in technology transfer arrangements was noted in Gallini and Wright (1990). A word of caution, however, is in order. The above mentioned studies noted that "efficiency of the agent" is difficult to operationalize and measure. The observed insignificance of the skill level, as a determinant of the royalty rate, may be due to the insufficiency of measurement. This is explicit in Yun (1999, p. 106).

of the other through their association in the organization. A reduction in k, given the costs of the scientist, implies that the scientist is accepting a greater share of the cost. Hence, he must receive a greater share α of the value generated.

The following variant reflects some of the economic implications of an increase in the size of the organization. The profit of each firm can be represented by

$$\pi_s = \alpha(m+u) - m^2/2\delta$$

so that $m = \alpha\delta$ as before. The NBF, or the large firm as the case may be, produces

$$m^* = n\alpha\delta$$

if it has n links with upstream firms. Given the possibility of dissonance alluded to earlier the investment and spending by the larger firm will be kn^2n^2, then it follows that

$$\pi_n = n(1-\alpha)(m+u) - km^2n^2$$

and the net value of the alliance is

$$N = n\alpha\delta - n\alpha^2\delta/2 - kn^2\alpha^2\delta^2 - \lambda n\alpha^2\sigma^2$$

The optimal choice of α will therefore be

$$\alpha = \delta/\left(\delta + 2\lambda\sigma^2 + 2kn\delta^2\right)$$

It can also be shown that the optimal n, that maximizes N, is given by

$$N = \left[\delta(2-\alpha) - 2\lambda\sigma^2\right]/4k\alpha\delta^2$$

Hence, n increases as δ rises initially, but highly skilled downstream firms are unlikely to find networking with larger firms profitable. Instead, as Danzon et al. (2005, p. 321) pointed out, "small firms take advantage of asymmetric information to out-license least promising compounds (while) retaining their more promising compounds to be developed internally." It should also be noted that the large firms tend to prefer a lower n.

The following observations are also pertinent. (a) The fundamental basis of contracting will be lost if the scientist need not interact with the NBF in the process of transferring the informal knowledge associated with scientific knowledge. This is reflected in $n \to 0$ as $\delta \to \infty$. That is, under these conditions, formal transfer of knowledge and a payment of fees to each of the scientists will be adequate and efficient. (b) The maximum size of the organization occurs when

$$\delta = 4\lambda\sigma^2/(2-\alpha)$$

That is, the NBF accepts a lower informal interaction with the scientist the greater the royalty share it must pay. Stated differently, a greater α will induce the NBF to choose projects where they require only a lower continuous involvement of the scientist. Similarly, when the project is less risky, the NBF would be more willing to undertake it, and it would be willing to involve the scientist on a more continuous basis. It cannot, however, be claimed that the NBF will undertake only those products that require this value of δ.

Note that one of the advantages of the contract is the expectation of greater commitment. For, as Teece (1980, p. 232) pointed out, " internal trading changes the incentives of the parties (i.e., aligns them more closely with the goals) and enables … (them to attenuate) costly haggling … and other non-cooperative (disruptive) behavior." In particular, the association of a university scientist with a NBF will improve his competence to move towards a marketable product. There will be a reduction in the scientist's perception of risk in the project. Further, the association of a star scientist may improve the image of the NBF on the capital market thereby reducing the uncertainty in its valuation. It is therefore possible that the variance of u becomes $V(u)=\sigma^2/\delta$. The corresponding optimal value of α is

$$\alpha = \delta^2/\left(\delta^2 + 2k\delta^3 + 2\lambda\sigma^2\right)$$

The organization is at an advantage whenever the variance can be reduced through such collaboration.

3.3 Cost Sharing

It is by now clear that sharing fixed costs at every stage of the organization becomes important. First, such risk sharing may reduce the liability of both the parties. Second, the NBF sharing costs of clinical trials, drug approvals, and so on induce the NBF to offer the requisite intangible knowledge in addition to the formal knowledge. It will then provide a commitment to the large company in so far as it transmits all the scientific information that it has truthfully. Part of the reason is of course its own interest in recovering investment. In the process of sharing costs, the NBF also gains control of the operations of the large firm. As a result, the NBF can scrutinize the decisions of the large firm and ensure alignment with its viewpoint.

Let s be the share of the NBF in the cost km^2. It will be assumed that this will have the effect of reducing the variance to σ^2/s. More pertinent to the argument will be the changes in the cost to the large firm. The following observations are relevant. (a) The firm has to pay the NBF an extra share of output by way of royalties due to the increase in his share of capital and the increase in the bargaining power. (b) The firm has to provide greater effort and perhaps incur more costs to convince the NBF to provide greater commitment ab initio. (c) The costs of negotiation, management, and conflict resolution increase with s. This may arise purely due to differences in expectations, management, and organizational values. The costs of making collective decisions can be quite substantial when the firms have diverse preferences.

The share of the total cost to the NBF will be skm^2. Its profit will now be

$$\pi_{\mathrm{f}} = \alpha\left(m+u\right) - m^2/2\delta - skm^2$$

Given the risk aversion, the value he attaches to π_{f} is

$$V_{\mathrm{f}} = \alpha m - m^2/2\delta - skm^2 - \lambda\alpha^2\sigma^2/s$$

Observe that the NBF will not accept a large s because he incurs additional cost. Further, there is a possibility that the NBF experiences liquidity constraints while raising the resources required for investments. Both these considerations suggest that the NBF will prevail on the choice of s. Hence, he can be expected to choose s and m to maximize V_{f}. This results in

$$s = \left(\lambda/k\right)^{1/2}\left(\sigma/\delta\right), \text{ and}$$
$$m = \alpha\delta^*, \text{ where } \delta^* = \beta\delta, \text{ and } \beta = -2\left(\lambda k\right)^{1/2}\sigma$$

The efficient choice of s so obtained has the following properties. (a) The NBF will accept a higher s to counteract the effect of a low δ. That is, he will signal greater commitment to the firm. (b) There is a direct relationship between s and $\lambda\sigma^2$. A greater λ and/or σ^2 necessitates the NBF indicating a greater commitment to the firm. (c) As m increases, the firm may seek greater security and commitment. The NBF will therefore agree to a larger s. It must however be acknowledged that an increase in s beyond a point may be a disadvantage to the firm because the NBF gains control. However, the choice of an efficient s, whose effect is through the variance, generally neutralizes the effect of a low δ.

3.4 Public Scientific R&D

As noted in Sect. 3.1, the development and commercialization of biotechnology have been knowledge intensive. No private firm has adequate scientific manpower or the laboratory tools to undertake the fundamental activities in the early phases of development. Perforce they must be developed and incubated in specialized research institutions and transferred to private firms through appropriate organizational mechanisms.[3] As Ramani (2002) pointed out, approaches to public policy focused on two ends of commercialization, viz., public research organizations and final

[3] Sonka and Pueppke (1999) noted that "much of the market application of biotechnology, in general, has involved small, entrepreneurial firms driving innovation. Often, these firms exploited publicly available knowledge to overcome their lack of (skill). Relative to agricultural technology,

product manufacturers. The effort was to retain the decision-making autonomy of each of the institutions involved, to the extent possible, and hope that formal interaction between them will develop to benefit society at large. However, as Ramani pointed out, "the indispensible intermediate link to (translate) scientific knowledge into technological competence was largely skipped."

The patent regime was an attempt to set up this link. The important development in biotechnology was in the form of the Bayh-Dole act in the USA. Of fundamental importance is the grant of patents to knowledge developed by scientists in public institutions. This enabled scientists in public institutions to recover the costs of R&D and appropriate the market value of their inventions either by creating startups on their own or license the use of their patents to private firms. As Fischer and Byerlee (2002) pointed out, "many governments (are) asking public research organizations to recover part of their costs by commercializing their products and services including sales of research products (e.g., sale of basic seeds), sales of non-research products and services (e.g., soil tests), and various forms of joint ventures.

In sum, there has been an acknowledgement that, in the context of knowledge-intensive biotechnology industry, neither the public sector nor the private sector is in a position to undertake all the requisite components of the value chain entirely by themselves. As a result, cooperation in varying degrees is called for depending on the organizational culture specific to a country and the industrial activity under consideration.[4]

An approach to the problem is to allow a private firm, which is perhaps more competent in handling the commercialization stage, to pursue it. Two alternatives are available:

1. The scientist or the public institution transfers knowledge and allows the private firm to make all the decisions.
2. They form a joint venture with both of them sharing costs and returns.

In general, as Fischer and Byerlee (2002) remarked, "joint venture agreements are common for private public collaboration. Each party contributes specific assets or knowledge, and shares benefits according to an apriori agreement. Since the

---

an important role of publicly supported research may be to create knowledge that can be used to fuel innovation in the market place."

[4]Even private firms may encounter financial constraints given the high risks of biotechnology projects. The Government of India (through its organ DBT) created BCIL (Biotechnology Consortium of India) with participation from IDBI, ICICI, and 30 other firms in the public sector. "It stipulated startups, arranged technology transfer and supported their efforts to attract adequate finances." For details, see Ramani (2002). On the other hand, France allowed publicly supported scientists and institutions to become shareholders in the firms associated with their laboratories. They may, as a result of such arrangements, gain control on knowledge leaks and performance of private firms. When the financial constraint is a problem, the scientist may also be allowed to seek venture capital and/or equity financing. However, this will reduce his control to some extent. It may also place a limit on the discoveries that can be moved to the commercial stage due to differences in perceptions about appropriability.

application of many products of biotechnology requires incorporation into locally adapted germplasm, there are many opportunities for the public sector to enter joint ventures with the private sector, especially when serving emerging commercial markets of interest to the private sector."

Assume that a scientist from a public institution discovered scientific knowledge that is expected to have an eventual commercial value. Consider the case where n such product developments can be based on this knowledge. Suppose, in the symmetric case, that each of the products is expected to generate a value m However, these developments have been subject to significant risk. The three major sources of such risk are:

1. Risks of rejection by the regulators
2. Competition from non-GM varieties
3. Rejection by the consumers

It may be postulated that the actual value generated is $(m+u)$ with u being a random variable with expected value $E(u)=0$ and variance $V(u)=\sigma^2$.

The essential choice for the scientist is the fraction α of the number of products, n, that he prefers to develop on his own. It will be assumed that the development of the remaining $(1-\alpha)n$ products will be licensed to private firms. Assume that production of each of the products entails a variable cost. For the scientist it can be represented by $m^2/2\delta^*$. On the other hand, it will be assumed to be $m^2/2\delta$; $\delta>\delta^*$ for the private firm.

Note that two different forces determine the variable costs of production. First, the level of output itself accounts for the variable costs. This can be captured by m^2. That is, it is postulated that there will be diminishing returns to the use of factors of production as m increases. Second, the scientist may not be as efficient as the private firm when it comes to commercialization. δ and δ^* therefore represent the degrees of efficiency of the scientist and the private firm. Postulate that the scientist or the private firm, as the case may be, incurs the entire cost. The private firm can compensate the scientist, for providing patented knowledge as well as the transfer of informal knowledge, by offering a fraction p of the value generated from the sale of the product.

It is important to examine the costs to the scientist in the case where a license is granted to a private firm. For all practical purposes, he has to:

1. Offer informal knowledge in the use of technology.
2. Monitor and control the private firm to guard against imitation and reengineering.

It can be expected that such costs will increase more than proportionately with m. Similarly, the costs will increase the farther the scientific invention is to the final product. This cost will therefore be represented by km^2. In general, k may be higher[5]:

[5] Note that the cost of licensing to a private firm is $km^2+m^2/2\delta$. On the other hand, if the scientist creates his own startup, it will be $m^2/2\delta^*$. Hence, licensing will be feasible only if $\delta^*<\delta/(1+2k\delta)$. k will also decrease as more private firms acquire competence either through learning by doing or

1. The more the requirements of knowledge transfer
2. The farther away the invention is to a product of commercial value
3. The lower the IPR protection
4. The greater the costs of financing and/or financial constraints

The profit for the scientist can be written as

$$\pi_s = \alpha n(m+u) + p(1-\alpha)n(m+u) - \alpha nm^2/2\delta * - (1-\alpha)nkm^2$$

It will be assumed, following the conventions of the principal agent models of the Kawasaki and McMillan (1987) vintage, that the scientist is risk averse. Hence, the value he assigns to π_s will be

$$V_s = \alpha nm + p(1-\alpha)nm - \alpha nm^2/2\delta * - (1-\alpha)nkm^2 - \lambda n^2\left[\alpha + p(1-\alpha)\right]^2\sigma^2$$

where λ is the degree of risk aversion of the scientist.

In a similar fashion, the profit of the $(1-\alpha)$n private firms is given by

$$\pi_n = (1-p)(1-\alpha)n(m+u) - (1-\alpha)nm^2/2\delta$$

The private firms are also involved in many other production activities. Consequently, they can effectively diversify their risk. That is, they will be generally risk neutral. The value of the license to them will be

$$V_n = (1-p)(1-\alpha)nm - (1-\alpha)nm^2/2\delta$$

Contract theory generally supports assigning decisions to the party with better information. Hence, the natural choice for modeling is to leave the decision regarding m to the private firms since they have better information. Clearly, the scientist is in the best position to choose α. Given that the scientist has a patent on knowledge, he can be expected to choose the terms of the license. In particular, he will choose the sharing fraction p as well. Each of the private firms derives a positive net profit as the number of product applications increases. Hence, they may not place any limit on n. But the scientist experiences diminishing returns with respect to increases in n. Consequently he will choose the efficient level of n as well.

Consider the efficient choice of m. It is given by $m=(1-p)\delta$. This represents the incentive constraint of each of the agents. That is, the private firm's output choice increases with its efficiency and the share of the revenue it gets.

---

hiring young scientists who acquired the skills through training and education. k may also decrease as n increases and/or α tends to unity. It should be noted that a private firm may consider σ^2 to be high because they are not sure about the extent and/or efficiency of informal knowledge transfer that they receive. To an extent, therefore, σ^2 may decrease with an increase in k and/or α. An efficient choice of k may also be conceptualized.

The principal agent models generally postulate that the principal (in this case the scientist) maximizes the net value of the contract, viz., $N = V_s + V_n$, taking the participatory constraint of the agent into account. That is, he maximizes

$$N = n(1-p)\delta - \alpha n(1-p)^2 \delta^2/2\delta^* - (1-\alpha)nk(1-p)^2\delta^2 - (1-\alpha)n(1-p)^2\delta/2 \\ -\lambda n^2\left[\alpha + p(1-\alpha)\right]^2\sigma^2$$

Each of the decisions of the scientist will be considered assuming the others as parametric. Adopting this approach identifies the transitional dynamics in an efficient manner.

Ceteris paribus, the choice of n satisfies the equation

$$(1-p)\delta - \alpha(1-p)^2/2\delta^* - (1-\alpha)k(1-p)^2\delta^2 - (1-\alpha)(1-p)^2\delta/2 \\ -2\lambda n\left[\alpha + p(1-\alpha)\right]^2\sigma^2 = 0$$

The following observations are pertinent:

1. $\partial n/\partial\delta^* > 0$. That is, an increase in the skill level of the scientist generates more startups including the licenses granted.
2. $\partial n/\partial k < 0$. An increase in the cost of monitoring and control by the scientist will deter him from granting more licenses. In particular, any reduction in IPR protection will deter the scientist from entrepreneurship.
3. $\partial n/\partial\lambda\sigma^2 < 0$. A risk-averse scientist is unlikely to grant too many licenses because that reduces his valuation of the expected returns.

Consider the choice of α or the willingness of the scientist to create his own startup. The optimal choice of α is such that

$$-(1-p)\delta^2/2\delta^* + k(1-p)\delta^2 + (1-p)\delta/2 - 2\lambda\sigma^2 n\left[\alpha + p(1-\alpha)\right] = 0$$

The following results can be readily verified:

1. $\partial\alpha/\partial n < 0$. Clearly, the larger the number of possible applications, the more he will contract out given his competence for commercialization of technology.
2. $\partial\alpha/\partial\delta^* > 0$. That is, he keeps more applications to himself when he is more competent.
3. $\partial\alpha/\partial\delta < 0$ if $\delta > \delta^*$. Greater competence of the licensee relative to his own will obviously induce the scientist to contract out more often. It should also be noted that $\delta < \delta^*$ when the scientific knowledge is in early stages and requires extensive R&D before a marketable product emerges. In such a case, the scientist will prefer to startup on his own.
4. $\partial\alpha/\partial k > 0$. That is, the more the monitoring and control necessary and the more the requirement of informal knowledge transfer, the more the scientist will prefer to create his own startup. The same applies when IPR protection is low.

5. $\partial\alpha/\partial\lambda\sigma^2 < 0$. Once again, it is plausible that a highly risk-averse scientist will not invest in his own startups.
6. $\partial\alpha/\partial p < 0$. It is expected that the scientist will license out more often if his share of revenues increases.

It can also be inferred that the scientist will be the sole entrepreneur if δ is fairly large in comparison to $\lambda\sigma^2$ and n and/or k is fairly large.

Consider the issue of the relationship between the number of startups (including licenses) and the net value generated in the process of commercialization. Ceteris paribus, it can be verified that $\partial N/\partial\delta^* > 0$ and $\partial n/\partial\delta^* > 0$. Consequently, an increase in the competence of the scientist will improve N as n increases. However, it cannot be generally shown that $\partial N/\partial n > 0$ in all contexts. This is not surprising since entrepreneurial success in generating a higher value of N is contingent on the entrepreneurs being supported by the availability of capital, finances, and so on. It can be surmised that this result will hold even in the steady state.

The analysis suggests that a scientist in a public institution has a greater motivation to become an entrepreneur and create a startup if (a) the eventual expected value of the discovery is substantial, (b) patent protection for proprietary knowledge is inadequate, (c) there is extensive necessity for knowledge development before a product of utility to the consumer emerges, and/or (d) there is a significant involvement of the scientist in the transfer of informal knowledge to private firms. On their part, private firms will accept a licensing contract only if they have adequate expertise and/or low-risk aversion. The institutional arrangements for financing biotechnology activity also tend to suggest that some form of joint venture will be the superior choice.

3.5 Conclusion

Biotechnology innovations proceed in cumulative steps ending with a product that is of use to the ultimate consumer. The scientists tend to protect their discoveries of fragments of cell structures and proteins through secrecy. This slows down scientific progress. To circumvent this constraint, a patent regime was put in place to provide intellectual property rights to discoverers of intermediate stages of science. Progress towards a useful end product therefore necessitated contracting. The successive stages of biotechnology developments also necessitated involvement of the discoverers of the earlier stages over prolonged time periods. This knowledge intensity was another reason for contracts. There was also a recognition that much of the scientific development and bioprocessing can fail. Similarly, the failure may occur at the stage of clinical testing or field trials of crops. These inherent risks are the primary reason for contractual sharing of such risks.

For all practical purposes, contracts were utilized to accelerate technological development. The primary goal was perhaps to minimize the costs of delivering a usable end product. However, this process had some undesirable consequences.

First, most scientists prefer to develop promising inventions in secrecy, and only dubious developments were licensed. Second, there has been a tendency to pass on high-risk inventions for contractual development. This is also a result of the risk-sharing propensities of contracting parties. Third, there was no specific method of establishing the cost reduction that the Coase logic advocated. Fourth, it has been difficult to conceptualize a uniform and efficient regulatory mechanism since the variability across developments has been quite pronounced.

In sum, the patent regime and contractual sharing of risks resulted in spreading risks. Conceptualizing efficient regulatory practices to achieve the much wanted cost reduction while reducing the intrinsic risk has been a challenging task.

References

Arora A (1996) Contracting for tacit knowledge: the provision of technical services in technology licensing contracts. J Dev Econ 50:233–256

Bottazi G, Dossi G, Lippi M, Pammoli F, Ricaboni M (2001) Innovation and corporate growth in the evolution of the drug industry. Int J Ind Organ 19:1161–1187

Danzon PM, Nicholson S, Pereira NS (2005) Productivity in pharmaceutical biotechnology R&D: the role of experiences and alliances. J Health Econ 24:317–339

DeCarolis D, Deeds DL (1999) The impact of stocks and flows of organizational knowledge on firm performance an empirical investigation of the biotechnology industry. Strateg Manag J 20:953–968

Fischer K, Byerlee D (2002) Managing intellectual property and commercialization in public research organizationms. In: Byerlee D, Ecaverria RG (eds) Agricultural research policy in the era of privatization. Inter-American Development Bank, Washington, DC

Gallini NT, Wright BD (1990) Technology transfer under asymmetric information. Rand J Econ 21:147–160

Kaufman PJ, Lafontaine F (1994) Costs of control: the sources of economic rents for McDonald's franchisees. J Law Econ 37:417–454

Kawasaki S, Mcmillan J (1987) The design of contracts: evidence from Japanese subcontracting. J Jpn Int Econ 3:1–30

Liebeskind JP, Oliver AL, Zucker L, Brewer M (1996) Social networks, learning and flexibility: sourcing scientific knowledge in biotechnology firms. Organ Sci 7:428–443

Powell WW, Koput KW, Smith-Doerr L, Owen-Smith J (1999) Network position and firm performance: organizational returns to collaboration in biotechnology industry. In: Andrews S, Knoke D (eds) Networks in and around organizations. JAI Press, Greenwich

Ramani S (2002) Who is interested in biotech? R&D strategies, knowledge base, and market sales of Indian biopharmaceutical firms. Res Policy 31:381–398

Schimmelpfenning DE, Gray CE, Brennan MF (2004) The impact of seed industry concentration on innovation: a study of the US biotechnology market leaders. Agric Econ 30:57–167

Sinka S, Pueppke S (1999) Exploring the public's role in agricultural biotechnology research. AgBioforum 2:33–36

Teece DJ (1980) Towards an economic theory of multiproduct firm. J Econ Behav Organ 1:237–247

Yun M (1999) Subcontracting relations in the Korean automotive industry: risk sharing and technological capability. Int J Ind Organ 17:81–108

Chapter 4
Information Asymmetry

Abstract Information asymmetry has a pivotal role in determining the nature of contractual arrangements of international joint ventures. In recognition of the risks associated therein, MNCs utilize resources to identify the information pertaining to the supply chain management and/or offer informal knowledge in the use of the technology transferred to their joint venture partners. There is, however, inadequate theoretical explanation of the channels through which such policies affect the choice of contract parameters (in particular, royalty rates) and how they influence the performance of joint ventures. This study argues that such policies reduce the variance associated with information asymmetry and thereby neutralize the deficiencies due to the lack of skills. This enables the MNCs to offer a uniform royalty contract to all their joint venture partners as reported in the empirical literature.

4.1 Nature of Information

Policy reforms in many developing countries paved the way for multinational firms transferring new technology to them and participating in their production and distribution processes. In general, such technology transfer consists of providing machinery, equipment, plant settings (installation and operating manuals), and procedures for maintenance. This is usually designated as formal knowledge. See, for instance, Arora (1996, p. 234). The MNCs expect a clearly defined level of output from the given resources if the formal knowledge is sufficient to operate the technology efficiently.

However, the MNCs experience information asymmetry with respect to the supply chain management. In particular, they are not fully aware of the production conditions (for instance, the quality of raw materials and labor) in the foreign country. Similarly, they do not have the knowledge regarding the market demand for the new product (because consumers in the foreign country are not familiar with its value to them). The MNCs as well as the foreign firms expect adverse selection as a result of such information asymmetry. That is, irrespective of which firm the MNC contracts with, the expected output will not be realized. In general, there is an ex

Based on content from "Information Asymmetry in International Joint Ventures" first published in *Indian Economic Journal*, 54(2), 2006, pp. 7–20. Content reproduced here with permission from Indian Economic Association.

T.V.S.R. Rao, *Risk Sharing, Risk Spreading and Efficient Regulation*,
DOI 10.1007/978-81-322-2562-1_4

ante recognition that the realized output will be random. This risk can be characterized by the variance in output.[1]

On the other hand, the foreign firm may not have complete knowledge and competence to absorb the new technology and produce output efficiently. In particular, they may not have the informal knowledge, in addition to the formal knowledge alluded to above, for efficient assimilation, utilization, and adaptation of technology. Such knowledge consists of rules of thumb, heuristic adaptations to local production conditions, and other tricks of trade. See, for instance, Arora (1996, p. 234).[2] Once again, the MNC may not have the a priori information about the distribution of such talents, to assimilate technology, among the potential foreign firms that it chooses. The information asymmetry makes the production process inefficient if the foreign firm is expected to learn these aspects on its own through learning by doing.

Confronted with different types of information asymmetry, the MNCs may choose contract parameters (in particular, the royalty rates) based on the information about the supply chain or the capacity of the foreign firm to absorb the new technology. The royalty rates offered to the foreign firms will differ from one another. Empirical evidence does not generally support this expected behavior. Instead, the MNCs recognize that when dealing with many foreign firms, it may be impractical for them to discriminate among them in setting the royalty rates. Therefore, they tend to define a uniform royalty rate for all of them. The problem for economic analysis is to justify such a practice and identify the efficient choice of the uniform royalty rate.[3]

Consider the possibility that the MNCs conceptualize alternative policies. Assume that the randomness is in the supply chain management of foreign firms. The MNCs may then make some initial investment in understanding the nature and extent of the markets for inputs and products. This tends to reduce the randomness due to such information asymmetry.

Similarly, when the MNC recognizes the necessity for intangible knowledge for the efficient management of the foreign firm, it may offer to (a) train the personnel in the foreign country in the use of technology; (b) depute specialists to provide the

---

[1] It should be clearly noted that the expected level of output will not change ex ante. Based on the external market conditions that are not known a priori, there will be a distribution of actual output that materializes depending on the choice of the joint venture partner. Hence, the only appropriate specification of the realized output is that it will be a random variable with mean defined by the design specification of the technology and some variance that is a consequence of the asymmetric market conditions.

[2] The following example from the chemical industry is illustrative. As Arora (1996, p. 235) stated it, "transfer of chemical technology will typically involve training the licensee in a variety of issues such as how to handle and store chemicals, how to control the production process and return it to operation after (an) unscheduled breakdown caused by (an) accident or impurities in the feedstock." A similar distinction between formal knowledge and know-how can be found in Wang and Blomstrom (1992), Andersen (1999, p. 628), Anand and Khanna (2000, p. 112), and Javorcik (2004, p. 51).

[3] Several studies pointed out that firms choose such uniform rates in practice. See, for example, Nichols (1983), Svejnar and Smith (1984), Chisholm (1997), Yun (1999), Okamuro (2001), McCalman (2004), and others.

requisite technical assistance in establishing production, quality control, and testing; (c) provide assistance in the design and layout of the manufacturing unit; (d) assist in the adaptation of drawings and designs; and (e) transmit technical information about improvements in product and manufacturing processes.

However, there is inadequate theoretical analysis of the channels through which such policies affect the performance of the firm.[4] In particular, it is as yet necessary to examine the possibility of alternate policies sustaining the preference for uniform royalty rates. The primary purpose of this study is to set up such an analytical structure. The fundamental result of this paper is that the change in the variance of the realized output is the principal channel of transmission of MNC decisions to the choice of contract parameters (in particular, royalty rates) and the performance of the joint venture. This has fundamental implications for the empirical analysis of joint venture contracts.

Analytical work along these lines generally utilizes the principal agent model originally proposed by Kawasaki and McMillan (1987) (KM hereafter). Section 4 2 presents a pertinent variant of this model. This structure, as well as other variants of it, suggests that the share of output received by the foreign firm is related to the efficiency of the agent and his degree of risk aversion.[5]

However, much of the empirical evidence suggests that it is predominantly determined by the risk aversion of the agent alone. See, for instance, Chishlom (1997, p. 196) and McCalman (2004). There is also some indirect evidence in Liu and Wang (2003, p. 950).[6] In Sect. 4.3, it is shown that the change in variance achieved through the provision of informal knowledge in the use of technology by the MNC, in contrast to the expected value formulation, can sustain this stylized fact.

It is sometimes suggested that the deficiencies in information are purely due to the lack of appropriate machinery and hence formal knowledge itself. In particular, the MNCs claim that the import and tariff policies prevent the MNC from supplying the appropriate machinery, embodying the technology, at the right time. However, it can be shown that sharing formal knowledge, by way of the MNC providing some fixed capital and machinery to the foreign firm, cannot sustain the stylized facts even if such a change in variance is postulated.[7] This is the theme of Sect. 4.4.

---

[4] See, for example, Marjit et al. (1995), Das (1999), and Das and Katayama (2003).

[5] Svejnar and Smith (1984) noted that the MNCs may devise policies that can effectively eliminate the deficiencies in the skill level of the foreign firm.

[6] The existence of ex ante rents in technology transfer arrangements was noted in Gallini and Wright (1990). Even in the context of franchise contracts, the royalty rates were shown to be independent of the skill level. See, for example, Kaufmann and Lafontaine (1994, p. 314). Instead, they observed that a franchise (such as McDonalds) keeps the sharing fraction constant. From a practical point of view, this enables them to attract only highly skilled franchisees and/or those with a low degree of risk aversion for the constant royalty rate leaves greater ex ante rents with the franchisees.

[7] In two related studies, Rao and Sharma (2005, 2006), this feature was considered to be an aspect of moral hazard. Another set of policies will be necessary under moral hazard if it is anticipated. It was, however, shown that the changes in the variance are the channel for transmission even in such a context.

In other words, it can be argued that expenditures directed toward rectifying the observed deficiency in informal knowledge alone can yield the desired results.[8] The pertinent question for analysis is the relative efficiency of the alternative policy options that have been considered. This will be attempted as well. Section 4.5 then summarizes the results. Further work, especially as it relates to moral hazard, will also be suggested.

4.2 Benchmark Model

Consider the context of a multinational firm (an IPR and/or patent holder designated as *P* hereafter) entrusting production and/or distribution to a foreign firm (an agent referred to as *F*). Assume that an output *e* is planned and that *F* incurs a variable cost $e^2/2\delta$, where δ is the efficiency of the agent.[9] However, assume that the realized output will be random due to external factors that *F* cannot control.[10] Denote the actual output by $(e+u)$ where *u* is a random variable[11] with $E(u)=0$ and $V(u)=\sigma^2$. In its simplest form, the KM model postulates that[12]

$$\begin{aligned}\pi_F &= \text{profit of the agent} \\ &= p(e+u) - e^2/2\delta\end{aligned}$$

where p = share of output accruing to *F*. *P* agrees to share the risk primarily because he is likely to incur greater costs and/or experience greater risk if he organizes production on his own. Typically, the KM model postulates that *F* is risk averse. Hence, the value of the contract to *F* can be written as

[8] Liquidity effects, observed in Chishlom (1997, p. 193) and Okamuro (2001, p. 360), may also be an explanation for such sharing. Such a modification can also be expected to sustain the results developed in Sect. 4.3. See footnote 17 below.

[9] Quadratic approximations for costs appear to perform quite well in empirical practice. This is the basic reason for such a choice in models related to the KM formulation. Some of the results developed in the rest of the paper may not hold for very general specifications of the cost functions. Empirical analysis based on these models must add other relevant variables and make some modifications in functional forms.

[10] It may be argued that *P* is initially making a plan to create a joint venture with *F*. Under these conditions, the effect of randomness will impinge on *P* primarily. The nature of the changes in the results will be spelt out in footnote 14 below.

[11] Under the assumption of information asymmetry, the randomness may be either in the market conditions or the knowledge regarding the skills of the foreign firm. To begin with, it will be assumed that the MNC has no control on either of these sources of randomness.

[12] The following observation is pertinent. In this formulation, an ex ante choice of *e* commits *F* to a definite variable cost. However, he cannot be sure of the output and revenue realized. Hence, *F* is likely to be risk averse. He seeks an insurance against this risk by asking *P* to share it with him. The share of output accruing to *F* can be interpreted as an incentive as well as an insurance effect. See, for example, Aoki (1988).

$$V_F = pe - e^2/2\delta - \lambda p^2\sigma^2$$

where λ is the degree of risk aversion of F. The KM model postulates that F chooses e, for a given p, to maximize V_F. That is, F will choose[13]

$$e = p\delta$$

On the contrary, the MNC has many more avenues of generating income and thereby hedging its risk, given its diversified portfolio. Hence, P is postulated to be risk neutral. The value of the contract to P is

$$V_P = (1-p)e$$

The other essential feature of the KM model is its assumption that P chooses p so as to maximize the net value of the contract, viz.,

$$\begin{aligned} N &= V_F + V_P \\ &= e - e^2/2\delta - \lambda p^2\sigma^2 \end{aligned}$$

taking the participatory constraint of F into account. That is, p is chosen to maximize

$$N = p\delta - p^2\delta/2 - \lambda p^2\sigma^2$$

Hence, the optimal sharing fraction is

$$p = \delta/\left(\delta + 2\lambda\sigma^2\right)$$

Observe that if the agent is very efficient and/or risk neutral, he will take the risk, keep the entire output, and pay upfront fees to the MNC for p tends to 1 as λ tends to 0 or δ tends to ∞.

Clearly, the model does not include any controls, which F or P can choose, to eliminate the lack of skill of F and the exogenously defined randomness. They are merely adjusting p and e keeping the randomness in perspective.[14]

---

[13] Note that F is likely to have more or better information about the markets in the foreign country. Hence, this will be a natural choice whenever there is information asymmetry.

[14] As noted in footnote 10 earlier, it can be argued that the MNC experiences the risk in the search for a joint venture partner. As such, it may not want to leave the decision regarding the output to the foreign firm. That is, the roles of the two firms may be reversed when it comes to the decisions regarding m and p. Maintaining all other assumptions as before, it can be shown that the optimal choices will be

$$e = 2\delta\lambda\sigma^2/\left(\delta + 2\lambda\sigma^2\right)$$

and

4.3 Scientific Knowledge

The analysis of efficient policy choices of the MNCs must take into account both aspects of information asymmetry alluded to earlier. First, suppose the MNC experiences difficulties in assessing the market demand for its products in the foreign market a priori. Clearly, it may make some investment in obtaining the requisite information. Second, consider a situation wherein *P* feels that foreign firms will not be in a position to manage the technology efficiently unless the informal knowledge about the technology is transferred along with the formal knowledge. It then becomes necessary for *P* to incur some expenditure for providing the requisite informal knowledge. To examine the effect of such an expenditure on the contract parameters in the KM framework, it is necessary to specify the channels of transmission.

One possibility is that the requirements of informal knowledge as well as market information are firm specific. Expenditure by the MNC, in resolving either form of information asymmetry, may be expected to move each of the firms closer to the expected level of output. That is, the probability of the actual output (for a given cost) being higher increases. The change in expected value is one approach to characterizing the effect of the MNC policy. Note, however, that this description also implies that the variance in the output decreases. The question that needs to be addressed is which of these specifications is closer to explaining (or justifying) the observed pattern of behavior? Another way of characterizing the channels of transmission is to acknowledge the possibility that all foreign firms are in need of such informal knowledge in varying degrees. That is, the MNC providing such knowledge affects the performance of all potential joint venture partners. In particular, the distribution tends to be closer to the ex ante expected level of output. It is therefore far more plausible to postulate that such MNC policies, directed toward reducing the information asymmetry that they experience, reduce the variance of the output.

These specifications will now be considered sequentially. The main focus of attention is on the correspondence of these theoretical specifications with the empirically acknowledged stylized facts. It can be readily noted that the effects of these

---

$$p = \delta/\left(\delta + 2\lambda\sigma^2\right)$$

Clearly, the output choice of *P* will be larger whenever

$$2\lambda\sigma^2 > \delta$$

This result is valid when *F* is highly risk averse and/or not very efficient in assimilating the new technology. The natural question is which of these choices is superior? The maximized net value per unit cost provides the best measure for comparison. For the choice in the text, this value is

$$v = 1 + 2\lambda\sigma^2/\delta$$

while the alternative here yields

$$v = 1 + \delta/2\lambda\sigma^2$$

Hence, the choice in the text is superior whenever *F* is more risk averse. Since the choice of *p* is the same in either case, the conclusion of the text remains intact.

policies are symmetric. Hence, only the informal knowledge dimension will be considered in detail.

Consider firm-specific informal knowledge to begin with. It can be expected that such expenditures on informal knowledge will also be subject to diminishing returns. Hence, for a given level of output e, it can be assumed that P spends an amount me^2.

The corresponding variable cost can be written as

$$v_F = e^2/2\delta m$$

That is, a large value of m enables the foreign firm to assimilate the new technology more efficiently. Consequently, there will be a reduction in the variable cost at which output e can be delivered. The basic assumption underlying this approach is that such an expenditure cannot alter the exogenous randomness in the market conditions and the degree of risk aversion of F. Hence, it is necessary to maintain that the realized level of output is random with $V(u)=\sigma^2$. As a result, the profit of F is[15]

$$\pi_F = p(e+u) - e^2/2\delta m$$

The efficient choice of output is therefore

$$e = p\delta m$$

The net value of the contract becomes

$$\begin{aligned} N &= e - e^2/2\delta m - \lambda p^2\sigma^2 - me^2 \\ &= p\delta m - p^2\delta m/2 - \lambda p^2\sigma^2 - p^2\delta^2 m^3 \end{aligned}$$

Consequently, the optimal choices of m and p are such that

$$\begin{aligned} &2 - p - 6m^2 p\delta = 0, \text{ and} \\ &\delta m\left(1 - p - 2p\delta m^2\right) = 2\lambda p\sigma^2 \end{aligned}$$

Hence, it can be inferred that[16]

$$p = 2/\left(1 + 6m^2\delta\right)$$

and the choice of m is such that

[15] Clearly, P must be compensated for the additional expenditure. The obvious mechanism is to adjust p suitably. Some authors suggest that P will claim a fixed amount upfront for the transfer of informal knowledge. See, for example, Brickley (2002). However, a change in p is more realistic if the expenditure by P depends on the skill level of F. This approach will be adopted in the sequel.

[16] It should also be noted that F does not get the full benefit to himself if an increase in me^2 is interpreted as increasing output if he efficiently uses the tacit knowledge. For, $p<1$.

$$\delta m\left(-1+2m^2\delta\right)=4\lambda\sigma^2$$

Note that, to make the analysis meaningful, it should be assumed that

$$-1+2m^2\delta>0$$

since δ, m, and $\lambda\sigma^2$ are positive. From the viewpoint of economic theory, this indicates that ceteris paribus the MNC would be willing to deal with only those foreign firms whose skill level δ exceeds $1/2m^2$. It is also natural that the more MNC would be willing to work with a lower-skilled foreign firm, the more it is willing to spend on the transfer of tacit knowledge.

It can also be readily verified that

$$\partial m/\partial\delta=-m\left(-1+4m^2\delta\right)/\delta\left(-1+6m^2\delta\right)<0$$

and, similarly,

$$\partial m/\partial\lambda\sigma^2=4/\delta\left(-1+6m^2\delta\right)>0$$

The MNC has to incur a lower cost to transfer tacit knowledge to F if it is more efficient. For any given m, an increase in $\lambda\sigma^2$ decreases N. To restore a higher net value of the contract, the MNC is compelled to increase m and reduce the variance further. Partially differentiating the equation $p=2/(1+6m^2\delta)$ with respect to δ and $\lambda\sigma^2$ successively, it can be shown that

$$\partial p/\partial\delta>0 \text{ and } \partial p/\partial\lambda\sigma^2<0$$

These results are consistent with the KM formulation. However, contrary to expectations, p cannot be independent of δ.[17] That is, P cannot effectively counteract the inefficiency if its expenditure affects only the expected value of output or the variable cost.

[17] The context of liquidity constraints is somewhat analogous. Postulate that P makes an a priori judgment that the randomness is due to liquidity constraints and not the shortage of tacit knowledge. Assume that F is experiencing liquidity constraints primarily because his skills and collateral are inadequate. One approach available to F is to locally obtain finances at a higher interest rate. On the other hand, P may agree to raise finances in its parent country if some saving is possible. Suppose, P incurs an extra cost me^2 and expects F to accept the variable cost $e^2/2\delta$ as before. Or, alternatively, P may allow F to raise the requisite finances and reimburse me^2 of expenditure. The greater the value of m offered, the lower the σ^2 due to the randomness created by the liquidity constraints. Hence, the optimal choice of m will be exactly the same as before. Once again, it is evident that the endogenous randomness specification compensates for the lack of skill on the part of F to raise the requisite finances. However, note that the basis for this formulation will be lost if the liquidity constraints are external to the operation of F. Further, it cannot be taken for granted that adequate finances will be available at the efficient m determined by the model. Some further refinements are in order.

The possibility that the transfer of tacit knowledge reduces the variance may now be examined. Assume that me^2 of expenditure by P leaves the variable cost unaltered at $e^2/2\delta$ while making $V(u)=\sigma^2/m$. Then, the value of the contract to F becomes

$$V_F = pe - e^2/2\delta - \lambda p^2\sigma^2/m$$

The efficient choice of e will now be

$$e = p\delta$$

and the net value of the contract is

$$N = pd - p^2\delta/2 - mp^2\delta^2 - \lambda p^2\sigma^2/m$$

The optimal choices of m and p are determined by the equations[18]

$$\delta^2 m^2 = \lambda\sigma^2, \text{ and}$$
$$p = 1/(1+4\sqrt{\lambda}\sigma)$$

Hence, the choice of m that neutralizes the effect of low skill level is

$$m = \sqrt{\lambda}\sigma/\delta$$

It will be lower the higher the skill level. However, a higher $\lambda\sigma^2$ necessitates a greater m. The most important finding is that p is now independent of δ. Clearly, an efficient choice of m neutralizes the deficiency due to the lower skill level of the foreign firm.[19,20]

[18] The MNC has no way of knowing a priori what the degree of risk aversion is. Consequently, they cannot devise any policies to moderate it. As a result, if they fix a p^* (constant) a priori, only foreign firms with low risk aversion will agree to joint ventures. The inframarginal firms derive a positive value from such contracts.

[19] Whereas P cannot effectively identify and monitor the effort of F (given the assumption of information asymmetry P only knows the variable cost as F reveals it and acts on that basis), the same is not true of the variance for it is a result of the general environment in which the foreign firm operates and is not specific to its own decisions. As such, it can be identified and monitored. In other words, me^2 efficiently reduces the variance for any given level of motivation and its implementation is certain because P gains control over it. Hence, the lack of skill, only if it manifests in the form of higher variance, can be effectively neutralized by the provision of tacit knowledge.

[20] P generally has a superior technology and hence a better product, in comparison to products of rival firms in the foreign country. It transfers this technology to F through the joint venture. F derives a market advantage due to this technical superiority.

4.4 Fixed Investment

P generally agrees to offer a part of the fixed capital equipment to *F* in addition to the transfer of technology for it may not be possible to achieve the desired quality and efficient level of output without it.[21] Further, though risk sharing ex post is still an alternative, it will be more efficient for *P* (the party with better information) to devise mechanisms to reduce the risk. Specific investments of *P* in the joint venture can be expected to reduce the variance of the random effects. This is the insurance effect alluded to in Aoki (1988) and Okamuro (2001) in a related context.

An analytical framework, to specify the efficient contract arrangements in such a context, can be outlined as follows. Let

F_f = investment of *F* in the fixed capital of the firm
F_p = investment of *P*

These quantities will be measured as per unit of time. *F* combines F_f with some variable factors in the production process. Assume that

$$\begin{aligned} v_f &= \text{variable factors employed by } F \\ &= e^2/2\delta F_f^{\alpha}; \alpha < 1 \end{aligned}$$

where e = efficient level of output and

δ = technological and organizational capabilities of *F*.

The above specification implies that the production process is governed by a Cobb-Douglas production technology with decreasing returns to scale.

The basic purpose of *P* in offering *Fp* to *F* is that of reducing the variance of u.[22] That is, u is such that

$$\begin{aligned} E(u) &= 0 \text{ and} \\ V(u) &= s^2/F_p \end{aligned}$$

Such a reduction in variance enhances the value of the joint venture to the risk averse *F*.

[21] This practice is prevalent in the context of franchising. See, for instance, the case of McDonalds outlined in Kaufman and Lafontaine (1994). Portfolio investment and equity sharing have a different purpose altogether. It will not be considered in this study.

[22] It can be shown that the alternative, of writing

$$v_F = e^2/2\delta F_f^{-} F_P,$$

yields similar results. Das and Katayama (2003) specify

$$v_F = e^2/2\delta \left(F_F + F_p\right)^{-}$$

Even this variant yields qualitatively the same conclusions.

The value of the contract to F can now be represented by

$$V_{\mathrm{f}} = pe - F_{\mathrm{f}} - \left(e^2/2\delta F_{\mathrm{f}}^{\alpha}\right) - \left(\lambda p^2\sigma^2/F_{\mathrm{p}}\right)$$

F chooses e and F_{f} such that

$$e = p\delta F_{\mathrm{f}}^{\alpha} \text{ and}$$
$$\alpha e^2 = 2\delta F_{\mathrm{f}}^{\alpha+1}$$

Hence, it follows that

$$F_{\mathrm{f}} = \left(\alpha\delta p^2/2\right)^{-1/(\alpha-1)}$$

and the cost of producing e units of output will be

$$C_{\mathrm{f}} = F_{\mathrm{f}}(\alpha+1)/\alpha$$

The net value of the contract is

$$N = e - F_{\mathrm{p}} - \left(\lambda p^2\sigma^2/F_{\mathrm{p}}\right) - \left(\alpha\delta p^2/2\right)^{-1/(\alpha-1)}(\alpha+1)/\alpha$$

P has the choice of F_{p} and p while taking the participation constraints of F into account. Hence, it follows that

$$F_{\mathrm{p}} = \sqrt{\lambda}p\sigma$$

The choice of p satisfies the equation

$$A\delta^{-1/\alpha-1}p^{-2\alpha/(\alpha-1)}(p-1) = 2\sqrt{\lambda}\sigma$$
$$\text{where } A = (\alpha/2)^{-\alpha/(\alpha-1)}(\alpha+1)/(\alpha-1) < 0$$

It can be readily verified that

$$\partial p/\partial\lambda\sigma^2 < 0$$

That is, P gets a greater share of output since he is taking more risk. Similarly,

$$\partial p/\partial\delta = p(p-1)/\delta\left[2\alpha-(\alpha+1)p\right] > 0$$

since the second-order condition for maximum necessitates $[2\alpha-(\alpha+1)p]<0$. The economic content of the second-order condition can be elucidated as follows. Note that there exists some δ^* corresponding to $p=2\alpha/(\alpha+1)$. Hence, P will accept a joint venture with F if and only if his efficiency level exceeds δ^*.

Recall that the provision of F_P can be viewed as a transfer of formal knowledge alone. F will not be in a position to assimilate it efficiently if his skill level is low for, as noted earlier, some informal knowledge is necessary. That is, investments of this form, even when efficiently chosen, cannot neutralize the deficiency in the skills of F. The contract choice, and the royalty rate in particular, remains a function of both δ and $\lambda\sigma^2$. This completes the demonstration of the conjecture that, unless it takes an appropriate form, even a reduction in randomness cannot explain the stylized facts.

4.5 Summing Up

Confronted with information asymmetry, the MNC, when it enters an international joint venture, makes attempts to identify specific sources of risk and create contractual arrangements to eliminate them. Providing tacit knowledge, explicitly incurring the requisite cost, is one of the major choices. This is expected to compensate the lack of skills of the foreign firm. In practice, the MNC also finds it practical to fix a common royalty rate for all such foreign transactions. However, the royalty rates may depend on the risk aversion since it is individual specific and it may not be possible to alter it through MNC policies.

While these aspects of the contracts are intuitively clear, the economic theory underlying the decisions has not been consistent with these stylized facts. Variants of the principal agent models, emanating from Kawasaki and McMillan (1987), deal with risk explicitly. However, the traditional approach to dealing with the effect of economic choices through expected values persists. This has been a hindrance. This study has shown that the channels of transmission are more likely to be through a change in variance. This approach has the advantage of being consistent with the stylized facts.

Surely, each aspect of information asymmetry needs to be tackled through policies that are most pertinent. Sharma and Rao (2007) examined other policy options for reducing adverse selection. However, the basic theme of this paper carries over.

The role of equity financing also appears to be similar for both the control and commitment effects of equity holding by the foreign firm or portfolio investors in that country have been alluded to in the literature. Intuitively, an efficient choice of the equity share for F can be expected to reduce the variance of output and/or revenue and thereby mitigate the adverse effects of low IPR protection. See, for example, Rao and Sharma (2005, 2006).

On the whole, the conceptualization of the changes in variance as a result of various policy options appears to be a promising theoretical development in understanding the nature of contract choice in international joint ventures.

References

Anand BN, Khanna T (2000) The structure of licensing contracts. J Ind Econ 48:103–135

Andersen PH (1999) Organizing international technical collaboration in subcontractor relationships: an investigation of the knowledge-stickiness problem. Res Policy 28:625–642

Aoki M (1988) Information, incentives and bargaining in the Japanese economy. Cambridge University Press, Cambridge

Arora A (1996) Contracting for tacit knowledge: the provision of technical services in technology licensing contracts. J Dev Econ 50:233–256

Brickley JA (2002) Royalty rates and upfront fees in share contracts: evidence from franchising. J Law Econ Organ 18:511–535

Chishlom DC (1997) Profit-sharing versus fixed-payment contracts: evidence from the motion pictures industry. J Law Econ Organ 13:169–201

Das SP (1999) Direct foreign investment versus licensing. Rev Dev Econ 3:85–97

Das SP, Katayama S (2003) International joint ventures and host-country policies. Jpn Econ Rev 54:381–394

Gallini NT, Wright BD (1990) Technology transfer under asymmetric information. Rand J Econ 21:147–160

Javorcik BS (2004) The composition of foreign direct investment and protection of intellectual property rights: evidence from transition economies. Eur Econ Rev 48:39–62

Kaufman PJ, Lafontaine F (1994) Costs of control: the source of economic rents for McDonald's franchisees. In: Masten SE (ed) Case studies in contracting and organization. Oxford University Press, NewYork

Kawasaki S, McMillan J (1987) The design of contracts: evidence from Japanese subcontracting. J Jpn Int Econ 1:327–349

Liu X, Wang C (2003) Does foreign direct investment facilitate technological progress? Evidence from Chinese industries. Res Policy 32:945–953

Margit S, Broll U, Mallick I (1995) A theory of overseas joint ventures. Econ Lett 47:367–370

McCalman P (2004) Foreign direct investment and intellectual property rights: evidence from Hollywood's global distribution of movies and videos. J Int Econ 62:107–123

Nichols S (1983) Agency contracts, institutional mode, and the transition to foreign direct investment by British manufacturing multinationals before 1939. J Econ Hist 43:675–686

Okamuro H (2001) Risk sharing in the supplier relationship: new evidence from the Japanese automotive industry. J Econ Behav Organ 45:361–381

Rao TVSR, Sharma R (2005) Equity participation in international joint ventures. Decision 33:1–20

Rao TVSR, Sharma R (2006) Commitment and control in international joint ventures. In: Narayana N (ed) Issues in globalization and economic reforms. Serials Publications, New Delhi

Sharma R, Rao TVSR (2006) Information asymmetry in international joint ventures. Indian Econ J 54:7–20

Sharma R, Rao TVSR (2007) Technology transfer in international joint ventures. Indian J Econ 87:663–678

Svejnar J, Smith SC (1984) The economics of joint ventures in less developed countries. Q J Econ 99:149–167

Wang JY, Blomstrom M (1992) Foreign investment and technology transfer. Eur Econ Rev 36:137–155

Yun M (1999) Subcontracting relations in the Korean automobile industry: risk sharing and technological capability. Int J Ind Organ 17:81–108

[illegible]
[illegible] (2005) [illegible]
[illegible] (2003) [illegible]
[illegible]
[illegible] (1997) [illegible]
[illegible]
[illegible]
[illegible] (2008) [illegible]
[illegible]
[illegible]
[illegible]
[illegible]
[illegible]
[illegible]
[illegible]
[illegible]
[illegible]
[illegible]
[illegible]
[illegible]

Chapter 5
Technology Transfer

Abstract Information asymmetry and adverse selection are intrinsic to technology transfer across national boundaries. The MNCs therefore offer informal knowledge in the use of technology, in addition to formal technological details, to their joint venture partners. They also share in the capital investments to elicit greater commitment. Theoretical explanation of the channels through which such sharing affects the contract parameters is however inadequate. In particular, the existing models are mostly deterministic and do not account for hidden action on the part of the foreign firms and the associated uncertainty. The principal agent model offers a more suitable framework for analysis. Utilizing the framework of the principal agent model, this study argues that such policies reduce the variance associated with the risk and thereby neutralize deficiencies due to information asymmetry. From a strategic management perspective, this conclusion suggests that MNC policies directed to assessing and reducing overall environmental uncertainties, especially those related to firms in the industry and government policies, will be superior to the provision of firm-specific informal knowledge.

5.1 The Setting

Technological development by MNCs generally centers around resources (both physical inputs and entrepreneurial skills) available in their country and their management culture. They design machinery, procedures for installation and operation, and specifications for maintenance with this environment in perspective. MNCs expect a clearly defined level of output from given resources if such tangible (formal) knowledge is adequate to operate the technology efficiently. See, for example, Arora (1996, p. 234). MNCs generally transfer the formal knowledge to foreign firms and hope that they can develop adequate informal procedures, specific to their industrial environment, to operate the technology efficiently.

However, two types of information asymmetry are intrinsic to such technology transfer. First, MNCs do not generally have adequate knowledge about the availability of appropriate resources to organize production efficiently and the size of

Based on content from "Technology Transfer in International Joint Ventures" first published in *The Indian Journal of Economics*, 87(347), 2007, pp. 673–678.

T.V.S.R. Rao, *Risk Sharing, Risk Spreading and Efficient Regulation*,
DOI 10.1007/978-81-322-2562-1_5

markets in foreign countries. By way of contrast, entrepreneurs in the foreign country will be better informed about these aspects. Second, foreign firms may not have the skills or the management culture to absorb and implement the new technology efficiently. MNCs will not be in a position to ascertain this at the time of negotiating contracts. This information asymmetry makes it necessary to conceptualize a joint venture based on comparative advantage.

Joint ventures experience adverse selection due to information asymmetry inherent in such arrangements. First, the MNC may not have an adequate knowledge of the competence (skill level) and commitment of the specific foreign firm with whom they form the joint venture. This results in the expected output not being realized or an increase in the average cost of production. More pertinent to the argument is the fact that MNCs will not be in a position to ascertain this change in expected value ex ante. Hence, there will be fundamental randomness that can be reflected in the variance in output.[1] Second, MNCs do not have adequate information about the more general economic environment in which the joint venture operates (e.g., the attitudes of consumers toward the new product and the foreign country government toward participation of MNCs in their production and distribution processes). This results in adverse selection irrespective of the motivation and commitment of the specific foreign firm. Such losses are more difficult to predict and are random. Hence, it would be realistic to argue that adverse selection due to environmental uncertainty manifests itself in the form of an increase in the variance of output.[2]

In practice, formal knowledge about technology will not be sufficient for proper assimilation, utilization, and adaptation of new technology even if the foreign firm has the skills and commitment and the foreign country government policies are not inhibitive for some rules of thumb, informal adaptations to local production conditions, and other tricks of trade may be necessary for the efficient use of technology and effective marketing of the product.[3] In general, whatever may be their level of motivation and commitment, most of the foreign firms may find it difficult to assimilate such information if they are expected to acquire it through learning by doing. That is, inadequate informal knowledge may also be an environmental problem resulting in adverse selection.

The MNC chooses contract parameters (in particular, royalty rates) with these sources of adverse selection in perspective. However, the MNC generally deals with many foreign firms. Instead of discriminating between them in the choice of royalty rates, it would be more practical to set a uniform rate. Such a practice was reported in the context of franchise contracts. See, for example, Kaufmann and Lafontaine (1994). Similarly, as Chisholm (1997) noted, the royalty rates to the distributors of

[1] Note that this is only in an ex ante sense. There may not be much of any ex post variation in output over time for any one joint venture.

[2] This variance is across different firms ex ante. Information asymmetry may therefore make an MNC choose an inefficient firm while forming a joint venture.

[3] As Arora (1996, p. 235) put it, "transfer of chemical technology will typically involve training the licensee in a variety of issues such as how to handle and store chemicals, how to control the production process and return it to operation after (an) unscheduled breakdown caused by (an) accident or impurities in the feedstock."

movies and theaters are fixed ex ante and the contract negotiation concerns the number of days over which a movie is exhibited. Such a practice implies that only those agents with a high skill level and/or low risk aversion will accept the contract. For, given such royalty rates, the ex ante rents accruing to the agent will be larger the higher his skill level. In general, such policies of the MNCs are not firm specific. They apply to all foreign firms uniformly. Environmental uncertainty persists even if some firm-specific adjustments are incorporated.

Another alternative available to the MNC is to devise policies that eliminate the sources of adverse selection. In particular, assume that there is a necessity for informal knowledge. The provision of informal knowledge may be considered as one incentive mechanism to improve the skills and elicit commitment from the foreign firm. However, it can only partially reduce environmental uncertainty for the costs of reducing the variance further may not be commensurate with the perceived benefits. This problem is far more pertinent when it is necessary to structure firm-specific transfer of informal knowledge. Hence, as in the previous situation, MNCs devise general policies toward all joint venture partners and expect more efficient firms that can generate ex ante rents to accept partnership in joint ventures. Once again, it is pertinent to note that environmental uncertainty cannot be fully eliminated even if some firm-specific fine-tuning of policies is attempted.

A third alternative available to the MNC is to entice the foreign firm to share in the fixed capital investment. For instance, the MNC may offer firm-specific informal knowledge only if the foreign firm agrees to pay for it. There is a possibility that this policy elicits even greater motivation from the foreign firm. A similar argument holds even in the context of more pervasive deficiencies. Suppose the foreign firm is expected to share in the investment necessary to identify and generate technological adaptations to local raw materials. It can be expected that the foreign firm has greater motivation because it must now recover these sunk costs. The more conventional argument is that by forcing such sharing the MNC can exert greater control on the foreign firm when there is randomness.

As noted earlier, whatever may be the sources of inefficiency and however carefully the MNC policies are chosen, there may be a problem of generating the desired motivation and commitment. In such a case, the only recourse to the MNC is to offer older technologies that may not require a high degree of skill and effort from the management of the foreign firm. The nature of the technology chosen necessarily depends on whether the problem is at the firm level or more general to the foreign country. On the whole, it can be concluded that appropriate identification of the sources of deficiency, suitable policy measures to elicit commitment or control as the source of problems suggests, and efficient implementation of such policies will be necessary to restore efficiency of technology transfer to joint ventures.

The following details are therefore obvious. (a) The realized level of output of a joint venture is random. This may be either due to the decisions and actions of the foreign firm or intrinsic to the more general environment in the foreign country. The variance in output captures this aspect accurately. (b) Confronted with adverse selection, MNCs devise general policies that they will apply equally to all foreign firms in their joint ventures. The primary reason for this is that fine-tuning policies to suit the requirements of specific firms may involve greater costs in relation to perceived marginal benefits. Further, such general policies can be expected to entice firms to enter joint ventures in the hope of obtaining ex ante rents. (c) Irrespective of the details of such policy specification, there will be some residual randomness in the operation of joint ventures.

However, as of now, there is inadequate information about the channels through which policies of MNCs affect the choice of contract parameters and the performance of joint ventures. The basic observation from the above reasoning is that most of the policies attempt to reduce the variance in output resulting from adverse selection. As Svejnar and Smith (1984) noted, such policies may neutralize the deficiencies due to the lack of skill and commitment of the foreign firms. One basic objective of the present study is to provide a theoretical demonstration of this result. It will also be shown that policies operating exclusively on specific firms and hence the expected levels of output cannot result in contract parameters that are independent of skill levels of specific firms. This differs from the general belief that policies of MNCs operate only through expected values and the randomness remains purely exogenous and determined by the environment in which the joint ventures operate.

The rest of the study is organized as follows. Section 5.2 outlines a basic modification of the KM model. The provision of informal knowledge will be examined in Sect. 5.3. It will be shown that it neutralizes the deficiencies in firm-specific skills if the provision of informal knowledge reduces the variance attributable to more general environmental problems. Section 5.4 considers sharing fixed costs as an alternative incentive mechanism. The control exercised through the choice of technology is the theme of Sect. 5.5. The concluding section highlights some related issues (such as the possibility of moral hazard) and the necessity to develop similar results with respect to the choice of foreign country government policies.

5.2 Analytical Framework

The benchmark model of the principal agent framework to study the problem under consideration is Kawasaki and McMillan (1987). However, some important modifications are necessary to address the pertinent questions.

It will be assumed that a multinational firm (an IPR and/or patent holder designated as P hereafter) entrusts production and/or distribution of a product based on his invention to a foreign firm (an agent referred to as F). Assume that an output e is planned. Corresponding to this, P undertakes an investment ke^2, where k is a constant, in physical capital.[4] Therefore, it is implicitly postulated that there are diminishing returns to the use of physical assets. Further, the more efficient the technology, the lower will be the capital requirements for a given output. Hence, a lower value

[4] It will be assumed that this is the cost of using the capital equipment per unit of time to facilitate the static analysis that follows. Note, however, that capital costs can be fully recovered only if the integrity of the joint venture can be sustained over a sufficiently long time.

of k indicates the transfer of superior technology.[5] Assume that P finances the entire capital and hence operates a wholly owned subsidiary. However, due to the information asymmetry with respect to production and market conditions in the foreign country, he entrusts the operational management to F. In his turn, F incurs a variable cost $e^2/2\delta$, where δ is the skill level of F. It should also be acknowledged that P will get to know the variable cost only to the extent that F is willing to reveal it. Diminishing returns with respect to variable factors are implicit in this formulation. However, unlike Das (1998) and Desai et al. (2001), complementarity between the fixed and variable factors is postulated.[6]

In practice, it is more realistic to assume that a low δ makes the output, for a given variable cost incurred by F, random. Denote the actual output by $(e+u)$ where u is a random variable with $E(u)=0$ and $V(u)=\sigma^2$. The variance is assumed to be exogenous to the decision-making process of P and F. That is, information asymmetry with respect to production and marketing conditions and the vagaries of the policies of the foreign country may be the primary sources of randomness. It should also be noted that this represents the risk perception of the MNC.

After the output is produced and sold, the two parties share it.[7] Let p be the share of $(e+u)$ offered to F. Fundamentally, the assumption is that P seeks an insurance against the risk by asking F to share it with him. Consequently, the share of output accruing to P can be interpreted as an insurance effect.

In its simplest form, the KM model postulates that

$$\begin{aligned}\pi_F &= \text{profit of } F \\ &= p(e+u) - e^2/2\lambda\delta\end{aligned}$$

Let λ be the degree of risk aversion of F. The value of the contract to F can be written as

$$V_F = pe - e^2/2\delta - \lambda p^2\sigma^2$$

The KM model assumes that F chooses e, for a given p, to maximize V_F. That is, F will choose

$$e = p\delta$$

---

[5] Technological development by the MNC will not generally pay attention to the variable costs in its implementation under various production conditions. Hence, substitution between capital and variable factors will not be acknowledged explicitly.

[6] It can be shown that allowing substitution between capital and variable factors does not yield royalty rates commensurate with the stylized facts if randomness is acknowledged.

[7] The fixed costs are assigned to P and the variable costs are borne by F. Hence, sharing output is the only relevant contract parameter.

On the contrary, P has many more avenues of generating income and thereby hedging his risk, given his diversified portfolio (of products as well as financial assets). Hence, P is postulated to be risk neutral.[8] The value of the contract to P is

$$V_{\mathrm{P}} = (1-p)e - ke^2$$

The other essential feature of the KM model is its assumption that P chooses p so as to maximize the net value of the contract, viz.,

$$\begin{aligned} N &= V_{\mathrm{F}} + V_{\mathrm{P}} \\ &= e - e^2/2\delta - ke^2 - \lambda p^2 \sigma^2, \end{aligned}$$

taking the participatory constraint of F into account. Hence, the optimal royalty rate is given by

$$p = \delta / \left(\delta + 2k\delta^2 + 2\lambda\sigma^2\right)$$

Note that the choice implies $p=0$ if and only if $\delta=0$ or $\lambda\sigma^2 \to \infty$. The intermediate cases, where $0<p<1$, are more likely in practice. The assumption that the randomness is exogenous therefore implies that the efficient contract merely adjusts p and e keeping it in perspective. The pertinent observation is that such an efficient p is not independent of δ. Clearly, the model does not incorporate any mechanisms that can neutralize the effect of information asymmetry.

5.3 Informal Knowledge

Assume that the MNC transfers the latest technology. Consequently, k is exogenously given. Consider a situation wherein P feels that foreign firms will not be in a position to manage the technology efficiently unless the informal knowledge is transferred along with the formal knowledge. It then becomes necessary for P to incur some expenditure for providing the requisite informal knowledge. To examine the effect of such an expenditure on the contract parameters in the KM framework, it is necessary to specify the channels of transmission. One possibility is that the requirements of informal knowledge are firm specific. Transfer of such informal knowledge increases the expected value of output for a given variable cost. Or, equivalently, the variable cost of producing a given level of output can be expected to decrease. The second possibility is that all foreign firms are in need of such

[8] The a priori expectation would have been one of relatively greater risk aversion of P for the risks associated with information asymmetry make it difficult to recover sunk investments. It can be easily verified that such a modification of the KM model yields similar results. However, the basic theme of this study is that P can modify the effects of randomness through his actions. Hence, the risk will primarily impinge on F if such choices are efficient.

informal knowledge in varying degrees. That is, the MNC providing such knowledge reduces the variance of the output. These specifications will now be considered sequentially.

Consider firm-specific informal knowledge to begin with. It can be expected that such expenditures on informal knowledge will also be subject to diminishing returns. Hence, for a given level of output e, it can be assumed that P spends an amount me^2. The corresponding variable cost can be written as

$$v_{\mathrm{F}} = e^2 / 2\delta\left(k+m\right)$$

for the efficiency in the use of technology is a result of the use of the informal knowledge in conjunction with the formal aspects of technology transfer. Note that this specification is also consistent with the notion that there will be diminishing returns with respect to m. Clearly, the basic assumption underlying this approach is that such an expenditure cannot alter the exogenous randomness in the market conditions and the degree of risk aversion of F. Hence, it is necessary to maintain that the realized level of output is random with $V(u)=\sigma^2$. As a result, the profit of F is[9]

$$\pi_{\mathrm{F}} = p\left(e+u\right) - e^2 / 2\delta\left(k+m\right)$$

The efficient choice of output is therefore

$$e = p\delta\left(k+m\right)$$

The net value of the contract becomes

$$\begin{aligned} N &= e - e^2 / 2\delta\left(k+m\right) - \lambda p^2\sigma^2 - \left(k+m\right)e^2 \\ &= p\delta\left(k+m\right) - p^2\delta\left(k+m\right)/2 - \lambda p^2\sigma^2 - p^2\delta^2\left(k+m\right)^3 \end{aligned}$$

Consequently, the optimal choices of m and p are such that

$$\begin{aligned} &2 - p - 6\left(k+m\right)^2 p\delta = 0 \text{ and} \\ &\delta\left(k+m\right)\left[1 - p - 2p\delta\left(k+m\right)^2\right] = 2\lambda p\sigma^2 \end{aligned}$$

From the first equation, it can be inferred that

$$p = 2/\left[1 + 6\left(k+m\right)^2\delta\right]$$

[9] Clearly, P must be compensated for the additional expenditure. The obvious mechanism is to adjust p suitably. Some authors suggest that P will claim a fixed amount upfront for the transfer of informal knowledge. See, for example, Brickley (2002). However, a change in p is more realistic if the expenditure by P depends on the skill level of F. This approach will be adopted in the sequel.

The second equation therefore indicates that the choice of m is such that

$$\delta(k+m)\left[-1+2(k+m)^2\delta\right]=4\lambda\sigma^2$$

Note that, to make the analysis meaningful, it should be assumed that

$$-1+2(k+m)^2\delta>0$$

since δ, $(k+m)$, and $\lambda\sigma^2$ are positive. From the viewpoint of economic theory, this indicates that ceteris paribus the MNC would be willing to deal with only those foreign firms whose skill level δ exceeds $1/2(k+m)^2$. It is also natural that the more MNC would be willing to work with a lower-skilled foreign firm, the more it is willing to spend on the transfer of tacit knowledge.

Differentiating both sides of the equation governing the choice of m partially with respect to δ, it can be readily verified that

$$\partial m/\partial\delta=-(k+m)\left[-1+4(k+m)^2\delta\right]/\delta\left[-1+6(k+m)^2\delta\right]<0$$

and, similarly,

$$\partial m/\partial\lambda\sigma^2=4/\delta\left[-1+6(k+m)^2\delta\right]>0$$

The MNC has to incur a lower cost to transfer tacit knowledge to F if it is more efficient. For any given $(k+m)$, an increase in $\lambda\sigma^2$ decreases N. To restore a higher net value of the contract, the MNC is compelled to increase m and reduce the variance further.

Partially differentiating the equation representing the choice of p with respect to δ and $\lambda\sigma^2$ successively, it can be shown that

$$\partial p/\partial\delta>0 \text{ and } \partial p/\partial\lambda\sigma^2<0$$

These results are consistent with the KM formulation. However, contrary to expectations, p cannot be independent of δ.[10] That is, P cannot effectively counteract the

[10] The context of liquidity constraints is somewhat analogous. Postulate that P makes an a priori judgment that the randomness is due to liquidity constraints and not the shortage of tacit knowledge. Assume that F is experiencing liquidity constraints primarily because his skills and collateral are inadequate. One approach available to F is to locally obtain finances at a higher interest rate. On the other hand, P may agree to raise finances in its parent country if some saving is possible. Suppose, P incurs an extra cost me^2 and expects F to accept the variable cost $e^2/2\delta$ as before. Or, alternatively, P may allow F to raise the requisite finances and reimburse me^2 of expenditure. The greater the value of m offered, the lower the σ^2 due to the randomness created by the liquidity constraints. Hence, the optimal choice of m will be exactly the same as before. Once again, it is evident that the endogenous randomness specification compensates for the lack of skill on the part of F to raise the requisite finances. However, note that the basis for this formulation will be lost if the liquidity constraints are external to the operation of F.

inefficiency if its expenditure affects only the expected value of output or the variable cost.

The possibility that the transfer of tacit knowledge reduces the variance may now be examined. Assume that me^2 of expenditure by P leaves the variable cost unaltered at $e^2/2\delta$ while making $V(u)=\sigma^2/(k+m)$. Then, the value of the contract to F becomes

$$V_{\mathrm{F}} = pe - e^2/2\delta - \lambda p^2\sigma^2/(k+m)$$

The efficient choice of e will now be

$$e = p\delta$$

and the net value of the contract is

$$N = p\delta - p^2\delta/2 - (k+m)p^2\delta^2 - \lambda p^2\sigma^2/(k+m)$$

The optimal choices of $(k+m)$ and p are determined by the equations

$$\delta^2(k+m)^2 = \lambda\sigma^2 \text{ and}$$
$$p = 1/\left(1+4\sqrt{\lambda\sigma}\right)$$

Hence, the choice of m that neutralizes the effect of low skill level is

$$(k+m) = \sqrt{\lambda\sigma}/\delta$$

It will be lower the higher the skill level. However, a higher $\lambda\sigma^2$ necessitates a greater m. The most important finding is that p is now independent of δ. Clearly, an efficient choice of m neutralizes the deficiency, due to the lower skill level of the foreign firm, through its effect on the variance of output.

5.4 Sharing Fixed Costs

It was pointed out in the previous section that the MNC may find it necessary to offer informal knowledge to F in order to neutralize the lack of skills on the part of F. However, the MNC financing the entire capital investment of the joint venture may not elicit adequate commitment from F in the use of the equipment transferred. The MNC may then insist that the foreign firm share a fraction s of $k\sigma^2$ to elicit compliance. This may make F feel more committed because recovery of his share of the fixed costs will now be at stake.

Assume that the share of F has the effect of reducing the variance to σ^2/s. More pertinent to the argument will be the changes in the cost to P. The following observations are relevant. (a) The MNC may have to pay F an extra share of output by way of royalties due to the increase in his share of capital and F's bargaining power.

(b) Gomes-Casseres (1989), Al-Saadon and Das (1996), and Chen and Hennert (2002, p. 4) pointed out that due to information asymmetry with respect to production and marketing conditions in the foreign country the MNC has to incur proportionately higher costs as s increases. (c) The MNC has to make much greater efforts and incur greater costs to convince F to provide the commitment if ab initio the transfer of highly efficient technology enables F to capture some rents. The MNC may experience diminishing returns to its efforts to persuade F to comply. This was noted in Al-Saadon and Das (1996). (d) The costs of negotiation, management, and conflict resolution increase with the share of the foreign firm. This may arise purely due to differences in expectations, management and cultural values, and attitudes of labor. Gomes-Casseres (1989, pp. 7ff; 1990, p. 3) and Cai (2003, p. 75) contain explicit statements to this effect. In particular, Cai observed that "joint ownership may result in considerable governance costs. When multiple parties jointly own a firm, they have to reach agreements on how to use the assets effectively. The costs (of) making collective decisions can be quite substantial, especially when these owners have diverse preferences." (e) There will be greater scrutiny of the decisions of P as s increases. This has the effect of reducing the flexibility of P with respect to transfer pricing and resource allocation across subsidiaries in different countries. The significance of such an opportunity cost was acknowledged in Gomes-Casseres (1989) and Das (1998). It will be postulated that αske^2 represents the total costs with the understanding that $\alpha s > 1$. The share of F will be restricted to ske^2 of capital alone. Note that the profit for F will now be

$$\pi_F = p(e+u) - e^2/2\delta - ske^2$$

Given his risk aversion, the value he attaches to π_F is

$$V_F = pe - e^2/2\delta - ske^2 - \lambda p^2\sigma^2/s$$

Observe that a risk-averse F will not accept a large s because he incurs an additional cost of greater commitment to reduce production risk. Further, there is a possibility that F experiences liquidity constraints while raising the resources required for capital investments. Both these considerations suggest that F will prevail on the choice of s. Hence, he can be expected to choose s and e to maximize V_F. This results in

$$\begin{aligned} s &= (\lambda/k)^{1/2}(\sigma/\delta) \\ e &= p\delta^*, \text{ where} \\ \delta^* &= \beta\delta \text{ and} \\ \beta &= 1 - 2(\lambda k)^{1/2}\sigma \end{aligned}$$

The net value of the contract is

$$\begin{aligned} N &= e - e^2/2\delta - \alpha ske^2 - \lambda p^2\sigma^2/s \\ &= p\delta\beta - p^2\beta^2\delta/2 - 2\beta(\lambda k)^{1/2} p^2\delta\sigma \end{aligned}$$

P will therefore choose

$$p = 1/\left[1 + 2(\lambda k)^{1/2}\sigma\right]$$

The efficient choice of *s* so obtained is consistent with several observations in the literature. (a) Das (1998, p. 139) pointed out that *F* would accept a higher s to counteract the effect of a low δ. That is, he will signal greater commitment to *P*. (b) Fan and Li (2000) noted the direct relationship between *s* and $\lambda\sigma^2$. Even in this context, a larger λ and/or σ^2 necessitates *F* indicating a greater commitment to *P*. (c) A large market in the foreign country can be expected to provide an incentive for *P* to transfer more efficient technology. Along with it, the MNC may seek greater security and commitment. *F* will therefore agree to a larger *s*. A larger *s* may also be due to the greater bargaining power of *F* given the IPR protection. It must however be acknowledged that an increase in s beyond a point may be a disadvantage to *F* because *F* gains control.

On the whole, it can be concluded that an efficient *s*, whose effect is through the variance, generally neutralizes the effect of a low δ. The commitment effect induced by *P*, rather than the voluntary motivational changes of *F* postulated by the changes in expected values, appears to be more reliable.

5.5 Technology Choice

Note that the technology transferred need not be entirely exogenous in practice. Instead, as noted in Sect. 5.1, the MNC may find it more risky to transfer a more recent (and hence relatively more efficient) technology. The MNC may only offer technology of an older vintage. This can be introduced in the principal agent model by making k a choice of the MNC.

The choice of technology can be expected to have one of two effects on the choice of contracts. First, many studies argue that the basic change is in the expected value of output. For, by transferring an older technology, the MNC can make sure that the extent of inefficiency is reduced. In particular, the damage that the foreign firm can inflict on the MNC will be lower. Operationally, this can be represented as a reduction in the variable cost of production for a given level of output. More efficient technologies are subject to greater adverse selection and hence greater variable costs. Clearly, an efficient choice of technology is based on the trade-off between the fixed and variable costs. Second, it may be argued that given the technology and the operating procedures, variable costs are determined and the management of the foreign firm has very little choice. Adverse selection manifests itself only in the form of a change in variance. Specifically, the more efficient the technology, the greater the possibility of adverse selection and a greater variance. The pertinent question is as follows. Which of these two mechanisms is a priori more plausible and is also consistent with empirically observed stylized facts? It was pointed out in section 1 that the variance route is more plausible on a priori grounds for the motivational effect, implied by expected value changes, is much less reliable compared to the control effect implied in the changes of variance.

It is immediately obvious that the analytical details are analogous to those of section 3. The only difference is that k is the pertinent choice variable with m set as zero. Hence, all the results of that section carry over ceteris paribus. Note also that a joint choice of k and m leave the results intact.

5.6 Looking Back

An MNC is confronted with the possibility of adverse selection in its technology transfer. This generally depends on the level of skill of the foreign firm. The MNC then attempts to choose a technology that it can efficiently transfer. Such a choice may motivate the foreign firm to reduce its variable cost for a given level of output. However, this effect is not very reliable and cannot eliminate the deficiencies of a low skill on the choice of royalty rates. On the other hand, given the skill level and the motivations of F, the MNC may be in a position to reduce the variance inherent in the environment in which the joint venture operates. The MNC, having greater control on this effect, will find it more reliable. This will also render the efficient choice of the royalty rate to be independent of the level of skill. A similar result can also be established with respect to the sharing of capital investments between the joint venture partners.

Two other observations are in order. First, other policy choices, such as equity participation, can be adopted by the MNC. The results can be shown to be invariant though the analysis requires a major modification. Second, the necessity for changes in randomness to sustain this result cannot however be taken for granted for there may be other channels through which the effects of policy choices can be transmitted to the choice of contract parameters and the performance of the joint venture. But, as of now, no other theoretical explanation is available.

It is often suggested that the MNC may experience moral hazard if the IPR protection of the foreign country is inadequate for, in any form of joint venture, the foreign firm may not operate efficiently and in consonance with the expectations of the MNC. In particular, after the MNC makes the investment, the foreign firm, or its workers, may reengineer the technology, create a competitive firm, and compete for the same market as the joint venture. Similarly, the government of the foreign country may change its policies with respect to profit taxation, transfer prices, and tariffs so as to drain profits of the MNC. It may also redefine the limits of equity participation or confiscate the assets altogether. Das (1998) designated this as policy moral hazard. Utilizing an analytical structure similar to the present study, it can be shown that policies affecting variance of output can mitigate moral hazard effectively.

On the whole, the conceptualization of changes in randomness resulting from the policy options of the joint venture partners appears to be a promising theoretical development in understanding the nature of efficient contracts in international joint ventures.

From a strategic management perspective, the results of the present study suggest the following. MNC policies directed to assessing and reducing overall environmental uncertainties, especially those related to firms in the industry and government policies, will be superior to the provision of firm-specific informal knowledge.

References

Al-Saadon Y, Das SP (1996) Host-country policy, transfer pricing and ownership distribution in international joint ventures: a theoretical analysis. J Ind Organ 14:345–364

Arora A (1996) Contracting for tacit knowledge: the provision of technical services in technology licensing contracts. J Dev Econ 50:233–256

Brickley JA (2002) Royalty rates and upfront fees in share contracts: evidence from franchising. J Law Econ Organ 18:511–535

Cai H (2003) A theory of joint asset ownership. Rand J Econ 34:63–77

Chen SFS, Hennert JF (2002) Japanese Investor's choice of joint ventures versus wholly-owned subsidiaries in the U.S.: the role of market barriers and firm capabilities. J Int Bus Stud 33:1–18

Chishlom DC (1997) Profit-sharing versus fixed-payment contracts: evidence from the motion pictures industry. J Law Econ Organ 13:169–201

Das SP (1998) On the choice of international joint ventures: the role of policy moral hazard. Policy Reform 2:135–150

Desai MA, Foley CF, Hines JR (2001) International joint ventures and the boundaries of the firm. Available at www.stern.nyu.edu/clb/Desai01.pdf

Gomes-Casseres B (1989) Ownership structures of foreign subsidiaries. J Econ Behav Organ 11:1–25

Gomes-Casseres B (1990) Firm ownership preferences and host government restrictions: an integrated approach. J Int Bus Stud 25:1–22

Kaufman PJ, Lafontaine F (1994) Costs of control: the sources of economic rents for McDonald's franchisees. J Law Econ 37:417–454

Kawasaki S, McMillan J (1987) The design of contracts: evidence from Japanese subcontracting. J Jpn Int Econ 1:327–349

Pan Y, Li X (2000) Joint venture formation of very large multinational firms. J Int Bus Stud 31:179–189

Svejnar J, Smith SC (1984) The economics of joint ventures in less developed countries. Q J Econ 99:149–167

Chapter 6
Equity Participation

Abstract International joint ventures are subject to moral hazard and instability. Low IPR protection and inadequate enforcement account for such problems. Principal agent models account for the moral hazard in terms of the randomness in revenue generated. Equity sharing arrangements, which have important commitment and control effects, can be expected to eliminate the moral hazard and produce royalty arrangements consistent with empirically observed stylized facts This study demonstrates that the change in the variance is the primary channel through which the commitment and control effects affect the choice of such royalty payments.

6.1 The Issues

An MNC generally transfers technology across international boundaries to facilitate production and distribution of products based on its innovations. The process of such technology transfer may lead to moral hazard due to the inadequacy of IPR protection and/or its enforcement in the foreign country.[1] This policy of the government may be a consequence of its attempts to protect the economic interest of a majority of local entrepreneurs who may not be in a position to compete with the MNCs.[2] This may reduce the profit of the MNC.[3] Das (1998) designated this as policy moral hazard.

Based on content from "Equity Participation in International Joint Ventures" first published in *Decision*, 33(1), 2006, pp. 1–20. Content reproduced here with permission from Indian Institute of Management Calcutta.

[1] It must be acknowledged that there are several other sources of moral hazard. Each distinct source necessitates a different policy of the MNC. Such results will be reported elsewhere while preserving the basic argument of this study.

[2] Das (1999, p. 139) observed that "policies in reality may include profit tax, production subsidy or taxes, export taxes, tariff or tariff exemption on the import of specialized inputs. There may be quantitative or value restrictions such as domestic content or export requirements. It may also be intangibles like government's pressure in officially approving standard rules and regulations."

[3] Government policies are not specific to any one joint venture. Hence, it is more realistic to assume that they are given to any one MNC. In its turn, the MNC chooses the contract mode and contract parameters efficiently keeping these policies in perspective. This approach will be utilized in this study. However, government policies change if and when observed policies of the MNCs are deemed harmful. It can be shown that an analysis based on this reverse causation yields similar results. The results will be reported elsewhere.

T.V.S.R. Rao, *Risk Sharing, Risk Spreading and Efficient Regulation*,
DOI 10.1007/978-81-322-2562-1_6

Confronted with this possibility, the MNC changes some of its policies to counteract the adverse effects. In particular, the MNC may offer a share of equity to the portfolio investors in the foreign country. Falvey and Fried (1986, p. 249) pointed out that equity holding of this nature has a commitment effect.[4] As Konrad and Lommerud (2001, p. 476) put it, "(s)elling shares in a foreign affiliate to residents in that country may indeed reduce the hold-up problem …, and may therefore be in the interest of both the multinational and the host country." For, "since the host country's government cares about its citizens' income from portfolio investment, the government is less willing to use high powered incentives to extract the firm's revenue" (p. 476).[5] The operation of the commitment effect necessitates assigning a greater equity share to the portfolio investors in the foreign country as the level of IPR protection decreases.

A somewhat different argument can be found in the literature. Equity ownership may counteract the effect of low IPR protection by allowing the MNC to retain control on the operations of the joint venture. For, as Dhanraj and Beamish (2004, p. 296) noted, "equity has been interpreted as a measure of control and dominance in a joint venture, with the implication that the more absolute control, the less potential for conflict as decisions can be made by the majority partner." This argument implies that the more the moral hazard, the greater the necessity will be for the MNC to hold a larger share of equity.[6]

It is also clear that while the control effect operates only after a threshold level of shareholding, the commitment effect manifests itself at all levels of equity holding by portfolio investors of the foreign country. Further, the theory of incomplete contracts often indicates that an ex ante resolution of the risks (through the commitment effect) due to moral hazard will be superior to ex post resolution (through the exercise of control) after experiencing a violation of the contract. However, note that the realization of the commitment effect depends on the motivation of the government of the foreign country. The control effect impinges more directly on the MNC. Hence, there will be some contexts in which the control effect neutralizes moral hazard

[4] Al-Saadon and Das (1996), Pan and Li (2000), and Noe et al. (2002, p. 1253) contend that a large market for output in the foreign country may attract sufficient commitment. Equity sharing may not be necessary. Low levels of equity participation may be sufficient even if it is used as an instrument. Similarly, equity sharing may affect the performance of the joint ventures through other channels. See, for instance, Folta and Janney (2004).

[5] On p. 476 they also pointed out that "(b)y selling shares in the affiliate the multinational captures part of its sunk investment. Moreover, the information rent goes to the multinational parent, because the parent (has) the information advantage." This is also a motivation for the foreign firm to exhibit greater commitment to the venture.

[6] However, as Dhanraj and Beamish (2004, p. 247) pointed out, control power, if it exists, may be for other reasons as well. On the other hand, the MNC cannot extend its control to policy decisions of the foreign country through equity sharing. Vishwasrao (1994) has a detailed analysis of some of the pertinent issues.

more efficiently.[7] In general, the commitment effect may not materialize until the MNC and the foreign firm had repeated contacts with each other.[8]

However, as Das and Katayama (2003) noted, theoretical analysis of the decision-making process within the joint venture and the channels of its transmission to the performance of the firm is inadequate. One strand of thought, exemplified by Desai et al. (2001), Das (1998), and Das and Katayama (2003), postulates a conventional production function involving factors of production that both the MNC and the foreign firm control. This is inadequate in so far as the effort of the foreign firm is known to the MNC only to the extent that the foreign firm reveals it. This information asymmetry can be explicitly incorporated in principal agent models originally proposed by Kawasaki and McMillan (1987) (KM hereafter). Das (1999) and Das and Katayama (2003), in particular, approach the problem from this perspective. However, the production function specification persists. Further, neither the commitment nor the control effect of equity participation is reflected in these models. The basic purpose of this study is to restructure the principal agent framework keeping both these aspects in perspective.

The principal agent models generally specify the realized output and revenue as random variables. Consequently, the observed variations may be changes in expected values and/or variance.[9] However, much of the literature conceptualizes the changes only through the expected value and considers the variance to be entirely exogenous and not affected by the decisions of the MNC.[10] On the other hand, the characterization of the commitment and control effects suggests that the expected value and/or variance may be affected. A specification of the nature of this randomness will therefore be a fundamental prerequisite for analysis. This is the basic modification in the modeling structure of the present study.

The royalty rate, viz., the share of output or revenue accruing to the foreign firm, is clearly the other essential contract parameter. The KM variant of the principal agent model generally indicates that the royalty rate depends on the level of IPR protection and the degree of risk aversion of the foreign firm. However, as Svejnar and Smith (1984) noted, the MNC adjusts its policies and contract parameters so as to neutralize the effects of low IPR protection and/or moral hazard created by government policies. That is, royalty rates, when efficiently chosen, will be indepen-

---

[7] Quite clearly a philosophical problem remains. The MNC cannot control or force the foreign firm to accept certain things that it does not feel comfortable with or is not motivated to accept. Hence, the control effect has the same limitation as the motivation effect. However, it appears a priori plausible that the MNC will be more confident about the control effect in contrast to the commitment effect.

[8] See, for example, Okamuro (2001), Besancenot and Vrancenau (2002), and Rangan and Drummond (2004).

[9] From the viewpoint of the MNC, there is an expected level of output from given resources. This expected level of output may not materialize if there is low IPR protection and pervasive moral hazard. The basic change is in the variance.

[10] This may be more readily justified in the context of information asymmetry postulated in such models, for the randomness in demand for the product of the venture may be due to consumer's inability to judge the value of the new product being introduced.

dent of the level of IPR protection. Further, such a choice can also be justified from a practical point of view, for, fundamentally, such a policy enables the MNC to attract only those foreign firms from countries with high IPR protection and/or those with a low degree of risk aversion. In addition, such a choice of royalty rates leaves greater ex ante rents with the foreign firms. The existence of such ex ante rents in technology transfer arrangements was documented in Gallini and Wright (1990). Consistent with these observations, much of the empirical evidence indicates that the royalty rate is determined by risk aversion alone. See, for instance, Chisholm (1997, p. 196) and McCalman (2004). There is also indirect evidence in Liu and Wang (2003, p. 950). However, the existing models of economic theory have not been able to specify the channels of transmission and of the MNC policies to the choice of contract parameters, so as to make them consistent with such stylized facts. The present study demonstrates that the commitment and control effects must operate through a reduction in variance to sustain this observation. Changes in expected values would be insufficient.

The rest of the study is organized as follows: Section 6.2 sets out the basic conceptualization of the nature of randomness and outlines the channels through which equity sharing neutralizes the effect of low IPR protection. Section 6.3 presents a fundamental modification of the KM framework with the issues of this paper in perspective. Section 6.4 offers a demonstration of the economic theory underlying the commitment effect. In Sect. 6.5 it will be argued that the control effect of equity participation is efficient only when specific firms have the ability to adapt themselves. It is not reliable in a general context. Section 6.6 provides a summary of results and points out several possible extensions of this study.

6.2 Economic Intuition

To begin with note that if the changes in output and revenue of the joint venture are only in the expected values, the deviations must be specified as a predefined function of the level of IPR protection and/or the choices of the MNC. However, the very essence of the problem is that the MNC does not have any such a priori knowledge. Hence, economic theory specifies the revenue as a random variable.

The most general specification of the principal agent models is that the variance is independent of the level of IPR protection. By assumption, the decision-making process of the MNC and the foreign firm cannot have any effect on the variance of the random output. This will be designated as exogenous randomness. However, as noted in Sect. 6.1, the MNC may be in a position to identify some sources of randomness to be intrinsic to the functioning of the agent (in particular, it may be committed based on long-standing association in related activities). Similarly, they may devise policies, such as equity sharing, to modify the adverse effects of the lack of strong IPR protection. That is, at least a part of the variance is endogenous to the decision-making process of the principals and the agents. Such arguments appear, albeit in a rudimentary form, in Kawasaki and McMillan (1987, p. 330), Che and Hausch (1999, pp. 127 ff), and Das and Katayama (2003, p. 382). It can therefore be argued that endogeneity of randomness must be an integral part of the specification of the relevant economic theory.

A more practical argument also suggests that endogenous randomness is the most appropriate channel of transmission. Suppose a high degree of risk is due to low IPR protection. The MNC may offer a share of equity to the portfolio investors in the foreign country. In the interest of such investors, the foreign country government may offer a higher IPR protection. This will alter the expected value of output only if there is a corresponding change in the motivation of the foreign firm, for, in the ultimate analysis, only the decisions of the foreign firm can alter the expected values. However, the MNC cannot take this for granted,[11] for the MNC has no direct control on the motivation of the foreign firm, nor can it efficiently monitor it. On the other hand, such equity participation and the resulting improvement in IPR protection provide a favorable environment in which the joint venture operates. This will directly contribute to an efficient reduction in variance whatever the level of motivation of the foreign firm will be. It is this feature which neutralizes the effect of low IPR protection when it operates through the variance channel.

It can be surmised that the adverse effects of a low IPR can be neutralized if it affects the variance and equity sharing is efficiently chosen. The level of IPR protection will no longer be relevant for determining the optimal choice of royalty rates.

This analytical framework offers the most plausible explanation for the observation of Svejnar and Smith (1984).[12] Note, however, that the MNC has no obvious way of reducing the degree of risk aversion exhibited by the foreign firm. Hence, the royalty rate will necessarily depend on the degree of risk aversion of the foreign firm. It should also be evident that any other specific difficulties, associated with the functioning of the joint venture, necessitate clearly defined policy action to counteract them. The challenge for economic analysis is to detail the appropriate combinations even if the specification of endogenous randomness is acknowledged.

6.3 Basic Model

The benchmark model of the principal agent framework to study the problem under consideration is Kawasaki and McMillan (1987). However, some important modifications are necessary to address the pertinent questions.

It will be assumed that a multinational firm (an IPR and/or patent holder designated as P hereafter) entrusts production and/or distribution of a product based on his invention to a foreign firm (an agent referred to as F).[13] Assume that an output e

[11] In a related context, Yun (1999, p. 88) noted that MNC policies to reduce risk will not be successful if the foreign firm does not have any motivation to adapt to such changes.

[12] The necessity for endogenous randomness to sustain this result cannot be taken for granted. But, as of now, no other theoretical explanation is available.

[13] In general, the knowledge about the new technology may be transmitted to the foreign firm in one of the three forms. First, merely transferring the blueprints and formal knowledge about the organization of the production process may be sufficient. The foreign firm will then set up the requisite

is planned. Corresponding to this P undertakes an investment ke^2, where k is a constant, in physical capital.[14] Therefore, it is implicitly postulated that there are diminishing returns to the use of physical assets. Further, the more efficient the technology, the lower the capital requirements will be for a given output. Hence, a lower value of k indicates the transfer of superior technology. However, due to the information asymmetry with respect to production and/or market conditions in the foreign country, he entrusts the operational management to F.[15] In his turn, F incurs a variable cost of production[16] $e^2/2\delta$, where δ is the degree of IPR protection offered by the foreign country,[17] for, conceptually, F will free ride on the reputation of P and increase the cost of producing a given e if δ is lower.[18] It should also be acknowledged that P gets to know the variable cost only to the extent that F is willing to reveal it. Diminishing returns with respect to variable factors is implicit in this for-

---

production facilities. Second, the new technology may be embodied in the machine structure that the MNC provides. In this case, the MNC has two options. It can provide the machinery and make all the investment. It then claims a royalty. Alternatively, it may sell the equipment to the foreign firm. The MNC is generally reluctant to do this because it suspects that reverse engineering will take place and its technological advantage will be eroded eventually. Third, in some cases, mere provision of the blueprints and/or equipment is not adequate for its efficient use. The MNC also offers its expertise in production and the necessary informal knowledge. A joint venture is the more efficient mechanism for the transfer of such technology. This study assumes that the MNC provides the equipment and accepts the implied costs and investment to maintain control of the technology due to the apprehension about low IPR protection.

[14] It will be assumed that this is the cost of using the capital equipment per unit of time to facilitate the static analysis that follows. Note, however, that capital costs can be fully recovered only if the integrity of the joint venture can be sustained over a sufficiently long time.

[15] Contract theory generally supports assigning decisions to the party with better information. Hence, the natural choice in modeling is to leave the decision regarding e to F. It should also be noted that the MNC generally prefers to leave the decision-making autonomy to the foreign firm. It will generally be much too expensive for the MNC to involve itself in the entire decision process. Hence, they are more likely to maintain control of strategic decisions and delegate operational choices to the foreign firm.

[16] Two different forces determine this variable cost of production. First, the level of output itself accounts for the variable costs. This can be captured by e^2. If there is some apprehension about market conditions, this can be written as θe^2; $\theta > 1$. Second, due to low IPR protection, there is a possibility that the expected revenue, viz., e, will not accrue to the joint venture. Since e is fixed a priori in the present model, this effect can be captured by the changes in variable cost. Hence, the specification $e^2/2\delta$. Including a θ does not alter the qualitative features of the model.

[17] It is possible to view a low δ as a representation of the low level of skill and/or a manifestation of information asymmetry of P with respect to markets and production conditions in the foreign country. The results related to such adverse selection will be reported elsewhere.

[18] Low IPR protection implies that lower costs are involved in the imitation of the new technology. This may result in rampant infringement of MNC technology by existing employees, for they may leave the joint venture to start their own firm. In practice, many studies reported such a high employee turnover as the major source of imitation. A low IPR protection may also result in the foreign country confiscating the assets of the MNC. This will be an extreme case of increasing variable cost or reducing profits to zero.

mulation. However, unlike Das (1998) and Desai et al. (2001), complementarity between the fixed and variable factors is postulated.[19]

In practice it is more realistic to assume that a low δ makes the output, for a given variable cost incurred by F, random. Denote the actual output by $(e+u)$ where u is a random variable with $E(u)=0$, and $V(u)=\sigma^2$. The variance is assumed to be exogenous to the decision-making process of P and F. That is, the vagaries of the policies of the foreign country, and the associated low IPR protection, may be the primary source of randomness. It should also be noted that this represents the risk perception of the MNC.

After the output is produced and sold, the two parties share the output.[20] Let p be the share of $(e+u)$ offered to F. Fundamentally, the assumption is that P seeks an insurance against the risk by asking F to share it with him. Consequently, the share of output accruing to P can be interpreted as an insurance effect.

In its simplest form, the KM model postulates that

$$\begin{aligned}\pi_F &= \text{profit of } F\\ &= p(e+u) - e^2/2\delta\end{aligned}$$

Let λ be the degree of risk aversion of F. The value of the contract to F can be written as

$$V_F = pe - e^2/2\delta - \lambda p^2\sigma^2$$

The KM model assumes that F chooses e, for a given p, to maximize V_F. That is, F will choose

$$e = p\delta$$

This is generally designated as the participatory constraint of the agent. On the contrary, P has many more avenues of generating income, thereby hedging his risk, given his diversified portfolio (of products as well as financial assets). Hence, P is postulated to be risk neutral.[21] The value of the contract to P is

---

[19] It can be shown that allowing substitution between capital and variable factors does not yield royalty rates that commensurate with the stylized facts even if endogenous randomness is acknowledged.

[20] The fixed costs are assigned to P and the variable costs are borne by F. Hence, sharing output is the only relevant contract parameter.

[21] The a priori expectation would have been one of the relatively greater risk aversions of P. For, the risks associated with low IPR protection make it difficult for him to recover his sunk investments. This will be especially relevant if he cannot counteract the randomness by his choices. It can be easily verified that such a modification of the KM framework yields similar results. However, the basic theme of this study is that P can modify the effects of randomness through his actions. Hence, the risk will primarily impinge on F if such choices are efficient. Consequently, the original KM specification will be maintained.

$$V_{\mathrm{P}}=(1-p)e-ke^2$$

The other essential feature of the KM model is its assumption that P chooses p so as to maximize the net value of the contract, viz.,

$$\begin{aligned} N &= V_{\mathrm{F}} + V_{\mathrm{P}} \\ &= e - e^2/2\delta - ke^2 - \lambda p^2\sigma^2 \end{aligned}$$

taking the participatory constraint of F into account.[22] Hence, the optimal royalty rate is given by

$$p=\delta/\left(\delta+2k\delta^2+2\lambda\sigma^2\right)$$

Note that the choice implies $p=0$ if and only if $\delta=0$ or $\lambda\sigma^2\rightarrow\infty$. That is, the MNC will not enter into a joint venture with a foreign firm if there is no IPR protection at all and/or the foreign firm is highly risk averse. The intermediate cases, where $0<p<1$, are more likely in practice. A more important feature of the choice of p may now be noted. Observe that the foreign firm incurs a cost $p^2\delta/2$ in the joint venture. On the other hand, the cost to P will be $kp^2\delta^2+\lambda p^2\sigma^2$ since the risk aversion of F adds to his costs. The efficient choice of p is in proportion to these costs. Note that as IPR protection increases, and therefore the value of δ, the cost to P increases faster. Hence, the only meaningful change in p will be a reduction. That is, ceteris paribus, it is expected that $\partial p/\partial\delta<0$. This is valid if and only if $\lambda\sigma^2<k\delta^2$. This inequality implies that the MNC will enter into a joint venture if and only if either δ is sufficiently high or λ is low. The results of the rest of the study will assume that this condition is satisfied. The assumption that the randomness is exogenous therefore implies that the efficient contract merely adjusts p and e keeping it in perspective. The pertinent observation is that such an efficient p is not independent of δ. Clearly, the model does not incorporate any mechanisms that can neutralize the effect of low IPR protection.

6.4 Commitment Effect

Any MNC entering a foreign country experiences information asymmetry with respect to local production conditions, the nature and extent of markets, business practices of foreign firms,[23] and the policies of the government of the foreign coun-

[22] The joint venture may initially maximize the joint surplus and then share it based on their bargaining power. However, note that joint surplus maximization cannot be defined without taking the participatory constraint of F into account. This is ingrained in the assumption that F has autonomy in its decision regarding e. Otherwise the MNC has the control of all the decisions and the model will be entirely different.

[23] As Allen and Phillips (2000) noted, equity participation may also help the MNC in alleviating information asymmetry. In other words, the MNC may be in a position to overcome adverse selection as well.

try. As Gomes-Casseres (1990, p. 20) noted, "a theory about multinational enterprise behavior should consider not only the costs and benefits perceived by the firm, but also the impact of relations between the firms and governments." From an operational viewpoint, these relationships determine policies of P (in particular, equity sharing agreements) to elicit commitment. The efficient choice of equity sharing must take these considerations into account.

The only major change in the KM model of the previous section is the introduction of equity financing. Suppose, instead of P financing the entire investment ke^2, it is entrusted to portfolio investors in both the countries.[24] A share s of this may be assigned to the portfolio investors in the foreign country. The gains to the MNC are as follows. (a) The most direct benefit is that the cost ke^2 is borne by the portfolio investors instead of P. However, it retains control of the technology and a share of the residual property rights. (b) As Nichols (1983) remarked, the MNC will get to know the production and marketing conditions by interacting with F and obtaining information from it through its book of accounts. (c) In consonance with the commitment effect alluded to above, the MNC may get some favorable treatment with respect to the policies of the foreign country. This was also noted in Das (1998, p. 136). (d) Allowing equity participation by portfolio investors of the foreign country promotes cooperation and mutual trust between the partners of the JV and the fear of increasing punishment for devious behavior from the portfolio investors. See, for example, Pan and Li (2000, p. 181) and Cai (2003, p. 64). Or, more generally, as Teece (1980, p. 232) pointed out, "internal trading changes the incentives of parties and enables … (them to attenuate) costly haggling … and other non-cooperative (disruptive) behavior."[25]

However, the gains are obtained only at a cost, for the MNC should explicitly pay a share of profits in the form of dividends. However, Svejnar and Smith (1984), Falvey and Fried (1986), Noe et al. (2002), and Cai (2003, p. 63) pointed out that the royalty payments will not be necessarily proportional to equity shares since there are several other costs associated with such arrangements. The costs, to the joint venture, of such equity sharing can be identified as follows. (a) Gomes-Casseres (1989), Al-Saadon and Das (1996), and Chen and Hennert (2002, p. 4) pointed out that the MNC may not have adequate knowledge about the inputs available and the marketing conditions in the foreign country. Hence, to negotiate any equity sharing (and hence eliciting commitment), the MNC has to incur proportionately higher costs as the volume of output increases. In general, as Noe et al. (2002, p. 1284) noted, any form of information asymmetry increases the costs of obtaining cooperation through equity participation.[26] (b) The MNC has to make much greater efforts and incur higher costs to convince F to provide the commitment if ab initio the transfer of highly efficient technology enables F to capture rents through reneging. The MNC may experience diminishing returns to its efforts, including equity

[24] Note that the partners in the joint venture sharing costs will have somewhat different implications. Hart and Moore (1998) contain some comparative analysis of the relative efficiency of cooperative vs. outside equity ownership.

[25] A more detailed analysis of these transaction costs can be found in Beamish and Banks (1987).

[26] The cost increase may eventually manifest itself in the form of a greater bargaining power and a higher royalty rate.

participation arrangements, to persuade F to comply. This was noted in Al-Saadon and Das (1996). (c) Consider the operation of capital markets. Capital markets in the foreign country may not be well developed. F may be facing liquidity constraints as well. Hence, Noe et al. (2002, p. 1252 ff) surmised that raising equity in the foreign country (and, in particular, higher levels) involves proportionately greater costs than in the parent country of the MNC. More likely than not, portfolio investors in the foreign country will expect greater returns from such joint ventures. This, in itself, increases costs as the share of equity of the foreign investors increases. Further, as Sinha (2001) pointed out, P finds it more expensive to buy out shares from portfolio investors in the foreign country. Such opportunity costs may be substantial. (d) The costs of negotiation, management, and conflict resolution increase with the share of the foreign portfolio investors. This may arise purely due to differences in expectations, management and cultural values, and attitudes of labor. Gomes-Casseres (1989, pp. 7 ff, 1990, p. 3), Desai et al. (2001, p. 3), and Cai (2003, p. 75) contain explicit statements to this effect.[27] (e) There will be greater scrutiny and auditing of the decisions of the joint venture as the share of equity of the foreign investors increases. This has the effect of reducing the flexibility of P with respect to transfer pricing and resource allocation across subsidiaries in different countries. The significance of such an opportunity cost was acknowledged in Gomes-Casseres (1989), Das (1998), and Desai et al. (2001).

On balance, it must be acknowledged that equity sharing creates additional costs to the joint venture and the royalty payments to the foreign firm are not necessarily proportional to the equity sharing arrangement.[28] The formal demonstration of the channels through which equity participation affects the choice of the royalty rate and the performance of the firm can now be outlined. In particular, it will be shown that the effect of low IPR protection can be eliminated only when it operates through the variance in output.

Clearly, the cost of offering equity to the portfolio investors in the foreign country impinges exclusively on P. Denote the cost by αske^2. Fundamentally, α is different from 1 or the rate of dividends paid. Further, as the above argument suggests, it is an increasing function of s. Similarly, the total cost depends on the volume of capital investment in the joint venture.

Two possibilities should be acknowledged. First, an increase in s attempts to neutralize the effect of a low δ through changes in expected values. In particular, an increase in s may motivate F to be more accountable to portfolio investors from the foreign country and thereby provide greater efficiency in the management of the JV. This may be expected to move the actual output closer to the expected output.

---

[27] In particular, Cai (2003, p. 75) observed that "joint ownership may result in considerable governance costs. When multiple parties jointly own a firm, they have to reach agreements on how to use the assets effectively. The costs in making collective decisions can be quite substantial, especially when these owners have diverse preferences."

[28] As Desai et al. (2001, p. 5) noted, "joint ventures can avoid moral hazard problems through prior agreements, and can arrange to receive profit shares in nondividend forms that need not be allocated in proportion to ownership shares."

Second, the channel of transmission may be the variance instead, for, in consonance with the viewpoint of the present study, the commitment effect will be interpreted as a variance reduction. That is, the probability of the actual output (for a given cost) being higher increases. This description implies that the variance in output decreases, for the distribution of actual output tends to be closer to the expected level. The question that needs to be addressed is as follows: which of these specifications is closer to explaining the observed pattern? Consider the first alternative. Note that the equity sharing arrangement does not impose any significant cost on F. Consequently, the profit for F is

$$\pi_F = p(e+u) - e^2/2\delta s$$

Hence, the efficient choice of e will be

$$e = p\delta s$$

The net value of the contract can be represented by

$$\begin{aligned} N &= e - e^2/2\delta s - \alpha s k e^2 - \lambda p^2 \sigma^2 \\ &= p\delta s - p^2 \delta s/2 - \alpha k p^2 \delta^2 s^3 - \lambda p^2 \sigma^2 \end{aligned}$$

Consequently, the optimal choice of s and p are such that

$$2 - p - 6\alpha k s^2 p\delta = 0, \text{ and}$$
$$\delta s(1 - p - 2\alpha k p\delta s^2) = 2\lambda p\sigma^2$$

From the first equation, it can be inferred that

$$p = 2/(1 + 6\alpha k s^2 \delta)$$

The second equation therefore indicates that the choice of s is such that

$$\delta s(-1 + 2\alpha k s^2 \delta) = 4\lambda\sigma^2$$

Note that to make the analysis meaningful, it should be assumed that

$$-1 + 2\alpha k s^2 \delta > 0$$

since δ, s, and $\lambda\sigma^2$ are positive. From the viewpoint of economic theory, this indicates that ceteris paribus the MNC would be willing to deal only with those foreign firms in countries where the IPR protection exceeds $1/2\alpha k s^2$. It is also natural that the MNC would be willing to transfer more efficient technologies only when the IPR protection is high. Similarly, a lower commitment to equity participation will be acceptable to the MNC if the IPR protection is higher.

Differentiating both sides of the equation representing the choice of s partially with respect to δ, it can be readily verified that

$$\partial s/\partial\delta = -s\left(-1+2\alpha ks^2\delta\right)/\delta\left(-1+6\alpha ks^2\delta\right) < 0,$$

and, similarly,

$$\partial s/\partial\lambda\sigma^2 = 4/\delta\left(-1+2\alpha ks^2\delta\right) > 0$$

The MNC would be compelled to offer a greater equity share to elicit commitment if the IPR protection is low.

Partially differentiating the equation determining p with respect to δ and $\lambda\sigma^2$ successively, it can be shown that

$$\partial p/\partial\delta > 0, \text{ and } \partial p/\partial\lambda\sigma^2 < 0$$

These results are consistent with the KM formulation. However, contrary to expectations, p cannot be independent of δ. That is, P cannot effectively counteract the lack of IPR protection if its choice of equity participation only affects the expected value of output or the variable cost.

The possibility that equity participation reduces the variance may now be considered. Assume that a share s of equity leaves the variable cost unaltered at $e^2/2\delta$ while making $V(u)=\sigma^2/s$. Then, the efficient choice of e for F is once again given by

$$e = p\delta$$

and the net value of the contract is

$$\begin{aligned} N &= e - e^2/2\delta - \alpha ske^2 - \lambda p^2\sigma^2/s \\ &= p\delta - p^2\delta/2 - \alpha skp^2\delta^2 - \lambda p^2\sigma^2/s \end{aligned}$$

The optimal choice of s and p is determined by the equations

$$\begin{aligned} &\alpha ks^2\delta^2 = \lambda\sigma^2, \text{ and} \\ &p = 1/\left[1+4(\alpha k\lambda)^{1/2}\sigma\right] \end{aligned}$$

Hence, the optimal choice of s that neutralizes the effect of a low IPR protection is

$$s = \left(\lambda\sigma^2/\alpha k\right)^{1/2}/\delta$$

Desai et al. (2001) anticipated this result though they could not explicitly demonstrate it.

This efficient choice of s is consistent with several observations in the literature. (a) Das (1998, p. 139) pointed out that the MNC would be willing to offer a higher s to counteract the effect of a low δ. On the other hand, Noe et al. (2002, p. 1254 ff) interpreted the same causation as indicating that F will accept a higher s if δ is low so as to signal commitment. That is, the inverse relation between s and δ can be both an incentive and a signal.[29] (b) Pan and Li (2000) and Pan (2002, p. 375) noted the direct relationship between s and $\lambda\sigma^2$. (c) A greater dependence on the resources of F and a large market in the foreign country can be expected to provide a greater bargaining power to F. See, for instance, Gomes-Casseres (1989), Al-Saadon and Das (1996), and Noe et al. (2002, p. 1254). Consequently, as Gomes-Casseres (1989) pointed out, α increases and P would be willing to offer a lower s.

One caveat has been proposed. Desai et al. (2001) and Dhanraj and Beamish (2004, p. 303) argued that the advantages due to an increasing s may not be monotonic.[30] Instead, an increase in s beyond a point may be a disadvantage to P because F gains control. Some flip-flops in the choice of s may be observed in practice. Also see McCalman (2004).

On the whole, it can be concluded that an efficient s, whose effect is through the variance, generally neutralizes the effect of a low δ. The commitment effect, induced by government policy, affecting all the joint ventures in the foreign country, rather than the voluntary motivational changes of F postulated by the changes in expected values, appears to be more reliable.

6.5 Control Effects

Due to the lack of adequate IPR protection, the MNCs may try to entice the government of the foreign country to modify it by offering an efficient level of equity sharing with its portfolio investors. From this perspective the source of the difficulty is not specific to any one joint venture. In a similar fashion, the commitment effect obtained from equity participation affects all firms in the foreign country uniformly. The control effect operates somewhat differently. First, it cannot have any influence on the foreign country government in relation to its strengthening the IPR standards. Second, the control effect operates in a firm-specific manner. In particular, there may be some firms in the foreign country who feel that they have the competence to

---

[29] A low δ may also be due to information asymmetry experienced by P. In such a case, P may have to concede a larger s to extract information. This was noted in Noe et al. (2002, p. 1264). On occasions, when the information asymmetry is acute, P may not be satisfied with a share p. He will then demand an upfront payment. See, for example, Brickley (2002).

[30] In particular, Dhanraj and Beamish (2004, p. 297) observed that "increments in the equity levels in the lower end will have a larger impact in reducing potential for opportunistic behavior than similar ones at the higher end." In other words, there will be diminishing commitment as equity holding of the foreign portfolio investors increases.

Information asymmetry may also be firm specific and depend on the products and technology under consideration. Clearly, firm-specific control may then be efficient.

form a JV with an MNC and increase their profits.[31] Given the low IPR protection, the MNC may insist on maintaining greater control of the JV as a protection against possible moral hazard. The control effect neutralizes the IPR problem only in such cases.[32] This asymmetry will be the main theme of this section within the framework of endogenous randomness alluded to in Sect. 6.2. The main emphasis will be on the control effect of equity sharing by portfolio investors in both the countries.[33]

Assume that the control effect, on a specific firm in the foreign country, operates via the expected value. Then, its level of efficiency increases by reducing the variable cost to $e^2/2\delta(1-s)$. The costs, of the MNC exercising control, will be similar to those alluded to in the previous section though they will be larger. In general, they will depend on the share of equity held by the MNC. Hence, they will be represented as $\beta(1-s)ke^2$. The profit of F then becomes

$$\pi_F = p(e+u) - e^2/2\delta(1-s)$$

Hence, F chooses

$$e = p\delta(1-s)$$

Maximizing the net value of the contract with respect to s and p results in the equations

$$(2-p) = 6\beta kp\delta(1-s)^2, \text{ and}$$
$$\delta(1-s)\left[(1-p) - 2\beta kp\delta(1-s)^2\right] = \lambda p^2\sigma^2$$

Therefore, the efficient choice of e can be solved from the equation

$$\delta\left[(2-p)/6\beta kp\delta\right]^{1/2}(1-2p) = 3\lambda p^2\sigma^2$$

Clearly, the choice of p will not be independent of δ. It is obvious that such a control effect cannot efficiently eliminate the lack of IPR protection.

---

[31] Information asymmetry may also be firm specific and depend on the products and technology under consideration. Clearly, firm-specific control may then be efficient.

[32] Pan and Li (2000, p. 181), Delios and Beamish (1999), Mjoen and Tallman (1997), and Cai (2003) noted that control will be effective only when the capital assets are transaction specific. As Noe et al. (2002) and Gomes-Casseres (1989) noted, information asymmetry with respect to production and marketing conditions in the foreign country may be another source of the necessity for control.

[33] Miller et al. (1997) and Mjoen and Tallman (1997) are among the several authors who pointed out that equity participation is only one of the many ways in which the MNC may exercise control over the JV.

Consider the alternative that firm-specific control operates through the variance instead. However, the overall level of IPR protection conditions the extent of variance. Equity participation and control exerted by the MNC on the specific joint venture may still be able to reduce the variance created by such moral hazard. Suppose the variance reduces to $\sigma^2/(1-s)$. As before, it can be verified that

$$e = p\delta$$

represents the participation constraint of F. Similarly, the optimal choices of $(1-s)$ and p will be

$$(1-s) = (\lambda/\beta k)^{1/2}(\sigma/\delta), \text{ and}$$
$$p = 1/\left[1+4(\lambda\beta k)^{1/2}\sigma\right]$$

The control effect overcomes the effect of low δ and the deleterious effects of low IPR protection as surmised above. This is the essential result of this section.

6.6 Retrospect

Consider the technology transferred by an MNC to a foreign country. It can be surmised that the expected output from a given technology and operating procedures will be fixed. However, the actual output depends on the organizational arrangements in the foreign country. In particular, the level of IPR protection may affect the motivation of the foreign firm. It is therefore natural to view any deviations in output as embodied in the variance. The policies of the firms and the foreign country government can affect this variance. This is one of the fundamental propositions of the present study.

Conceptually, a pragmatic choice of policy instruments and efficient levels of them can be expected to eliminate moral hazard through a suitable reduction in the variance. If this is possible, the MNC may adopt a royalty rate independent of the level of IPR protection in all foreign countries to which it transfers the technology. One possible mechanism through which it achieves this is equity sharing by foreign investors. However, the risk aversion of the foreign firm is its own idiosyncrasy and may not be amenable to alteration through the policy choices of the MNC. The royalty rates, though not a function of the level of IPR protection, may yet depend on the degree of risk aversion of the foreign firm. This is the second proposition of the study.

The pertinent question then refers to the channels through which MNC policies neutralize the effect of IPR protection on the efficient choice of royalty rates. Consider the commitment effect of equity participation by the investors in the foreign country, which operates on all the joint ventures. For all practical purposes, it implies that the foreign government improves IPR protection in the interest of investors in its own country. Thus, equity participation that the MNC elicits from the foreign equity investors is an incentive effect for the foreign firm to maintain efficient performance. This constitutes the third proposition of the present analysis.

However, equity participation can also have a control effect. For, the equity holders in their own interest, try to obtain information about the decisions of the management, assess their efficiency, and influence the choices in the optimum direction. Such a control effect can only be firm specific. The fourth basic proposition of this study is that such control effect can also explain the stylized facts observed by Svejnar and Smith (1984).

Observe that both the commitment effect and the control effect suggest that only a foreign firm with appropriate competence and in countries with adequate IPR protection will enter the joint venture. However, in consonance with the results on incomplete contracts, the motivational changes brought about by incentives may be much less efficient compared to compliance elicited through control.

It was assumed throughout this study that when confronted by a low IPR protection, the MNC offers to share equity with the portfolio investors in the foreign country. The analysis then surmised that this results in a change of the foreign government policies in such a way that the variance is reduced. This, in its turn, neutralizes the effect of a low δ. However, the changes in government policy have not been modeled explicitly. It would be worthwhile to try this.

The quadratic approximation to costs is a typical feature of the KM model. It is the simplest representation of the existence of diminishing returns. Considerable empirical work, on subcontracting and franchise contracts, indicates that this is a good workable approximation. See, for example, Kawasaki and McMillan (1987), Yun (1999), Okamuro (2001), and Brickley (2002). It is therefore surmised that this will be a useful approximation even in the present context. Modifications of this specification may suggest themselves as empirical investigation proceeds. Similarly, Pratt's measure can be utilized as a measure of relative risk aversion. This, and its variations, may be applicable in specific empirical contexts. In particular, as Dhanraj and Beamish (2004) pointed out, a more general functional specification may be necessary to explain the observed cycles (flip-flops) in the choices of s.

Neither the commitment nor the control effects are completely reliable. Some amount of mutual understanding and trust will be required to overcome the propensities for opportunistic behavior of either of the parties. See, for example, Madhok (1997) and Rauch (2001). Repeated contracting and positive feedback, as noted in Okamuro (2001) and Besancenot and Vrancenau (2002), are pertinent. A dynamic generalization of the KM framework may in fact provide a more meaningful representation of the variety of patterns of organization of the joint ventures as they emerge in practical contexts.

References

Allen JW, Phillips GM (2000) Corporate equity ownership, strategic alliances, and product market relationships. J Financ 55(6):2791–2815

Al-Saadon Y, Das SP (1996) Host-country policy, transfer pricing and ownership distribution in international joint ventures: a theoretical analysis. Int J Ind Organ 14(3):345–364

Beamish PW, Banks JC (1987) Equity joint ventures and the theory of the multinational enterprise. J Int Bus Stud 18(2):1–16

Besancenot D, Vrancenau R (2002) Manager honesty and foreign investment in developing countries. Res Econ 56(3):231–250

Brickley JA (2002) Royalty rates and upfront fees in share contracts: evidence from franchising. J Law Econ Organ 18(2):511–535

Cai H (2003) A theory of joint asset ownership. Rand J Econ 34(Spring):63–77

Che YK, Hausch DB (1999) Cooperative investments and the value of contracting. Am Econ Rev 89(1):125–147

Chen SFS, Hennert JF (2002) Japanese investors' choice of joint ventures versus wholly-owned subsidiaries in the U.S.: the role of market barriers and firm capabilities. J Int Bus Stud 33(1):1–18

Chishlom DC (1997) Profit-sharing versus fixed-payment contracts: evidence from the motion pictures industry. J Law Econ Organ 13(1):169–201

Das SP (1998) On the choice of international joint ventures: the role of policy moral hazard. J Policy Reform 2:135–150

Das SP (1999) Direct foreign investment versus licensing. Rev Dev Econ 3(1):86–97

Das SP, Katayama S (2003) International joint ventures and host-country policies. Jpn Econ Rev 54(4):381–394

Delois A, Beamish PW (1999) Ownership strategy of Japanese firms: transactional, institutional, and experience influences. Strateg Manag J 20(10):915–933

Desai MA, Foley CF, Hines JR (2001) International joint ventures and the boundaries of the firm. Available at www.stern.nyu.edu/clb/Desai01.pdf

Dhanraj C, Beamish PW (2004) Effect of equity ownership on the survival of international joint ventures. Strateg Manag J 25(3):295–305

Falvey RE, Fried HO (1986) National ownership requirements and transfer pricing. J Dev Econ 24(2):249–254

Folta TB, Janney JJ (2004) Strategic benefits to firms issuing private equity placements. Strateg Manag J 25(3):223–242

Gallini NT, Wright BD (1990) Technology transfer under asymmetric information. Rand J Econ 21(Spring):147–160

Gomes-Casseres B (1989) Ownership structures of foreign subsidiaries. J Econ Behav Organ 11(1):1–25

Gomes-Casseres B (1990) Firm ownership preferences and host government restrictions: an integrated approach. J Int Bus Stud 25(1):1–22

Hart O, Moore J (1998) Cooperatives vs. Outside ownership, NBER working paper 6421. National Bureau of Economic Research, Cambridge, MA

Kawasaki S, McMillan J (1987) The design of contracts: evidence from Japanese subcontracting. J Jpn Int Econ 1(3):327–349

Konrad KA, Lommerud KE (2001) Foreign direct investment, intra-firm trade and ownership structure. Eur Econ Rev 45(3):475–494

Liu X, Wang C (2003) Does foreign direct investment facilitate technological progress? Evidence from Chinese industries. Res Policy 32(6):945–953

Madhok A (1997) Cost, value and foreign market entry mode: the transaction and the firm. Strateg Manag J 18(1):39–61

McCalman P (2004) Foreign direct investment and intellectual property rights: evidence from Hollywood's global distribution of movies and videos. J Int Econ 62(1):107–123

Miller R, Glen J, Jaspersen F, Karmokolias Y (1997) International joint ventures in developing countries. Financ Dev 34(1):26–29

Mjoen H, Tallman S (1997) Control and performance in international joint ventures. Organ Sci 8(3):257–274

Nichols S (1983) Agency contracts, institutional mode, and the transition to foreign direct investment by British manufacturing multinationals before 1939. J Econ Hist 43(3):675–686

Noe TH, Rebello MJ, Shrikhande M (2002) Structuring international cooperative ventures. Rev Financ Stud 15(4):1251–1282

Okamuro H (2001) Risk sharing in the supplier relationship: new evidence from the Japanese automotive industry. J Econ Behav Organ 45(4):361–381

Pan Y (2002) Equity ownership in international joint ventures: the impact of source country factors. J Int Bus Stud 33(2):375–384

Pan Y, Li X (2000) Joint venture formation of very large multinational firms. J Int Bus Stud 31(1):179–189

Rangan S, Drummond A (2004) Explaining outcomes in competition among foreign multinationals in a focal host market. Strateg Manag J 25(3):285–293

Rauch JE (2001) Business and social networks in international trade. J Econ Lit 39(4):1177–1203

Sinha UB (2001) International joint ventures, licensing and buy-out under asymmetric information. J Dev Econ 66(1):127–151

Svejnar J, Smith SC (1984) The economics of joint ventures in less developed countries. Q J Econ 99(1):149–167

Teece DJ (1980) Towards an economic theory of the multiproduct firm. J Econ Behav Organ 1(3):237–247

Vishwasrao S (1994) Intellectual property rights and the mode of technology transfer. J Dev Econ 44(2):381–402

Yun M (1999) Subcontracting relations in the Korean automotive industry: risk sharing and technological capability. Int J Ind Organ 17(1):81–108

Chapter 7
Cost Sharing

Abstract Why and how do contracting parties share variable and/or fixed costs? How are the revenue and cost sharing agreements affected by an expectation of premature termination? How will fixed assets be shared if dissolution occurs without prior notice? These and other related questions will be examined utilizing a synthetic principal agent framework. The analysis centers around three effects of cost sharing: integrity effect, incentive effect, and control effect. Though somewhat fragmented, the available empirical literature, pertaining to many areas of application, will be summarized to disentangle the forces behind cost sharing in contractual relations.

7.1 Fixed vs. Variable Costs

An enterprising individual (who will be designated as the principal hereafter) purchases capital equipment incurring a fixed cost (F). He/she expects to generate revenue x per unit of time over its life span of T units of time by incurring some variable costs. However, very often, the entrepreneur does not have the expertise to organize production on his/her own. He/she rents (or leases) the capital equipment to an agent for a certain length of time in most cases. The agent utilizes the capital assets to generate the expected revenue. The contract generally involves the agent incurring the variable cost and both of them sharing the revenue obtained from the use of the machine at each point of time. In some situations, the payment to the agent may not be adequate to recover the variable cost. Modifications of revenue sharing contracts have been conceptualized in such contexts. A two-part tariff, or a minimum bills contract, is the popular option. See, for instance, Masten and Crocker (1985) and Masten (1988). A different scenario has been noted as well. Depending on the liquidity position of the agent and other strategic considerations that will be noted below, the principal may bear the entire cost and expect the agent to offer his/her labor in generating the revenue. The agent may be paid a wage instead of a share in revenue.

Conceptually, there may be some fixed costs, in addition to the cost of acquiring and operating machines, that the agent must incur per unit of time in order to

Based on content from "Sharing Fixed Costs in Franchise Contracts" first published in *Indian Economic Journal*, 51(2), 2003, pp. 24–34. Content reproduced here with permission from Indian Economic Association.

T.V.S.R. Rao, *Risk Sharing, Risk Spreading and Efficient Regulation*,
DOI 10.1007/978-81-322-2562-1_7

produce any output at all. This may include costs attributable to the efficient choice of the supply chain for inputs and marketing outlets for the sale of output. Consider the following somewhat more specifically. Starting a restaurant involves not only the land and buildings but also the purchase of cooking equipment, cutlery, and so on. The first set of assets involves long-run fixed costs while the second dimension refers to short-term fixed costs. The share of current revenue accruing to the agent must cover this fixed cost as well.

Consider the fixed costs of the principal while acquiring the capital equipment. A fraction of the cost F must be recovered every unit of time through the revenue generated from the production of output. Simple rules, like a two-part tariff or a minimum bills contract, may be put in place. However, the issues involved here are qualitatively different from the variable cost considerations alluded to earlier. In particular, the variations in market demand that are entirely outside the control of the agent necessitate the take-or-pay provision. In general, this arrangement is necessary when the output produced cannot be put in inventory (as in the case of electricity supply) or inventory tends to be expensive (as in the case of natural gas or drinking water supplied to households) for there is still a compulsion that production levels at every point of time must correspond to demand as it materializes. Both these contract forms, it should be obvious from their description, involve sharing fixed costs as well.

Once the contract is in place, the agent may fail to maintain the machine properly so as to reduce his/her share of cost in a cost sharing contract and/or he/she may try to produce more revenue (per unit of time) than what is normally expected so as to improve his/her share in a revenue sharing agreement. In either case, he/she depreciates the machine faster than anticipated and terminates the contract well before the rental agreement expires.[1] See, for example, Arcand et al. (2006). The principal's ability to ensure continuity of production and recover the fixed cost depends on the condition in which the machine is handed over, specificity of capital in the particular line of production (in particular, the idiosyncratic nature of capital equipment), and the degree of difficulty in reaching another contract. Hubert (1995), for instance, pointed out that a principal (an owner of a house) has to incur non-negligible costs in locating a suitable new agent (a renter). If a situation of this nature is anticipated, the contract may involve the agent paying a part of the fixed cost of the machines as well. Revenue or cost sharing agreements may be interlinked due to the possibility of premature dissolution of the contract.[2]

In sum, sharing both variable and fixed costs may be necessary in most principal agent contexts. This may be in addition to the revenue sharing agreements depend-

---

[1] Raff et al. (2009), Dybvig et al. (2009), Braido (2008), and Jacoby and Mansuri (2009) noted, in this context, that the principal may stipulate periodic maintenance of the machines since the principal cannot directly observe the extent to which assets are run down.

[2] Technology transfer agreements in joint ventures are such that the agent initially enters the contract to gain the know-how. At some point in the execution of the contract, the agent may feel that he/she accumulated enough knowledge so that he/she can operate efficiently if he/she is independent. The agent may then terminate the contract prematurely. The principal realizes that early termination of the contract increases the losses that the agent can inflict on him. See, for example, Habib and Barral (2007). Expected remaining value considerations may then be dominant in the ex ante specification of the sharing of fixed costs.

ing on the specific contractual situation under consideration.[3] The following observation should be reiterated. In much of the literature, the sharing of fixed costs is defined in relation to the costs (both variable and fixed) for production and distribution incurred during a specified interval of time while the production contract is in execution. The effect of expected premature termination of the contract did not receive the attention it deserves.

The principal agent models explicitly define efficient sharing of risk while specifying the proportion of output that the principal claims. In general, these models assume that the contract will run through the entire span of the life of the machines. In output sharing contracts, the principal may anticipate that the agent will choose levels of production beyond the expected average. This may depreciate the productive capacity of the machines faster and/or increase the risk of failure. Adjustments in sharing fractions have been conceptualized to account for this contingency.

Note that this approach fails to appreciate the need to recover the remaining value of capital assets at the time of dissolution of the contract. The revenue sharing plus fixed cost share approach to the contract must be modified to account for this aspect explicitly.[4] Clearly, this will depend on the losses anticipated at the time of contract termination. In some practical contexts, like franchise contracts, the principal usually expects the agent to share F upfront to guard against losses of premature dissolution of contract. Observe that the remaining value of the asset alone is at stake. Hence, an agreement concerning the dissolution of the contract may be defined independent of revenue share and exclusively focus on sharing the remaining value of the assets.

One thing is clear. Suppose the principal anticipates premature contract failure. In such a case, he/she can make an attempt to recover some fixed costs while the contract is in operation through two sources. First, he/she may claim a larger share of revenue generated. Second, he/she may expect the agent to share a portion of the fixed cost of acquisition of the asset. The efficient choice, as observed earlier, depends upon the nature of the asset. It will be useful to investigate the reasons for one choice rather than the other.

From an analytical perspective, it must be acknowledged that there is an interlinkage between the current production level and the occurrence of contract dissolution. However, there is as yet no rigorous theoretical foundation to examine the interlinkage between revenue and cost sharing contracts when contract dissolution is expected ex ante. Hence, a synthetic model will be necessary to appreciate the efficient sharing of fixed costs.

---

[3] There may be several other choices in a contract. This study will consider only the sharing of costs and revenue. Further, some accounting and legal constraints may be important in determining the contract parameters in the context of project financing. They will not be considered explicitly.

[4] One exception may be the professional partnerships for their capital assets usually consist of human capital that is malleable. However, even in such contexts, the brand equity and reputation are not easy to recover. Typical studies along these lines include Bradford and Martin (2000), Huddart and Liang (2005), Lerox (2005), Levin and Tadelis (2005), and Omelas and Turner (2007).

Structuring efficient contracts of this nature must acknowledge that their design depends on whether the agent or the principal is expected to initiate dissolution. For example, the principal may be liable to pay the remaining expected share of revenue at the time of severance if he/she initiates it. On the other hand, the agent has to forego his/her share of the fixed cost if he/she decides to withdraw from the contract. Anticipating this possibility, of his/her seeking dissolution and the costs associated with it, the principal chooses the output share and the share of fixed costs efficiently. As of now, the existing literature does not account for this distinction.

It has been pointed out that in some contracts, such as marriage, it may not be meaningful to conceptualize efficient sharing of fixed assets at the time of contract dissolution ex ante. Instead, the contract must be dissolved efficiently ex post. Such issues have been considered in Crampton et al. (1987), Choate and Maser (1992), Dearden and Einolf (2003), Smith (2005, 2007), Turner (2013), Galavoti et al. (2009), and Grosskopf (2009). It is necessary to understand the intricacies of contract design in this context. Clearly, identifying the differences of this case from the others is essential.

The present study sets up a principal agent model as a synthetic analytical structure to examine each of the issues alluded to above.[5] The rest of the presentation is organized as follows. The different sources of risk, their effects on the choice of contract parameters, and the need for and consequences of cost sharing will be outlined in Sect. 7.2. Section 7.3 details a basic principal agent model[6] and deals with sharing variable costs in particular. The most important result is the demonstration that cost sharing is superior to minimum bills contracts or other adjustments in revenue sharing. Section 7.4 considers fixed cost sharing mechanisms when the principal expects premature contract termination. Section 7.5 defines optimal contracts and adjustments in revenue and cost sharing acknowledging the interlinkage between use of assets while the contract is in progress and possibilities of premature dissolution. Section 7.6 deals exclusively with sharing fixed assets when a contract is dissolved without any prior notice. Empirical findings are summarized in Sect. 7.7. Since this is a fertile area for future research, Sect. 7.8 highlights some aspects that require further analysis.

7.2 Risk Sharing

To begin with, it must be acknowledged that the delegation of the use of assets to the agent involves both productivity-augmenting effects and some risks.[7] Clearly, the gains are attributable to the agent being a specialist in production. The risks are

---

[5]It was pointed out in Chen et al. (2007) that experimental evidence indicates a shortage of the principal agent models at the end points where the revenue shares are too high or too low. Even so, it has been a useful analytical tool in most practical contexts. Empirical experiences with the model have also been generally encouraging.

[6]Kaufman and Lafontaine (1992) noted that franchisors may leave a larger share of revenues to franchisees in the long-run interest of a continuing relationship.

[7]The distinctions between the several sources of risk have been detailed in Tjemkas (2008).

usually of three types. First, the choice of the agent may not result in the most efficient agent getting the contract. That is, there is some risk due to adverse selection. Second, neither the principal nor the agent may be in a position to calibrate the revenue-generating potential of the production for which the fixed assets are utilized. In other words, some risks are intrinsic to the market environment. The agent and/or the principal may know a priori the sources of such risks and the extent to which they affect the recovery of revenue. However, neither of them may be in a position to predict some systemic risks. Third, after the contract is signed and depending on the incentives and controls built into the contract, the agent may not operate the assets efficiently. That is, the agent will make the principal bear some risks that may include systemic risks. In general, the conceptualization of contracts is such that the principal is passing on some risks to the agent. The principal may also pass on some risks backwards to the sources of finance he/she utilizes while acquiring the fixed assets.

For all practical purposes, the revenue generated is the only source from which the costs can be recovered. Hence, the most important contract parameter is the share of revenue accruing to the agent. In most practical contexts, the agent is expected to bear the entire variable cost. Hence, the share assigned to him must be adequate to motivate him to be efficient and not merely to recover the variable costs. To be sure, situations are conceivable where the efficient share of revenue determined by the principal agent relationship is not adequate to cover the variable costs for systemic risks that neither the principal nor the agent can control effectively may be the sources of the problem that define the capacity of the agent to generate adequate revenues. In such a case, the principal may offer a higher share, provide a loan to the agent if the problem is considered to be transitory, or agree to share the variable costs with the agent. If the problem is somewhat persistent, a higher revenue share may not have the desired motivational effects. For, on occasions, it has been pointed out that the agent getting a share of revenue may induce him to concentrate on the level of production while inflating costs beyond the efficient level. See, for instance, Baker (2006). As a result, the principal will be at a disadvantage. The agent can be motivated to be efficient if he/she is expected to share a part of the cost or bear the entire cost in the limit. However, note that the ability of the agent to bear these costs and generate an adequate return for his/her efforts poses a constraint on the extent to which he/she can bear the costs. The downside of the cost consciousness is the possibility that the agent does not maintain the efficiency of the capital assets entrusted to him. On the other hand, the principal may have some advantages due to the control effect that such cost sharing bestows on him.[8]

Note that both the systemic risks and the adaptations of the agent in the use of capital assets ultimately determine the structure of the efficient contract. The agent, confronted with systemic risks, may make efficient adaptations to the level of diligence he/she exercises in the use of assets. He/she may be in a position to bear all such costs along with the variable costs of production. Sometimes the principal must share these costs to maintain the contract at the desired level of efficiency.

[8]Yun (1999) contains a synthetic model in which the relative efficiency of revenue sharing versus cost sharing can be disentangled.

Such a definition of efficient mechanisms should not be merely static. Instead, it must factor in the need to maintain the production efficiency of assets over their life span.

It is therefore important to recognize that maintaining efficient production at a point of time may yet be incongruent with its maintenance over time. For, as noted above, the agent may run down assets and terminate the contract prematurely. The agent may not be averse to this if he/she has other alternatives that he/she can switch to. Having sunk investments will adversely affect only the principal. Sharing fixed costs with the agent offers the principal advantages of controlling and motivating the agent in the efficient long-term use of capital assets. It is obvious, from the above description, that the agent's share of revenue may not be adequate for him to bear the burden of sharing fixed costs. However, some broader issues seem to be pertinent.

Several combinations of shares of output, variable costs, and fixed costs are discernible in practice. First, in the context of house ownership, requirements are such that the principal can only charge a fixed rent and bear all the costs. In particular, he/she cannot conceptualize the agent sharing the fixed cost of purchase. Further, he/she cannot expect the agent to bear even the costs of maintenance. It may result in the asset being run down and premature termination of the contract. Second, a landlord will not ask a tenant to share the fixed costs of acquiring the land primarily due to reasons of ownership but offers a share of output to the agent due to motivational considerations. Fixed wage to the agent or fixed rent to the principal depends on other considerations. Third, consider the case of a producer of movies or music CDs. Two forms of contract are obtained.[9] (a) The principal bears the fixed cost of production while the agent bears the fixed cost of exhibition and pays a fraction of the revenue to the producer. (b) The principal (a producer of movies) expects the agents (distributors though not theaters) to share a part of the fixed cost of production and share revenues in addition. In this context, the share of the fixed cost is of the form of monopoly rent for good movies instead of the fear of their being depreciated faster. To an extent, it can be expected to elicit commitment from the distributor to exhibit the movie over an adequate length of time. Fourth, in franchise contracts, the sharing of fixed cost is primarily due to the fear of depreciating the brand equity of the principal's assets. However, the principal may also recognize the possibility that the agent may not have adequate wealth or avenues to raise the requisite finances. The principal, recognizing the liquidity constraint of the agent, typically agrees to share a part of the total investment in fixed assets. Such sharing may be due to other reasons as well. (a) The principal, especially when he/she is dealing with many agents, may consider establishing the brand name of the product and maintaining it as a necessity. Piecemeal efforts by agents may not be efficient. Instead, system-wide production and selling efforts may have to be coordinated by the principal. (b) The principal may wish to maintain some control over the production process and the distribution effort (as in franchises) to ensure that the brand name is not eroded. (c) The principals wish to see that the agents are capable of

[9] Fairly detailed presentations of the various issues are available in Dana and Spier (2001), Mortimer (2002), and Vogel (1996).

innovations and customer-specific investments for they are important for future growth. See, for example, Okamuro (2001, p. 378). (d) As Palay (1984, p. 266) noted, the more specialized the transaction-specific investment, the more the risk of opportunistic behavior during negotiation and execution of the contract. The principal may ask the agent to share some fixed costs as a protection against the possibility that the other party will act opportunistically to usurp potentially appropriable quasi-rents. In the context of purchase of durable goods, the firm (principal) agrees to share a part of the fixed cost of purchase, in the form of a warranty in case of premature failure of the durable, essentially because they have to maintain their brand value to ensure stability of their market share. Fifth, in the context of marriage, both partners may pay for the purchase of assets and their use. If there is a divorce, the dissolution agreement is exclusively determined ex post and usually on the basis of costs of raising children, employment prospects of the spouses, and so on. Ex ante specification of the share of remaining value or remaining liability is rare though not ruled out altogether. The analysis of sharing fixed costs in contractual relationships must keep these aspects in perspective.

In the final analysis, it must be acknowledged that the efficient contract depends on the effort and efficiency of the agent, his/her degree of risk aversion, the expected output that can still be salvaged at the time of contract dissolution, and the asset specificity that prevents the use of machines in alternative lines of production. Even the remaining value of assets and the price at which shares of the principal will be valued at the time of dissolution affect the choice. In practice, the principal, who may be dealing with many similar agents simultaneously, may not be willing to offer agent-specific contracts. Instead, he/she prefers to offer a uniform contract to all of them to self-select. In other words, the agents will adapt their efficiency and risk aversion to match the policy on offer or only those agents who find it advantageous will enter the contract. To the extent that they can, both the principals and the agents may endeavor to reduce the impact of systemic risk as well. The analysis will be modified to account for these adjustments as well.

In sum, the sharing of fixed costs may be due to (a) an integrity effect, (b) an incentive effect, and (c) a control effect. The integrity effect, in its turn, has three dimensions.[10] First, only competent agents will agree to the contract if the principal expects the agent to share a larger proportion of fixed costs. The competence may be with respect to product design, operating complex production structures, and/or doing the job more diligently and efficiently. In short, maintaining quality, cost minimization, and innovativeness may be possible as the agent's share of fixed costs increase. Second, the agent will accept the contract only if he/she has adequate wealth and/or the ability to raise adequate finances to share the fixed costs expected

[10] It should be clear that these effects can be a result of choices other than cost sharing. For example, in franchise contracts, the commitment of the agent is calibrated through interviews, insisting that the agent should not run another business at the same time and so on. In fact, no specific fixed cost can be assigned to a brand name nor can some accounting value offer a convincing measure to form the basis for sharing. Perforce, other mechanisms will become necessary. This argument applies to all the three effects considered here.

from him. Third, the efficient share of revenue cannot provide him adequate income unless the agent can generate sufficient revenues. In other words, survival and the ability to recover costs place a limit on how much cost he/she can share. The incentive effect notes that a share of revenue contract tends to make the agent neglect cost minimization. On the other hand, excessive emphasis on cost minimization may lead to the agent neglecting maintenance of assets and future value generation. In this context, an increase in the share of fixed costs induces the agent to perform better in both these directions. The control effect, in its turn, has three dimensions. First, the principal wishes to maintain the contract over the entire lifetime of the assets. He/she can be sure if the agent shares a large enough proportion of fixed costs. Second, when the agent bears a large enough share of the fixed costs, he/she can be expected to be more diligent, maintain assets better, and be more sensitive to systemic risks and make appropriate adaptations. Third, by inhibiting the tendency to terminate the contract earlier, when the agent is bearing a higher share of fixed cost, the principal's motivation to make larger investments to achieve growth can be maintained. In some cases, especially when the dissolution occurs unexpectedly, the principal or the agent may wish to maintain long-run contractual relationships. Fixed cost sharing may depend entirely on such considerations.[11] All other influences will be outlined in the sequel.

It would be pertinent to outline the actions or decisions of the agents and the principals that are designed to ensure the emergence of these effects. In general, these actions can be divided into two groups: soft options (that tend to have immediate and direct effect) and hard choices (that affect decisions regarding production, investment, and effort and have an indirect effect as they work through the system).

What actions or decisions of the agents and the principals ensure the emergence of these effects? The decisions can be divided into two groups: soft options (direct effects) and hard choices (that work through the decisions about output, investment, etc., or the system)

The soft options for the agent can be detailed as follows:

(a) Choose only those contracts commensurate with his/her wealth position, which enable him to bear the costs and generate the necessary income.
(b) Develop adequate skills and expertise to entice the principal to continue the relationship.
(c) Exhibit sufficient loyalty.
(d) Seek an appropriate share of revenues.
(e) Inform the principal of his/her decisions voluntarily so that the principal can verify compliance.
(f) Be alert to the options available and use exit policy whenever feasible.

---

[11] A tenant usually expends resources as an agent of the landlord. Suppose, now, that an unexpected drought or a flood destroys the crops. In the long-run interest, the principal not only does not insist on his/her share of the crop but also compensates the agent all the costs that he/she incurred.

(g) Threat of premature termination.
(h) Signal threats to run down the value of assets through callous use and/or producing excessive output.

For the principal, the softer options are:

(a) To set a high enough share of revenue to the agent
(b) To leave some ex ante rents to the agent
(c) To offer the agent a fixed wage in addition to revenue share
(d) To ask for a fixed rent in addition to revenue share
(e) To offer loans to the agent in case of temporary distress
(f) To offer to train the agent in relation-specific skills
(g) To supervise the activities of the agent periodically
(h) To use threat of eviction in case of noncompliance
(i) To discuss expansion plans with the agent and offer to extend investments in his/her activity
(j) To participate and/or supervise activities that ensure that the value of fixed assets is preserved

The hard options can be detailed as follows. For the agent, they consist of:

(a) Sharing fixed costs of the principal
(b) Asking the principal to share some of his/her costs

The principal can choose from the following:

(a) Share fixed costs of the agent.
(b) Make the agent share the fixed costs of the principal.
(c) Transfer risk through capital markets.
(d) Contract dissolution.

The criteria for efficient choice of the necessary instruments can be the following:

(a) Transaction costs
(b) Cost of providing incentives
(c) Cost of control
(d) Necessity to maintain contractual relations over time

It may appear that they will exhaust soft options before using hard choices. However, in practice, hard choices have been used very often. Hence, it is necessary to study them in detail.

The foregoing presentation provides the synthetic basis against which the rest of the analysis will be structured.

7.3 Modeling Framework[12]

The simplest output sharing contract can be formulated as follows. Let the principal specify the revenue x that he/she expects the agent to produce.[13] For, normally, the principal knows the capacity of the machines and the output he/she can expect. Assume that the agent bears the entire variable cost of production $x^2/2\delta$. In this formulation, δ represents the agent's efficiency in the use of machines. On the other hand, the agent, who is conscious of the recovery of the costs that he/she has to incur, can be expected to demand a greater share of the revenue with an increase in cost.[14] Let the agent claim a proportion p of revenue. Both of them will maximize their respective gains. However, the principal must take the agent's participatory constraint into account while defining the revenue that he/she expects the agent to produce.

In practice, the contract is subject to the risks mentioned earlier. Consequently, the realized revenue will be random. It may be denoted by $(x+u)$ where u is a random variable with expected value zero and variance σ^2. Observe that the gain to the agent is therefore

$$g_a = p(x+u) - x^2/2\delta$$

In general, such agents will be risk averse [15] since most of the agents work exclusively for the principal. Further, they will not have any other source of income. Therefore, the agent is highly susceptible to risks and randomness. Hence, the value of the contract to the agent can be written as

$$v_a = px - x^2/2\delta - \lambda\sigma^2 p^2$$

Similarly, the gain to the principal is

$$g_p = (1-p)(x+u)$$

---

[12] The following presentation utilizes simple algebraic functional forms to exhibit the basic thrust of the arguments succinctly. Claims of generality are relegated to the background.

[13] It may be argued that x should represent the physical output instead of revenue. The principal will then get a share of this output. He/she can recover some revenue only by selling output. However, he/she may not be able to do it except at a great cost to himself/herself. In such a case, he/she may demand a fixed rent instead. Such an argument was advanced in Fukunaga and Hufman (2009). To maintain generality of the contract form, x will be interpreted as revenue that the agent recovers by selling the product.

[14] Alternately, the agent, who is conscious of an increase in costs as x rises, may be conceptualized to choose x instead. The principal may then be induced to offer a larger share of revenue to the agent. The analysis of such an alternative will be quite similar.

[15] It may be argued that the principal is more likely to be risk averse since he/she has to depend on the agent for the efficient use of the fixed assets. Similarly, the agent may be risk neutral since he/she has the option of terminating the contract without any loss to himself/herself whenever the equipment fails.

He/she can be expected to be risk neutral. As Okamuro (2001, p. 262) pointed out, it may be assumed that the principal has a greater risk-bearing capacity for he/she is likely to have a more secure financial base and tends to be highly diversified. This feature allows him to recoup the loss in any one line of business from the gains in another.[16] Hence, to him, the value of the contract will be

$$v_{\mathrm{p}} = (1 - p)x$$

Maximizing v_{a} with respect to p results in

$$p = x/2\lambda\sigma^2$$

Ceteris paribus, higher risk aversion of the agent reduces his/her share of revenue. For, it should be expected that the principal, who is taking greater risks, needs to be compensated by a higher share of revenue. It can be deduced that

$$v_{\mathrm{p}} = \left(1 - x/2\lambda\sigma^2\right)x$$

is maximum if and only if

$$x = \lambda\sigma^2$$

From the viewpoint of the principal, an increase in the degree of risk will yield adequate revenue at each point of time only if he/she targets a higher level of revenue. The corresponding $p = ½$. In many of the empirically relevant contracts of this nature, this equal sharing of revenue has been observed.

Note that this efficient contract can be sustained if and only if $v_{\mathrm{a}} \geq 0$. It can be readily verified that this can be achieved if and only if $\delta \geq 2\lambda\sigma^2$. Some modification of the contract will be necessary if $\delta < 2\lambda\sigma^2$. The take-or-pay contract will stipulate that the agent must be paid a higher p such that

$$2\delta\lambda\sigma^2 p^2 - 2p\delta + \lambda\sigma^2 = 0$$

In other words, the agent expects a certain minimum payment whenever the efficient sharing mechanism does not enable him to achieve a positive value given his/her share of revenue. This choice is only a second best.

The following example indicates that variable cost sharing contracts have been in vogue. Consider the case of a sugar mill owner who contracts with a farmer for the delivery of sugarcane. Assume that the farmer is expected to bear the entire variable cost of transportation. The principal pays a fixed price for sugarcane or a fraction of revenue from the sale of sugar. The farmers generally complain that they have not been able to recover the variable costs. The practical option is for the sugar mill to share the variable cost with the farmer.

---

[16] In the ultimate analysis, the principal is a residual claimant. He/she does not have much choice except accepting profits as well as losses. To an extent, this is the implication of his/her risk neutrality.

Clearly, one of the reasons for $v_a < 0$ is the variable cost of production. Hence, the principal may agree to share a fraction $(1-s)$ of the cost. It can be readily verified that the optimal choices of p and x given s are

$$p = \delta/2\left[\delta + (1-s)\lambda\sigma^2\right] \text{ and } x = \delta\lambda\sigma^2/2\left[\delta + (1-s)\lambda\sigma^2\right]$$

Ceteris paribus, an increase in s increases both x and p. This is the incentive effect on the agent. The corresponding value of the contract to the agent is zero if and only if

$$s = \delta/2\lambda\sigma^2$$

This is consistent with the intuition that a highly risk averse agent will prefer to place the entire burden of cost on the principal and accept a wage contract. The corresponding choices of p and x reduce to

$$p = \delta/\left(\delta + 2\lambda\sigma^2\right) \text{ and } x = 2\delta\lambda\sigma^2/\left(\delta + 2\lambda\sigma^2\right)$$

Observe that $p > ½$ if and only if $\delta > 2\lambda\sigma^2$. In other words, a relatively efficient agent can extract a larger share of revenue in return to the control exerted by the principal. However, the equilibrium level of production is lower leading to the conclusion that the incentive effect of sharing costs results in the agent exhibiting more diligent use of the assets.[17]

It should also be noted that the above values of p and x can be rewritten as

$$p = s/(1+s) \text{ and } x = \delta/(1+s)$$

Hence, in equilibrium, the agent will be paid a lower share of the revenue as his/her costs decrease. Similarly, the decrease in marginal cost, resulting from the agent bearing a lower share of costs, increases the level of production. Integrity effects are therefore evident.

It can be shown that this cost sharing arrangement is superior to the take-or-pay contract. Note that the net value of the contract is[18]

$$\begin{aligned} v^* &= v_a + v_p \\ &= x - x^2/2\delta - \lambda\sigma^2 p^2 \end{aligned}$$

---

[17] Braido (2008), however, qualifies this argument. As he/she put it, it is difficult to say that the contract resulted in low output due to the lack of agent's effort instead of systemic risk. In general, both these factors are at work.

[18] Why is the maximization of net revenue sacrosanct? Note that the total opportunity cost of conducting the production operations from the perspective of the principal will be $x^2/2\delta + \lambda\sigma^2 p^2$ for the principal will accept the agency relationship only if it will be more expensive if he/she undertakes production on his/her own. Hence, the contract will be efficient if the net value is maximized taking the agent's participation constraint into account.

and the agent's participation constraint is $p = x/2\lambda\sigma^2$. Hence, in the incentive-compatible equilibrium, v^* is maximized for the values of p and x obtained in the cost sharing agreement.

Four further observations are in order. First, suppose $v_a < 0$. The principal may transfer the risk to some outside financing agent instead of providing a loan or sharing the cost. There is no choice for the principal except sharing cost if the outside agents can also estimate that the contract is a losing proposition in the long run. Second, the agent is generally concerned about the risk at each point of time rather than v_a per se. In such a case, the principal may lend him some money temporarily instead of sharing cost. The agent's motivation may be reduced instead of showing any improvement if such short-term financing is available. Cost sharing may yet be the most efficient alternative. Third, if the agent has sufficient wealth or cash reserves, it may not be necessary for the principal to share the short-term risk to which the agent is exposed. Fourth, $v_a < 0$ arises either because x is low or due to low p. They may, in turn, be low because the systemic risk σ^2 is high. In such a case, managing the risk, or reducing the variance, may also be one of the alternatives. Sharing costs may not be a compulsion if this can be achieved. The point in all these cases is that interlocking of several forms may arise in such contracts. The project financing literature considers a rich variety of such possibilities.

Jullien et al. (1999) observed that the agent may become more diligent if systemic risk increases. This will enable him to claim a larger p for any given $\lambda\sigma^2$. Maximizing p yields

$$\delta = c\lambda\sigma^2$$

where c is the relative ease with which the agent can adapt to external risks. It is therefore intuitively plausible that the agent will bear a greater share of the cost if he/she can adapt his/her efficiency in the use of assets more easily. Note, further, that the efficient choice of p will now be

$$p = c/(c+2) > ½ \text{ whenever } c > 2$$

When the agent finds it easy to adapt his/her efficiency in the use of assets to systemic risk, he/she will do so and claim a larger share of revenue. The original efficient contract will be restored when c tends to infinity. That is, the control effect dominates this efficiency effect in most practical contexts. Conceptually, the choice of s is also expected to have an effect on the efficiency of the agent. For, if he/she makes full adjustment, he/she can claim the largest share of revenue. Considering $\delta = \delta(s)$ and maximizing p, it can be shown that the agent will choose $\delta = \beta\,(1-s)$ where β represents the extent to which the principal's share of costs exerts monitoring influence on the agent. Note that the corresponding optimal contract is

$$s = \beta/(\beta + 2\lambda\sigma^2),\ p = \beta/2(\beta + 2\lambda\sigma^2),\ \text{and}\ x = 2\lambda\sigma^2\beta/(\beta + 2\lambda\sigma^2)$$

For all practical purposes, the principal gains by leaving all the costs to the agent if he/she has very little monitoring influence. In sum, the efficient share of costs that the agent bears depends on the costs of his/her making efficient adaptations of δ and the principal's ability to discipline the agent.

Assume that *f* is the fixed cost of using the machines per unit of time. This may include the depreciation of machines and all other fixed costs involved in organizing production every unit of time. To develop the contrast with the above result, assume that the principal bears a proportion $(1-s)$ of the fixed costs as well as the entire variable cost.[19] Then, the gain to the agent is[20]

$$g_{\mathrm{a}} = p(x+u) - \mathrm{sf}$$

and his/her valuation, as before, will be

$$v_{\mathrm{a}} = px - \mathrm{sf} - \lambda\sigma^2 p^2$$

His/Her choice of *p*, ceteris paribus, will turn out to be

$$p = x/2\lambda\sigma^2$$

Consider the gain to the producer. It is given by

$$g_{\mathrm{p}} = (1-p)(x+u) - x^2/2\delta - (1-s)f$$

so that his/her valuation is

$$\begin{aligned} v_{\mathrm{p}} &= (1-p)x - x^2/2\delta - (1-s)f \\ &= \left(1 - x/2\lambda\sigma^2\right)x - x^2/2\delta - (1-s)f \end{aligned}$$

The efficient choice of *x* is

$$x = \delta\lambda\sigma^2/\left(\delta + \lambda\sigma^2\right)$$

and, similarly,

---

[19] Suppose, instead, that the agent is expected to bear the entire variable cost. Then, as noted earlier, the efficient choice is not viable if $\delta < 2\lambda\sigma^2$. In such a case, the agent cannot be expected to share any fixed cost at all. The practical context where a retailer is selling music CDs of a producer is a case in point. Usually the principal bears the entire fixed cost for the dealers have significant cost of maintaining inventory and marketing. A part of the problem may also be a result of the producer insisting that the agent holds a large stock in anticipation that a huge market can be generated.

[20] In addition to the effect of sf on the agent's gains, it has implications for the control exercised by the principal to preserve the value of fixed assets over the life of the machines. See, for example, Jacoby and Mansuri (2009). This will be considered afresh in the sequel.

$$p = \delta / 2(\delta + \lambda\sigma^2)$$

The agent will not accept the contract if $v_a \leq 0$. On the other hand, the principal is a residual claimant. Note that for the optimal choices of p and x

$$v_a = \lambda\sigma^2\delta^2 / 4(\delta + \lambda\sigma^2) - \text{sf}$$

so that the maximum sf he/she will accept will be

$$\text{sf} = \lambda\sigma^2\delta^2 / 4(\delta + \lambda\sigma^2)$$

Clearly, the cost commitment of the agent remains the same as in the previous case. However, the equilibrium level of output will decrease. In other words, sharing fixed costs will have the effect of the more diligent agent accepting a greater share of the fixed costs and using the assets more carefully so as to preserve their value over time. Such a choice is superior to sharing variable costs.

Let the revenue expected from the use of the fixed asset be highly variable. Then, it is better for the owner to seek a share of the fixed cost. Similarly, suppose the agent is highly risk averse. Then, he/she is likely to use the asset more diligently and not reduce the value of the asset. If this materializes, the owner need not ask the agent to bear a share of the fixed cost. Arcand et al. (2006) noted a result of this nature.

Note, further, that p and x can be rewritten as

$$p = (\text{sf}/\lambda\sigma^2)^{1/2} \quad \text{and} \quad x = 2(\text{sf}\lambda\sigma^2)^{1/2}$$

That is, an increase in the agent's share of fixed cost entices him to produce greater output and expects a larger share of revenue to cover the cost.

On the whole, these cost sharing mechanisms assume that the contractual integrity can be maintained throughout the entire life span of the assets. A different conceptualization is necessary to accommodate the possibility of premature dissolution of the contract.

7.4 Premature Termination

Two practical contexts may be detailed to motivate the analysis of this section. First, consider the context of a bank that takes deposits and utilizes the money to offer loans to others. The central bank, as the policy coordinator of all banks and a lender of last resort, anticipates that an amount y of loans cannot be recovered. When the bank fails to collect these loans, the central bank offers a bailout $p(y+v)$. As before, v is a random variable. It will be assumed that the expected value of v is zero and its variance is σ_v^2. They incur a cost $(y+v)^2/2\varepsilon$ in trying to rescue the loans. Clearly, ε is a representation of the quality of assets as reflected in the central bank's ability to recover them. In order to cover these costs, the central bank expects the bank to make a deposit αy with it.[21] Second, the context of an accident insurance is similar. An insurance company expects that a value y of the equipment remains at the time an accident may occur. However, it may occur when $(y+v)$ of value is yet to be realized. To send it for repairs, they must incur a cost $(y+v)^2/2\varepsilon$. The premium they expect the insured to pay will depend on y.

The formal modeling of the general context can be detailed as follows. When a principal delegates production to an agent, he/she expects that the machine may fail while y units of revenue is yet to be realized.[22] However, he/she cannot be sure of this. The actual loss may be $(y+v)$ where v is a random variable with expected value zero and variance σ_v^2. The principal therefore contemplates making the agent bear αy of this as his/her share of the fixed cost ex ante.[23] This has the effect of motivating the agent to use the asset so as to keep the losses at a minimum. The assumption is that, while the contract is in progress, output is shared to cover the variable costs of the agent, the cost of maintaining the production capacity of the fixed asset, and depreciation of the machine. The only issue with premature termination, from the principal's point of view, is the amount of fixed cost that he/she should make the agent bear so as to reduce the likelihood of premature termination and maximize his/her gain if premature dissolution does occur.[24]

Two possibilities will now be considered distinctly. Assume that the agent terminates the contract. Normally, the only gain to him is in avoiding the share of revenue that he/she would have paid the principal if the contract remained in force till the end. This can be represented by $(1-p)$ $(y+u)$. However, when he/she terminates the contract, the agent cannot expect the principal to repay the share of fixed cost that he/she incurred while entering the contract. Consequently, the gain to the agent is

$$g_a = (1-p)(y+v) - \alpha y$$

[21] A detailed analysis of central bank regulatory policy along these lines can be found in Rao (2010).

[22] Habib and Barral (2007) and Braido (2008), in particular, noted that the agent's action may affect the quality of the fixed asset since excessive use or careless use may lead to early breakdown. As Braido (2008) and Ganglmair (2009) pointed out, there is a danger of underinvestment in this context if fixed cost sharing is defined ex ante.

[23] This is a credible damage measure for the agent has to forego this amount if he/she decides to terminate the contract prematurely. An alternative is considered more efficient in franchise contracts. For example, denying the franchisee a permission to start a new franchise may be adequate. This alternative is necessitated because the franchisee does not generally share in the fixed costs of the franchiser.

[24] Dybvig et al. (2009) expressed this in the following way. Sharing current output is not sufficient to define an efficient contract. It should also reveal a signal (e.g., sharing of fixed costs) about his/her commitment to use assets diligently before production and sharing risk. The agent provides an informative signal which contains information that is correlated with future returns. These controls are not only for eliciting the desired effort but also for choosing the intended revenue generation as a function of the signal.

He/she can be expected to be risk averse for he/she expects the principal to choose a larger α if he/she expects a higher value of y at the time of the termination of the contract.[25] Hence, the value of the contract to the agent is

$$v_a = \left[(1-p)-\alpha\right]y - \lambda\sigma_v^2(1-p)^2$$

Realistically, the principal will choose α given the expected y choice of the agent. Consequently, for any y that the agent chooses, the maximum α that the principal can expect him to accept will be such that $v_a = 0$. That is,

$$\alpha = (1-p) - \lambda\sigma_v^2(1-p)^2/y$$

Consider the gain to the principal. He/she gains αy in the sense that he/she need not refund it in the event of the agent terminating the contract. However, he/she has to find another agent and/or related production lines from which he/she can recover the remaining value of the fixed assets. Such costs depend on the degree of malleability (or not being idiosyncratic in the same line of production) of the capital equipment. They can be represented by $(y+v)^2/2\varepsilon$ with ε representing the degree of malleability of capital.[26] The gain to the principal will be

$$g_p = \alpha y - (y+v)^2/2\varepsilon$$

Clearly, he/she is likely to be risk neutral to the possibility of premature termination. The value of the contract to the principal will be

$$v_p = \alpha y - \left(y^2 + \sigma_v^2\right)/2\varepsilon$$

The principal may be expected to maximize v_p by choosing p for, in the ultimate analysis, he/she has to bear the costs of reorganization and recovery of the remaining value of machines through their utilization in production. However, he/she must keep the agent's participatory constraint in perspective. The optimal p is therefore such that

$$(1-p) = y/2\lambda\sigma_v^2$$

The agent's choice of y may now be considered. He/she is likely to choose it in such a way that $v_p = 0$. That is, the y satisfies the equation

$$\alpha y = \left(y^2 + \sigma_v^2\right)/2\varepsilon$$

---

[25] Raff et al. (2009) argue that the share of fixed assets should depend on the value of assets as well.

[26] Chao et al. (2009), for instance, argued that the principal asking the agent to share these costs has a better control effect from the principal's perspective.

The following observation is important. Note that

$$\partial y/\partial\alpha = y\varepsilon/(y-\alpha\varepsilon) < 0 \text{ if and only if } \alpha > y/\varepsilon$$

That is, ceteris paribus, the imposition of a larger share of fixed costs on the agent will have the desired control effect only if α is large enough. Low levels of α are more likely to have incentive effects instead of control effects.

Ceteris paribus, the purpose of the principal choosing a higher value of α is to reduce the possibility of early termination. In the present framework, this will occur if and only if

$y<\alpha\varepsilon$. Now, note that, in equilibrium,

$$\alpha = y/4\lambda\sigma v^2$$

That is, in the final analysis, the principal will choose a larger α if he/she expects the y to be larger. The equilibrium choice of y can be shown to be

$$y=(2\lambda)^{1/2}\sigma_v^2/(\varepsilon-2\lambda\sigma_v^2)^{1/2}$$

and $y<\alpha\varepsilon$ if and only if $\varepsilon>4\lambda\sigma_v{}^2$

Note that the principal will not insist on sharing fixed costs if the equipment is fully malleable. Further, as Dailami and Hauswald (2007) pointed out, there will be no need for a positive α if external or systemic risks can be eliminated through appropriate actions of the principal and/or the agent.

The alternative that the principal may terminate the contract prematurely may now be examined. In this context, the agent will be entitled to the remaining share of revenue that he/she would have received if the contract continued. This is the general nature of severance payments to the agent. However, the principal will not repay the share of the fixed cost that the agent had to pay at the time of contract writing. Hence, the gain to the agent can be written as

$$g_\text{a} = p(y+v)-\alpha y$$

Assume, as before, that the agent is risk averse. The value to the agent is

$$v_a = (p-\alpha)y-\lambda\sigma_v^2p^2$$

The agent cannot have any influence on the choice of y since the principal is terminating the contract. Hence, the only choice is p. Maximizing v_a with respect to p results in

$$p=y/2\lambda\sigma_v^2$$

Note that the principal retains αy paid by the agent. But now he/she has to incur a cost $(y+v)^2/2\varepsilon$ to salvage the remaining revenue. Hence, his/her gains are

$$g_p = \alpha y - (y+v)^2/2\varepsilon$$

He/she can be expected to be risk neutral since he/she can choose α, based on the y where he/she expects to terminate the contract, to his/her advantage. That is, the value of the contract to the principal is

$$v_p = \alpha y - (y^2 + \sigma_v^2)/2\varepsilon$$

Clearly, the principal can be expected to choose y. The optimal choice will be

$$y = \alpha\varepsilon$$

The optimized value of v_a can be shown to be

$$v_a = 1/4\lambda - \sigma_v^2/2\varepsilon$$

so that the contract is viable if and only if $\varepsilon > 2\lambda\sigma_v^2$. Consider

$$v_p = \alpha^2\varepsilon/2 - \sigma_v^2/2\varepsilon$$

Hence, the minimum α that the principal will accept is

$$\alpha = \sigma_v/\varepsilon$$

The equilibrium contract is

$$y = \sigma_v,\ p = 1/2\lambda\sigma_v,\ and\ \alpha = \sigma_v/\varepsilon$$

Note that

$\partial y/\partial\alpha = 1/\varepsilon > 0$. Hence, it follows that the principal will choose a larger value of α the sooner he/she plans to terminate the contract. Further, as asset specificity increases, irrespective of whether risks originate in internal or external (systemic) sources, there is little room for hedging risks or transferring them through the channel of financial intermediation. Such unmanageable risks must be shared by the agent. See, for instance, Dailami and Hauswald (2007). Similarly note that when assets are specific, as in a project financing context, output contract fulfillment and revenue generation are interlocked with the financial arrangements to acquire assets and provide variable costs. Suppose the management is able to credibly manage the output risk and lower σ_v^2. In such cases, it may not be necessary to contemplate cost sharing arrangements.

7.5 Interlinkage[27]

In many practical contexts, there is an interlinkage between the use of fixed assets in current production and preserving the value of assets. The following examples are typical.

Example 1 A producer of music CDs incurs a certain amount of fixed cost. He/she then supplies fixed amounts to each of the retailers in his/her network. The retailers, in their turn, incur some costs while selling CDs to customers. The producer claims a fraction of the sales revenue. However, the producer recognizes that the retailer will return some CDs saying that he/she cannot find any more market. Recognizing this contingency, the producer asks the retailer to make a non-refundable deposit. Clearly, the producer must incur some additional cost (such as offering discounts) to sell the CDs. Therefore, the producer can be expected to take the possibility of dissolution into account while fixing the royalties that he/she will offer on the sale of CDs.

Example 2 A landlord accepts a tenant. Normally, the tenant is expected to bear all the variable costs. He/she will be offered a share of revenue. However, the tenant may find it advantageous to reduce costs. He/she may do so by not paying attention to soil conservation measures, pest control, and so on. He/she will eventually render the land fallow (or at least of lower productivity) and return it to the landlord. Anticipating this possibility, the landlord may ask the tenant to spend a certain amount on such measures (and share a part if need be). The landlord will adjust the revenue share offered to the tenant taking the possibility of contract failure into account.

The principal anticipates contract failure given the revenue sharing incentive structure. He/she, therefore, stipulates a certain volume of production and a share of fixed costs. Since the agent must bear the variable costs of production, he/she stipulates a certain share of revenue and a severance payment in case the principal initiates the dissolution. This accounts for the interlocking explicitly.[28]

The following analytical structure illustrates the sharing of fixed costs and the interlinkage it creates while determining the share of revenue offered to the agent.

---

[27] Arcand et al. (2006), Li and Wolfstetter (2010), and Fukunaga and Hufman (2009) argued that the agent may run down assets fast and terminate the contract if he/she has to bear all the costs and share output. He/she essentially chooses the output levels and timing of termination to maximize his/her return. On the other hand, cost sharing in the short run may result in better use of assets. Premature dissolution of contracts can be eliminated.

Sappington (1991, p. 55) observed that there is an interlinkage between rewarding good performance and the alternative of penalizing bad performance. The agents may still not self-select adequately to adhere to the efficiency expected by the principal. He/she, therefore, advocates a Vickrey auction to choose the appropriate agent.

[28] Sappington (1991, p. 55) observed that there is an interlinkage between rewarding good performance and the alternative of penalizing bad performance. The agents may still not self-select adequately to adhere to the efficiency expected by the principal. He/she, therefore, advocates a Vickrey auction to choose the appropriate agent.

As before, assume that the agent recovers revenue $(x+u)$ after incurring a variable cost $x^2/2\delta$. Note that this quantity x is the total revenue over the tenure of the contract instead of per unit of time as postulated earlier. The agent receives a share p of $(x+u)$. Hence, the value of this part of the contract to the agent is

$$v_a = px - x^2/2\delta - \lambda\sigma^2 p^2$$

Assume that he/she decides to dissolve the contract while y units of revenue are yet to be realized. Anticipating this contingency, the principal expects him to bear αy of the fixed cost.[29] The value of dissolution to the agent is

$$v_a = (1-p)y - \alpha y - \lambda(1-p)^2\sigma^2$$

It is obvious that $x+y=A$ where A is the total output expected from the capital assets over their life span. Note further that if output produced is $x+u$, the remaining value will be $y-u$.

The agent must choose the value of x at which he/she prefers dissolution of the contract. Note that if he/she produces one more unit of x, he/she gains $p-x/\delta$. Similarly, the decision entails a loss $[\alpha+(1-p)]$ that he/she would have experienced from termination. Hence, his/her gains will be maximized if

$$2p = 1+\alpha + x/\delta$$

In an analogous fashion, it can be verified that the net marginal gain to the principal will be zero if

$$y/\varepsilon = p-1+\alpha$$

The efficient equilibrium choices of p and x will therefore become

$$p = [\delta(1+\alpha)+A+\varepsilon(1-\alpha)]/(2\delta+\varepsilon) \text{ and}$$
$$x = A-\delta[2A+\varepsilon(1-3\alpha)]/(2\delta+\varepsilon)$$

The principal may fix α in one of two ways. First, he/she may choose it in such a way that the contract is dissolution proof.[30] That is, he/she will choose $x=A$. This choice results in

$$\alpha = (\delta - A)/3\delta$$

[29] Raff et al. (2009) pointed out that the principal needs credible signals to calibrate the probability of early termination of the contract. They suggest that the current level of revenue generated and the costs incurred by the agent in the process should form the basis.

[30] This saves the principal from specifying the sharing of assets at the time of contract termination if it were to occur. Comino et al. (2010) in fact argue that the incentive to do better and continue rather than dissolve the contract increases if there is no ex ante specification of how assets will be shared when termination occurs. Perhaps the choice depends on asset specificity.

This choice is not a function of ε, the malleability of capital equipment, simply because the contingency of termination does not arise if $x=A$. Observe that the resulting

$$p=(2\delta+A)/3\delta$$

It will not be equal to ½ for any relevant range of values of A and δ. In fact, observe that p tends to 2/3 as δ tends to infinity. Higher values of p protect the principal from premature termination. See, for example, Kaufman and Lafontaine (1994, p. 420), Lafontaine (1992), and Brickley (2002). Second, a more general approach may be to choose $v_a=0$ as outlined earlier. It can be shown that $\alpha=\alpha(\varepsilon)$ such that $\partial\alpha/\partial\varepsilon<0$. That is, the principal will choose to ask the agent for a lower share of the fixed assets when the capital assets are more malleable. In general, the interlinkage alters the values of all the contract parameters.[31]

The case where the principal prefers dissolution of contract can be examined in an analogous fashion. No new insights seem to emerge. It should, however, be noted that dissolution may occur for any random u if it is sufficiently large and the agent cannot sustain the contract any further. That is, the above contract specification is dissolution proof only on an average. Such a possibility was noted in Quadrini (2007).

7.6 Post-dissolution

In the previous section, it was acknowledged that premature dissolution can be expected in some contracting contexts. It was also demonstrated that the choice of contract parameters, including those that are applicable while the contract is in operation, will be affected by the expectation of termination and the possible sharing of the remaining value of assets.

In many practical contexts, it has been observed that long-term contracts are subject to entirely unexpected and premature termination due to a variety of reasons. Primary among them are the changes in technology, the availability of alternative investment prospects to either party, or simply disagreements and mistrust. It is difficult to know a priori why and when a contract will be called off. The recovery of the remaining value of assets becomes an important issue.

Chiu (1998) and Cai (2003) pointed out that the degree to which an agent can recover his/her share of assets at the time of contract termination depends on (a) the investment opportunities available to him outside the contract in which he/she is

---

[31] Kraft (2008) has the following additional observations. First, greater asset specificity (or a low value of ε) is expected to make the agent choose a larger y. Second, when the uncertainty is high, it will be expected that there will be premature dissolution and a need to have a larger α. Third, an agent choosing a high value of x signals his/her intentions to dissolve the contract prematurely. Consequently, αy should increase.

currently locked in, (b) extent to which he/she is able to keep himself/herself informed about alternatives, and (c) the potential threat he/she can pose to the principal (in terms of exit and liquidation) even before contract termination occurs. More specifically, the sharing of fixed costs depends on these external factors rather than the dynamics within the contract.

In some contexts, as noted in the foregoing sections, the agents share a part of the fixed costs of assets attributable to the contract. Suppose, now, the contract is terminated at a totally unexpected time well ahead of the time required for the agent to recover his/her fixed cost through the revenue sharing agreement. It was assumed that the agent loses his/her share of fixed costs. However, it has been observed in the context of long-term contracts that the principal repays the agent if he/she finds it necessary to maintain contractual relations in the future.[32]

Consider the contract between a movie producer and a distributor. Normally, the producer extracts a part of the fixed production cost from the distributor ex ante. Consider the possibility that the movie turns out to be a flop at the box office. In such a case, neither of them may be in a position to recover sunk costs. It may appear that the distributor has to lose the remaining value of the deposit he/she made. However, the producer cannot consider the issue as one of short-term contracting. In the interest of the continuity of the long-run relationship, he/she may compensate the distributor to the extent he/she has to or he/she can.[33] However, both of them acknowledge that losses are intrinsic to business.

In a marriage relationship, both spouses finance the assets they acquire. It may be perfectly normal to conceptualize a payment for life insurance. But it is not equally pleasant to discuss sharing arrangements in case of divorce ex ante. There is generally no thought given to the issue of how they can recover their investments in case of divorce. However, they have to face the issue if the situation demands it.

The canonical model of sharing post-dissolution can be developed in the following manner. The crucial observation is that the left-out value of the assets, or the cost liabilities of children in the context of divorce, will be notoriously difficult to

---

[32] In many firms, severance pay is offered to a manager when he/she is displaced. It may depend on the share of the remaining value of assets he/she would have received if the contract remained in force. It may be made a function of the remaining value per se and the bargaining power of the manager. There is, however, no suggestion that the quantum of severance pay is related to a commitment to maintain the agent post-dissolution. Usually such contract arrangements are defined ex ante at the time of hiring the manager. The control effects of such post-dissolution contracts are in doubt. For, there is a suggestion that the managers may not work efficiently if the severance pay is high. However, note that the decisions of the managers may depend more on current payments and severance pay may indeed not have any effect on their performance. Similarly, the choice of severance pay may not influence their decisions if the managers do not have many opportunities elsewhere. In general, it is difficult to identify all the factors that determine severance pay and its efficacy as a control mechanism.

[33] Clearly, the distributor, though the weaker party, has some monopoly power in the long run for the producers must depend on him to exhibit their movies. The distributor therefore makes a first claim on what he/she can extract from the producer in the interest of maintaining long-term contractual relationships.

ascertain. They tend to be random. Let y be its expected value. The agent will normally claim a share q of the value $(y+u)$. That is,

$$g_a = q(y+u)$$

The agent, not being very sure of future prospects at the time of dissolution of the contract, tends to be risk averse. The value of his/her share is then

$$v_a = qy - \lambda\sigma^2 q^2$$

The agent is expected to claim a share that maximizes v_a. The resulting q is

$$q = y/2\lambda\sigma^2$$

The principal, on his/her part, must take this participatory constraint into account in his/her decision-making process. His/Her assessment of the salvage value of assets depends on the malleability of the assets and the costs he/she must incur in recovering the value. Assume that this cost can be represented by $(y+u)^2/2\varepsilon$. Then, the gains are

$$g_p = (1-q)(y+u) - (y+u)^2/2\varepsilon$$

A risk-neutral principal will consider the value of the contract to be[34]

$$v_p = \left(1 - y/2\lambda\sigma^2\right)y - \left(y^2 + \sigma^2\right)/2\varepsilon$$

The optimal y, from his/her perspective, will be

$$y = \varepsilon\lambda\sigma^2/\left(\varepsilon + \lambda\sigma^2\right)$$

The resulting equilibrium q is

$$q = \varepsilon/2\left(\varepsilon + \lambda\sigma^2\right)$$

Hence, this static formulation cannot sustain the repayment by the principal of the entire fixed cost incurred by the agent. For this choice $v_a \geq 0$. The residual claimant, the principal, may lose. But he/she may not have any legal recourse.[35]

[34] Allen (1992) argues that when the contract is in force, the principal may choose y to maximize $v = v_a + v_p$. Contractual integrity can be maintained if neither the principal nor the agent can expect to do better. However, note that post-dissolution the principal is not likely to have the motivation to maximize the collective gain.

[35] There are several difficulties with this approach to modeling post-dissolution contracts. Firstly, y may represent the expected costs for the agent in recovering the value of his/her fixed assets. Secondly, when the agent makes an investment in some fixed assets, his/her ability to recover their

In general, due to transaction costs that the principal must incur, $q<½$. It reaches a value $q=½$ only when the assets are perfectly malleable. Similarly, when the assets are essentially idiosyncratic, such sharing is not possible. As noted at the outset, the principal making payments depends on who made the investment in the fixed assets to begin with. The other important aspect is that, say in the context of divorce, the agent may claim that the costs of educating the children or other costs that the agent incurred while acquiring the assets must be factored in while calculating q. This tends to be subjective. Ganglmair (2009) noted the possibility of the agent acquiring such monopoly power. More pertinent is the argument that anticipating such behavior may tend to reduce the relation-specific investment. To be sure, it is not easy to conceptualize and identify the efficient amount of investment in fixed assets.

7.7 Empirical Findings

Several testable implications of the above analysis for the sharing of fixed costs can now be identified:

(a) Integrity effect

1. The lower the wealth of the agent, or capacity to bear, the lower the share of fixed costs he/she can accept.
2. The lower the abilities of the agent, the lower will be the share of fixed costs he/she will accept. The abilities may be with respect to creating product designs, organizing efficient production, marketing skills, or access to finances.
3. The greater the systemic risk, the less likely the agent will agree to bear a share of fixed costs. In general, if the equilibrium share of revenue is low, the agent cannot continue the activity. The principal must reduce the cost burden of the agent.
4. The greater the revenue-generating potential of assets, the lower will be the necessity for the agent to share variable and/or fixed costs.
5. In some cases, the principal has an advantage in creating centralized marketing and selling effort. This will induce the principal to determine the quantum of investment. Very often, brand equity is the only asset built up through such investment. The agent must be motivated to preserve the brand equity. The principal expects the agent to share the investment and leave him an adequate share of the monopoly rent that he/she generates.

---

value and his/her risk aversion may dominate the determination of shares. In other words, a large λ may necessitate a larger q. Thirdly, a large λ may not be adequate to represent the bargaining power of the agent for such power may depend on the idiosyncratic nature of his/her assets, opportunities available to him elsewhere, and the malleability of the principal's fixed assets. Further developments of this theory are in order.

6. The share of variable costs that the principal bears depends on the adequacy of the efficient share of revenue in maintaining the agent. It also depends on the transient or permanent character of systemic risks.

(b) Incentive effect

1. The share of the fixed cost that the agent is expected to bear depends on the motivation necessary to improve his/her diligence in the use of assets. It will eventually manifest itself in the form of an increase in output and a reduction in the possibility of premature termination.
2. If the systemic risks and/or risk aversion of the agent are large, the principal bearing a larger share of the fixed assets motivates the agent to be more efficient while the contract is in operation. The incentive effect will be prominent when the fixed assets of the principal are highly malleable.

(c) Control effect

1. The lower the malleability of fixed assets, the more the principal wants the agent to bear fixed costs.
2. Suppose the agent is expected to bear the entire fixed cost ex ante. If unexpected premature dissolution of contract occurs and maintaining the long-term integrity of the contract is important, the principal must reimburse the remaining value to the agent.

The empirical evidences available are generally of three types. First, there are some historical descriptions of a contract. That is, the evidence is anecdotal and specific. It is doubtful if the same pattern will be experienced in other related contexts. Second, some evidence is based on case studies. Usually, there is no attempt at generalization. Third, there have been some rigorous econometric tests. Even these tend to be situation specific. As such, they defy any generalization. For, contracting practices tend to be industry and context specific. Since these empirical experiences do offer some useful information, the details will now be presented. It is important to note that the number of studies on any one aspect, as reported here, does not convey any information about the importance of one of these effects over the other. In fact, there is virtually no attempt to examine the nature of changes in revenue sharing and contract termination contingent on the controls exercised by the principal. This remains a fertile ground for future research.

Availability of data has also been a constraint. Masten and Saussier (2002, p. 289) pointed out the following. "As the number of provisions (objectives of the principals and agents as well as the instruments available to them) analyzed increases, the number of explanatory variables and the size of the data set needed for statistical identification multiplies. Often, sufficient numbers of observations to analyze more than two or three provisions at a time simply do not exist." Further, as Aggarwal (2007, p. 476) reiterated, "most of the theoretically (defined) variables are either not observed or only partially observed. Given this problem, the empirical methodology used most often is to regress control choice on a range of proxies relating to the characteristics of the contracting parties (and other variables conditioning the environment in which the contracts are defined and implemented)."

That is, reduced form specifications dominate empirical work. The estimation of all the parameters in the structural model may not be necessary to obtain the requisite information about the contracts.

Return to the simplest model of Sect. 7.2 to illustrate the econometric methods utilized in practice. Consider the case where a firm has n different contracts. Clearly, the differences in p and x are due to the variations in δ and $\lambda\sigma^2$. The econometric problem is to examine whether the actual choices of the firm correspond to these theoretical expectations. The data usually consists of the actual output x_a from each of the contracts at each point of time. To begin with, note that since

$$x_a = 2\delta\lambda\sigma^2/\left(\delta + 2\lambda\sigma^2\right)$$
$$1/x_a = 1/\delta + 1/2\lambda\sigma^2$$

Assume that proxies for δ, λ, and σ^2 can be defined and measured. Then, the regression

$$x_j^* = a + b\delta_j^* + c\left(\lambda\sigma^2\right)_j + \text{error}$$

where x_j = average of x_{aj} over time, $x_j^* = 1/x_j$, and so on for $j = 1, 2, \ldots, n$ and the hypothesis $a = 0$, $b = 1 = c$ will provide the desired test. The practical difficulty with this approach is the choice of proxies.

Assume that g_p from each of the contracts at each point of time is also available. Then, the parameters δ_j, λ_j, and σ_j^2 can be estimated. Estimation begins by observing that[36]

$$V\left(x_a\right) = \text{variance of } x_a = \sigma^2$$

For each $j = 1, 2, \ldots, n$

Hence, this can be used to estimate σ_j^2. Secondly, note that

$$V\left(g_a\right) = S^2 = \left(1 - p\right)^2 \sigma^2$$

as implied by the specification of the principal agent model. Consequently, most of the studies propose to estimate p as

$$p = 1 - S/\sigma$$

Given that

$$p = s/\left(1 + s\right)$$

[36] Asanuma (1989), Asanuma and Kikutani (1992), Yun (1999), and Gonzales-Diaz et al. (2000) considered variations on this method of estimation.

the parameter s can also be estimated for each j separately. The other two parameters of interest are λ and δ. Observe that

$$x_a = 2\lambda\sigma^2 p$$

Hence, λ_j can be estimated as the average over time of $(x_{aj}/2\sigma_j^2 p_j)$ for each j. Further, from the definition of the efficient choice of s, it follows that

$$\delta = 2\lambda\sigma^2 s$$

so that all the necessary δ_j values can be computed. It is now possible to estimate a cross-section regression to test the desired hypothesis. Some variations on these themes have been utilized in practice.

Many recent developments of econometric practices and empirical evidence, based on related models, have been surveyed in Masten and Saussier (2002) and Chiappori and Salanie (2003). Significant work is still in progress.[37] However, as of today, many econometric problems remain unresolved:

(a) Integrity effect

Whenever a principal contemplates a contractual relationship with an agent, he/she considers the nature of the fixed assets first. They may consist of plant and machinery, buildings, productive agricultural land, a special product (like the Coca-Cola concentrate), capabilities to scale up technologies, or simply a brand name (say McDonalds). He/she would surely not share the ownership of some of these assets, e.g., a house, agricultural land, or a brand name. Perforce, the principal must bear the entire fixed cost of ownership. He/she may still delegate the use of such fixed assets to an agent. If he/she does, he/she must ensure, for instance, that his/her brand name is preserved. He/she will ask the agent to share some fixed costs in the form of a franchise fees. Note that some complimentary investment may be necessary to generate revenue. In general, this is of a short-term nature. The principal needs to ensure integrity of the contract. To do so, he/she expects the agent to bear the entire cost. This may yet be insufficient to make sure that the agent is capable of using the assets properly. He/she may share some fixed costs of training, developing samples or molds, or promotional expenses. A competent agent will not hesitate to bear some part of these costs. From the principal's viewpoint, the good agents self-select if sharing fixed costs is stipulated. As in the case of automobile assemblers, the principal may assess that the agent, though technically competent and can be trusted to use his/her fixed assets diligently, lacks the wealth or ability to raise finances to take the burden of fixed costs. The principal may then choose to share a part of the fixed costs that the agent is expected to incur. In other words, the financial health of the agent is of concern to the principal in ensuring contractual integrity. The agent may, however, deal with many principals and not exclusively with one. For example, Sona steering supplies to Maruti, Hyundai, and so on.

[37] Prominent work includes Hernandez (2003), Zheng et al. (2008), Brown and Bellemare (2009), and Fukunaga and Hufman (2009).

The principal is then not sure of how much of the fixed investment of the agent is meant to cater to his/her requirements. He/she will then refuse to share the fixed costs of the agent. The competence of the agent, the nature of fixed costs of the agent, and the agent's financial position will determine his/her share. The principal has the option of adjusting the share of revenue instead of sharing fixed costs. The choice depends mostly on the extent to which the principal depends on a particular agent. If he/she can switch between agents freely (as in the case of automobile ancillaries like tires, instrument panel, etc.), the principal prefers to operate through revenue shares rather than sharing fixed cost. In fact, much of the empirical evidence suggests that the principals try to avoid long-term commitment in the form of sharing fixed costs even when they recognize that the agent needs help in maintaining contractual integrity. The following specific studies may now be noted:

1. Korringa (1996) considered the case of footwear suppliers of Agra. In this industry, sample making (including manufacturing a small lot for sale) plays a crucial role. The transition from sample to the final manufacture is also a lengthy process. Some agents are quite competent. The principal buyer usually pays the entire fixed cost if the agent is competent and can deliver good designs on time, etc. But, in some cases, the agent may not have the ability to generate the designs. Korringa then noted that such agents are generally expected to bear the fixed as well as the variable costs. This is efficient from the viewpoint of the principal. It was noted that even bigger agents may not have the capacity to bear the burden of investments if the designs change frequently. In all such cases, the principal bears the entire fixed cost. They can control quality only by resorting to such practices. The principal buyers view contractual integrity only in terms of the agent's ability to deliver promises on a long-term basis. Further, the principal buyer is accepting fixed costs only when they are relatively small. Even in the context of automobile ancillaries, Yun (1999) noted that the principals pay the entire fixed cost to the agent only for small inexpensive dies and molds.
2. Chaudhury (1999) found some contrasting experiences. In Durgapur, a large majority of subcontractors are engaged in fabrication of boiler parts such as ducts, casting, and machining works. The ancillary units wanted a guarantee that once they install costly machinery and start manufacturing the proposed items, the parent firm will continue purchasing from them. Parent firms, like the Durgapur Steel Plant, pointed out that ancillaries were generally risk averse, unwilling to invest in new ventures, and lack the drive for technical upgradation and growth in general. They preferred to restrict contracts to only those agents that can deliver products they need at the prices they are willing to offer. In Jamshedpur, TELCO considered the sole supplier or upgradation as an advantage. They offer designs, molds, etc., to their subcontractors and also bear a substantial portion of the fixed costs of training workers to adapt to their requirements. They control quality through such practices. Along with the prices paid for parts this has the effect of assuring their commitment to contractual integrity. As a group, the Tatas provided regular support and technical assistance to ancillaries supplying to them. TELCO has different divisions to render technical help to ancillary suppliers from the stage of drawing and

design through to execution processes, viz., inspection, metallurgy, and ancillary development, engineering research, etc. TELCO is particular about quality. Hence, they invested in this aspect of ancillary production. The Tata enterprises encouraged, guided, and actively helped their subcontractors (in raising investment and finances also) as a deliberate policy. They are willing to make advance payments for future deliveries as well. When large investments by the agent are a necessity, such sharing of fixed costs may be considered a requirement to maintain contractual integrity. The other point emerging from this study is that the specificity of the principal's requirements may compel them to deal with a few agents. In all such cases, the principal attempts to achieve long-term integrity of the contract by sharing fixed costs.

3. Okamuro (2001) reported a similar experience. For, he/she found that the parent takes a larger share of investment of the agent if their dependence on him increases. The agents obtain financial aid from the parent and exchange with them engineers and other employees for training and technology transfer. When coupled with specificity of the principal's requirements and the role of a specific agent in fulfilling them, the principal deems dissolution and exit-based relations to be too expensive. Parent firms are willing to stabilize the profit rate of their suppliers because they want to (a) keep them capable of innovations and customer-specific investments, (b) avoid losing their own specific investments through closure of supplier or bankruptcy, and (c) leave some relational quasi-rents acknowledging relation-specific skills.
4. Lafontaine (1992) and Kaufman and Lafontaine (1994) argue that McDonalds' practice of leaving a larger share of revenue is superior to monitoring the use of fixed assets given to the agent or making them share fixed costs (which do not have the incentive effect to increase current revenue). They reckon that a larger share may be due to the liquidity problems of the agent. Suppose the share is high. The cost, to the agent, of reducing effort is not only the reduction in revenue to himself/herself but increased chance of termination (if the principal is not satisfied).
5. When the number of buyers from an agent is large, it may not be possible to ensure that the benefits of sharing fixed costs exclusively accrue to the specific principal who makes the investment. In this context, the principal generally expects the agent to make the investment. The Tirupur knitwear case outlined in Swaminathan and Jeyaranjan (1999) is typical of this kind of experience. However, contrary to the expectations mentioned earlier, there is no evidence to suggest that the agents have been offered higher revenue shares to maintain a satisfactory level of income for them.
6. However, the classic case of Fisher Body vs. General Motors provides a contrasting experience. Fisher Body, owned and operated by the Fisher brothers, was producing car bodies for several assemblers including General Motors and Ford.[38] FB created all the capital assets that were necessary for their manufacturing operations. The major reason was that the capital assets were not exclu-

[38] Klein (1998, 2007), Coase (2000, 2006), Casadesus-Masanell and Spulber (2000), and Goldberg (2008) contain a detailed account of this classic Fisher Body vs. General Motors case.

sive to the requirements of GM. In 1919, GM bought 60 % equity stake in FB. The prices that GM paid for car bodies of FB were calculated by using 17.6 % markup over the operating and transportation costs incurred by FB. Since FB creates and operates the necessary capital equipment, this markup was expected to offer them an adequate return. Late in 1925, GM, as a part of its expansion plan, wanted to close the FB plant in Detroit and build a new body plant in Flint, near its assembly plant. FB objected to this. They wanted to expand their Detroit plant for FB had customers, other than GM, and it would have been less costly to supply them from Detroit rather than Flint. The added disincentive was that they would lose on the markup on transportation costs, embodied in the original GM agreement, if they relocated to Flint. In 1926, GM acquired the rest of the 40 % equity and made the Fisher brothers their employees. They then created a new plant at Flint. In sum, leaving the entire fixed investments to the agent may disturb contractual integrity.

7. In the context of insurance, Pauly and Blavin (2008) found that the agent would be inclined to share a larger proportion of variable costs of repair if he/she finds that the quality of service offered by the insurance company is not satisfactory. A deductible insurance is of this nature. This is somewhat akin to the integrity effect.
8. Tremcar, a Canadian firm, is in the milk transportation business.[39] They produce steel tanker trucks. Component manufacture, assembly shop, attending to warranties, after-sales service, and repairs are the essential aspects to ensure success of their business. As business grew, its owner Tremblay realized that the investment and coordination needed diversification. Some of his/her employees had entrepreneurial talent and could make the requisite investments. He/she allowed them to do so because their loyalty to Tremcar was necessary and sufficient for success. Sharing fixed costs, by way of creating new firms, was necessary to maintain contractual integrity as the size increased and both investments and management became difficult.
9. Equity sharing licenses substitute for revenue or profit share contracts. The former will be more direct as incentive effect to produce better and more results. Firms generally agree to share fixed cost of inventors to enable them to progress faster. This enables the inventor to carry on if he/she does not have the income to sustain activity. A profit or revenue share is not enough in such contexts. See, for instance, Burhop and Lubbers (2009).
10. Raff et al. (2009) offered a reasonable summary. They claim that, in general, the share of the fixed cost of the principal = f(agent's ability to contribute valuable assets such as market specific assets, distribution networks, production capabilities, value of its own productive assets that need protection). Allowing the agent a high share of fixed assets and high share of revenue induces him to reveal his/her capabilities and value of his/her assets. It also allows him to receive adequate returns to make the contract remain in force. This, as stated earlier, is the essence of the integrity effect.

[39] This presentation is based on Mireault (2003).

(b) Incentive effect

1. Dailami and Hauswald (2007) provided empirical evidence for the following. In the context of resources like liquefied natural gas (LNG), the assets are specific. If the agent does not buy adequate amounts, the recovery of fixed costs will be difficult.

   Some outside major underwriting the principal's debt is somewhat akin to the landlord paying a subsistence loan to a tenant in bad times to be repaid later. However, it is an incomplete protection. Hence, asking that the agent share fixed costs before writing output and price contracts is efficient.
2. The empirical evidence in Muris et al. (1993) indicates that Coca-Cola bottlers operated on the following contractual terms. Initially the breakable and returnable bottles required local handling. This prompted the setting up of independent bottling plants that made the necessary investment. The control rested with the bottling plants. The bottling plants agreed to invest in plant and equipment, to keep plant and equipment in such a condition as will be sufficient to meet satisfactorily the demand, and to increase such investment as the demand for Coca-Cola in bottles may require. The concentrate manufacturers also made specific investments in their production. In some cases, they also made investments in bottler-specific needs. Independent distributors and concentrate manufacturers were protected from termination so long as they adhered to quality prescriptions. The contracts were perpetual for short-term contracts would be insufficient to protect bottling plants from long-term investment. However, the owners of bottling plants did not agree to sharing advertising and marketing costs since the benefits did not accrue to them exclusively. Independent bottling plants did not agree to make investments in new products (unless they already proved successful) either. Fundamentally, the share of fixed costs incurred by the agents offered them incentive to remain efficient though some problems were discernible.
3. Return to the Kaufman and Lafontaine (1994) empirical analysis. They found that McDonalds generally buys the land and buildings and gives them to the agents against a payment of franchise fees. When buying a new franchise, agents are required to provide 40 % of the capital requirements on their own. This ensures that the agent has a large personal stake in the franchise. Agents are expected to invest in updates and equipment used by the outlet. Such arrangements, it is expected, will have the desirable effect of increasing revenue and preserving the value of assets. McDonalds' supplements this incentive effect with a large enough share of revenues to leave adequate ex ante rents with the agents.
4. Yun (1999) considered the context of automobile ancillaries. He/she found that contracting mechanisms have been designed to induce subcontracting practices under which agents cooperate closely in technical aspects or share investments. The following salient points may be noted. First, a die is specific to a particular product and cannot be used at its full value for other purposes and therefore represents a highly risky investment for the agent. As such, developing a die can constitute a major element of investment for a subcontractor. The principal

usually shares the cost of financing the development of a die. That is, in many cases, the principals pay for their own investments and capital assets though the agents use them. However, though the principal may have the incentive to invest in agents, it will not succeed if the agent's ability to learn is minimal. This suggests that sharing fixed costs with the agent may not always have the intended incentive effect.

5. Kaufman and Lafontaine (1994) found that if the principal creates a threat of not offering more investments, it may have a better incentive effect on the agent. This works better than offering a share of rents ex ante as an incentive mechanism. Refusing to give a new franchise is like withholding investment rather than asking the franchisee to share investment. For all practical purposes, this is also an incentive effect from the sharing of fixed costs.

(c) Control effect

Much of the early literature made attempts to find evidence for the control influences of revenue sharing agreements. In particular, the general hypothesis was that the agent, who receives a higher share of revenue, will be induced to take up more relationship specific investments and preserve the value of fixed assets. There is very little support for this hypothesis. The second hypothesis was that if the agent is made to share fixed investment and he/she is made a residual claimant, i.e., share profits instead of revenues, he/she will be induced to perform more efficiently both in generating higher current revenues as also in his/her efforts to conserve fixed assets. See, for example, Hsiao et al. (1998). However, the cost increase, even if he/she is capable of bearing it, may reduce output and possibly his/her share of revenue as well. The third hypothesis that has been subjected to empirical test is that an upfront rent, along with revenue sharing, may replace the residual claimant status more efficiently. Again, there is very limited empirical evidence for this hypothesis. The fourth hypothesis attempted is that the threat of the agent to terminate the contract is often due to opportunities available to the agent elsewhere instead of the terms of the contract per se. See, for instance, Tommasi and Weinschelbaum (2004) and Brown and Bellemare (2009). In such contexts, if the principal attempts to impose a share of fixed costs, it may be counterproductive. Instead, he/she may do well to offer him a bigger share of revenues. The fifth strand of thought generally occurs in the landlord vs. tenant contracts though it has far wider ramifications. Given a revenue share, the agent may be motivated to maximize current income at the expense of preserving the value of fixed assets. The alternative available to the principal is to make the necessary investments in the activities of the agent.[40] There is some empirical support for this alternative. The sixth approach begins by arguing that revenue and cost shares cannot really offer the most efficient control. At best, they may be necessary but not sufficient. The more potential control is the threat of the principal to terminate the contract if performance, both current output and value-preserving activities, is below par. Though Banerjee and Ghatak (2004) offered

[40] Note that this only meant an integrity effect when the principal has no investment in fixed assets utilized in the transaction. The shoe manufacturing context alluded to earlier is a case in point.

some empirical support for this view, its efficacy depends on the costs that the principal must incur to verify the compliance of expectations. In general, a variety of control options have been utilized with varying degrees of success.

The following empirical evidences are fairly representative:

1. Chiappori (2000) reported a positive correlation between the ability of the agent and his/her timing to terminate the contract. Assume that the agent adjusts his/her degree of diligence in the execution of contracts to the externally generated systemic risks. Then, the evidence suggests a positive correlation between systemic risk and the timing of dissolution. The agent will then be asked to share a larger proportion of fixed costs.
2. deJanvary A and Sadeulet (2007) observed that when the systemic risks are high and the agent is risk averse, he/she would be more prone to terminate the contract earlier and revenue sharing arrangements are not sufficient. Some cost sharing mechanisms will rein them in.
3. Jacoby and Mansuri (2009) found several interesting features. First, the ability of the agent to maintain the quality of land depends on soil fertility, his/her own efficiency in farming, his/her initial wealth position, and risk aversion. An efficient farmer working on a bad plot may invest more on control measures. Second, the agent may spend more on conservation measures if he/she can get a loan from the principal and repay from his/her revenue share. Third, the principal's option to supervise the agent's actions is more efficient. Fourth, high-powered options, like sharing fixed costs, may have only limited effect. They will be used only when the assets are highly transaction specific.
4. Tommasi and Weinschelbaum (2004) found that contract termination occurs mostly due to superior alternatives for the agent outside the contract. The most efficient control device is to make the agent share a part of the fixed costs.
5. Zheng et al. (2008) observed that, contrary to expectations, higher systemic risk and the agent's risk aversion tend to reduce the agent's share of fixed costs and greater revenue shares to sustain the contract over time.
6. Ahmadjian and Oxley (2006) contains some interesting empirical observations. Revenue sharing is not adequate to preserve the value of fixed assets only when the systemic risks are high. In such a case, depending on the value and durability of assets, the principal will ask the agent to accept a partial equity stake. Conversely, when the agent is making investments in fixed assets initially, the principal will begin to acquire a partial equity stake. Such partial equity stakes are generally low and do not provide any control to the principal. They are more in the form of incentives. The agent having to share the cost of fixed assets, however, has a control effect. The extent of such control appears to depend on relation-specific and difficult-to-manufacture parts supplied by the agent, the degree to which the principal depends on these parts in his/her manufacturing activity, and the specificity of assets to the transaction. Dependence balancing, i.e., the relative equity sharing of the principal and the agent in the fixed assets of the other, depends on specificity, cost of supervision, and the perceived risk of termination.

7. Agents tend to concentrate on short-term soil conservation measures when revenue sharing contracts have been utilized. Landlords tend to invest in contractible soil conservation measures. However, this increase in cost tends to reduce output and the share of the agent. Expecting the agent to bear a fixed amount of the cost of acquiring fixed assets has a better control effect.[41]
8. Banerjee and Ghatak (2004) contains references to several empirical facts. First, eviction threats focused on higher share of revenue or fixed rent do not have the desired effect of controlling the erosion of the quality of fixed assets. Second, threats directly based on the inadequacy of investments in soil conservation measures are more efficient. This makes the control task of the principal very difficult.

In general, though many mechanisms have been tried out and their efficacy evaluated empirically, there is no robust guideline to achieve efficient control on the agent. It is perhaps necessary to identify the actions of the agent that point to possible premature dissolution and supervise them directly. The efficiency of such a choice depends on the costs of supervision and control. Indirect, and high-powered, measures like sharing fixed costs may economize on transaction costs but their efficiency in preventing early dissolution of the contract cannot be taken for granted.

(d) Post-dissolution contracts

In general, the contracting parties have several options at the time of unexpected contract dissolution. Chief among them are the following:

(a) The fixed assets may be sold off and the value recovered shared between the parties.[42]
(b) Merge the assets with some other transaction, by selling a major part of equity ownership (usually called a spinoff), and share the expected revenues.
(c) One of the partners, who continue to use the assets, retains a majority ownership of assets and allows another agent to use the assets to generate revenue. This is usually designated as a carveout. The question of what to pay the partner who is leaving the contracted has to be decided on some other basis.
(d) In some cases, the cost of continuing operations and maintaining assets takes the center stage. Costs may then be shared. The value of fixed assets and their revenue-generating potential per se may not enter the contract determination.

Only a few empirical studies are available. The basic results can be summarized as follows:

1. Palay (1984, p. 276) noted that the supplier of freight cars (specialized containers to transport specific products of a company) and their services are usually

[41] Otsuka et al. (1992) contains a summary of results pertaining to the tenant vs. landlord context.

[42] The sell-off may be generally to a third party. However, there is a possibility that either the principal or the agent proposes to buy the other's expected share or sell his/her share to the other. The efficient choice depends on the monopoly power and perceptions of fairness. deFrutos and Kitsteiner (2008) contains one such analysis.

expected to bear the fixed costs of their acquisition though the user specifies the requirements that must be satisfied. Suppose, now, that the user company changes its technology or design specification of its products to a point where the old racks are no longer usable. However, the firm recognizes that they have to still depend on the same agent to provide the transportation services according to their modified specifications. Given this long-term contractual dependence, users of freight cars repaid the entire unamortized value (based on book values rather than market resale) of the machines. Similarly, firms tend to pay the total cost of contracted output to the agent when unexpected reductions in output are recorded. In other words, extreme conditions of uncertainty may not allow any other contracting options. This pattern is expected when the principal has to maintain good long-term relations with the agents on whom the long-term integrity of his/her business depends.

2. In franchises and joint ventures, the agent loses his/her fixed assets almost entirely unless they can be used in some other related activity. This was noted in the context of McDonalds franchises and distributors of soft drinks. Similarly, when Godrej broke up with Procter and Gamble, the former lost most of its marketing outlets and so on. It was also noted that the agents usually agree to technology transfer contracts to learn about the technology of the principal. Once they find ways of adapting the technology, they dissolve the contract. The parent loses some of his/her fixed assets in the contract. Many instances of the agent behaving opportunistically have been recorded.
3. The context of an agent negotiating a merger or acquisition has been reported in Bates and Lemmon (2004) and Jeon (2011). When an agent contracts to undertake the negotiation, he/she generally sets up termination fees. For, despite the effort and costs the agent incurs, the merger deal may not succeed. He/she wants to make sure that the termination fee is adequate to compensate him for the effort. Their empirical results show that smaller targets and targets with lower institutional ownership tend to offer larger termination fees. They also find that low or moderate termination fees serve as an efficient contractual device while large fees reflect target managers' self-interest and are less beneficial to augmenting shareholder wealth.
4. Studies of Smith (2005, 2007) and Walker and Zhu (2006) regarding post-divorce sharing indicate that child support is the key variable that links income before and after divorce. It is the main factor that causes changes in net income caused by marital dissolution. If the expected changes in income, which would result if the marriage relationship continued, turn out to be significantly large, they will affect post-divorce income. Otherwise, small income changes in marriage, even if divorce is anticipated, have no effect on post-divorce income. Galavoti et al. (2009) suggest that such results hold even in routine industrial contexts.

For all practical purposes, it can be concluded that the agent, claiming to be the weaker party, defines the sharing to satisfy his/her requirements. The principal, who is generally a residual claimant, does not have much bargaining power to counter such claims. As noted earlier, such tendencies are evident even when premature termination of the contract is expected.

7.8 In Sum

Whenever a firm enters into a contract with an agent to do some of its work, the preference would be to choose the most efficient agent that has the expertise to design and produce the desired output, who is motivated to do the job efficiently, and who can bear the necessary variable and/or fixed costs. The principal will then agree to pay the agent a price for the product or a share of revenue. The principal will be the residual claimant. In practice, however, such agency relationships are rare.

Much of the difficulty is with respect to the ability of the agent to provide the requisite short-term investment and the purchase of the necessary fixed assets. The firm may be required to provide the fixed assets in cases where the wealth position of the agent does not enable him to make the investment.

The principal will make the agent accept the fixed costs if he/she has some monopoly power. The principal will have such power if the talents of the agent are transaction specific (i.e., the agent does not have any other avenues to use his/her talent). The threat of eviction to make the agent comply will indeed be very strong in such contexts. On the contrary, the agent may have other opportunities to use his/her talents. In such a case, the agent gains monopoly power and expects the principal to bear most of the fixed costs. The relative bargaining power determines the sharing of fixed costs.

Some product markets experience higher systemic risks by their very nature. In such cases, irrespective of the initial wealth position of the agent and his/her monopoly power, he/she will be risk averse to making investments in fixed assets and become a residual claimant. The principal must finance fixed assets since his/her initial wealth allows him to take more risk.

Capital markets generally have the role of absorbing risks in such transactions. If the principal and/or the agent have access to such external finance, they may not have to make the investments on their own.

An agent will prefer a wage employment in the extreme case where the agent has talents that are not specific, has no resource base, and is highly risk averse.

Now suppose the principal makes all the investment. He/she would then be concerned about the use of the fixed assets. Depending on the opportunity available to either one of them outside the contract under consideration, they may prefer to dissolve the contract prematurely. One alternative available to the principal is to claim a larger share of revenue while the contract is in operation. A more efficient alternative is the sharing of fixed costs whenever it is feasible. Such sharing depends on the expected loss at contract dissolution and the malleability of capital assets. Observe that there are two sides to this problem. The agent may be expected to share the fixed assets of the principal. This will be basically to elicit a control effect in the use of assets. On the other hand, the principal may share some of the fixed assets of the agent. The incentive effect dominates in such cases. However, there can be several fixed assets for which such sharing is impractical. It would be necessary to devise other mechanisms to achieve contractual efficiency and integrity.

In general, it appears that both the parties try to achieve monopoly power over the other by accepting a certain share of the fixed costs. The agent, who has the relatively weaker position, expects the principal to bear the risks, assures him of adequate returns to entice him to continue in the contract, and uses assets only to the extent that they cater to his/her income generation requirements. The residual claimant status does not offer the principal any tangible monopoly power over the agent. In particular, the revenue and cost sharing arrangements seem to be insufficient to make the agent comply fully with the principal's expectations for the assets of the agent are far less specific so that he/she can hold out the threat to dissolve the contract if he/she does not get what he/she wants. The principals are at a disadvantage as residual claimants. Formal design of contracts does not seem to have the ability to make the agents comply with the principal's requirements if they are not so predisposed.

Arguments regarding the ability, willingness, and monopoly power seem to dominate the contractual sharing of fixed assets post-dissolution as well.[43]

In any case, there is a need to generate more empirical results on the relationship between revenue and cost sharing, the efficiency of contract execution, and the propensities to dissolve contracts prematurely. There are many other softer instruments that the principals generally utilize to achieve the three desired effects. Evaluation of fixed cost sharing must take these influences into account.

A fairly comprehensive summary of the various forces that govern contractual sharing of fixed costs in principal agent relationships reveals that the following factors are significant:

(a) The initial wealth of the agent
(b) The income-generating potential of fixed assets
(c) The ability of the agent to generate adequate income from the assets
(d) The nature and intensity of systemic risks and the agent's risk aversion
(e) The ability and willingness of the agent to absorb systemic risks given the income he/she needs to ensure contractual integrity
(f) The alternatives available to the agent and/or the principal and the relative monopoly power
(g) The quantum and specificity of the short-term fixed assets that the agent must use to generate revenue out of the fixed assets of the principal
(h) The specificity of assets to the transaction or the degree of their malleability in other uses
(i) The nature of assets and whether or not sharing ownership is meaningful
(j) The efficacy of revenue and cost sharing arrangements as incentive and control mechanisms to minimize early contract termination

---

[43] Looking back at the empirical studies on cost sharing, it may be noted that sharing while the contract is in operation and, at the other end of the spectrum, post-dissolution sharing dominate. Very little information is available regarding the intermediate choices and interlinkage between sharing while the contract is in progress and expected dissolution. It is, however, obvious that both the incentive and control effects operate in practice. More, and detailed, information on this is a practical necessity.

(k) The possibility and efficacy of utilizing other softer instruments instead of the more powerful cost sharing mechanisms
(l) The nature of long-term relationships that they need to maintain to ensure contractual integrity
(m) The requirement of both the principal and agent having control on the use of the assets generated and used by the other

A comprehensive empirical evaluation of these and other related factors has not been possible so far.

The following observations regarding the usefulness of the principal agent models as an analytical device are in order. Invariably such models generally fix a principal and his/her activity and investment and assume that many agents are available to choose from. The principal is then expected to select contract parameters based on agent characteristics. Alternately, the principal may choose a single contract and expect the agents to self-select. The primary shortage of these models is that they do not incorporate the alternatives available to the agent and his/her relative bargaining power. However, there are several limitations regarding the range of choices available to both the parties that can be endogenized in these models.

The task that remains before the analyst is indeed very large. Progress has been piecemeal, incremental, and not very definitive to offer flawless guidelines for the future.

References

Aggarwal RM (2007) Role of risk sharing and transaction costs in contract choice: theory and evidence from groundwater contracts. J Econ Behav Organ 63:475–496

Ahmadjian C, Oxley J (2006) Using hostages to support exchange: dependence balancing and partial equity stakes in Japanese automotive supplier relationships. J Law Econ Org 22:213–233

Allen DW (1992) What does she see in him? The effect of sharing on the choice of spouse. Econ Inq 30:57–67

Arcand JL, Ai C, Ethier E (2006) Moral hazard and Marshallian inefficiency: evidence from Tunisia. J Dev Econ 83:411–445

Asanuma B (1989) Manufacturer-supplier relationship in Japan and the concept of relation-specific skills. J Jpn Int Econ 3:1–30

Asanuma B, Kikutani T (1992) Risk absorption in Japanese subcontracting: a microeconometric study of the automobile industry. J Jpn Int Econ 6:1–29

Baker R (2006) Risk aversion in maintenance: overmaintenance and the principal agent problem. IMA J Manag Math 17:99–113

Banerjee AV, Ghatak M (2004) Eviction threats and investment incentives. J Dev Econ 74:469–488

Bates TW, Lemmon ML (2004) Breaking up is hard to do? An analysis of termination fee provisions and merger outcomes. J Financ Econ 69:469–504

Bradford WD, Martin RE (2000) Partnerships, profit sharing, and quality competition in the medical profession. Rev Ind Organ 17:193–208

Braido LHB (2008) Evidence on the incentive properties of share contracts. J Law Econ 51:327–350

Brickley JA (2002) Royalty rates and upfront fees in share contracts: evidence from franchising. J Law Econ Org 18:511–535

Brown ZS, Bellemare MF (2009) The structural estimation of principal-agent models by least squares: evidence from land tenancy in Madagascar. Available at http://purl.umn.edu/48908

Burhop C, Lubbers T (2009) The historical market for technology licenses: chemicals, pharmaceuticals, and electrical engineering in imperial Germany. Available at http://ssrn.com/abstract=1463249

Cai H (2003) A theory of joint ownership. Rand J Econ 34:63–77

Casadesus-Masanell R, Spulber DF (2000) The fable of fisher-body. J Law Econ 43:67–104

Chao GH, Iravani SMR, Savaskan RC (2009) Quality improvement incentives and product recall cost sharing contracts. Manag Sci 55:1122–1138

Chaudhury DR (1999) Interfirm industrial linkages in India: subcontracting practices in Durgapur and Jamshedpur. In: Bagchi AK (ed) Economy and society. Sage Publications, New Delhi

Chen KY, Huberman B, Kalkanci B (2007) Does principal agent theory work in real life? Available at http://www.hpl.hp.com/research/ide/papers/agency/agency.pdf

Chiappori PA (2000) Econometric models of insurance under asymmetric information. In: Dionne G (ed) Handbook of insurance. Kluwer Academic Publishers, London

Chiappori PA, Salanie B (2003) Testing contract theory: a survey of some recent work. In: Dewatripont M, Hansen LP, Turnovsky SJ (eds) Advances in economics and econometrics – theory and applications. Cambridge University Press, New York

Chiu S (1998) Noncooperative bargaining, hostages, and optimal ownership. Am Econ Rev 88:882–901

Choate GM, Maser SM (1992) The impact of asset specificity of single-period contracting. J Econ Behav Organ 18:372–389

Coase RH (2000) The acquisition of fisher body by general motors. J Law Econ 43:15–31

Coase RH (2006) The conduct of economics: the example of fisher-body and general motors. J Econ Manag Strateg 15:255–278

Comino S, Nicolo A, Tedeschi P (2010) Termination clauses in partnerships. Eur Econ Rev 54:718–732

Crampton P, Gibbons R, Klemperer P (1987) Dissolving a partnership efficiently. Econometrica 55:615–632

Dailami M, Hauswald R (2007) Credit-spread determinants and interlocking contracts: a study of Ras Gas project. J Financ Econ 86:248–278

Dana JD, Spier KE (2001) Revenue sharing and vertical control in the video rental industry. J Ind Econ 49:223–245

Dearden JA, Einolf K (2003) Strategy-proof allocation of fixed costs. Rev Econ Des 8:185–204

deFrutos MA, Kitsteiner T (2008) Efficient partnership dissolution under buy and sell choices. Rand J Econ 39:184–198

deJanvary A, Sadeulet E (2007) Optimal share contracts with moral hazard on effort and in output reporting: managing the double laffer curve effect. Available at are.berkeley.edu/~alain

Dybvig PH, Fransworth HK, Carpenter JN (2009) Portfolio performance and agency. Rev Financ Stud 23:1–23

Fukunaga K, Hufman WE (2009) The role of risk and transaction costs in contract design: evidence from farmland lease contracts in U.S. agriculture. Am J Agric Econ 91:237–249

Galavoti S, Mutos N, Oyama D (2009) On efficient partnership dissolution under ex post individual rationality. Available at http://ssrn.com/abstract=1348236

Ganglmair B (2009) Early contract termination and specific investment. Available at http://ssrn.com/abstract=983040

Goldberg VP (2008) Lawyers asleep at the wheel? The GM-fisher body contract. Ind Corp Chang 17:1071–1084

Gonzales-Diaz M, Arrunada B, Fernadez A (2000) Causes of subcontracting: evidence from panel data on construction firms. J Econ Behav Organ 42:167–187

Grosskopf O (2009) Dividing the surplus upon termination: the case of relational contracts. Available at works.bepress.com/ofer_grosskopf/3/

Habib MA, Barral PM (2007) The role of knowhow acquisition in the formation and duration of joint ventures. Rev Financ Stud 20:189–233
Hernandez MV (2003) Structural estimation of a principal agent model: moral hazard in medical insurance. Rand J Econ 34:670–693
Hsiao C, Nugent J, Perrigne I, Qiu J (1998) Share versus residual claimant contracts: the case of Chinese TVEs. J Comp Econ 26:317–337
Hubert F (1995) Contracting with costly tenants. Reg Sci Urban Econ 25:631–654
Huddart S, Liang PJ (2005) Profit sharing and monitoring in partnerships. J Account Econ 40:153–187
Jacoby HG, Mansuri G (2009) Incentives, supervision, and sharecropper productivity. J Dev Econ 88:232–241
Jeon JQ (2011) How much is reasonable? The size of termination fees in mergers and acquisitions. J Corp Financ 17:959–982
Jullien B, Salanie B, Salanie F (1999) Should more risk averse agents exert more effort? Geneva Pap Risk Insur Theory 24:19–28
Kaufman PJ, Lafontaine F (1994) Costs of control: the sources of economic rents for McDonald's Franchises. J Law Econ 37:417–454
Klein B (1998) Vertical integration as organizational ownership: the fisher body-general motors relationship revisited. J Law Econ Org 4:199–213
Klein B (2007) The economic lessons of fisher body-general motors. Int J Econ Bus 4:1–36
Korringa P (1996) Economics of collaboration. Sage Publications, New Delhi
Kraft H (2008) Continuous-time delegated portfolio management with homogeneous expectations: can agency conflict be avoided? Fin Mkts Portfolio Mgmt 22:67–90
Lafontaine F (1992) Agency theory and franchising: some empirical results. Rand J Econ 23:263–283
Lerox J (2005) Strategy proof profit sharing in partnerships: improving upon autarky. Available at http://www.ruf.rice.edu/~econ/papers/2005papers/leroux05.pdf
Levin J, Tadelis S (2005) Profit sharing and the role of professional partnerships. Q J Econ 120:131–171
Li J, Wolfstetter E (2010) Partnership dissolution, complementarity, and investment incentives. Oxford Econ Pap 62:529–552
Masten SE (1988) Minimum bills contracts: theory and policy. J Ind Econ 37:85–97
Masten SE, Crocker KJ (1985) Efficient adaptation in long term contracts: take-or-pay provisions for natural gas. Am Econ Rev 75:1083–1093
Masten SE, Saussier S (2002) Econometrics of contracts: an assessment of developments in the empirical literature on contracting. In: Brousseau E, Glachant JM (eds) The economics of contracts. Cambridge University Press, Cambridge
Mireault D (2003) Spinoffs at tremcar: partnerships for growth. Available at http://zonecours.hec.ca/documents/H2006-P5-672552.53457A-spin-offatTremacar.pdf
Mortimer JH (2002) The effects of revenue sharing contracts on welfare in vertically separated markets evidence from the video rental industry. Available at http://ssrn.com/abstract=336244
Muris TJ, Schieffman DT, Spiller PT (1993) Strategy, structure, and antitrust in the carbonated soft-drink industry. Quorum Books, New York
Okamuro H (2001) Risk sharing in supplier relationships: new evidence from the Japanese automotive industry. J Econ Behav Organ 45:361–381
Omelas E, Turner LJ (2007) Efficient dissolution of partnerships and the structure of control. Games Econ Behav 60:187–199
Otsuka K, Chuma H, Hayami Y (1992) Land and labor contracts in agrarian economies: theories and facts. J Econ Lit 30:1965–2018
Palay TM (1984) Comparative institutional economics: the governance of rail freight contracting. J Legal Stud 13:265–287
Pauly MV, Blavin FE (2008) Moral hazard in insurance, value-based cost sharing and the benefits of blissful ignorance. J Health Econ 27:1407–1417

Quadrini V (2007) Investment and liquidation in renegotiation proof contracts with moral hazard. J Monet Econ 51:713–751
Raff H, Ryan M, Staher F (2009) Whole versus shared ownership of foreign affiliates. Int J Ind Organ 27:572–581
Rao TVSR (2010) Financial crisis, efficient bailouts, and regulatory policy. Macroecon Financ Emerg Mark Econ 3:167–188
Sappington DEM (1991) Incentives in principal-agent relationships. J Econ Perspect 5:45–66
Smith I (2005) Fairness and inefficient divorce. Econ Lett 88:159–163
Smith I (2007) Property division on divorce with inequity aversion. Int Rev Law Econ 27:111–128
Swaminathan P, Jeyaranjan J (1999) The Knitware cluster in Tiruppur: an Indian industrial district in the making. In: Bagchi AK (ed) Economy and organization. Sage Publications, New Delhi
Tjemkas BV (2008) Growing and sharing the pie: a study of performance in strategic alliances. Available at http://dare.ubn.kun.nl
Tommasi M, Weinschelbaum F (2004) Principal-agent contracts under the threat of insurance. J Inst Theor Econ 163:379–393
Turner JL (2013) Dissolving (In) efficient partnerships. Social Choice and Welfare 41:321–335
Vogel HL (1996) Entertainment industry economics. Cambridge University Press, Cambridge
Walker I, Zhu Y (2006) Child support and partnership dissolution. Econ J 116:C93–C109
Yun M (1999) Subcontracting relations in the Korean automotive industry: risk sharing and technological capability. Int J Ind Organ 17:81–108
Zheng X, Vukina T, Shin C (2008) The role of farmer's risk aversion for contract choice in the U.S. Hog industry. J Agric Food Ind Organ 6:1–20

Chapter 8
Warranties and Risk Sharing

Abstract This study examines the extent to which warranties can represent risk sharing arrangements between consumers and the firm. In particular, we argue that this approach can explain limited warranties and limited warranty duration. The existing literature on warranties is ambivalent about the relationship between quality of products and warranties. In contrast, we argue that there is a definite relationship between warranties, technological complexity of products, and the degree to which consumers exercise due diligence in the use of the product. We also examine the relationship between warranty and the intensity of use by the consumer. It has also been demonstrated that risk aversion can explain the choice of extended warranties though the result is somewhat circumscribed. We also show that warranties and risk sharing aggravate the lemons problem instead of mitigating it.

8.1 Risk and Warranty

Economic theory pertaining to product warranties is rather extensive.[1] Generally, as Emons (1989a) pointed out, the insurance motive, the signaling motive, and the incentive motive have been utilized to explain the nature of warranty contracts. However, Emons (1989a, p. 48) noted that "these basic motives are not able to explain the variety of warranty practices which can be found in real world economies, such as limited warranty coverage, limited warranty duration, or inter firm differences in warranties."

In response to this, many recent studies acknowledge a double-sided moral hazard in the purchase, by a consumer, of a durable good and the warranty offered by the firm. In particular, it has been acknowledged that the firm may be tempted to pass on low-quality products without any warranty. On the other hand, the consumer may not exercise due diligence in the use of the product if warranty is high. These features, of the likely decisions of the firm and consumer attitudes, suggest that the warranty offered by the firm will never really cover the entire loss to the

Based on content from "Limited Warranties, Extended Warranties and Risk Sharing" first published in *The Indian Journal of Economics*, 90(357), 2009, pp. 747–772. Content reproduced here with permission from University of Allahabad.

[1] A review of many aspects of this problem can be found in Murty and Djamaludin (2002).

T.V.S.R. Rao, *Risk Sharing, Risk Spreading and Efficient Regulation*,
DOI 10.1007/978-81-322-2562-1_8

consumer in case of product failure. In other words, both of them sharing the risk of product failure may be an efficient mechanism to reduce moral hazard. Some studies adopt this approach to the design of warranty because it can address issues of limited warranty. However, there is an ambiguity with respect to the relationship between warranty and product quality.

Another aspect of warranties is generally highlighted. Suppose a durable good breaks down. One option available to the consumer is to approach someone, other than the firm that sold the product, for repairs. Usually, these firms acquire the requisite knowledge and can easily provide the necessary service. However, they may eventually copy some of the technological details of production. Hence, there is a possibility that the original firm loses some of its market over time. The alternative, of warranties, implies that the original firm undertakes the repairs and can protect some of its proprietary knowledge. This information advantage of the firm may in fact offset some costs of honoring the warranty. See, for example, Masten and Snyder (1989, 1993). Consequently, conceding limited warranty, not exceeding this cost saving, may be advantageous to the firm. We make this one of the pivots around which the design of warranties can be conceptualized.

The more pertinent argument that plays the other pivotal role is the following. We begin by acknowledging that the consumer can exercise some diligence in the use of the product to counteract the effects of his risk aversion. The degree to which he can make this adjustment depends on the technological complexity of the product. However, suppose he can and does make a perfect adjustment. In such a case, the product can fail only if it is defective at the manufacturing stage. A full warranty would then be justified. Inadequate or partial adjustments attract only limited warranties. Note that, compared to the quality versus warranty interaction, this relationship is more definitive. In fact, warranties can be defined without any reference to quality. This is the basic theme of the present study.

Limited warranties can also be justified from the viewpoint of contract execution. For example, the firm may prescribe standards of diligence in the use of the product as well as schedules for preventive maintenance. Full warranty may be justified if the consumer follows all these specifications earnestly. However, when a failure does occur, the firm may not be in a position to verify that consumer negligence is not the cause of the failure. But, the warranty must be honored. Hence, the optimal choice for the firm is to offer only a limited warranty. This was clearly articulated in Wehrt (2000).

Another distinct feature of warranties is the use of extended warranties. When the firm is not sure about the consumer type, viz., whether he is careful in the use of the product or not, there may be an advantage in limiting warranty to begin with, assessing the consumer type, and then modifying the warranty on the basis of the information acquired. This is another aspect of limited warranties. We will examine its relationship with risk sharing and consumer diligence.

Warranties generally consist of an upfront payment (covering the costs of repair of some specified components, replacing the equipment, etc.) and/or a proportionate sharing of costs. For example, consider the warranties on an automobile. Some parts, like the engine, are under full coverage. However, the consumers would be expected to bear the costs of moving the vehicle to the designated service station. Similarly, the consumer will also be expected to pay for some components that need replacement while the engine performance is being corrected. For, there may be wear and tear irrespective of the engine performance. Of course, some parts like tires, air filters, etc., may not be covered under any warranty. Limited warranties with respect to the length of time, over the expected lifetime of the product, are also quite common because some consumers use the product more intensively than others. We will show how limited warranty duration is related to risk sharing when some consumers use the product more intensively than others.

One other aspect of warranties, as a risk sharing arrangement, is worth noting. Both the firm and the consumers may find it advantageous to deal with more risks and lower-quality products if the arrangement is successful. The more confident the consumers of their ability to use risky products, the more likely the market exhibits greater volatility. We will examine this aspect of risk sharing as well. Warranties are neither necessary nor sufficient to mitigate this hazard.

The principal agent models have this structure since they emphasize risk sharing. It would be useful to at least investigate the extent to which gaps in the theoretical studies can be filled if this approach is adopted. We develop all our results utilizing this modeling methodology.

The present study is structured against this backdrop. In Sect. 8.2, we set out the basic model. This provides us a fundamental basis to justify limited warranties on the basis of risk sharing. However, it cannot fully explain the one or a few combinations of warranties that the firm offers. In Sect. 8.3, we consider the possibility that the consumer makes an adjustment in the level of care in his use of the product as a reaction to his risk aversion. It can be then shown that the maximum warranty offered by the firm corresponds to full adjustment. However, the extent of this warranty depends on the technological complexity of the product and the corresponding degree of difficulty the consumer experiences while making the adjustment. The analysis also provides some insights into the relationship between quality and warranty based on the due diligence exercised by the consumer. The firm may prescribe preventive maintenance as an alternative to the voluntary care exercised by the consumer. We develop, in Sect. 8.4, the implications of this for the efficient choice of warranty. We argue that this may be either complementary or substitutable to voluntary care. However, the channels of transmission are the same as in Sect. 8.3. In Sect. 8.5, we consider limited warranty duration as an alternative risk sharing mechanism when some consumers use the product more intensely. We will show that higher intensity of use results in lower warranty and/or warranty over a limited duration. This analysis also enables us to examine discriminating monopoly practices. We then show, in Sect. 8.6, that extended warranties reduce original warranties and that extended warranties will be lower unless the consumer is expected to pay. However, a third party offering extended service warranty cannot be construed as a risk sharing device. It is only a way of creating monopoly profits. Section 8.7 acknowledges that firms generally deal with many consumers even in a durable goods market. The fundamentally new result is about the role of the costs of coordination that the firm experiences and their effect on the extent of warranty.

Section 8.8 deals with the lemons problem. The basic result is that both the consumers and the firm, based on their motivations to improve their gains, bring about more products of lower quality. An overall summary in Sect. 8.9 concludes the study.

8.2 Model Structure

Consider the context of a buyer of a durable consumer good. He may, generally, suspect that the product fails during its expected lifetime. Let y denote the expected loss in output due to the failure. It would be convenient to postulate that this includes the costs incurred in sending the product to the designated service station even if the firm promises repairs under warranty. The actual loss, in practice, may be random. Let $y_a = y + u$ be the actual loss. In this formulation, u is a random variable with expected value $E(u) = 0$ and variance $V(u) = \sigma^2$. Assume, for the present, that this randomness is entirely due to the quality of the product. It would be analytically convenient to designate σ^2 as an index of the quality or durability of the product. Alternatively, y itself may be looked upon as a measure of quality.[2]

The warranty contract may compensate the consumer a fraction $p(y+u)$. Note that the consumer may not be in a position to fully recover the loss in revenue even if the product is fully repaired.[3] Let the gain to the consumer be

$$g_a = p(y+u)$$

since the standard practice under product warranties is for the firm to bear the costs of repair fully. Normally, it can be assumed that the consumer is risk averse to the possibility of breakdown. The value of g_a to the consumer can therefore be written as

$$v_a = py - \lambda p^2 \sigma^2$$

where λ is the degree of risk aversion of the consumer.

---

[2] MacLeod (2007), for instance, noted that the quality of a product is its characteristic that the buyer would like the seller to select. It may not be the ex post or realized quality performance of the product. As such, considering y as the choice variable of the firm is in order. Murty and Blischke (2000, p.44) also noted that the quality of a product need not be one dimensional. "Other dimensions of quality include maintainability, availability, repairability, and many aspects of product performance that may, under certain circumstances, be covered under warranty."

[3] The practical import of this warranty arrangement can be illustrated as follows. Suppose an automobile manufacturer expects a car that he manufactures to give a maximum of 50,000 km. Assume that he also knows that it can breakdown after 20,000 km. That is, he expects that $y = 30{,}000$. He may, for instance, offer a warranty for only 25,000 km. Similarly, suppose a firm knows that the maximum life of its product is 5 years. Let its expected life at the time of failure be 2 years. That is, $y = 3$. The firm may offer a warranty for only 2.5 years. Of course, on some occasions, it has been observed that the firm pretty much knows that the product will not break down within the warranty offered. Emons (1989b) considered this possibility earlier.

The consumer is not in a position to recover $(1-p)(y+u)$ of the loss even under warranty. It is important to recognize the following. Suppose the product fails. The consumer brings it to the designated service station of the firm, gets it repaired, and takes it back. In this process, the consumer recovers $p(y+u)$ of his loss. The rest is not really a component of revenue accruing to the firm despite the fact that it incurred a cost for repairs. It is still considered as a component of g_p here because the Masten and Snyder argument, noted above, suggests that the firm would have lost at least this much if the consumer takes the product to some other firm for repairs. In that sense, it is the opportunity value of the warranty to the firm.

The firm must incur a cost for repair whenever the product fails. This cost depends on the due diligence exercised by the consumer while using the product. It also depends on the extent of the risk covered under the warranty. In particular, the greater the remaining life of the product, the greater will be the cost of warranty compliance. Let the cost be represented by $y^2/2\delta$ where δ is an index of consumer diligence.[4] The gain to the firm is

$$g_p = (1-p)(y+u) - y^2/2\delta$$

The firm can be expected to be risk neutral because its diversified activities enable it to cover the losses in one product from the gains in another. Even otherwise such gains are an unexpected windfall to it. The value to the firm is therefore

$$v_p = (1-p)y - y^2/2\delta$$

Consider the choice of the consumer. Usually the consumer knows that there will be some failure irrespective of which of the many products available on the market he buys. Hence, he is more concerned about loss recovery. This depends on p. Stated differently, a consumer, who suspects that a product is of low quality, will agree to buy the product only if the warranty is high enough. In general, since the consumer does not know the y, corresponding to any of the products that he is expected to choose from, he may not be in a position to express a preference for y. Hence, he would choose that p which maximizes v_a. This maximization results in

$$p = y/2\lambda\sigma^2$$

Note that the net gain from the contract to both the parties taken together is

$$\begin{aligned} N &= v_a + v_p \\ &= y - y^2/2\delta - \lambda p^2\sigma^2 \end{aligned}$$

---

[4] Some products do not seem to offer any warranties. Dybvig and Lutz (1993) argued that this will be observed whenever δ is small enough to make $y < y^2/2\delta$ for, then, the cost of providing the warranty far exceeds the collective benefit to both the consumer and the firm.

For all practical purposes, the opportunity cost of recovering the loss y due to the failure of the product is $y^2/2\delta+\lambda p^2\sigma^2$. That the firm accepts the warranty indicates that the cost of entrusting repairs to another firm would be higher.

From the viewpoint of the firm, the more important decision is the choice of y. For, it should be in a position to recover the costs incurred for the repairs whatever may be the choice of p. Consequently, the firm can be expected to choose y to maximize N. Shavell (2004, p. 220) justifies this in the following way. "The type of warranty that a firm would offer is the one that would maximize the full price of its product as perceived by consumers. A firm not offering that warranty would lose its customers to competitors. This means that if customers do not misperceive risks, the warranty that is sold will be the one that results in the lowest full price and therefore is socially the best." The resulting choice of y is

$$y = 2\delta\lambda\sigma^2/\left(\delta + 2\lambda\sigma^2\right)$$

so that the ex post choice of warranty will be

$$p = \delta/\left(\delta + 2\lambda\sigma^2\right)$$

Ceteris paribus, this implies that a consumer who is highly risk averse will seek a lower warranty.[5]

In actual practice, there is an impression that the firm fixes a warranty and the consumer has the choice of one of the products among the many that are available (thereby indicating a preference for y). The choices described in the foregoing model are ex ante. The above observation refers to ex post implementation. More pertinently, the consumer may infer the quality of the product from the warranty offered and make his choice of the product accordingly. The analytical distinction between ex ante and ex post will not be an impediment to this practical reality.

Another dimension of practical detail needs emphasis. The market consists of a large number of buyers. Each of them will have a different δ and λ. To conceptualize separate warranties for each one of them will be expensive for the firm. Hence, the firm is more likely to choose a few values of p a priori and allow consumers to choose the warranty they desire. See, for instance, Emons (1989b).

To appreciate this, rewrite the choice of p in the form

$$\delta(1-p) = 2p\lambda\sigma^2$$

That is, given a p and σ^2, there will be several combinations of δ, λ, and hence groups of consumers who exhibit these attributes that satisfy this equation. Only such consumers will buy the product.

[5] In practice, for a given δ, a highly risk-averse consumer may yet seek a higher p. He wants a good-quality product with significant warranty. We will consider this possibility in the sequel.

The following analysis provides some further insights into the choice of p. The consumer may have a reservation level m_a of value. Then,

$$\begin{aligned} v_a &= py - \lambda p^2\sigma^2 \\ &= \lambda\sigma^2\delta^2 / \left(\delta + 2\lambda\sigma^2\right)^2 \geq m_a \end{aligned}$$

The minimum p acceptable to such consumers will be

$$p_m = \left(m_a / \lambda\sigma^2\right)^{1/2}$$

Similarly, the firm may have a reservation level of profit m_p. Then,

$$\begin{aligned} v_p &= (1-p)y - y^2/2\delta \\ &= 2\delta\left(\lambda\sigma^2\right)^2 / \left(\delta + 2\lambda\sigma^2\right)^2 \geq m_p \end{aligned}$$

Hence, the best product that the firm will offer will have a quality

$$y_m = \left(2\delta m_p\right)^{1/2}$$

Assume, now, that the firm chooses $p_1 > p$. Consider a consumer who cannot (or who does not wish to) use the product carefully. That is, he exhibits a low δ. If he is also highly risk averse, he will end up choosing a product with lower warranty. On the other hand, a consumer who is less risk averse and more willing to use the product carefully would be inclined to seek a greater warranty. Note, however, that the information contained in the model is inadequate to fix the product variety, warranty combinations that the firm should offer. Emons (1989b) examined this possibility in a different framework.

One other result should be noted. Observe that y tends to zero as σ^2 reduces to zero. In other words, both σ^2 and y contain the same information about the quality of the product. Further, when σ^2 is small and the firm feels confident about its product, it will offer the maximum warranty. Similarly, the firm will offer the maximum warranty if it is confident that the consumer will fully comply with the maintenance schedules that it prescribes.[6]

[6] Experimental evidence seems to suggest that the p defined by the model may not hold when it is close to 0 or 1. There can be bunching around these values for, when the firm is quite confident that its product is of good quality, it may offer a near full warranty. See, for example, Coricelli and Luini (2003). Heal (1977) also suggested earlier that risk sharing may lead to excessive warranty for he argued that a risk-neutral firm will bear the entire risk which a risk-averse consumer experiences. This is generally not valid.

8.3 Different Approach

Up to this point in the analysis, it was assumed that δ and λ are independent characteristics of a consumer. However, it would be realistic to expect that a highly risk-averse consumer would also pay a great deal of attention to maintaining the product to ensure continuous service.[7] That is,

$$d\delta / d\lambda\sigma^2 > 0$$

More generally, assume that η, the elasticity of δ with respect to $\lambda\sigma^2$, is positive. It can be readily verified that

$$dp/d\lambda\sigma^2 = 2\delta(\eta - 1)/\left(\delta + 2\lambda\sigma^2\right)^2$$

This expression will be zero if $\eta = 1$. This indicates that the consumer makes a perfect correction in his care corresponding to every change in $\lambda\sigma^2$. Consequently, the consumer need not demand any change in the warranty offered by the firm. In general, product failures would only be due to intrinsic technical details of production and the product warranty should reflect this feature. Suppose $\eta < 1$. That is, the consumer is less than cautious while using the product. He cannot then demand an increased warranty from the firm. Instead, he will accept a lower p thereby acknowledging that his negligence toward maintenance is a part of the reason for the failure of the product. Analytically, the case where $\eta > 1$ is more illuminating. To be sure, the more careful consumer recognizes that the product failure, if it were to occur, cannot be a result of his negligence. He then demands a greater warranty from the firm. Thus, even under risk sharing arrangements, there will be an increase in warranty when $\lambda\sigma^2$ increases. The ceteris paribus clause under the risk sharing formulation could not sustain this result.[8]

[7] Cooper and Ross (1985), Emons (1988), and Dybvig and Lutz (1993) acknowledged that the consumers can adjust the care with which they use the product. Thus, the consumers can exert some influence on the failure of the product depending on the way they use it. The issue is this. What determines the adjustments in δ? $\lambda\sigma^2$ is surely one of the determinants. Emons (1988) argued that p, viz., the warranty offered, may itself determine the choice of δ. Similarly, following the argument of Murty and Blischke (2000), it can be argued that even the firm makes adjustments in several characteristics of its product when it recognizes the pertinent dimensions of consumer risk aversion. This may include the warranty and the σ^2 itself. We will not consider these alternatives in detail here.

[8] In much of the existing literature, the usual argument is that the firm <u>signals</u> good quality by offering greater warranty. Similarly, greater warranty will provide an <u>incentive</u> to the consumer to buy a product when he is not sure of the quality a priori. The present result appears far more plausible for, when $\eta > 1$, the consumer is exercising more than adequate caution to neutralize his risk aversion. Hence, it becomes necessary for the firm to signal its compliance by offering a greater warranty. This need not depend on the quality of the product. Similarly, if $\eta < 1$, the consumer is not adequately diligent. A higher warranty will then provide an incentive to the consumer to use the product better. In either case, the consumer may consider warranty as an insurance that the firm

Since y is another measure of product quality, let us examine the changes in p as y varies. Consider the total derivatives

$$\mathrm{d}p/\mathrm{d}\lambda\sigma^2 = 2\delta(\eta-1)/(\delta+2\lambda\sigma^2)^2 \text{ and}$$
$$\mathrm{d}y/\mathrm{d}\lambda\sigma^2 = 2\delta(\delta+2\eta\lambda\sigma^2)/(\delta+2\lambda\sigma^2)^2$$

From this, it can be inferred that

$$\mathrm{d}p/\mathrm{d}y = (\eta-1)/(\delta+2\lambda\sigma^2)$$

All the results developed above remain intact. If $\eta < 1$, the firm will offer better warranties for good products. $\eta > 1$ would attract more warranties for bad products. This suggests that some limits on due diligence of the consumer would indeed be worthwhile.

Observe that the maximum p that the firm would be willing to offer occurs when $\eta = 1$. That is,

$$\delta = \mathrm{C}\lambda\sigma^2$$

where C is a constant and will be the combination that the consumer chooses. Corresponding to this,

$$p = \mathrm{C}/(\mathrm{C}+2)$$

This is a monotonic increasing function of C and tends to 1 as C tends to ∞. In other words, a consumer who exercises the utmost caution in using the product will demand complete warranty.[9] It should also be noted that this choice of p is independent of δ and $\lambda\sigma^2$ whatever may be the value of C. C would indeed vary with the complexity of the product.

For the sake of analytical completeness, consider the case where the firm expects the consumer to bear the entire cost of repairs. That is, the firm claims that the failure of the product is entirely due to his carelessness and that there is no manufacturing defect in the product. The gain to the consumer now becomes

$$g_{\mathrm{a}} = p(y+u) - y^2/2\delta \text{ and}$$
$$v_{\mathrm{a}} = py - y^2/2\delta - \lambda p^2\sigma^2$$

offers to convince him that it is sincere about maintaining the product if it were to fail. Of course, there is no guarantee that any of these mechanisms result in the desired outcome.

[9] Cooper and Ross (1985) noted that the consumers would demand greater warranties when their cost of effort in maintaining the product is higher.

Moreover, under this dispensation, the consumer is more concerned about the y that determines his expenses. Correspondingly, he chooses

$$y = p\delta$$

The net value of the contract is

$$\mathrm{N} = y - y^2/2\delta - \lambda p^2\sigma^2$$

and the efficient choice of p is

$$p = \delta/\left(\delta + 2\lambda\sigma^2\right)$$

as before.

It can be verified that the total derivative

$$\mathrm{d}p/\mathrm{d}y = 2(\eta - 1)/\left(2\eta - \delta + 2\lambda\sigma^2\right)$$

Once again, if $\eta > 1$, the firm will offer more warranty for lower-quality products.[10] This will be valid when $\eta < 1$ only if $\delta > 2(\eta + \lambda\sigma^2)$. Suppose the firm offers a bad product. It will involve a lower cost of production. Since the consumer is not sufficiently careful, he will ask for repairs more often. But the firm has nothing to lose because the consumer is expected to bear the cost. There is no motivation to offer better products because frequent repairs cannot be avoided if $\eta < 1$.

In the ultimate analysis, the firm may indeed offer the maximum warranty irrespective of the quality of the product. Nevertheless, it depends on C that reflects the difficulty in the consumer using the product diligently. The firm may make a technologically complex product in such a way that the buyer can use it with great ease and very little maintenance and justify a relatively low warranty. On the other hand, even some low-value products may involve complex technologies and demand a great deal of caution in their use. Such products attract larger warranties irrespective of their quality. It appears that the costs of due diligence, to the firm as well as the consumer, rather than the quality of the product determine the warranty offered in practice.

In much of the literature, the emphasis is on the relationship between the quality of the product and warranty. In particular, it is expected that a producer of better-quality products offers greater warranty. This created confusion because in practice high warranties have been offered for even poor-quality and/or low-value products. It is justified on the argument that the firm does not really expect the consumer to claim warranty on low-valued products (because the costs they incur exceed the value of warranty) and that, when the product is of poor quality, the consumer is

[10] The converse is also true. The best known example is that of high-quality Japanese cars that offer very low warranty.

more likely to use it carefully. The role of risk aversion was considered in the following manner. Heal (1977) argued that if the firm is risk neutral and the consumers are risk averse, then the former should absorb all the risk and offer full warranty. The present study has taken the following viewpoint. Suppose the consumer is risk averse. He should use the product carefully so that it does not breakdown. But, there is no guarantee that he is using the product carefully and with his risk aversion in perspective. If he does, then full warranty is justified for the product's failure is not due to the carelessness of the consumer. Instead, it is essentially due to the intrinsic quality of the product. If he does not, he should be asked to share some risk. The present argument suggests that warranty depends basically on the extent to which the consumer is willing and able to adjust his pattern of usage to his degree of risk aversion. Higher warranty will be offered to those that show greater adjustment. If the adjustment is perfect, then failure is essentially a technical feature of the product. The firm must accept the liability, and warranty will be complete coverage of loss. It should then be noted that, when adjusting δ to $\lambda\sigma^2$, the consumer experiences some costs. The firm is also facing some costs due to warranty. If the former are large, then warranty must be large irrespective of the intrinsic value of the product. In other words, the maximum warranty offered should be related to the degree of difficulty that the consumer experiences in making this adjustment. If it is very large and the product is complex, most of the failure is due to the nature of the product and this justifies large warranty. On the other hand, if it is low, failure can be attributed to the consumer negligence. In that case, the required warranty would be low.

8.4 Preventive Maintenance

Up to this point in the analysis, it was assumed that the consumer voluntarily undertakes activities that ensure proper use of the product. But, as we have shown in the previous section, this may force the firm to offer an excessive warranty at least in some cases. We now examine the possibility that the firm, which has a fair idea about the value of y, insists that the consumer accepts preventive maintenance so that the losses can be kept close to y when the product fails.[11] Similarly, σ^2 may be determined entirely by the technological and design features. Let the firm expect the consumers to spend ky^2 on preventive maintenance. Whatever may be the consumer's voluntary disposition for the use of the product, this enables the firm to reduce the incidence of failure due to consumer neglect. The firm may, then, be willing to offer a greater warranty.

As before, when the consumer chooses p ex ante, the efficient equilibrium choice will be

[11] Maintenance issues have been considered extensively. See, for example, Dybvig and Lutz (1993) and Murty and Blischke (2000).

$$p = \delta / \left(\delta + 2\lambda\sigma^2 + 4k\lambda\sigma^2\right)$$

Ceteris paribus, the consumer demands only a smaller warranty.[12] The consumer actually feels that his expenditure on preventive maintenance reduces the possibility of failure and, as a result, he does not need as much warranty.[13] However, note that

$$v_a = p^2\lambda\sigma^2\left(1 - 4k\lambda\sigma^2\right) / \left(\delta + 2\lambda\sigma^2 + 4k\lambda\sigma^2\right)$$
$$\geq 0 \text{ iff } k \leq 1/4\lambda\sigma^2$$

The maximum preventive maintenance that the consumer will accept is therefore[14]

$$k_{\mathrm{m}} = 1/4\lambda\sigma^2$$

It may be argued that preventive maintenance will enable the firm to calibrate the caution exercised by the buyer. The consumer, who is aware of this, may be more careful in the use of the product as k increases. That is, the consumer may increase his voluntary efforts to use the product safely. We then have a possibility that $\mathrm{d}\delta/\mathrm{d}k > 0$. Then, it can be verified that

$$\mathrm{d}p/\mathrm{d}k = 2\lambda\sigma^2\delta\left[2(\eta - 1)k + \eta\right]/k\left(\delta + 2\lambda\sigma^2 + 4k\lambda\sigma^2\right)^2$$

Clearly, p will increase with k if and only if

$$2k/(2k+1) < \eta < 1$$

because $2k/(2k+1)$ tends to 1 as k tends to infinity. If $\eta > 1$, the overall level of consumer diligence has gone up. The firm would prefer to increase warranty. A similar argument holds even if $\eta < 2k/(2k+1)$. In sum, the consumer can expect the firm to offer a greater warranty if and only if the overall level of caution exercised by the consumer increases commensurate with his risk aversion.[15] This result does not, in any way, depend on the quality of the durable good per se. Most of the studies

---

[12] If the firm is the decision maker with respect to the warranty, we expect p to increase with k for the firm knows that there will be fewer failures if the consumer follows the prescribed preventive maintenance schemes. But, here the consumer expressed incentive constraints that are binding on the firm.

[13] Suppose we interpret ky^2 as the cost, to the consumer, of availing warranty. In such a case, the consumer may express a preference for a lower p as k increases.

[14] For all practical purposes, the cost, to the consumer, of preventive maintenance is $ky^2 + \lambda p^2\sigma^2$. The advantage of warranty is py. Hence, warranty is advantageous if and only if $py > \mathrm{k}y^2 + \lambda p^2\sigma^2$. This results in the condition $k \leq 1/4\lambda\sigma^2$.

[15] The consumer may decide to reduce his voluntary level of caution since preventive maintenance can substitute for this. Similar results can be developed in this case as well.

reported ambiguous results with respect to the relationship between warranty and quality because they did not acknowledge this phenomenon.

One other possibility exists. An expenditure ky^2 on preventive maintenance may have the effect of reducing the variance of u to σ^2/k for, now, defects, if any, can be detected and corrected in time. This alternative yields

$$p = \delta / \left[k\delta\left(1 + 4\lambda\sigma^2\right) + 2\lambda\sigma^2 \right]$$

Consequently, p will increase if and only if $k < 1/(1 + 4\lambda\sigma^2)$. The costs of preventive maintenance overweigh the advantages of increasing the warranty if k is larger than this quantity.

Generally, firms prescribe preventive maintenance for the entire duration of the warranty. They would probably insist on greater preventive maintenance the more warranty they offer. In other words, preventive maintenance schedules and warranty may not be directly related to the output lost if and when the product fails. Let us, therefore, denote the cost of preventive maintenance by kp^2. Clearly, the consumer bears the cost. The efficient choice of p for the consumer is

$$p = y/2\left(k + \lambda\sigma^2\right), \text{ and the optimal } y \text{ is}$$

$$y = 2\delta\left(k + \lambda\sigma^2\right) / \left[\delta + 2\left(k + \lambda\sigma^2\right)\right]$$

so that

$$p = \delta / \left[\delta + 2\left(k + \lambda\sigma^2\right)\right]$$

Consider all the consumers who buy the product for given p and k. The δ, $\lambda\sigma^2$, and combinations they represent will be along the straight line

$$\delta(1 - p) = 2p\left(k + \lambda\sigma^2\right)$$

The slope

$$\mathrm{d}\lambda\sigma^2 / \mathrm{d}\delta = (1 - p)/2p$$

Since $\mathrm{d}\lambda\sigma^2/\mathrm{d}\delta$ remains invariant, the existence of k does not change the consumers that buy the product. If, however, $\mathrm{d}\delta/\mathrm{d}k > 0$, it can be shown that the level of warranty increases whenever $\eta > 1$. On the contrary, when $\eta < 1$, the warranty increases only if $k/(k + \lambda\sigma^2) < \eta < 1$. The results are, for all practical purposes, analogous to the above case.

A finer point of the analysis may now be reported. It is possible to define an optimal value of k in the case under consideration for the consumer can maximize v_a by choosing $k = (\lambda\sigma^2)^{1/2}$. With this choice in perspective, it can be shown that

$$p = y/4\left(\lambda\sigma^2\right)^{1/2}$$
$$y = 4\delta\left(\lambda\sigma^2\right)^{1/2} / \left[\delta + 4\left(\lambda\sigma^2\right)^{1/2}\right]$$

so that

$$p = \delta / \left[\delta + 4\left(\lambda\sigma^2\right)^{1/2}\right]$$

Hence, the level of warranty will be higher, compared to the base case, if $k > 2$. High risk aversion can be adequately compensated by preventive maintenance in all such cases.

In sum, preventive maintenance will also impact the level of warranty offered through its effect on the caution exercised by the buyer. It does not have much to do with the quality of the product per se.

8.5 Warranty Duration

The usual warranty offered for technologically complex products like automobiles has a somewhat different structure compared to the one we considered so far. Normally, the warranty would be for a fixed time period or a prescribed number of kilometers of driving, whichever comes first.[16] This section is designed to appreciate the economics underlying this choice of warranty contract.

Suppose the product is designed and manufactured to produce Y units of output per unit of time for T years. However, the firm may find that there are two types of users.[17] One group of consumers uses the product more intensively. That is, for them, Y* per unit of time exceeds Y. The second group of consumers uses it to produce less than or equal to Y units of output per unit of time. The intensive user may surmise that the product will fail t units of time ahead of its expected life. When the product fails and the firm restores it under warranty, he cannot expect to get more than *pt*Y of output from the product for the rest of its life. Stated differently, the warranty offered by the firm may stipulate that only this much of output will be promised after the product is restored. The consumer should not expect more since the product was initially designed to produce Y units of output per unit of time. Postulating the usual randomness associated with the fulfillment of this promise after repairs means that the gain to the consumer will be

[16] It was generally pointed out that the output from household durables is not measurable. It cannot be objectively verified either. In such contexts, the only possible warranty is over a duration less than the expected life of the durable.

[17] Issues pertaining to warranty duration in such contexts have been examined in Emons (1989b).

$$g_a = p(tY + u)$$

Correspondingly, the value becomes

$$v_a = ptY - \lambda p^2 \sigma^2$$

Assume, as before, that the consumer chooses p. This choice will be

$$p = tY/2\lambda\sigma^2$$

The basic difference in the present context is the cost to the firm, of repairs under the warranty, when the product fails. It can be expected that it will be $t^2Y^{*2}/2\delta$ because the intensive use of the product may damage parts extensively. Hence, the gain to the firm is

$$g_p = (1-p)(tY + u) - t^2 Y^{*2}/2\delta \text{ and}$$
$$v_p = (1-p)tY - t^2 Y^{*2}/2\delta$$

The net gain from the contract then becomes

$$N = tY - \lambda p^2 \sigma^2 - t^2 Y^{*2}/2\delta$$

The firm can be expected to choose t to maximize N. Such a choice is given by

$$t = 2\delta\lambda\sigma^2 Y/\left(\delta Y^2 + 2\lambda\sigma^2 Y^{*2}\right)$$

Hence, it follows that

$$y = tY = 2\delta\lambda\sigma^2/\left(\delta + 2\lambda\sigma^2 x^2\right)$$

where

$$x = \text{intensity of use}$$
$$= Y^*/Y$$

Consequently, the choice of p is

$$p = \delta/\left(\delta + 2\lambda\sigma^2 x^2\right)$$

Clearly, these choices reduce to the results obtained earlier if $x = 1$. In general, this contract choice applies only when $x > 1$.

To protect less intensive users under this warranty mechanism, the firm may stipulate that the warranty holds for:

(a) T–$(1-p)t$ units of time
(b) TY–$(1-p)t$Y of output

depending on which of these occurs first. Let us designate this as the limited warranty duration contract.

As in the previous section, assume that a risk-averse consumer may yet make attempts to utilize the product diligently. It can be verified that

$$\mathrm{d}p/\mathrm{d}y = x^2(\eta-1)/(\delta+2\lambda\ \sigma^2x^2\eta)$$

Hence, if $\eta > 1$, the consumer demands greater warranty for relatively bad products, and if $\eta < 1$, the consumer expects higher warranty only for good products.

As before, note that p is maximized when $\eta = 1$. The maximum p that the firm will offer is

$$p = \mathrm{C}/(\mathrm{C}+2x^2)$$

where, as usual,

$$\delta = \mathrm{C}\lambda\sigma^2$$

The issue that needs to be considered is about the firm's choice of x. It can be readily shown that only $x=1$ can maximize N. The firm may, instead, maximize its own expected gains. Note that

$$v_{\mathrm{p}} = 2\mathrm{C}x^2\lambda\sigma^2/(\mathrm{C}+2x^2)^2$$

The optimal choice of x is therefore

$$x = (\mathrm{C}/2)^{1/2}$$

The firm will offer this warranty if and only if $\mathrm{C} > 2$. Corresponding to this choice, the optimal tY is

$$t\mathrm{Y} = \lambda\sigma^2$$

The economic logic underlying this derivation is as follows. Suppose the consumer is risk averse. He may also find it relatively expensive to exercise due diligence in the use of the product. He would then be prone to utilize the product intensively and get the maximum output from it before it breaks down. Anticipating this behavior, the firm finds that its interests will be secure if it expects

$$x = (\mathrm{C}/2)^{1/2}$$

The firm defines the warranty offered accordingly.

There is another observation in the literature. In general, since t is smaller, on the presumption that $x > 1$, the low-intensity consumer tends to lose in the implementation of this warranty. However, the firm knows that all users will not utilize the product with the same intensity. It may gain by discriminating among these groups by offering a choice of warranty. Consider the alternative to be

$$p = C/(C+2) \text{ and } y = 2C\lambda\sigma^2/(C+2)$$

Observe that the value of the limited warranty duration contract, to the low-intensity consumer, will be larger if and only if

$$\lambda\sigma^2/4 > C^2\lambda\sigma^2/(C+2)^2$$

That is, we require

$$3C^2 - 4C - 4 < 0$$

This would be valid only if $C < 2$. Hence, it can be concluded that the low-intensity user will prefer the limited warranty duration contract. This is the only type of contract that will be observed in practice. The low-intensity user prefers it. The high-intensity user cannot expect any better warranty. In general, this analysis does not validate the argument that the consumers will self-select if different warranty arrangements are offered to them.

Results, pertaining to preventive maintenance, can also be developed along similar lines. They will not be presented here because there is no fundamental change in the conclusions.

However, note that the argument of the previous section, viz. that the warranty offered varies with the consumer's degree of difficulty in exercising due diligence rather than the quality of the product, remains intact.

8.6 Extended Warranties

On occasions, firms offer extended warranties for their products. In general, extended warranties are offered when the product does not fail within the stipulated initial warranty. Very often, extended warranties enhance the period of coverage or cover more output. Usually, the additional output under extended warranties offers lower coverage in comparison to the original warranty. Such extended warranties, or service contracts, may also be offered to the consumer, if he so chooses, at some cost. They are not offered as a package unlike the original warranty that is integral to the purchase of the product. Thus, as Lutz and Padmanabhan (1998) noted, an extended warranty is an additional insurance against product failure.

The major objective of the firm, while designing extended warranties, may be to set up a discriminating monopoly situation by separating the more risk-averse consumers from the others. Firms may also reduce initial warranties to force consumers into buying extended warranties. Earlier studies suggest that the firm may reduce the original warranty if it is not sure about the consumer exercising the expected due diligence in the use of the product.

In some cases, third-party insurers offer extended warranties, either as complementary to or in competition with the firm, so that there is a clear indication that profit making is a major motive underlying such service contracts. The existence of an outside insurer providing extended warranty may have an influence on the original warranty policy of the firm. It will increase if they are viewed as competitors.

Reduction in the original warranty, and preference for extended warranties, also suggests a risk sharing arrangement for the consumer may reduce the caution exercised in the use of the product if the original warranty is high. In such cases, the firm can ascertain the consumer type by offering a lower warranty initially and extending it to more diligent users on its expiry. The consumer, on the other hand, may feel that a lower-quality product is being sold if the initial warranty is low. The availability of an extended warranty may be an assurance that the firm is indeed offering a good-quality product.

We will only consider the risk sharing feature of extended warranties. In such a context, extended warranties may deter independent third parties from acquiring proprietary technological knowledge.

To capture the risk sharing effect, postulate that the firm does not charge the consumer for extended warranty. Let the extended warranty coverage be until such a time when the product may have the capacity to deliver $y^* < y$ units of output. As before, the firm covers only a fraction of this. It may then be noted that the additional gain to the consumer is

$$g_a = q(y^* + u)$$

where q is the fraction that the extended warranty offers. The intrinsic nature of the product does not change in any way just because the firm is now offering extended warranty. Hence, the random variable u is the same as before. It can also be surmised that the risk aversion of the consumer does not change materially. Consequently, the value of the extended warranty to the consumer is

$$v_a = qy^* - \lambda q^2 \sigma^2$$

The q that the consumer desires will be

$$q = y^* / 2\lambda\sigma^2$$

Consider the gain to the producer. The product has already survived the original warranty. Hence, even if it did not fail, there would have been some wear and tear that would have an effect on servicing the product during the tenure of the extended warranty. These costs[18] can be approximated by $(y+y^*)^2/2\delta$. Hence, the additional gain to the producer is

$$g_p = (1-q)(y^* + u) \quad (y+y^*)^2/2\delta$$

Hence, the value to the firm (or the expected profit) will be

$$v_p = (1-q)y^* - (y+y^*)^2/2\delta$$

As before, net value maximization yields

$$q = p^2 \text{ and } y^* = 2p^{*2}\lambda\sigma^2$$

Clearly, the extended warranty is lower. Fundamentally, this is a result of the increase in cost, to the firm, of servicing the extended warranty At least on some occasions, it may be due to the expectation that the consumer will not remain as cautious as before given his good experience with the product during the period of initial warranty. In fact, it may be expected that η, the elasticity of δ with respect to $\lambda\sigma^2$, will be less than unity. Hence, larger extended warranties will be offered only for very good products.

We now examine the choice of warranty to understand the relationship between y and y^* if they are determined jointly by the firm a priori. It is reasonable to postulate that the consumer has no reason to think of the extended warranty while the original warranty is in force irrespective of whether the product fails or not. Consequently, the consumer's choices are

$$y = 2\lambda p\sigma^2 \text{ and } y^* = 2\lambda q\sigma^2$$

Consider the net value of the contract. It will depend on the cost incurred by the firm. Note that it will be a function of y^*. This component of cost will be written as $y^{*2}/2\delta$. However, the product is already worn out even if the original warranty was not utilized. We will postulate that the other component of cost[19] is $(y+y^*)^2/2\delta$. Hence, it follows that

$$N = y + y^* - \lambda\sigma^2(p^2 + q^2) - y^{*2}/2\delta - (y+y^*)^2/2\delta$$

The optimal choices of y and y^* will then be

[18] Some alternative specifications appear equally plausible. However, the qualitative results will not change materially.

[19] There is no clear a priori economic basis on which these costs can be defined. As such, this specification can be contested. The point of the following analysis is that at least one plausible cost structure that can sustain the observed empirical regularities can be traced.

$$y = 2\delta\lambda\sigma^2\left(\delta + 2\lambda\sigma^2\right)/\left[\left(\delta + 2\lambda\sigma^2\right)^2 + 2\delta\lambda\sigma^2\right]\text{and}$$
$$y^* = 2\delta^2\lambda\sigma^2/\left[\left(\delta + 2\lambda\sigma^2\right)^2 + 2\delta\lambda\sigma^2\right]$$

The corresponding choices of p and q are

$$p = \delta\left(\delta + 2\lambda\sigma^2\right)/\left[\left(\delta + 2\lambda\sigma^2\right)^2 + 2\delta\lambda\sigma^2\right]\text{and}$$
$$q = \delta^2/\left[\left(\delta + 2\lambda\sigma^2\right)^2 + 2\delta\lambda\sigma^2\right]$$

It is therefore obvious that $q<p$ and $y^*<y$. Further, the p chosen under extended warranty is less than the p chosen when no such extended warranty is offered. These results are in agreement with the results that Lutz and Padmanabhan (1998) and Murty and Blischke (2000) obtained by invoking discriminating monopoly.

We now consider the possibility that the firm charges the consumer for the extended warranty. Since the firm offers to restore qy^* units of output in case of failure, we assume the charges to be eqy^*. With this modification, it can be shown that

$$q = \delta^2/(\delta + 2\lambda\sigma^2[\delta\left(1-e\right)^2 + 2\lambda\sigma^2 \text{ and}$$
$$\left(1-e\right)y^* = 2q\lambda\sigma^2$$

Observe that for $e>0$ the resulting y^* and q are higher. This should be obvious because the firm is now able to recover a part of the cost of servicing the warranty.

Introduction of an independent insurer will have a somewhat different effect. His motivation will be profit maximization alone. It has no implications for any risk sharing. It should therefore be clear that the results of Lutz and Padmanabhan (1998) and Murty and Blischke (2000) depend basically on the changes in the market demand for the firm's product. They do not depend on risk sharing per se.

In sum, risk sharing has limited implications for extended warranties. However, some basic empirical realities may yet be explained by the risk sharing logic.

8.7 Many Consumers

In many practical contexts, the firm sells its durable goods to many consumers. However, all the earlier sections considered sale to any one consumer. Though this is possible in reality, the more general context of many consumers should be examined. Similarly, one of the reasons for the risk-neutral attitude of the firm, as postulated consistently through all the previous sections, arises partly because the firm is dealing with many heterogeneous consumers with several δ, λ combinations. The present section is an attempt to examine this aspect of practical reality.

As before, we will assume that each item of the product sold has a warranty y. The choice of each of the n identical consumers would still satisfy the equation

$$y = 2p\lambda\sigma^2$$

From the viewpoint of the firm, the increase in the number of consumers leads to increased costs. This can be represented by $(ny)^2/2\delta$ where n = number of consumers. The gain to the firm will then be

$$g_{\mathrm{p}} = n(1-p)(y+u) - (ny)^2/2\delta$$

Maintaining the assumption of risk neutrality, we have

$$v_{\mathrm{p}} = n(1-p)y - (ny)^2/2\delta$$

Similarly, the net value of the contract is

$$N = ny - n\lambda\sigma^2 p^2 - (ny)^2/2\delta$$

The firm now chooses y. Explicit optimization yields

$$y = 2\delta\lambda\sigma^2/(\delta + 2n\lambda\sigma^2)$$

Note that, from this, it can be inferred that

$$\partial(ny)/\partial n = 2\delta^2\lambda\sigma^2/(\delta + 2n\lambda\sigma^2)^2 > 0$$

for all values of n. Consequently, it is not possible to conceptualize an optimal value of n. This can be justified on the following economic intuition as well. Note that the firm would not like to leave out any consumer that wishes to buy its product for the maximized value of v_{p} is

$$v_{\mathrm{p}} = 2n^2\delta\lambda^2\sigma^4/(\delta + 2n\lambda\sigma^2)^2$$

and, as a result,

$$\partial v_{\mathrm{p}}/\partial n = 4n\delta\lambda^2\sigma^4(\delta + \lambda\sigma^2)/(\delta + 2n\lambda\sigma^2)^3 > 0$$

for all values of n.

Observe that each consumer can be expected to adjust the caution with which he uses the product based on his risk aversion and the degree of difficulty involved in doing so given the technological complexity of the product. Under these conditions, the firm would choose a common value of p

$$p = \mathrm{C}/(\mathrm{C}+2n)$$

for all the consumers.

Consider the possibility that the costs of coordination, to the firm, will increase with the number of consumers for any given choice of warranty.[20] We may denote this by cn^2. The net value of the contract will be modified accordingly. The optimal choice of n will now be such that

$$2nc = \lambda\sigma^2\delta^2/\left(\delta + 2n\lambda\sigma^2\right)^2$$

Assume that the firm chooses the maximum p as specified above. Given this choice, it can be readily verified that

$$\partial n/\partial c = -n/c < 0$$

so that coordination costs discourage the firm from expanding n indefinitely. The properties of the corresponding warranty choice do not change materially.

8.8 Why Lemons?

Cooter and Porat (2002) argued that risk sharing only spreads risks among the parties and that it cannot assure us that the overall risks are reduced. In other words, risk sharing contractual agreements may indeed encourage dealing in more risky transactions. It should therefore be expected that many bad products reach the market under the warranty arrangements that we have been considering.[21] We will present a brief outline of this result in this section.

Return to the basic model of Sect. 8.2. Given the optimal values of p and y, it can be shown that

$$v_a = \lambda\sigma^2\delta^2/\left(\delta + 2\lambda\sigma^2\right)^2$$

[20] Cooper and Ross (1985) pointed out that the firm will be at a disadvantage when they have too many diffused and heterogeneous customers.

[21] Emons (1988) also examined such a possibility. The argument was that an increase in warranty reduces the motivation of the consumer in maintaining the product properly. The economics underlying the argument in this section is quite different.

We will now investigate the propensity of the consumers to encourage the introduction of more risky and low-quality products. This can be inferred if v_a increases with $\lambda\sigma^2$. In fact, it can be verified that

$$\partial v_a / \partial \lambda\sigma^2 = \delta^2 \left(\delta - 2\lambda\sigma^2\right) / \left(\delta + 2\lambda\sigma^2\right)^3 > 0$$

if and only if $\delta > 2\lambda\sigma^2$. Hence, it can be concluded that the consumer gains if $\lambda\sigma^2$ is relatively low and/or he is more efficient in the use of the product. In either case, it cannot be denied that the consumer has an incentive to accept products of lower quality.

How does the firm react? Note that

$$\partial y / \partial \lambda\sigma^2 = 2\delta^2 / \left(\delta + 2\lambda\sigma^2\right)^2 > 0$$

That is, firms tend to choose high-risk, low-quality products and offer a higher warranty to increase their market share. Further, observe that

$$\partial v_p / \partial \lambda\sigma^2 = 4\delta^2 \lambda\sigma^2 / \left(\delta + 2\lambda\sigma^2\right)^3 > 0$$

Hence, the firm gains by choosing poor-quality products.

It may be concluded that the commercial interests of both the consumers and the firms tend to increase low-quality, high-risk durable goods on the market.

Let us now consider the case where there are many consumers on the market for a durable good. To begin with, note that the value addition to any one consumer is a decreasing function of n for

$$\partial v_a / \partial n < 0$$

In other words, each of the consumers may feel that they will lose. However, they will not resist the firm offering lower-quality products. Note that, for the entire group of consumers, the value is

$$n v_a = n \lambda\sigma^2 \delta^2 / \left(\delta + 2n\lambda\sigma^2\right)^2$$

and it can be verified that

$$\partial\left(n v_a\right) / \partial n = \lambda\sigma^2 \delta^3 / \left(\delta + 2n\lambda\sigma^2\right)^3 > 0$$

so that they gain collectively when n increases. Similarly, it can be shown that

$$\partial(nv_{\mathrm{a}})/\partial\lambda\sigma^2 = n\delta\left(\delta - 2n\lambda\sigma^2\right)/\left(\delta + 2n\lambda\sigma^2\right)^3 > 0$$
$$\text{if and only if } \delta > 2n\lambda\sigma^2$$

Hence, the consumers tend to support lower-quality products, albeit within limits.

Is there any advantage to the firm if n and/or $\lambda\sigma^2$ increases? To answer this question, note that

$$v_{\mathrm{p}} = 2n^2\delta\lambda^2\sigma^4/\left(\delta + 2n\lambda\sigma^2\right)^2$$

so that

$$\partial v_p/\partial n > 0$$

That is, the firm has sufficient commercial motivation to produce more and riskier products.

Consider the volatility of N as a result of these choices. It can be readily demonstrated that both $\partial N/\partial n$ and $\partial N/\partial\lambda\sigma^2$ are positive if and only if $\delta > 2n\lambda\sigma^2$. From this, it can be inferred that the more agile consumers encourage low-quality products and contribute to greater volatility of collective welfare.

8.9 Conclusion

The analysis of this study clearly demonstrates that limited warranties and limited duration warranties can be explained by the phenomenon of risk sharing. Firms can be expected to offer full warranty, for all product failures over the entire expected life of the product, only if the product is technically very complex and the consumer cannot prevent failure even if he exercises the utmost caution in its use. Quality of the product per se has a limited role.

One of the basic limitations of warranty specification is that the firm can never satisfactorily verify that the consumer is not misusing the product due to intensive use and is complying with all the service requirements that it specifies and that due diligence is exercised. The firm may reduce quality, offer a less than efficient warranty, and still make positive profits. Thus, warranties are an imperfect mechanism to mitigate moral hazard. If anything, the lemons problem may be exacerbated.

The cost specifications adopted in this study are, at best, symptomatic. It is difficult to provide any definite theoretical basis for these specifications. At the current stage of development, even empirical studies do not provide any more useful insights. We will perhaps gain by examining the implications of alternative specifications.

The most difficult issue for economic analysis, in the principal agent model framework, is the role of the product market in defining efficient risk sharing warranties. As of now, this is uncharted territory.

It would perhaps be fair to argue that some dimensions of warranties are exclusively due to the risk sharing propensities just as the others are explained by the signaling, incentive, or insurance motives. However, it is not clear if they are mutually exclusive and the territory of operation of each one of them can be delimited. A similar problem, with respect to quality, technological complexity in the use of the product, due diligence of the consumers, and the firm's reaction by changing the design and manufacture of the product, as they impinge on warranty decision, exists. There is a feeling that warranties may be neither necessary nor sufficient to achieve the stated purpose.

References

Cooper R, Ross TW (1985) Product warranties and double moral hazard. Rand J Econ 16:103–113

Cooter R, Porat A (2002) Anti insurance. Available at http://www.tau.ac.il/law/members/Porat-ariel/antiinsurance-pdf.pdf

Coricelli G, Luini L (2003) Double moral hazard: an experiment on warranties. Econ Manag Financ Mark 2:7–25

Dybvig PH, Lutz NA (1993) Warranties, durability, and maintenance: two-sided moral hazard in a continuous time model. Rev Econ Stud 60:575–597

Emons W (1988) Warranties, moral hazard, and the lemons problem. J Econ Theory 46:16–33

Emons W (1989a) The theory of warranty contracts. J Econ Surv 3:43–57

Emons W (1989b) On the limitation of warranty duration. J Ind Econ 37:287–301

Heal G (1977) Guarantees and risk sharing. Rev Econ Stud 44:549–560

Lutz NA, Padmanabhan V (1998) Warranties, extended warranties, and product quality. Int J Ind Organ 16:463–493

MacLeod WB (2007) Reputation, relationships, and contract enforcement. J Econ Lit 45:595–628

Masten SE, Snyder EA (1989) The design and duration of contracts: strategic and efficiency considerations. Law Contemp Probl 52:63–85

Masten SE, Snyder EA (1993) United States vs. United Shoe Machinery Corporation: on the merits. J Law Econ 36:33–70

Murty DNP, Blischke WR (2000) Strategic warranty management: a life-cycle approach. IEEE Trans Eng Manag 47:40–54

Murty DNP, Djamaludin I (2002) New product warranty: a literature review. Int J Prod Econ 79:231–260

Shavell S (2004) Foundations of economic analysis of law. Belknap Press of Harvard University, Cambridge, MA

Wehrt K (2000) Warranties. In: Bouckaert B, Geest GD (eds) Encyclopedia of law and economics. Edward Elgar, Cheltanham

References

Chapter 9
Accident and Health Insurance

Abstract Individuals tend to seek insurance to pass some risks on to the insurer when they expect large losses in the use of assets. The insurer can make his activity sustainable by pooling risks. If individuals can be expected to bear a greater fraction of the loss due to failure, they will be more diligent in the use of assets and reduce risks for which they are responsible. Similarly, efficient insurance policies may motivate individuals to reduce some forms of systemic risk especially when they are predictable. However, the increase in costs, associated with risks and the fulfillment of covenants designed to reduce them, invariably increases costs, reduces the equilibrium insurance coverage, and increases premiums. The residual systemic risk that cannot be absorbed by these policies and the necessity to generate wider and superior insurance service are at the basis of the call for regulation of the insurance business. The attempt made in this study is to examine the nature of efficient insurance in the presence of both types of risk, regulatory policy, and individual adaptations to them. Sharing risks through self-selection, optimal regulatory oversight, and insurance policies designed on such a basis can be efficient and offer a fairly wide coverage only against some individual-specific and limited systemic risks. In several contexts systemic risks and their origin cannot be predicted in advance. Efficient design of insurance to counter such risks may never really be possible since it is an ex ante specification.

9.1 Insurance and Risk

The possession and utilization of most assets promise to generate value to its owner (and sometimes to others in a society) over a certain length of time. Some individual effort in their use is necessary to make sure that the expected value is realized. Negligence on the part of the individual often prevents the generation of the full and

---

Based on content from "Efficient Contracts for Accident and Health", in B. Kamaiah, S.V. Seshaiah and G.R.K. Murty (eds.) first published in the edited volume *Select Issues in Macroeconomics: A Quantitative Approach* (Hyderabad: ICFAI University Press), 2014, pp. 231–259. Content reproduced here with permission from ICFAI University Press.

T.V.S.R. Rao, *Risk Sharing, Risk Spreading and Efficient Regulation*,
DOI 10.1007/978-81-322-2562-1_9

potential value.[1] Risks in the use of assets need not always be due to the negligence of individuals. External sources like an accident or fire may also lead to risks. When an asset fails to deliver value as expected, the individual has to incur some costs to restore its value. In the case of accidents, the individual is also liable for third-party losses. On occasions these losses may be so large that they are beyond the capacity of the individual to pay from current income. The prospect of such risk motivates individuals to enter into an insurance contract.

It involves the insured (the individual who purchases insurance as a shield against the loss in the value of his assets) to pay a premium to the insurer (an insurance company) with the understanding that the insurer will cover certain losses if and when they arise. Individuals do recognize that their careless use of assets increases the costs to the insurer, and it results in an increase in insurance premiums. Some individuals may find the insurance economical. There may then be self-selection. Another group of individuals may voluntarily exercise due diligence to keep the insurance premiums within limits. The insurer, on his part, expects that his operation can be viable if he pools risks arising out of the actions of many individuals. He also attempts to define some verifiable precautions like a deductible in the context of accident insurance, periodic checkup, use of some drugs to reduce the incidence of chronic conditions, and so on in the case of health insurance to motivate due diligence on the part of the insured. The insurance premium and the loss coverage can then be defined without reference to the diligence of the insured. Instead, they will depend only on the risks expected by the insurance company. In either case, the viability of the insurance company depends on how many individuals make claims and how it invests the premiums to generate additional finances. That is, the viability of the insurance contract, especially when confronted with unexpected risk, depends on the financial position of the insurer vis-à-vis the claims of the insured.

The insurer generally offers a contract that specifies the premium that the insured must pay, the extent of losses covered, and the quality of service rendered if and when a claim is presented. The insurer's choice of service stations in the context of accident insurance and hospitals for health insurance convey the quality of service to the insured. In any practical context, the quality of service will be multidimensional. The insured may then effectively choose a contract and the insurer who offers the quality of service they prefer. From the perspective of the insurer, individuals exhibit different degrees of diligence and risk aversion in the use of assets despite the covenants that they are expected to adhere to. Hence, the insurers find it difficult to calibrate these differences. Perforce, they utilize signals like claims in cases of accidents and health insurance to assess the individual types. An efficient design of contracts must keep these aspects in perspective. In general, there is a great deal of heterogeneity among insurance seekers, and it accounts for the wide variety of insurance policies available.

---

[1] Note that product failure may be due to design and manufacturing defects as well. The company selling the assets offers a warranty. This will also have the structure of insurance for all practical purposes. In practice, warranties offer coverage against only a limited set of potential losses. However, warranties will not cover accidents that cannot be attributed to the quality of the product per se. Hence, the individual opts for an insurance cover over and above product warranties. The insurance policies are, by their nature, generally sought by the individual rather than being offered by the manufacturer. The latter concept may not even exist in the context of health insurance.

The ultimate purpose of efficient insurance contracts must be to:

- Provide as much coverage as possible to each of the insured both qualitatively and quantitatively.
- Do so at the lowest possible rates.
- Make coverage available to as many as possible (especially with respect to health insurance).
- Ensure that the insurance companies remain financially viable so that the insured and the investors (other than the insured) are properly protected.

There is widespread belief that mature individuals (both the insured and the insurers) and market operation would induce honorable behavior and reduce individual specific as well as other risks so that efficient insurance contracts emerge. In particular, individuals seeking insurance may adjust their diligence and their degree of risk aversion. This reduces risks specific to individual decisions. However, individuals may not be in a position to anticipate some risks and find it very expensive to initiate corrective action on their own. In a similar fashion, insurance companies may define covenants to contain the risks that individuals generate. They may also calibrate risks better and act accordingly. However, it is obvious that such corrective self-regulation by individuals and market operation will be efficient only so long as the risks are within certain bounds.

It has been observed that individual adaptations, even when they materialize voluntarily, are subject to two other limitations. First, usually individuals, who tend to be careless in using assets, face greater risks and have the propensity to seek larger insurance cover. Individual behavior and attitudes are quite difficult to change through the use of conventional incentive and control mechanisms. This tends to make insurance companies offer lower-risk coverage, charge higher premiums, and cater to only the more diligent among those that seek insurance Second, from the viewpoint of the insurance companies, there will be an increase in costs if the insured drop guard. This may induce them to offer lower quality of service in addition to the problems mentioned above. Much of the literature concentrates on the first dimension and neglects the latter. Some results, like adverse selection having a major impact on the choice of coverage and premium in insurance contracts, may need to be modified. On the whole, there is perhaps only a limited range of individual decisions and adaptation that render self-regulation, by individuals and markets, efficient. Covenants, designed by insurance companies, tend to have limited effects on the efficiency of insurance contracts. In general, some risks are much less amenable to self-regulation of individuals and markets. Regulatory policies become a necessity in such contexts.

A market consisting of private insurance companies, essentially because it tends to be a differentiated oligopoly, cannot deliver some of the characteristics of efficient contracts alluded to above. In particular, it has been observed that the:

- Premium charged may be too large and discourage individuals who are in need of insurance.
- Quality of service may be inadequate (e.g., a health insurance contract may refuse to include a precondition in its coverage).

- Service stations and hospitals may induce, or inflate, the demand for their services.
- Management of finances and investments of insurance companies may not be optimal.

Risks emerging from the actions of individuals outside the insurance contract and the difficulty in making adaptations to them may explain the emergence of oligopoly markets and the consequences thereof.

Some pooling of risks, as in the case of an employer buying health insurance on behalf of his employees, and social health insurance systems sponsored by the government may mitigate some of these problems. In other cases an explicit regulation of the activities of the insurers may be warranted. In general, insurance regulation has been dealing with:

- Insurance premiums and rates charged
- Compulsory accident insurance
- Contracts between the insurer and the service provider
- Licensing based on the initial capital of the insurance company as a signal of its viability
- Solvency regulation dealing with the insurer's investment profile
- Minimizing individual specific as well as other forms of risks

The characterization of efficient regulation has been problematic. For instance, in the context of compulsory accident insurance enforcement (verification) has been costly, and there is a persistent feeling that such a policy increases the incidence of accidents, and consequently insurance premiums, thereby neutralizing the benefits of universal coverage.

The basic purpose of the present study is to develop modified principal agent models to examine efficient risk sharing in insurance contracts. The emphasis is on the role of individual specific vs. other forms of risk in designing insurance contracts. This differs from the conventional emphasis on adverse selection and moral hazard though these aspects are integrated in the analysis. More specifically, an attempt will be made to contrast accident and health insurance contracts from the perspective detailed above.

The rest of the study is organized as follows. Section 9.2 defines the different forms of risks that an efficient design of insurance contracts should take into account. The emphasis of this section is on the distinction between individual-specific versus systemic risks. Section 9.3 then outlines the basic principal agent model in the context of accident coverage. The efficiency with which individuals use assets has been described by their diligence in their use and the degree of risk aversion. Unlike other models in the literature, the quality of service rendered by the service provider is made an important aspect of the specification of an efficient contract. In general, it will be observed that covenants defined by the insurance policy and self-regulation may induce greater risk aversion rather than diligence. It will be demonstrated that they cannot neutralize systemic risk even if they tend to act against individual risk. Section 9.4 deals with health insurance. Two aspects have been highlighted. First, hospitals experience excessive costs due to under (or excessive) utilization of their expensive assets. This tends to inflate the supplier-induced demand for medical services.[2] Employer-supported insurance policies may mitigate this problem to some extent. Second, the more expensive health care, the more individuals seek insurance. This reduces the ability of the insurance companies to contain individual-specific risk. Systemic risk continues to be a challenge for efficient design of health insurance contracts as well. In Sect. 9.5, some aspects of regulatory policies will be highlighted. It will be argued that some regulatory policies will be needed as supplement to self-regulation by market participants even if individual specific and systemic risks are assumed to be given. The essential theme is to examine their efficacy in containing systemic risks. The idea is to demonstrate that even predictable systemic risks cannot be contained unless they are within certain limits. Similarly, there is no way to design efficient regulation to counter unexpected systemic risks. Section 9.6 highlights some basic limitations of the analytical framework adopted. In particular, the rich variety of contracts observed in practice[3] may not be amenable to analysis within simplified principal agent models and their behavioral postulates.

9.2 Nature of Risks

To begin with, it must be acknowledged that each individual exhibits distinct diligence and care in the use of an asset. Some individuals are predisposed to use an asset carefully, while others are not. This is an ex ante characteristic. An individual may not change his behavior significantly even after entering into an insurance contract. The greater the diligence with which an individual uses an asset, the lower will be the risk of failure. Hence, the level of diligence attributable to an individual is a measure of risk. For all practical purposes, it is specific to each individual. The behavior of some individuals changes ex post. For instance, after the insurance contract is signed, individuals may not exhibit diligence expected from them in the use of assets. This may lead to losses in excess of those anticipated ex ante. Individual-specific risks may also manifest in this form.

Individuals differ with respect to their propensities to take risks whatever may be their predisposition towards careful use of the asset. Some individuals are psychologically tuned to taking more risk than others. In particular, an individual, who is very careful in the use of assets, may yet be highly risk averse depending on his wealth position and the value of the asset. Greater risk aversion may lead to more careful use of assets. However, an individual, who knows that he is not very careful

[2]There is yet another dimension of the supplier-induced demand. It occurs when expensive drugs tend to be prescribed by a physician who also dispenses the medicines.

[3]As Klein and Wong (2009) noted, there is great heterogeneity of insurance seekers. A greater variety in the choice of contracts (with respect to coverage, service quality, and premium) may yet be the most efficient since a uniform insurance premium can reintroduce adverse selection.

in the use of the asset, may exhibit greater risk aversion. For all practical purposes, these two aspects are independent. From an analytical standpoint, this is also a dimension of individual-specific risk. Every individual will combine the effects of these risks with the cost of acquiring the asset and the expected costs of repair in case of an accident while conceptualizing an insurance contract.

Individuals seek insurance based on this private information. Insurance companies may specify policies based on individual-specific information if it is available. Similarly, when an individual takes an insurance policy, he is essentially sharing his risk with the insurer. He can expect that greater risks will make him bear a larger proportion of the risk. This feature, in itself, may be sufficient incentive for him to reduce individual-specific risk. Self-selection in private insurance markets may manifest itself in this form. Suppose all individuals can be expected to adapt their behavior optimally. Then, the insurance company may offer one contract to everyone. This will effectively eliminate the consequences of individual risk. However, this mechanism is not trustworthy. Individuals are not likely to initiate corrective action unless they are spurred into action by outside agents. Insurance companies may specify policies based on individual-specific information if it is available. However, they do not have this information and may find it rather expensive and impractical to elicit it even if they wish to make an attempt. As a result, they tend to offer one uniform policy or a limited set of options from which individuals can choose one. In this process of self-selection, individuals may not reveal their true type. It is actually possible that high-risk individuals seek greater insurance cover and/or show a willingness to pay a larger premium. Finkelstein and Poterba (2004) pointed out that many aspects of insurance contracts, not merely coverage or premiums, have seeds of adverse selection. This is another source of risk. It is a systemic risk in the sense that individual types are the basic source of such risk and no one in particular can be held responsible for it. The incidence of the risk will be initially on the insurer. He will design insurance contracts based on his perception and experiences with such a risk.

Observe that the efficient design of insurance contracts may depend on individual-specific characteristics and the systemic risk. The eventual impact of the changes in insurance on individuals, via the changes in insurance premium, coverage, and quality of service, suggests that they will also be sensitive to it. Some changes in the level of diligence in the use of assets and the degree of risk aversion may be expected. The magnitude and intensity of systemic risk may be reduced if individuals take collective responsibility. Whether or not such changes enable the insurer to design insurance policies without reference to the individual-specific and systemic risks remains an issue for analysis.

The insurance company may also create some risks as a result of its decision-making process. They may not, for instance, exercise proper caution in choosing the risks they insure. Similarly, they may make risky investments that do not lend themselves to desired recovery. Such risks are generally specific to one particular insurance company. But there can be risks imposed on them quite independent of their choices. For example, an economic downturn triggered by the reduction in the activity of another sector may make some of their investments vulnerable. Similarly, the emergence of the recent subprime crisis reduced the value of the investments of many insurance companies despite the caution each of them exercised in their portfolio choice. Such systemic risks may also make their operation quite vulnerable. Individuals, who insure with them, are subject to both these forms of risks. The insurance companies may exercise adequate control on their decisions when the likely risks are due to their actions. They may not be in a position to mitigate systemic risks through their actions. Similarly, they may not be in a position to counter some systemic risks even if all insurance companies take collective responsibility. Any analysis of efficient insurance contracts should deal with this aspect as well.

Some systemic risks are such that their magnitude and intensity can be reduced when individuals take collective responsibility. The existence of insurance and certain policies of insurance companies may also motivate them to cooperate. However, by their nature, some systemic risks cannot be predicted. Their sources and intensity will be revealed only ex post. Individuals cannot do much to adapt to such risks. Some regulatory policies may limit their impact. At least in some cases, even such policies may prove inefficient and inadequate.

In general, individuals and insurance companies enter into a contract before the emergence of risks. Suppose the sources and magnitude of some risks, irrespective of whether they are individual specific or systemic, can be estimated a priori. Both the participants in the contract may then design and implement corrective action. Perforce the magnitude and efficiency of the changes that they stipulate and implement depend on the costs of their design and enforcement. The requisite changes may not occur if the costs are too high relative to the expected benefits. When the costs increase with the magnitude of risk, individual action may therefore eliminate only a part of the risk. Large risks cannot be contained by individual action especially when the risks are systemic in nature. In such contexts the primary role of regulatory oversight will be to reduce the magnitude and incidence of systemic risks. When the source and extent of systemic risks cannot be determined ex ante, there is no way to modify the insurance contracts either through the actions of individuals or regulatory agencies. For all practical purposes, regulatory action must be exogenous to the design of insurance policies per se.

9.3 Accident Coverage

An automobile or a house can generally provide a certain amount of service to its user over a predefined horizon of time. However, it may be expected that an accident can occur while y units of service have yet to be realized.[4] The actual loss, in practice, may be random.[5] Let $y_a = y + u$ be the actual loss where u is a random variable

[4] Conceptually it would be simpler if even third-party liability is included here. In general, the insurance coverage is related to the expected loss in value. It will not be correlated with the cost of providing the service. The insurance premium will, however, be related to the cost of providing the service.

[5] In general, an insurance company insures almost any individual who seeks insurance with them. The only understanding is that they accept the conditions specified by the insurer. It is therefore

with an expected value $E(u)=0$ and variance $V(u)=\sigma^2$. u is entirely exogenous (systemic) and not due to the behavior or use by any one individual.[6] When an accident occurs, the insurance company sends the customer to a designated service station and gets the asset repaired.[7] There may be delays in recovering service. It is also possible that the repairs provided will be such that the entire $(y+u)$ can never be recovered. Let the actual recovery be $p(y+u)$. p is then an expression of the quality of service offered by the insurance contract.[8] Assume that the insurance premium which the individual pays is αy.

The gain to the individual will be

$$g_i = p(y+u) - \alpha y$$

In general, the insured can be expected to be risk averse. For, this feature makes him seek an insurance contract in the first place.[9] Hence, the value of g_i to him is

$$v_i = (p-\alpha)y - \lambda p^2\sigma^2$$

where λ represents his degree of risk aversion. Note that λ is one measure of risk. Its effect will be in the form of a reduction in the value of assets.

Assuming that there are many insurers, whose offer of service differentiates them from the others, the insured has the choice of p and the corresponding insurer. Maximizing v_i with respect to p yields

$$p = y/2\lambda\sigma^2$$

Suppose the asset is of high value and the expected loss when an accident occurs is also high. The insured will then seek better service quality in case of an accident.

---

entirely possible that a large variety of individuals with different attitudes towards the use of assets is insured. This can be represented by the randomness in y.

[6] The possibility that the actual loss is very little or there is no claim on the insurer must be acknowledged. $u<0$ in this specification signals this possibility.

[7] Clearly, it will be necessary to examine the contracts between the insurance company and the network of its service providers, for this may determine the quality of service and the cost of providing the service. Bourgeon et al. (2008) identified two aspects. First, the insurance companies prefer a long-term relationship with a service provider to avoid their monopolistic dominance. Second, there is a preference to contract with more than the optimum number of service providers to gain some monopoly power by lowering competition in insurance markets. However, this aspect will not be pursued in the present study.

[8] Note that the service station will initially set up its capital and other resources that are optimal to deliver the service y. They cannot suddenly create more infrastructures if the actual service requirement is high. Instead, they will try to cater to $(y+u)$ with the same infrastructure. The costs of providing the service will increase more than proportionately. This is one reason for the reduction in the quality of service. $u<0$ and underutilization of capacity can also increase the cost of providing service. This will be acknowledged in the following specification.

[9] Initially the impact of risk will be on the insurer. In general, the insurer attempts to transfer the risk on to the insured in the form of an increase in the insurance premium. The individuals can be expected to have much less ability to absorb these increments. As a result, they are likely to exhibit greater risk aversion relative to the insurer.

Let σ^2 be low. Then, the individual knows that the probability of loss is low. Given the insurance premium, he will then seek better service quality. Assume that λ is low. The insured is willing to take more risk. He will find it difficult to sustain this attitude if the quality of service is poor, for he realizes that he may be involved in more accidents and will lose a great deal of the value of the asset rapidly if p is low. This motivates him to seek a higher level of the quality of service.

The insurer must pay the service provider for the service $(y+u)$. As Chalkley and McVicar (2008) observed, cost-based payments are more efficient in comparison to those based on a fixed price per unit of service. It will be expected that the cost of repairs increases rapidly with $(y+u)$, since the facilities will be initially designed to cater to y at the lowest possible average cost. However, if the individual is careless in his use of the asset, the amount of damage and the necessity for repairs will be higher. Let the cost be $(y+u)^2/2\delta$ where δ is a measure of efficiency of use. Note that δ is also a measure of the individual-specific risk.[10] It manifests itself in the form of an increase in cost and a corresponding reduction in value to the insurer. The gain to the insurance company is

$$g_c = \alpha y - (y+u)^2/2\delta$$

In general, the insurer is dealing with a large and heterogeneous group of individuals. Hence, on an average he can offset risks from one against the lack of claim from others. That is, the insurer is expected to be risk neutral. Hence, the value of the contract to the insurer is[11]

$$v_c = \alpha y - \left(y^2 + \sigma^2\right)/2\delta$$

As noted earlier, the insurance company makes an assessment of the value of the asset before insuring it and determines the loss coverage (y) it is willing to offer. That is, y is the basic choice of the insurer. Maximizing[12] v_c yields $y = \alpha\delta$. That is, as Fenn et al. (2007) noted, an increase in α, or its very existence, increases the willingness to entertain larger claims.[13] However, a low δ, and the consequent increase

[10] In actual practice, the level of diligence of an insured individual may be difficult to judge from the available data. Usually the information available will be about age, how long the individual has been driving, history of accidents, and so on. δ is a reflection of such information. See, for example, Abbring et al. (2003).

[11] The insurance company will use the money, collected in the form of premiums, in various forms of investment (lending). These policies should be such that the company has adequate resources to pay insurance claims (their liabilities) as and when they arise.

[12] Strictly speaking, the insurance company maximizes its intensive margin once the response of the competitors is known. They can choose y alone. At the second stage, and consistent with the participation constraint of the individual insurance companies, the market will set α to maximize the extensive margin. No one insurance company may be in a position to fix it.

[13] Nell et al. (2009) argued that individuals tend to seek more health care if they are insured. That is, from the viewpoint of the insured, an increase in α tends to increase y ceteris paribus. The present model makes y supplier determined instead of the insured defining it ex ante. However, this result is valid in equilibrium. They also indicate that individuals tend to insure more if the cost of

in the cost of providing service, does not induce an increase in the supply of insurance. Substitution of the above choice of y in v_c results in

$$v_c = \alpha^2\delta/2 - \sigma^2/2\delta$$

In a competitive insurance market, the expected profit will be zero.[14] Hence, in equilibrium, the insurance premium can only be $\alpha = \sigma/\delta$. The corresponding choice of y will be $y = \sigma$. The equilibrium value of p reduces to $p = 1/2\lambda\sigma$.

The following observations regarding this equilibrium configuration are pertinent. First, a low value of δ induces the insurer to claim a larger insurance premium. This should not be interpreted to mean that low δ individuals will offer a larger premium ex ante. For, note that in practice and as assumed in the above model, the insured cannot generally express a preference for α. Instead, a more diligent individual, who uses the asset more carefully, is rewarded by having to pay a lower premium. Further, a higher expectation of systemic risk induces the insurer to seek a larger premium. Second, observe that as λ increases, the high risk aversion will induce the individual to be more careful in the use of the assets. Since the residual loss is low, he does not ask for better quality of service. The possibility that the individual may adjust λ based on the variations in δ will be examined below. Third, an increase in systemic risk, but not a low value of δ per se, is the only consideration that induces the insured to seek more insurance cover.[15] In other words, this theoretical framework is consistent with the empirical observation that there is no evidence of ex ante adverse selection in insurance contracts.[16] Fourth, consider the equilibrium value of v_i. It is given by

---

service increases. In the present framework, the demand for insurance is not affected by the cost of service since it is postulated that the individual does not pay for it anyway.

[14] Two observations are pertinent. First, suppose the insurance market is oligopolistic. Then, the insurer may discriminate among different groups of individuals by charging different insurance premiums so as to maximize v_c. Second, there is a general agreement that sharing risks results in spreading greater risks and creating further volatility in the system. However, it can be easily verified that in this model, irrespective of the nature of the insurance market, neither the insurer nor individuals gain by increasing the systemic risk. The real problem with insurance is that it cannot contain risks of large magnitude and not that it augments risks in the system by spreading risks among the participants.

[15] Suppose there is a ceteris paribus increase in the cost of service. Then, in the absence of insurance, the individual stands to lose. There is a justification to the argument that it induces a greater demand for insurance. However, the available empirical evidence is not sufficiently conclusive to consider it as a stylized fact. In particular, note that the present model does not sustain this expectation.

[16] The insurer generally obtains an accountant's valuation of the asset being insured before determining the coverage. To that extent, the insurer does not experience any adverse selection. However, on occasions, the remaining value of an automobile is associated with its age alone. Adverse selection is then possible. Similarly, observe that the insurer may not really base the decisions regarding the premium charged and the quality of service on the efficiency of use or risk aversion of individuals. Instead, one single specification will be applied to everybody. In such a case adverse selection with respect to these dimensions cannot be ruled out. Empirical tests, that utilize only insurance coverage, cannot capture these details.

$$v_i = 1/4\lambda - \sigma^2/\delta$$

Hence, an increase in σ^2 cannot improve his value. That is, the insurance mechanism does not allow him to pass the entire risk on to the insurer. Further, $v_i \geq 0$ if and only if $\delta \geq 4\lambda\sigma^2$. Only individuals who exhibit adequately high diligence will insure. It will not be available to individuals with low δ and/or high risk aversion.[17] The equilibrium choices exclude several individuals who seek insurance. Fifth, observe that v_i increases with an increase in δ and/or a reduction in λ. Hence, the insured may be prompted to reveal a higher value of diligence and lower risk aversion ex ante based on the variations in σ that they observe. This may induce the insurer to charge a lower premium as well as offer better quality of service.

Observe that as σ increases, the insurance companies seek larger premiums, lower the quality of service offered, and leave out several individuals who seek insurance otherwise. It would be pertinent to examine the possibility that individuals regulate themselves in the choices of δ and λ based on variations in σ and thereby induce insurance companies to offer more and better service.[18]

Jullien et al. (1999) suggested the possibility that as σ varies individuals may find it advantageous to adjust δ to maximize their gain.[19] In particular, if an accident occurs despite full cooperation from the insured, they will be entitled to full compensation in the form of the lowest insurance premium.[20] It can be readily verified that minimizing α with respect to σ assuming that $\delta = \delta(\sigma)$ results in

$$\delta = c\sigma$$

where c is a measure of the ease with which individuals can take better care of their assets.[21] The corresponding choice of α will be $1/c$. When individuals are capable of

---

[17] Note that this is quite the opposite of the results obtained in models that emphasize adverse selection alone. For, the typical conclusion of such studies is that the equilibrium consists of individuals with lower probability of accident purchasing no insurance and individuals with higher accident probability purchasing a fair level of insurance. This result can be obtained if the costs incurred by the service provider are $(y+u)/\delta$. For, in such a case, the equilibrium contract choices will be $p = 1/\delta = \alpha$ and $y = 2\lambda\sigma^2/\delta$. That is, the higher the δ, and hence the lower the probability of accidents, the lower will be the insurance coverage sought by individuals. The nature of the cost function, estimable in any given empirical context, has a crucial effect on the structure of the equilibrium contract.

[18] Suppose there is no systemic risk at all. Then, the specification of this equilibrium suggests that there will be no necessity for any insurance. Since δ is the only source of risk in such a context, it can be expected that individuals exercise due diligence in the use of assets and bear the consequences of their carelessness, if any.

[19] Self-selection and self-regulation have been recurring themes. See, for instance, Snow (2009).

[20] As Rutten et al. (2001) pointed out, government regulators usually force the insurer to charge a uniform (constant) insurance premium from the heterogeneous risk groups. Note that insurance contracts generally, including those involving deductibles, are not tailored to specific individuals. Instead of being exclusive, they tend to be uniform for all risk classes. High-risk individuals are de facto subsidized. This creates the specter of adverse selection.

[21] In practice, the costs of making adjustments of this nature appear to be very large. This may be one reason why insurance companies offer a wide variety of policies from which individuals can select. This reasoning is quite independent of adverse selection as the basis for such a variety.

utilizing the product better and agree to do so, the insurer offers the lowest premium.[22] Observe that for this configuration of choices

$$v_{\mathrm{i}} = (1/4\lambda\sigma) - (\sigma/c)$$

so that a reduction in c improves v_{i}. That is, a lower c induces individuals with lower δ to seek insurance. This cannot be considered as adverse selection since the insurance company is not losing anything.[23] The practical difficulty with this approach is that the insured generally experiences acute information asymmetry with respect to systemic risk. Even this phenomenon makes the cost of adjustment rather high. That is, the value of c will be rather small, and it would be difficult to satisfy the above inequality. Individual habits and inertia may be such that it may be difficult to achieve the anticipated changes in δ and c. Hence, this is not a reliable mechanism in practice. Similarly, they may adjust λ as σ^2 varies. In particular, suppose σ^2 is high. p will be smaller in equilibrium given λ. High risk aversion worsens the situation. Hence, when there is high systemic risk, the only way individuals can induce the insurer to offer better service is by lowering their risk aversion and agreeing to share the risk. Hence, maximizing p will yield

$$\lambda = \theta/\sigma$$

where θ is also an indicator of the relative ease with which the insured can adjust λ to variations in σ. Such cooperation results in the choice

$$p = 1/2\theta$$

by the insurer. Notice that these choices are independent of the environmental risk and the individual-specific characteristics.[24]

It would be pertinent to examine the possibility that the insured individual gains from such behavior. Note that $\lambda = \theta/\sigma$, $\alpha = \sigma/\delta$, $p = 1/2\theta$, and $y = \sigma$ so that

$$v_{\mathrm{i}} = \sigma/4\theta - \sigma^2/\delta > 0 \text{ if and only if } \sigma < \delta/4\theta$$

---

[22] Observe that the equilibrium values of y and p do not depend on δ. Hence, this is the only plausible interpretation of the adjustments in δ to variations in σ^2.

[23] The following argument is also pertinent. Suppose individuals are willing to cooperate and adjust δ and λ to variations in σ^2. This results in the insurance company offering one single insurance policy to everyone. Saying that this mechanism leads to adverse selection is somewhat of a contradiction because individuals agreed to comply in the first place. The argument will be valid only if the insurers themselves proposed such policies without ascertaining the willingness on the part of the insured to comply. Making δ and λ adapt to some form of deductible insurance may have to be utilized to establish the willingness of the insured to comply. This will be examined in the analysis that follows.

[24] The argument is premised on the assumption that individuals, who know that they have a greater risk of accident, will seek more complete coverage if many contract options are on offer. As Abbring et al. (2003) pointed out, low-risk individuals may lose the incentive to insure if a fixed contract is offered to everyone. Hence, such arrangements have a limited role in reducing the risk.

The insured will gain if and only if this condition is satisfied. Individuals' adaptation of risk taking to systemic risk is superior if and only if the systemic risks are relatively low. Note, further, that the optimal choices of δ and λ specified here are adjustments to an exogenously determined σ. Self-regulation by individuals, even if it manifests itself, can at best moderate individual risks. They cannot reduce the systemic risk per se.

Chiappori (2000) observed that if individuals self-select on the basis of their private information about the degree of risk, that is they will choose a high δ when they expect a high σ^2, then coverage and expected costs should be positively correlated. That is, y and δ will be positively related. Similarly, coverage and systemic risk should be positively correlated. That is, y and σ will be positively correlated. The above analysis is in line with these expectations.

In general, such self-regulation is superior only when the systemic risks are low. In essence, it may be argued that self-regulation and the operation of a competitive insurance market will result in a better value for individuals only when the extent of systemic risk is within certain bounds.

One alternative that suggests itself is regulation of the insured by insurance companies with a view to elicit cooperative behavior from them. For, an increase in insurance coverage increases the costs of the insurers. Hence, it will be natural to make the insured bear some of these costs. Usually this takes the form of specifying some restrictions in the use of assets, e.g., preventive maintenance. Assume that the insurer expects the insured to accept periodic preventive maintenance and bear ky^2 of costs. In general, they may ask the insured to get a certification from their network of service stations. The resulting gains to the insured will then be

$$g_i = p(y+u) - \alpha y - ky^2, \text{ and}$$
$$v_i = (p-\alpha)y - ky^2 - \lambda p^2\sigma^2$$

The choice of p will again be $p = y/2\lambda\sigma^2$. Similarly, the gain to the insurance company is

$$g_c = \alpha y + ky^2 - (y+u)^2/2\delta, \text{ so that}$$
$$v_c = \alpha y + ky^2 - (y^2+\sigma^2)/2\delta$$

Consequently, they will choose

$$y = \alpha\delta/(1-2k\delta);\ 2k\delta < 1$$

Since the resulting $v_c = 0$ when $\alpha = \sigma/\delta$, there will be no change in the insurance premium per se. However,

$$y = \sigma/(1-2k\delta), \text{ and } p = \sigma/2\lambda\sigma^2(1-2k\delta)$$

indicate that both the risk coverage and the quality of service will improve. The purpose of choosing k is to induce the insured to choose $\delta = \delta(k)$ in such a way that maximum coverage can be provided. Maximizing y results in $k\delta = a$ (a constant). It can also be verified that the cost of preventive maintenance decreases with an increase in the diligence exercised by the insured. The corresponding value of v_i will be positive if

$$\delta > 4\lambda\sigma^2 (1 - \mathrm{a})$$

That is, some more risks will be insured. It may be concluded that risks generated by individuals can be fairly effectively controlled, but these mechanisms cannot reduce systemic risks.

Another possibility should be considered now. Initially, the insured will reveal a high δ and low λ so that he can elicit a low insurance premium and better quality of service. Now, suppose, the insured lowers his guard after the contract is signed. Note that

$$v_c = \alpha^2\delta/2 - \sigma^2/2\delta$$

Consequently,

$$dv_c/d\delta = \alpha^2/2 + \sigma^2/2\delta^2$$

At the equilibrium choice $\alpha\delta = \sigma$, this becomes $\sigma^2/\delta^2 > 0$. Hence, a reduction in δ reduces v_c. The insurer will lose in the resulting configuration. This is the genesis of possible moral hazard in insurance contracts. The insurer may, on his part, initiate some mechanisms to elicit compliance from the insured. A deductible insurance is the usual mechanism to mitigate this moral hazard.

Three approaches to defining deductibles are discernible:

- A fixed amount (usually chosen by the individual).
- Proportional to u; that is, a rebate is offered when the individual did not make claims in the past or an increase in the premium when he did make a claim.
- Proportional to the cost of service.

Fenn et al. (2007) noted the fact that an individual who paid for insurance may induce excess claims and deductibles can control such tendencies. Blomqvist and Leger (2005), among others, documented the effect of different payment mechanisms and insurance schemes on the utilization of services. Pauly and Blavin (2008) suggested the following. (a) Cost sharing form of deductibles will not be the best for services with higher benefits relative to costs. (b) Fearing excessive cost patients may not seek efficient health care. Deductibles that share costs on the basis of value of services may avoid this. (c) Deductibles place a financial burden on the insured. However, it is necessary to expose the insured to such financial risk to avoid their lowering the level of caution relative to the cost of providing the service. (d) Suppose the valuation of service by the insured is higher than that of the service provider or insurer. The individual should then be asked to bear the excess in the form of a deductible. This can be illustrated as follows. In the context of an automobile accident, the insured may feel that the service provider assigned by the insurer is not restoring full value. The individual may then prefer to go to a service station that restores full value even if he has to bear a part of the cost in the form of a deductible. Technological innovations are available to record driver behavior on a real-time basis. Hence, the deductibles can be tuned to a variety of factors that eventually create the loss due to an accident.

The efficiency of these mechanisms will now be examined sequentially. Let β be the fixed amount of deductible in the insurance contract. It can be readily verified that the efficient contract consists of

$$\alpha = \left(\sigma^2 - 2\beta\delta\right)^{1/2}/\delta,\ y = \left(\sigma^2 - 2\beta\delta\right)^{1/2},\ \text{and}\ p = \left(\sigma^2 - 2\beta\delta\right)^{1/2}/2\lambda\sigma^2$$

Clearly, both the risk coverage and service quality are lower. Less serious accidents will not attract as much attention of the insurer as the more serious ones mostly because the costs are lower and the service station does not gain much. Similarly, the insured may prefer not to claim.[25] Note, further, that the optimized value will be

$$v_{\mathrm{i}} = 1/4\lambda - \sigma^2/\delta - 2\beta\delta/\lambda\sigma^2$$

It follows that some individuals with δ values above $4\lambda\sigma^2$ will not take the deductible insurance. δ should be high enough to entice individuals to enter the insurance contract. With higher δ, the individual feels that the probability of an accident is lower and he does not need as much insurance cover as before. Similarly, he will pay less by way of premium because he is bearing a part of the loss by himself. It can also be verified that v_{i} reduces whatever be the value of β. Hence, the individual prefers $\beta=0$.

Suppose, on the other hand, that the deductibles take the form βu. It can be shown that the efficient contract is

$$\alpha = \sigma/\delta, y = \sigma,\ \text{and}\ p = \left(1/2\lambda\sigma\right) + \beta$$

Hence, it follows that

$$v_{\mathrm{i}} = 1/4\lambda - \sigma^2/\delta + \beta\sigma \geq 0$$

for lower values of δ. Alternatively, higher-risk individuals will also be attracted to take the insurance. The insurance mechanism will therefore cover more individuals than before. The essential difference is that the insurer offers better quality of service.

There is a practical difficulty in making deductibles proportional to cost. In general, it is easy to verify that $u>0$ when an excessive claim is made and $u<0$ when

[25] The argument is basically that the cost of getting the service outside the insurance network may be less than the deductible in the insurance premium when claims are relatively small.

there is no claim.[26] But it is not equally easy to ascertain the cost changes. Since deductibles must be defined before observing u, they must be defined as $\beta y^2/2\delta$. With this proviso in perspective, note that $\alpha = \sigma(1-\beta)^{1/2}/\delta$ and $v_i \geq 0$ if and only if $\delta \geq 2\lambda\sigma^2(2-\beta)$. Even some less diligent individuals will take the insurance. For, accidents will be more frequent if the insured is less diligent. This will inflate costs and insurance premium. Hence, everybody will be more diligent. The premium will fall,[27] risk coverage will improve, and so will the quality of service.[28]

In retrospect, it can be claimed that a rebate for no claim and/or an increase in insurance premium when there is a claim can be most closely related to the extent of ex post moral hazard. It should not be a surprise that βu form of deductible is preferred by the insurer as well as the insured. See, for example, Felder (2008).

However, some disadvantages of this form of deductible insurance should be noted. In practice, the volatility in the use of the asset has two sources: the diligence with which the insured uses the asset (δ) and the systemic risk (σ^2) that is not under his control. It would be pertinent to investigate the efficient choice of β that improves δ. Two parameters are subject to the choice of the insured, viz., the level of diligence (δ) and his degree of risk aversion (λ). If he adjusts both of these appropriately, he can claim that the occurrence of an accident is purely exogenous to his choices and that he should be entitled to the lowest possible insurance premium (α) and the highest possible quality of service (p).[29] Note that the equilibrium choice of α does not depend on β. Hence, it is not possible to define a β that minimizes α by altering δ. In general, therefore, it would be unrealistic to expect the insured to alter δ based on the choice of β. Levels of diligence are hard to modify. The only possibility is that fearing a payment of higher premium when an accident occurs and a claim is made the insured may exhibit greater risk aversion due to the associated losses. It is reasonable to expect that the insurer will offer the best quality if λ adjusts fully. Consider the maximization of p assuming that $\lambda = \lambda(\beta)$. This results in the choice

$$\lambda^* = 1/(d - \sigma\beta)$$

---

[26] Empirical observation appears to indicate that no collision rebates tend to make individuals lower guard and thereby create more accidents. However, this appears implausible intuitively because no one would invite an accident just because they are covered by the insurance. The efficacy of deductible insurance has been difficult to judge.

[27] Chiappori (2000) pointed out that deductible insurance policies will be attractive only if the variable part of the insurance premium is reduced.

[28] Note that making the insured commit to periodic checkup and bear the cost $\beta y^2/2\delta$ is one alternative available to the insurer in his efforts to make the insured more diligent. Analytically these two concepts are similar. Also notice that this choice does serve the purpose of making the insurer cover some less diligent individuals as well.

[29] Pauly and Blavin (2008) argued that p should increase to 1. For, otherwise, the insured may exercise the option of taking the asset to the service station that restores its full value and bear the deductible that the insurance company is unwilling to pay. The efficient β according to this viewpoint is $\beta = 1 - (1/2\lambda\sigma)$. In practice p is observed to be around .5. This is clearly inadequate. It may compel the insured to propose a fairly high deductible to elicit better quality of service.

where d is a constant. If $\beta=0$, the value of $\lambda^*=\lambda$. Hence, $d=1/\lambda$. It follows that

$$\lambda^* = \lambda/(1-2\sigma\beta\lambda) > \lambda \text{ for all } \beta > 0.$$

Strictly speaking, insurance should offer risk coverage, but it need not leave any surplus in the hands of the insured. Hence, the optimal value of β is

$$\beta^* = (\delta - 4\lambda\sigma^2)/4\lambda\sigma(\delta - 2\lambda\sigma^2)$$

In other words, this form of deductible insurance does not really eliminate or reduce systemic volatility. It merely transfers it from one level to another. In general, the insurer trying to induce individuals to comply by using a deductible insurance policy fails to improve the system behavior and cannot, in any case, reduce the systemic risk. This feature signals the need for a more explicit regulatory policy from some outside agency.

9.4 Health Insurance

It is fairly obvious that many of the results in the previous section are applicable even in the context of health insurance. For, there are some parallels between the context of accidents and medical problems encountered by individuals. However, some features of providing health services necessitate specific attention.

One common feature is that the insurance coverage is related to the expected loss in value rather than the cost of providing the service. For, as Hernandez (2003) pointed out, when a patient thinks about whether or not to seek hospital or physician care he looks at the nature of the problem and the disutility it creates rather than the cost of getting the treatment. Hence, insurance is for certain illnesses rather than some amount of money. However, modeling insurance contracts for distinct illnesses is unrealistic because observed contracts are of a more general nature encompassing many types of medical services.

Individuals do have the ability to protect themselves from several diseases. However, carelessness in protecting themselves does lead to illness. This feature is captured by δ in the previous section. This is one aspect of individual risk. An individual, who is otherwise capable of protecting himself, may yet prefer to take the risk. This is the other source of individual-centered risk reflected in the specification of λ in section 2. Thus, there is a clear distinction between δ and λ as they pertain to an individual.

Even in the context of health issues, there will be some systemic risks over and above individual risks. To illustrate this, note that no one individual in particular can be blamed for the outbreak of an epidemic. Similarly, no one or a group of individuals can foresee the advent of incidents like the swine flu.

Individuals can exercise sufficient caution to protect themselves even when there is an outbreak of a major health condition (say, like the swine flu). The costs of doing so are relatively low. That is, the parameter c utilized in section 2 is rather large in the present context. This is in contrast to individual behavior in the context of accidents. Further, note that individuals generally become highly risk averse when an epidemic breaks out. Hence, in the context of personal health care, even θ tends to be large. Several systemic risks will be such that individuals can easily adapt their behavior to counter their effect to a large extent. For instance, note that after the outbreak of swine flu, individuals could adapt their caution to prevent it from affecting them. However, some health conditions may yet be beyond their ability to adjust. It is necessary for public health authorities to reduce the incidence of such systemic risks rather than expect individuals to adjust after it manifests itself.

One feature of medical problems is glaring. In most practical contexts, the effects are exclusively on the individual and do not affect others. This is unlike the third-party problems in the case of accidents. As a result, in most of the outpatient care, where the value addition and the cost of providing service are low, individuals pay for the health care. They do not depend on insurance. Only when the costs are likely to be high, perhaps due to the necessity for hospitalization, will individuals seek any insurance. As Nell et al. (2009) argued, individuals tend to seek larger insurance cover when the expected costs of required services increase. Rutten et al. (2001) pointed out that a crucial benefit of health insurance is that it provides access to otherwise unaffordable health care.

In general, individuals confront another aspect of systemic risk that is specific to health problems. By their nature, modern medical technologies are capital intensive and expensive. Hospitals tend to build up infrastructure to cater to a certain level of service (y) efficiently. Individual-specific and systemic risks, alluded to above, introduce some randomness into the service requirements. Deviations from the capacity levels of service tend to inflate costs significantly. Consequently, there will be risks introduced by the variations in costs. In their efforts to maximize their profits (or sustain their activities), both hospitals and physicians tend to create artificial (supplier-induced) demand.[30] This is generally looked upon as a mechanism to utilize the infrastructure more efficiently.[31] Clearly, this aspect of systemic risk is specific to the provision of medical services alone. Individuals may find it difficult to counter such risks which can be essentially systemic since no individual or insurer is causing them. It may be necessary for individuals to act collectively to negate such systemic risks.

[30] Boadway et al. (2004) pointed out that leaving patient care to hospitals is a double-edged sword; it may reduce transaction costs, but it may induce more than necessary treatment or high-cost treatment in collusion with equipment manufacturers and drug companies. This phenomenon may be observed even in those cases where the physician also dispenses medicines.

[31] Blomqvist and Leger (2005) argued that moral hazard from doctors and supplier-induced demand can be controlled if the hospitals and doctors become employees of the insurance company. In practice, this is observed in a few cases. Boadway et al. (2004) noted that much regulatory policy is devoted to alter hospital behavior and contain supplier-induced demand. However, as Rutten et al. (2001) pointed out, more attention must be devoted to identify mechanisms to improve physician efficiency. It is not possible to depend on only one instrument of choice to achieve the desired results.

The first aspect that requires attention is the increase in costs and implications for efficient insurance contracts. Observe that in the context of accidents, the individual-induced risk u is qualitatively of the same kind as y so that the specification of cost to the service provider $(y+u)^2/2\delta$ was justified. However, in the case of health care, this risk u may be systemic as well, and the costs are likely to be higher. They can be represented by $y^2/2\delta+mu^2$. The expected cost in the old scheme was $(y^2+\sigma^2)/2\delta$, while in the new scheme it will be $y^2/2\delta+m\sigma^2$. Hence, the costs will increase if $2m\delta>1$. This specification has no effect on the ex ante choice of p. The insured will choose $p=y/2\lambda\sigma^2$. Similarly, the choice of y by the insurance company will again be $y=\alpha\delta$. However, the competitive choice of α will now be $\alpha=(2m/\delta)^{1/2}\sigma$. It can be readily inferred that p, y, and α will increase if $2m\delta>1$. That is, both under utilization and over utilization of hospital capacity may lead to steep increases in cost. This causes α to increase. But it does not deter individuals from seeking more insurance coverage. For in its absence they fear the risk of having to pay more for health care from their own resources. One qualification is however in order. Suppose, as claimed by the hospitals, stabilizing demand around their capacity level reduces cost. Supplier-induced demand may then result in a reduction in σ. α and y will decrease, and the quality of service will improve. Hence, contrary to the usual arguments, this pattern of behavior on the part of the service providers may indeed be advantageous. Observe that $v_i>0$ if and only if $\delta>4\lambda\sigma^2$. That is, there is no possibility of more risks being covered by the insurance even after the supplier attempts to influence demand for the services of the hospitals to stabilize demand at capacity levels.

Felder (2008) noted that an optimal insurance contract may in fact stipulate that some payments for health care will not be a part of the insurance cover. This may be over and above outpatient care. One reason for this may be the fact that insurance premiums cannot increase proportional to cost. For note that in equilibrium

$$\alpha y = 2m\sigma^2 = y^2/2\delta + m\sigma^2$$

Hence, they may be induced to eliminate as many services as they can from insurance contract. The insurer may also increase the fixed cost component of the insurance premium to force individuals to stay with them over a longer duration. This may have the effect of stabilizing the demand for hospital services. However, it can affect the hospitals and insurers adversely in so far as the frequency and cost of treatment for some ailments like asthma or diabetics may increase during the tenure of the contract. The fixed component of the insurance premium per se will be inadequate against such a contingency.

The argument that individuals can counter some health risks is sound. It may apply even in the context of some systemic risks. However, following the arguments of the previous section, it can be shown that such diligence can neutralize only limited risks. Risk coverage improves in such cases, and some reduction in insurance premium can be achieved. However, especially large systemic risks and those that cannot be anticipated ex ante do not offer any such chance. In general, the efficacy of this mechanism also depends on the cost-effectiveness of such adaptations.

In general, if an individual had the experience of a particular ailment in the past, the probability of its recurrence increases. The implied increases in cost induce the insurer to deny coverage or charge a rather high premium. Individuals tend to seek health insurance over a longer duration of time to protect against this contingency. Longer-term contracts may also mean that when an individual is younger, he is likely to keep claims at a low level, and this feature subsidizes claims at a later stage. This may be an adequate inducement for insurers to offer long-term contracts. This lock in, or continuous affiliation, may however provide an incentive to the service providers (physicians or hospitals) to suggest more than necessary and expensive treatment to patients. This supplier-induced demand inflates risk premiums. On the whole, long-term contracts may be a mixed blessing from the viewpoint of the insured and the insurer.

However, if employers take insurance on behalf of their employees, the younger individuals subsidize the claims of older workers. Crocker and Moran (2002) emphasized this aspect explicitly. This alternative may also help stabilize the revenues of the insurance companies, reduce the total insurance coverage, and keep insurance premiums under control. It can also have the effect of reducing risks of the insurer. The important issue in this context is not about individual and/or systemic risks being absorbed by the mechanism. Instead, it pertains to the sharing of the insurance premium among the employees. In general, it is expected that the total risk coverage decreases below the sum of what each individual will seek if they acted in isolation. Premium will decrease proportionately. It can be written as

$$\alpha y = \left(\sum n_j^{\varepsilon}\right)^{\beta/\varepsilon}; \quad 0 < \varepsilon < 1, \beta < \varepsilon$$

where n_j is the number of employees of risk type $j; j = 1, 2, \ldots, n$

It can be readily verified that $\beta < \varepsilon$ is necessary to claim that there will be a reduction in risk coverage as a result of such a group insurance. The issue at hand is to efficiently determine the premium to be paid by an individual belonging to group j. Define

$$\alpha_j = \beta n_j^{\varepsilon-1} \left(\sum n_j^{\varepsilon}\right)^{\beta/\varepsilon-1}$$

Then, $\sum \alpha_j n_j = \beta \left(\sum n_j^{\varepsilon}\right)^{\beta/\varepsilon} = \alpha y$ if and only if $\beta = \alpha$. This will not be satisfied in general. More pertinent is the possibility that when $\beta > \alpha$ some surplus accrues to the employer. In such a case, an efficient distribution will be to define $\alpha_j^* = \theta \alpha_j$ such that $\alpha = \theta \beta$. It may be noted that in health insurance, the equilibrium distribution of premium is such that the rates individuals pay exceed the marginal cost so that consumer surplus accrues to insurers. However, they did not consider this alternative way of distributing premiums paid by the firm among its employees.

Health insurance coverage is generally subject to two problems as mentioned above, viz., the need to stabilize demand around capacity levels to minimize costs of providing service and to reduce systemic risks arising out of the heterogeneity of the behavior of the insured. Basically the high cost of service is the reason why an insurance company cannot offer more services. If they can control these costs or make individuals share the costs (in addition to the insurance premium) it would be possible to improve insurance coverage. Some medical conditions, like asthma or diabetics, require frequent treatment. The insurer may then specify that the insured go to hospitals specified in his network for periodic checkup. In general the insured will be expected to pay for such checkup. The hospitals may also find this satisfactory because their services will be used to capacity levels on a continuing basis. Cochrane (2009), for example, argued that this mechanism will eliminate the risk of excluding those with a precondition. It also helps insurance companies to specify uniform policies for all insured with respect to coverage and premium.

It is often suggested that an adequate system of risk-adjusted premium subsidies combined with ex post risk sharing could effectively guarantee fairness while reducing adverse and favorable selection in competitive health insurance markets. However, as noted above, the available instruments, in the operation of private markets for insurance, may be unequal to the task at hand. Regulatory oversight and social health schemes will be necessary to improve coverage and quality of service and lower insurance premiums.

9.5 Regulation

The analysis of the preceding two sections clearly indicates the following. First, private insurance mechanisms will not cover some risks and/or offer low enough insurance premiums even when individuals optimally change their level of diligence and risk aversion in the use of assets. Second, in the context of health, some group insurance policies may benefit both the insured and the insurer. Even so, large systemic risks will not be covered adequately. Further, some problems arise in the context of group members sharing the premium. Third, regulatory policy to reduce the incidence of systemic risks may help individuals and insurance companies to make appropriate adaptations and improve the nature of private insurance. Ex post adaptation to systemic risks is expensive and difficult to manage. Fourth, high systemic risks also attract larger premiums and reduce quality. Hence, regulating systemic risk is important. For instance, it is necessary for public health authorities to reduce the incidence of systemic risks rather than expect individuals to adjust after they manifest themselves. However, at some stage it is difficult to anticipate the emergence of systemic risk. Ex post protection by a public agency then becomes necessary for the survival of the insurance industry. Fifth, optimal health insurance must pay attention to the distribution of health care since optimal designs may exclude a large group that needs insurance but do not have the capacity to pay. Social insurance policies will need to be conceptualized in addition to privately financed policies. Designing institutional mechanisms to deliver such services, in addition to their efficient financing, has been the real challenge.

One alternative has been to entice private insurance companies to increase coverage, lower premiums, and improve the quality of service. Regulators, or public agencies, may provide cost subsidy for certain classes of basic services.[32] The second alternative is to regulate premiums directly. However, note that this may have an adverse effect on coverage and quality of service since the costs cannot be adequately absorbed in the operation of competitive insurance markets. The third alternative is to provide some basic health services through an independent network of government hospitals.

The receipt of insurance premiums and payments to insured in case of accidents are mediated through the insurance company. Hence, the way the insurer invests the money, and consequently its financial health, determines timely payments. If the insurance company can generate more resources by investing the premiums wisely, it is possible to reduce the premium or provide better service or wider coverage. But this process is subject to risks. The insurance company may choose the proper balance on its own. If they fail to do so and eventually create a systemic risk, they must be regulated. Cummins (2005) and Cowley and Cummins (2005) among others dealt with the financial and securitization aspects explicitly.

To begin with, consider the possibility that the regulator attempts to alter the behavior of private insurers in such a way that they take care of a larger group of individuals, offer better service, and charge lower premiums. See, for example, Snow (2009). Subsidizing the cost of service agents is one such mechanism. Assume that the public agency provides a fraction $(1-q)$ of the cost of service as a subsidy. The rest of the cost will be borne by the insurer. It can be readily verified that the equilibrium contract choice becomes $y=\sigma$, $\alpha=q\sigma/\delta$, and $p=1/2\lambda\sigma$. However, since

$$v_{\mathrm{i}} = (1/4\lambda) - (q\sigma^2/\delta)$$

the choice of q to maximize v_{i} is not obvious. Note that the most important effect of the choice of q is on the insurance premium. Hence, the regulatory agency may choose a δ above which it wants the service at the lowest possible premium. It will have the effect of maximizing v_{i}. Let $q=q(\delta)$ be chosen to maximize q/δ. Such a choice of $q=a\delta$ where a is a constant. That is, if the regulator chooses to make insurance available to all individuals with $\delta \geq \delta^*$, he will fix $q=a\delta^*$. The resulting v_{i}, viz.,

$$v_{\mathrm{i}} = (1/4\lambda) - (a\delta^*\sigma^2/\delta) > 0$$

if and only if $\delta > 4a\delta^*\sigma^2$. The regulator's objective is fulfilled if and only if $a < 1/4\lambda\sigma^2$. That is, the policy will be efficient only if the subsidies are large enough. Large values of a and/or σ^2 will not yield the desired result.

[32] Providing a direct subsidy to insured on the premiums they need to pay is the other alternative. But it is expensive to enforce. Hence, the option examined here is efficient.

The second alternative available to the regulator is to fix α^*. Clearly, α^* must be chosen such that $\alpha^*\delta = \sigma$ and maximize

$$v_i = (1/4\lambda) - (\sigma^2/\delta)$$

Hence, α^* should be made a function of σ to minimize δ. Such a choice is clearly

$$\alpha^* = b\sigma;\ b = \text{constant}$$

The corresponding δ choice will be $1/b$. When this choice is in place

$$v_i = (1/4\lambda) - b\sigma^2 > 0$$

only if $b < 1/4\lambda\sigma^2$. That is, even this policy regulation will yield the desired results only under certain conditions.

In general, regulatory policies of this nature operate efficiently only if some conditions are satisfied. In particular, large values of σ^2 will not be efficiently eliminated.

The regulator may directly segment the market and provide exclusive public health schemes to those in need. Suppose health services $p(y+u)$ will be offered and the public agency bears the entire cost $(y+u)^2/2\delta$. The gain to the society can be written as[33]

$$g = p(y+u) - (y+u)^2/2\delta$$

Maximizing v with respect to y results in the choice $y = p\delta$. The quality of service offered must be determined. Three alternatives may be conceptualized. First, p may be made a function of δ to maximize the coverage y. This results in the choice $p = b/\delta$ where b is a constant. The resulting

$$v = (p^2\delta/2) - (\sigma^2/2\delta) > 0$$

if and only if $b > \sigma/\delta$. That is, the policy is efficient only for some individuals. Second, p may be made a function of δ to maximize v. It results in

$$p^2\delta = \delta^* + \sigma^2(1/\delta - 1/\delta^*)$$

[33] In any equilibrium configuration, these costs will be financed by taxing all individuals in the society. This group of beneficiaries may end up paying only a fraction of the cost. Maximizing the net benefit to this segment may be a legitimate objective of public policy. The analysis can be modified if this approach is considered to be more appropriate.

The resulting v is positive if and only if $\sigma < \delta^*$. Once again large values of σ^2 cannot make such regulatory policy efficient. Third, p can be chosen to be a function of σ^2 to maximize v. It can be shown that

$$p^2 = \left(\sigma^2 / \delta^2\right) + \text{constant}$$

However, the regulator desires to achieve the best service ($p = 1$) for some low enough δ^*. The constant can be determined accordingly. Note that even under this alternative $v > 0$ only for some values of σ^2.

Observe that public health services are expected to have the effect of reducing systemic risks. That is, the tendency to reduce σ^2 may help making such policies efficient. However, modeling the externality offered by public health policy and the corresponding reduction in σ^2 is not obvious.

In general, it may be necessary to operate public health schemes along with private insurance to provide efficient health care to a large segment of the population. It should also be noted that there is a limit set by policy instruments available to the regulator to make dependence on him efficient.

Results pertaining to the investment and financial choices of insurance companies can be developed in an analogous fashion. See Rao (2009, 2010) for details. They will not be reproduced here essentially because the conclusions are rather similar to those presented here.

Insurance regulators have been dealing with a vast array of such activities. Risks generated by individuals, as they affect system performance, can be regulated. Exogenously created risks are hard to deal with using any form of ex ante regulatory instruments. In general, only one or a few instruments, either related to individual choice or regulatory behavior, will not produce the desired efficiency. A multi-pronged approach is necessary.

9.6 Limits of Insurance

In retrospect it can be claimed that the major results of this study are in line with sophisticated common sense. Suppose the risk originates in the actions of the individual. Then, it would be possible for the individual to initiate effective corrective action so long as the costs of doing so do not exceed the resulting benefits. Similarly, the insurance company may be in a position to initiate corrective action to induce the individual to comply with stability requirements. Self-regulation and market discipline in this sense are efficient within certain bounds. However, some regulatory mechanisms are necessary if risks exceed certain limits and/or it is very expensive for individuals to initiate corrective action. The context of systemic risks is much more difficult. For, individuals may not be in a position to anticipate such risk. No one individual may be in a position to initiate corrective action and may resist correction due to habit persistence. The need for regulatory action is much more pronounced. The main purpose of such mechanisms is to reduce systemic risks to acceptable limits. The form such mechanisms take depends on the purpose of regulation.

One example is the following. An individual may get ill if he does not pay attention to his personal hygiene. But he may develop illness if surroundings are not clean irrespective of his efforts to maintain personal hygiene. Hence, he may make efforts to keep the neighborhood environment clean. There are limits to which this can be achieved.

Insurance cannot be a substitute for such diligence. However, by its nature, personal care and contributing to healthy neighborhood conditions can be expensive. All individuals in a society may not be able to pay for the costs of efficient caution. Hence, it becomes essential for some over arching institution to ensure environmental cleanliness. Public health schemes become essential. The existence of economies of scale and scope also suggest collective action in addition to individual effort.

Systemic risks, or their proximate causes, do not have any general structure. Hence, they are difficult to predict. The historically accumulated information offers some useful guidelines. But, in many cases, they will reveal their structure only when they occur. It is always difficult to design contractual mechanisms to anticipate and neutralize systemic risks a priori. Efforts and precautions can be put in place to at best minimize systemic risks but not to eliminate them. Corrections, induced by individuals, insurance companies, or regulatory agencies. are per force ex post. This is a fundamental limitation of insurance mechanisms. Insurance companies also find it difficult to protect themselves against high and unexpected systemic risks. Conceptualizing a lender of last resort, in case they fail, only shifts the risk further instead of offering assistance in resolving it.

As Fuchs (2000) pointed out, several types of principal agent models of insurance exist: physician vs. patient and physician vs. managed care organizations (including public health services). Many details of health insurance, not merely absorbing risks or utilizing the limited set of instruments examined in the present study, still need careful analysis. One aspect is particularly glaring. The entire analysis of this study assumed that α represents the willingness of the individual to pay the insurance premium. In consonance with private individual choices, it was also presumed that expression of willingness is supported by the ability to pay. Private insurance contracts exclude individuals that cannot pay. In the context of health insurance, in particular, it may be argued that some basic health services should be covered by insurance irrespective of the ability of individuals to pay. This may also be a necessity to reduce the externalities on those that are in a position to pay. Some form of social health insurance or provision of public hospital services must be conceptualized. Private health insurance schemes surely pivot insurance policies on the diligence of the individual in the use of assets as postulated in the study. This may not be justifiable in the context of social health insurance or the provision of public health services. The extensions of the models, to take the ability to pay into account, are not altogether obvious to articulate.[34] Further investigation is necessary since this has important implications for regulatory policy.

All said and done insurance offers limited protection against risks. Its role in reducing systemic risks is also somewhat circumscribed.

References

Abbring JH, Chiappori PA, Heckman JJ, Pinquet J (2003) Adverse selection and moral hazard in insurance: can dynamic data help to distinguish? J Eur Econ Assoc 1:512–521

Blomquist A, Leger PT (2005) Information asymmetry, insurance, and the decision to hospitalize. J Health Econ 24:775–793

Boadway R, Marchand M, Sato M (2004) An optimal contract approach to hospital financing. J Health Econ 23:85–110

Bourgeon JM, Picard P, Pouyet J (2008) Providers' affiliation, insurance and collusion. J Bank Financ 32:170–186

Chalkley M, McVicar D (2008) Choice of contracts in the British National Health Service: an empirical study. J Health Econ 27:1155–1167

Chiappori PA (2000) Econometric models of insurance under asymmetric information. In: Dionne G (ed) Handbook of insurance. Kluwer Academic Publishers, London

Cochrane JH (2009) Health status insurance: how markets provide health security. Policy Anal 633:1–12

Cowley A, Cummins JD (2005) Securitization of life insurance assets and liabilities. J Risk Insur 72:193–226

Crocker KJ, Moran JR (2002) Contracting with limited commitment: evidence from employment based health insurance contracts. Rand J Econ 34:694–718

Cummins JD (2005) Securitization of life insurance assets and liabilities. J Risk Insur 72:193–226

Felder S (2008) To wait or pay for medical treatment? Restraining ex post moral hazard in health insurance. J Health Econ 27:1418–1422

Fenn P, Gray A, Rickman N (2007) Liability, insurance, and medical practice. J Health Econ 26:1057–1070

Finkelstein A, Poterba J (2004) Adverse selection in insurance markets: policy holder evidence from the U.K. Annuity Market. J Polit Econ 112:188–208

Fuchs VR (2000) The future of health economics. J Health Econ 19:141–157

Hernandez MV (2003) Structural estimation of a principal-agent model: moral hazard in medical insurance. Rand J Econ 34:670–693

Jullien B, Salanie B, Salanie F (1999) Should more risk averse agents exert more effort? Geneva Pap Risk Insur Theory 24:19–28

Klein RW, Wong S (2009) Catastrophe risk financing in the United States and the European Union: a comparative analysis of alternative regulatory approaches. J Risk Insur 76:607–637

Nell M, Richter A, Schiller J (2009) When prices hardly matter: incomplete insurance contracts and markets for repair goods. Eur Econ Rev 53:343–354

[34] It may be argued that restructuring the model allowing the individual to choose α instead of p, the insurer choosing the cost he is willing to pay, and the service provider choosing the quality of service commensurate with the costs he expects to be reimbursed will provide an answer. However, such a definition of α still represents willingness to pay rather than the ability to do so. A more fundamental change is necessary.

Pauly MV, Blavin FE (2008) Moral hazard in insurance, value-based cost sharing and the benefits of blissful ignorance. J Health Econ 27:1407–1417

Rao TVSR (2009) Securitization, ratings, and regulatory policy. Presented at the fourth annual conference on public policy and management. IIM, Bangalore, 10–12 Apr

Rao TVSR (2010) Financial crisis, efficient bailouts, and regulatory policy. Macroecon Financ Emerg Market Econ 3(2):167–188

Rutten F, Bleichrodt H, Brouwer M, Koopmanschap M, Schut E (2001) Handbook of health economics. J Health Econ 20:855–879

Snow A (2009) On the possibility of self-selection in competitive insurance markets. J Risk Insur 76:249–259

Chapter 10
Securitization and Volatility

Abstract The originator passing on the risks (or sharing risks) in financial transactions is the general end result of asset-based securitization. It can be shown that volatility (measured as the variance in the recovery of receivables) increases in at least four contexts. (a) The originator does not share the risk and consequently expands into high-risk activities to increase his business. This depends on the efficiency of the special purpose vehicle (SPV) in collecting receivables and how consideration is defined at the time of securitization. However, there will be limits on volatility beyond which the originator does not gain. (b) The size of any one securitized pool may be small compared to the total business of the SPV. Portfolio choice based on the risk-adjusted rate of return becomes important in such a context. In an expanding market, the originator and/or the SPV may find the risk-adjusted rate of return on securitization even higher with increasingly risky transactions. He will then expand into activities that increase the volatility of transactions. (c) The investor, who buys the pass-through certificates issued by the SPV, may find securitized transactions more attractive relative to conventional financial instruments either due to lower transaction costs, shorter time horizon over which they are recovered, or higher risk-adjusted rate of return. Even this has the effect of increasing the volatility of financial transactions. (d) The parties tend to utilize credit rating agencies to indicate the risks involved and reduce their adverse impact. However, their commercial interests may result in ratings that augment and spread risks instead of containing them within desirable limits.

10.1 Structure of Securitization

The relatively rapid growth of the economy over the past few years created a high demand for finances. Conventional sources of finance, say the stock market and the banking sector, have not expanded in tandem and/or some transactions cannot be

---

Based on content from "Securitization and Volatility of Financial Transactions" first published *The Indian Journal of Economics*, 90(356), 2009, pp. 187–202. Content reproduced here with permission from University of Allahabad.

T.V.S.R. Rao, *Risk Sharing, Risk Spreading and Efficient Regulation*,
DOI 10.1007/978-81-322-2562-1_10

negotiated by using such instruments. In particular, many new firms are not listed on any stock market. Similarly, some transactions, like futures trading in commodities, are not as yet fully amenable to negotiation through the stock market. One of the reasons for this is the fact that institutions like the NCDEX are relatively new and cover only a few of these transactions.

Novel methods of finance and a variety of financial instruments dealing with such transactions emerged. Structured finance, securitization in particular, belongs to this category. The securitization process can be illustrated by the following. Consider the loans extended in the context of sale of cars or commercial vehicles. A company, say Tata Motors, who offers the requisite finance to individual buyers, may initially borrow from the bank.[1] But the recovery can be only over an extended time horizon. Their quest for increasing business in a buoyant market will be set back if they have to depend on the banks for more loans. Securitization of receivables clearly offers a more attractive alternative because it enables the originator to increase the pool of finances and expand sales of the firm. The other reason for securitization may be the costs involved in the recovery of loans. The originator may feel that the transaction costs are too high if he undertakes the activity. Someone else that has an advantage in handling such financial transactions may feel that he can handle it more efficiently and profit from it. It would be more efficient if the underlying assets are transferred to such agents. For all practical purposes, this is the genesis of securitization in a variety of contexts.[2]

A typical securitized transaction has the following structure. A firm, called an originator, puts together a pool of its receivables for securitization. Over the last few years, for instance, Tata Motors chose thirty different tranches of receivables from the sale of cars and commercial vehicles for securitization. The firm sells them to a special purpose vehicle (SPV, usually a trust) for a consideration that is normally a fraction of the value of receivables. This also entails transfer of property rights of the underlying assets. That is, the transaction should be a true sale that removes the assets from the balance sheet of the originator. This alone gives the SPV the right to collect the receivables. In his turn, the SPV issues pass-through certificates (PTCs) to investors[3] to recover the money paid to the originator as consideration.[4] Basically the SPV shares and/or transfers the risk to such investors.

---

[1] Why does the firm undertake this instead of allowing the buyer to take the loan from the bank? One obvious reason is the reduction in transaction costs. The second reason may be the difficulty in the buyer obtaining the loan without adequate collateral.

[2] Commercial mortgage-based assets belong to the same category though their recovery would be over a longer duration. Process flow securitization of capital assets, whose recovery is contingent on production and sale based on such assets, is somewhat different.

[3] The reader may argue that the SPV may pay the necessary consideration to the originator, collect the receivables, and derive greater profits. Issuance of PTCs then needs justification. Note that if the SPV collects the receivables on his own his costs will increase and he will not remain risk neutral. A risk-averse SPV and the originator may then agree to net value maximization in choosing the consideration, the value of the pool of receivables securitized, and the number of items in the securitized pool. This alternative is not pursued here because conventionally the SPV is expected to share risks by issuing PTCs.

[4] The small saver has many investment opportunities in a growing economy. Why would he invest in PTCs of a trust that is not well known? The basic reason will be that such trusts consolidate all

There has been a general acknowledgment that the various participants in a securitized transaction should be convinced that the receivables are collectible. Consequently, the originator seeks a rating from the credit rating agencies to achieve this. It is generally expected that the costs of collecting the receivables will be lower if a high credit rating is available.

However, securitization comes with a price tag as in the case of all other financial instruments. The investors use their saving to participate in these transactions. Even the non-bank financial institutions belong to this category. They may invest in the PTCs issued by the SPV either because the recovery is over a shorter time interval or because they expect a higher risk-adjusted rate of return. In any case, the SPV has to spend some money to collect the receivables.

The originator may be willing and able to take a certain amount of risk if he collects the receivables on his own. If the PTC investors and the SPV are expected to share the risk, as is the case under securitization, there is always a possibility that the SPV and PTC holders will not agree to so much risk. Risk reduction may then be a precondition to achieve any sort of securitization. Received contract theory also suggests that different agents specializing in their respective expertise will reduce such volatility. However, the practical reality is that the SPVs tend to be more willing to accept the risk because they are better organized in collecting such receivables. The investors in the PTCs may also find this a more attractive option due to lower transaction costs, higher risk-adjusted rate of return, or shorter horizons over which they can recover their investment. Similarly, the credit rating agencies will not compromise on their business objective of generating higher revenues for themselves and the originators who seek their ratings.[5] IIF (2008) and the World Bank studies, such as Caprio et al. (2008), acknowledged this inadequacy of credit ratings. However, they contend that financial markets are mature enough to set terms of trade to eliminate arbitrage and overcome adverse selection. As a practical reality, they do not seem to exhibit the requisite efficiency. Hence, credit ratings themselves have not been adequate to protect the ultimate investors of PTCs from bearing the brunt of the risk in such transactions.[6] A general impression is created that all such structured finance activities, including securitization, derivatives, and options, create a great deal of speculative activity. This is expected to increase market volatility. It appears that an analytical approach, based on contract theory, to understand the tendency to

---

similar small savings and invest more efficiently than any one small saver can. The logic is similar to channeling saving through a stockbroker or a holding company.

[5] Caprio et al. (2008, p. 16) considered the possibility of drastically over rating and offering oversized tranches of structured financial instruments. They argued that part '\of the argument lies in the incentive conflict managers and line employees of such firms faced between preserving the long-run value of the firm's reputation and choosing bonuses and raises that short-term revenue expansion can generate. Errors in classification are slow to revel themselves. They can only be established after a long and variable lag." In general, the credit rating agencies can only provide the information about known skills. Hull et al. (2004) suggested that credit rating agencies cannot anticipate unexpected external exigencies that lower the value of securitized assets. They can only react to it by downgrading when the information is available. That is, credit ratings may be quite independent of the payments to the managers as well.

[6] Adelson (2007) detailed many requirements of an ideal credit rating system.

increased volatility is warranted. The rest of this paper attempts to develop such an analytical framework while developing appropriate concepts of volatility.

The analytical framework is set in a modified version of the principal agent models. It will be shown that volatility increases in at least three contexts. (a) The originator does not share the risk and consequently expands into high-risk activities to increase his business. This depends on how consideration is defined at the time of securitization. (b) In an expanding market, the originator and/or the SPV may find the risk-adjusted return higher even with increasingly risky transactions. (c) The investor, who buys the PTCs issued by the SPV, may find securitized transactions more attractive relative to more conventional financial instruments as noted earlier. The framework developed here is rich enough to allow an analysis of several other channels through which volatility may increase.

Consequently, there is a suggestion that some ex ante measures of regulation directed to the originator, SPV, and/or the credit rating agency must be specified so that high risks of securitization and the associated losses to the investors are kept under control. Ex post regulation must be conceptualized if failure occurs despite the due diligence recommended and adhered to since sudden changes in macroeconomic conditions may create a financial crisis. In such cases, the integrity of the financial system can be maintained in the short run only if the banking system reacts by creating adequate liquidity.

The rest of the presentation is organized as follows. The basic modeling framework dealing with securitization will be the subject of Sect. 10.2. Section 10.3 indicates the roots of risk spreading in the process of sharing risks. Section 10.4 then acknowledges that securitization may involve a large pool of assets. As a consequence, risk spreading will be highlighted. Section 10.5 investigates the possibility of a regulator requiring the originator to hold a reserve, based on the intrinsic risk and the volume of the securitized pool, with an agency they specify. Such reserves can be used to rescue the investors if the SPV is unable to collect the receivables in practice. The parties to the securitized transactions may also make adjustments to make them efficient. This will be detailed in Sect. 10.6.

10.2 Analytical Framework

Consider a transaction in which an originator is securitizing a pool of receivables. A basic feature of such a pool is that the amount that can be recovered will not be the same for every transaction in the pool.[7] For analytical purposes, it can be postulated that the recovery will be

---

[7] The SPV may take possession of the asset if the original buyer defaults. Hence, it may be argued that the randomness is not with respect to whether or not the receivables can be collected. Instead, the difficulty will be reflected in the transaction costs involved in the recovery of receivables. However, there will be costs in recovering the original loan amount. The treatment of this alternative, in models of the nature presented in this section, will be symmetric.

$$r + u;\ E(u) = 0,\ V(u) = \sigma^2$$

where r = average recovery and
u = a random variable[8] with expected value 0 and variance σ^2.
For the present, assume that σ^2 is independent of r.[9]

If the originator collects the receivables on his own, he incurs a direct cost and the cost of the business lost due to the unavailability of finances. This may be represented by $r^2/2\varepsilon$ where ε = his efficiency in managing the collection of receivables.

The gain to the originator will then be

$$g_0 = r + u - r^2/2\varepsilon$$

Assume that he is risk averse. Then, the value he associates with this transaction can be written as

$$v_0 = r - \lambda_0\sigma^2 - r^2/2\varepsilon$$

where λ_0 = his degree of risk aversion.

He can be expected to choose r to maximize v_0. It results in[10]

$$r = \varepsilon$$

and the optimal value

$$v_0 = \varepsilon/2 - \lambda_0\sigma^2$$

[8] It is generally argued that securitization must represent a true sale so that the assets can be removed from the balance sheet of the originator. However, depending on the original contract, there may be legal hurdles in the SPV collecting the receivables. The following case reported by the rating agency, Fitch India, will illustrate this. They were rating three tranches of mortgage loans securitized by Citibank. The SPV, Royal Trust, needed the help of Citibank to recover the receivables. In other words, a true sale may not be enough to make securitization successful. This may also be an aspect of the randomness.

[9] The variance σ^2 will probably be lower if the securitized transaction is rated by an agency. However, this can be achieved only at a cost. The originator may still deal in more risky assets and thereby increase the volatility of such financial transactions. This will not be pursued further in this study.

[10] It may be argued that a risk-averse firm will choose a lower r. This can be built into the model in one of two ways. First, σ^2 is an increasing function of r. Second, the costs of recovery depend not only on r but on the nature of receivables. That is, the costs of recovery may themselves depend on σ^2. However, such extensions do not seem to offer any additional insights regarding the volatility of the underlying financial transactions.

The alternative available to the originator is securitization. Consider the case where he claims a fixed fraction p of r as consideration. This is indeed the general practice.[11] The gain to the originator is[12]

$$g_0 = pr + r^2/2\varepsilon$$

since post-securitization he does not incur the cost of collection of the underlying receivables. This is entirely deterministic. Hence, its value to the originator is

$$v_0 = g_0$$

The SPV, in his turn, issues PTCs to collect pr. It is expected that the investor will provide this money through the purchase of PTCs. However, the SPV will eventually collect $r+u$ and pays a fraction $q(r+u)$ to the investors.[13] Consequently, the gain to the investors is[14]

$$\begin{aligned} g_i &= q(r+u) - pr \\ &= (q-p)r + qu \end{aligned}$$

In general, the investors are risk averse. Hence, the value of the transaction to them is

$$v_i = (q-p)r - \lambda\sigma^2 q^2$$

The investors are not sure about the rate of return that they can expect and/or repayment of the investment. They can be expected to choose q ceteris paribus. This choice results in

$$q = r/2\lambda\sigma^2$$

---

[11] One of the prevalent practices is to make it equal to the present discounted value of r after some adjustments for receivables outstanding beyond the stipulated time at which an installment must be paid. The choice of an appropriate discount rate will then be pertinent. The formulation will be symmetric.

[12] The gain to the originator is not merely the collection of the consideration based on the pool of receivables that are securitized. It also consists of the additional business that he can generate once the consideration is received. The following analysis does not take this aspect into account explicitly. However, it should be noted that securitization increases r and the propensity of the originator in offering more loans even if they tend to be more risky.

[13] The SPV may claim a fixed share $(1-q)r$ and pass on the entire risk to the investor. It can be readily verified that such a contract is inefficient. The net variability will also be higher.

[14] The originator, while considering the underwriting standards, may be prone to take more risk since he knows that he will securitize the pool of receivables and thereby pass on the risks to the SPV and/or the eventual investor. This will indeed provide him an opportunity to expand his business as well. Hence, it may be expected that the σ^2 post-securitization will be larger. This, in itself, may be one source of greater volatility of securitized financial transactions.

Note that q increases with r and decreases with an increase in λ and/or σ^2.

The SPV receives an amount $(1-q)(r+u)$. However, he must spend some money to collect the receivables. Denote this by

$$r^2/2\delta \quad \text{where} \quad \delta = \text{his efficiency}$$

For all practical purposes, the SPV does not gain anything unless $\delta > \varepsilon$. His gain can be denoted by

$$g_s = (1-q)(r+u) - r^2/2\delta$$

In general, the SPV is not taking any risk because he is not paying pr. Instead, he makes the investor pay for it. Hence, he is not very sensitive to the risk of losing that investment. Further, the SPV will be dealing with many such transactions. Hence, he can balance the residual losses in one transaction against gains from another. It can therefore be surmised that he will be risk neutral. The value of g_s to the SPV may then be written as

$$v_s = (1-q)r - r^2/2\delta$$

Note that, for all practical purposes, the SPV is underwriting the issue of PTCs. For, he is required to pay pr to the originator whether or not he can attract investors to buy his PTCs. Hence, from a pragmatic viewpoint, he should place a value on that effort as well. Such a valuation will be equal to v_i. For, in a way, that is the opportunity value to the SPV if he has to accept the burden of underwriting that fails to attract investors. Hence, from the perspective of the SPV, the net value of the contract is the sum of v_s and v_i.

An efficient contract then requires that he maximize

$$\begin{aligned} N &= v_i + v_s \\ &= (1-p)r - r^2/2\delta - \lambda\sigma^2 q^2 \end{aligned}$$

Two observations are in order. First, v_0 is not included in N since the originator, by claiming a fixed consideration, does not share the risk. Second, the SPV may only maximize v_s and eventually choose a Nash equilibrium contract. This can be shown to be less efficient (lower optimized N) compared to the present approach.

Surely, the SPV's first priority is not about how much he wishes to pay the investor since the SPV should first collect the receivables. Hence, it can be expected that he would be more worried about how much he can collect. Similarly, the possibility that the SPV may not be in a position to collect all the receivables is at the apex of the likely default that the investor envisages. It would therefore be logical to expect the SPV to make the choice with respect to r, the quantum of receivables in the securitized pool.[15]

[15] Note one finer point of analytical detail. Suppose we assign the choice of r to the investor and that of q to the SPV contrary to the argument in the text. It can be shown that such choices result

The SPV has to take the participation constraint of *i*, viz.,

$$q = r/2\lambda\sigma^2,$$

into account while choosing *r*, i.e., the pool of receivables that he will buy. This choice results in

$$r = 2\delta(1-p)\lambda\sigma^2/(\delta + 2\lambda\sigma^2)$$

It may then be noted that the originator chooses *p* to maximize v_0 keeping the reactions of the SPV and the investors in perspective. This optimization results in[16]

$$p = (\varepsilon - 2\theta)/2(\varepsilon - \theta) < 1$$

where[17]

$$\theta = \delta\lambda\sigma^2/(\delta + 2\lambda\sigma^2)$$

The optimized value of *N* becomes

$$N = \delta(1-p)^2\lambda\sigma^2/(\delta + 2\lambda\sigma^2) > 0$$

It can also be verified that $q>p$ whenever $\delta>\varepsilon$. This is in consonance with the expectation in contract theory that the party taking more risk should receive a larger payment.[18]

---

in a lower net value *N*. That is, such a contractual choice would be inefficient. This reinforces the practical aspect of the assumptions made in the text.

[16] The resulting value of *p* is not independent of δ. In practice, in repeated transactions, the originator does not know the efficiency of the SPV. Hence, he would prefer a *p* independent of δ. It can be shown that this result will emerge if $v(u)=\sigma^2/\delta$. That is, a smart SPV can collect receivables more efficiently in this sense.

[17] Observe that this inequality cannot be satisfied if $\varepsilon<\theta$ for, then, $p<1$ if and only if

$$\varepsilon - 2\theta > 2(\varepsilon - \theta)$$

This inequality cannot hold since $\varepsilon>0$. It must also be noted that $\varepsilon>2\theta$ if and only if $\lambda\sigma^2<\delta\varepsilon/2(\delta-\varepsilon)$. That is, the analysis would hold only when $\lambda\sigma2$ is sufficiently small. One reason for this is that $0<\theta<\delta$ for $0<\lambda\sigma^2<\infty$. Given this, inequality 2θ will exceed ε for sufficiently large values of $\lambda\sigma^2$. The second reason can be obtained from the definition of v_i. In particular, a ceteris paribus increase in $\lambda\sigma^2$ decreases the value of v_i. For high values of $\lambda\sigma^2$, the value of $v_i<0$ and the investors will not accept the contract.

[18] This regulatory constraint is also necessary to make the contract meaningful for the investor will not accept the contract if $q<p$.

10.3 Volatility of Transactions

Observe that

$$V(g_i) = q^2\sigma^2 \text{ and}$$
$$V(g_s) = (1-q)^2\sigma^2$$

where V is the variance.

Hence, the total variance of the financial transaction (which will be designated as its volatility) is

$$V = \left[q^2 + (1-q)^2\right]\sigma^2 < \sigma^2$$

for q is always less than 1. Hence, in general, securitization can be expected to reduce volatility.

Up to this point in the analysis, σ^2 is taken to be exogenously given. It is necessary to investigate the changes in the behavior of the contracting parties as it varies.

To begin with, note that

$$\partial V/\partial q = 2(2q-1) \text{ and}$$
$$2q = \varepsilon\theta/\lambda\sigma^2(\varepsilon - \theta) > 1 \text{ whenever } \delta > 2\varepsilon$$

Hence, it follows that[19]

$$\partial V/\partial q > 0$$

Similarly,

$$\partial q/\partial\lambda\sigma^2 > 0$$

Hence, $\partial V/\partial\lambda\sigma^2 > 0$

Consequently, any increase in $\lambda\sigma^2$ makes V larger. That is, there will be greater volatility of securitized transactions as $\lambda\sigma^2$ increases. It would therefore be natural to investigate the conditions under which the parties to the transaction prefer greater σ^2.

[19] The preceding footnote suggested that the analysis would be meaningful only if $\lambda\sigma^2$ is small. The inequality $\delta > 2\varepsilon$ indicates that the SPV should be significantly more efficient to create greater volatility. An efficient SPV, dealing with relatively low risk, can therefore be expected to prefer higher values of $\lambda\sigma^2$ and thereby create greater volatility in securitized transactions. However, very high values of $\lambda\sigma^2$ will not support such a choice. The volatility increases only within certain limits.

Fundamentally, securitization allows the originator to increase the volume of transactions. Since

$$\partial V/\partial q > 0 \text{ and } \partial q/\partial r > 0,$$

it can be concluded that

$$\partial V/\partial r > 0$$

That is, volatility increases with the volume of transactions. This provides the other reasoning leading to the greater volatility of financial transactions.

Note, however, that the originator may feel that securitization enables him to pass on the risks. This may embolden him to undertake more and/or bigger transactions even if they involve a larger σ^2. As noted earlier, this would imply a greater volatility related to financial transactions.

It is also clear that

$$\begin{aligned} v_i &= (q-p)r - \lambda\sigma^2 q^2 \\ &= \lambda\sigma^2 q^2 - 2\lambda\sigma^2 qp \end{aligned}$$

It can now be verified that

$$\begin{aligned} &\partial p/\partial q = -\lambda\sigma^2/\varepsilon < 0 \\ &\partial v_i/\partial q > 0 \end{aligned}$$

Since $\partial q/\partial\lambda\sigma^2 > 0$, it follows that

$$\partial v_i/\partial\lambda\sigma^2 > 0$$

In other words, the investors will stand to gain by increases in volatility. They will not resist the originator choosing more risky pools.

In a similar fashion, the originator may be expected to find avenues of increasing v_0. Recall that

$$v_0 = \varepsilon^2\theta/(\varepsilon-\theta)^2$$

Hence,

$$\partial v_0/\partial\theta = \varepsilon^2(\varepsilon+\theta)/(\varepsilon-\theta)^3 > 0$$

Further,

$$\partial\theta/\partial\lambda\sigma^2 = \delta^2/(\delta+2\lambda\sigma^2)^2 > 0$$

With this information in place, it can be readily verified that

$$\partial v_0/\partial\lambda\sigma^2 > 0$$

Therefore, the originator also gains by accepting more risky pools of receivables for securitization.[20]

In his turn, the SPV would like to increase his business.[21] Note that

$$r = \varepsilon\theta/(\varepsilon - \theta)$$

Hence,

$$\partial r/\partial\theta = \varepsilon^2/(\varepsilon - \theta)^2 > 0$$

It can then be inferred that

$$\partial r/\partial\lambda\sigma^2 > 0$$

In other words, even the SPV can be expected to prefer a larger σ^2.

These three results taken together indicate that securitized transactions generally tend to be more volatile.

Consider the possibility that the SPV and the investors agree to a Nash equilibrium instead. It can be shown that, in such a case, the sharing fraction will be

$$q_n = \delta/(\delta + 2\lambda\sigma^2)$$

It can be readily verified that the volatility of transactions will increase if such a choice prevails.

Up to this point in the analysis, one single optimized pool of receivables has been the focus of attention. In any practical context, the SPV may be willing to deal with

---

[20] It can also be shown that

$$\partial V/\partial\delta > 0 \text{ whenever } \delta > \varepsilon$$

That is, a more efficient SPV will tend to expand transactions to a point where there is greater volatility in the securitized pool.

[21] Should this be interpreted as increasing the value of v_s? This may not be the best interpretation because he is risk neutral. Instead, he will seek out more business, represented by r, and expect to improve his position on an average. It can be actually shown that

$$\partial v_s/\partial\lambda\sigma^2 < 0 \text{ whenever } \delta > \varepsilon$$

That is, he may not gain in any one transaction. An increase in average gains will then depend on some transactions being less risky than the others. Alternatively, since the SPV is handling many such transactions, he expects to increase his net return on all these transactions even if he gets a lower value on any one of them.

much larger investments than the optimal r specified in the above analysis.[22] It is therefore necessary to examine the more general portfolio choice problem of the SPV. Consider the portfolio choice of an SPV who decides to invest a total amount of T in financial instruments. He first chooses the investment that offers the highest risk-adjusted rate of return. If it is possible to invest the entire T in that instrument, his choice problem is solved. Suppose a smaller amount is all that is possible because there are not many securitized transactions that yield that risk-adjusted rate of return. He will then invest the maximum possible and turn to the next financial instrument that yields the second highest risk-adjusted rate of return. This lexicographic ordering indicates that the SPV may have a preference for R_s instead of v_s or r.

Consider the rate of return to the SPV. It can be written as

$$\begin{aligned} R_s &= v_s / r \\ &= (1-q) - r/2\delta \\ &= 1 - \left[\theta\varepsilon / (\varepsilon - \theta)\right]\left[1/\delta + 1/\lambda\sigma^2\right] \end{aligned}$$

It can be readily verified that

$$\partial R_s / \partial \lambda\sigma^2 = \theta\varepsilon R_s / (\varepsilon - \theta)\lambda^2\sigma^4 > 0$$

That is, the risk-adjusted rate of return to the SPV increases with $\lambda\sigma^2$. Hence, he is prone to take on more risky pools for securitization.

Similarly, the investor has a portfolio choice problem analogous to that of the SPV. With this interpretation, consider

$$\begin{aligned} R_i &= \text{rate of return to the investor} \\ &= v_i / pr \\ &= q/2p - 1 \end{aligned}$$

Following a procedure similar to the one above, it can be shown that

$$\partial q / \partial \lambda\sigma^2 > 0 \text{ and } \partial p / \partial \lambda\sigma^2 < 0$$

given the assumptions made so far. Hence, it can be inferred that

$$\partial R_i / \partial \lambda\sigma^2 > 0$$

That is, if $\lambda\sigma^2$ is small enough, R_i will increase with $\lambda\sigma^2$. It can therefore be argued that even the investors have reason to prefer pools with a high risk.

However, note that the originator has no similar incentive. His concern will only be to maximize v_0. As noted earlier, this induces him to prefer larger values of σ^2.

---

[22] The case where r is much larger than the desired investment of the SPV would be symmetric.

For all practical purposes, it may be claimed that, even with an increase in $\lambda\sigma^2$, the risk-adjusted rate of return may be favorable. This is the other inducement for the parties to create a greater volatility in securitized transactions.

10.4 Size of the Pool[23]

The analysis of the previous section assumed that the size of the pool of receivables securitized is given. However, it is intuitively obvious that volatility is likely to increase with the size of the pool given the risk associated with the recovery of any one asset in the pool. This will be formally demonstrated in this section.

Consider the case where the pool has n transactions. Assume, as before, that each transaction results in receivables of value $(r+u)$. It should be expected that the costs, to the originator and the SPV, of collecting the receivables will now become $r^2n^2/2\varepsilon$ and $r^2n^2/2\delta$, respectively.[24] The value of the transaction to the originator will then be

$$v_0 = npr + n^2r^2/2\varepsilon$$

Similarly, the value of his share to the investor becomes

$$v_{\mathrm{i}} = n(q-p)r - \lambda n^2q^2\sigma^2$$

so that the optimal choice of q will now be

$$q = r/2n\lambda\sigma^2$$

Analogously, it can be verified that

$$v_{\mathrm{s}} = n(1-q)r - n^2r^2/2\delta$$
$$N = n(1-p)r - n^2r^2/2\delta - r^2/2\lambda\sigma^2$$

and the efficient choice of r is

$$r = 2(1-p)\theta$$

where

---

[23] Observe the following. Given the average value of any one item in the pool being securitized, the total value of the transactions handled by the SPV may increase in one of two ways. First, there may be an increase in the number of items in the pool. Second, there may be an increase in the number of pools keeping the number of items in each pool constant. Hence, this section will consider increasing the number of items in a pool.

[24] It may be argued that these costs will only be $nr^2/2\varepsilon$ and $nr^2/2\delta$. It can be verified that the essential qualitative results remain the same as those reported in this section.

$$\theta = \lambda\sigma^2\delta n/\left(\delta + 2n\lambda\sigma^2\right)$$

The corresponding optimal choice of p is

$$p = (\varepsilon - 2n\theta)/2(\varepsilon - n\theta)$$

The following results can be readily verified:

(a) $\partial r/\partial n > 0$. That is, an increase in the size of the pool also induces the originator to increase the size of each transaction in the pool.
(b) $\partial p/\partial n < 0$. This implies that the originator will receive a smaller amount by way of consideration per transaction as the risk increases.
(c) $\partial v_0/\partial n > 0$ whenever $\delta > \varepsilon$. The originator stands to gain by increasing the number of transactions in the pool being securitized.

It can be concluded that both the SPV and the originator will favor larger pools and increase the volatility of these financial transactions.

There may, however, be an optimal n beyond which the size of the pool will not increase. Consider

$$N = n(1-p)r - n^2r^2/2\delta - r^2/2\lambda\sigma^2$$

The optimal n will then be

$$n = (1-p)\delta$$

The efficiency of the SPV and the consideration claimed by the originator place a limit on the number of transactions in the pool being securitized.

10.5 Credit Ratings[25]

The choice of credit ratings and their effect on volatility of securitized transactions will be outlined in this section. It can be shown that the ratings only tend to augment risks. Consequently, a regulator may monitor the credit rating agencies. However, this appears to be a blunt instrument that does not reduce the volatility by much.

Return to Sect. 10.2. δ may now represent the ratings of the pool of transactions by a rating agency. It can also be interpreted as the change in the efficiency of the SPV given the ratings. Given a good rating, the SPV may no longer be concerned about the possibility that he may not be able to collect all the receivables. That is, r is not his primary choice any longer. He will choose p taking the participatory constraint of the investors into account. The efficient choice of p is therefore

[25] Several variations of this theme have been detailed in Rao (2011).

$$p = 4\delta c\lambda\sigma^2 / \left[\delta + 2\lambda\sigma^2 \left(1 + 4c\delta\right)\right]$$

where it can be surmised that the credit rating agency charges cr^2 to provide the rating.[26] Observe that the originator is more prone to securitize risky assets since p increases with δ and $\lambda\sigma^2$ for all values of δ and $\lambda\sigma^2$.

It can also be verified that v_0, v_i, v_s, and cr^2 will increase with δ for all values of $\lambda\sigma^2$ so long as v_i remains positive. That is, both the originator and the credit rating agency stand to improve their returns by favoring higher ratings even for highly risky transactions. Both of them tend to create more risks with the originator initiating greater risks and the credit rating agency supporting it. As a result, concerns of moral hazard on the part of the credit rating agency have been voiced.

One caveat is in order. Note that the credit rating agency chooses δ to maximize its returns and consequently r. Observe that

$$\begin{aligned} r &= p/2c \\ &= 2\delta\lambda\sigma^2 // \left[\delta + 2\lambda\sigma^2 \left(1 + 4c\delta\right)\right] \end{aligned}$$

The agency will maximize r keeping in perspective its choice of δ which also depends on $\lambda\sigma^2$. Such a choice results in

$$\delta = 2\lambda\sigma^2 / \left(2C\lambda\sigma^2 - 1\right)$$

where C is a constant. It may be inferred that, irrespective of the cost involved in doing the ratings, the agency prefers to reduce δ as $\lambda\sigma^2$ increases in the interest of its long-run credibility. After all, it will be conscious of its losses, in terms of credibility, of wrong credit ratings. It may be verified that the optimal choice of p reduces to

$$p = 2c / \left(C + 4c\right)$$

which is independent of both δ and $\lambda\sigma^2$. As generally noted, this justifies the choice of p as the present discounted value of the receivables being securitized.

The choice of C generally reflects the effect of the costs that the credit rating agency incurs while fixing δ in response to the observed or estimated $\lambda\sigma^2$. In general,

---

[26] A true sale may not be sufficient to make securitization successful. For example, Fitch India reported the following. Citibank securitized three tranches of mortgage loans. Royal Trust was the SPV. They needed the help of Citibank to recover the receivables due to some legal issues of ownership transfer. These costs may be included in cr^2 if and when they arise. In general, ratings will account for such contingencies as well.

IIF (2008) contains a detailed discussion of the precautions that need to be exercised by the originators, SPVs, investors, rating agencies, and the regulators. For the originators, the emphasis is on risk management, stress analysis that takes into consideration the risk in its other assets, and valuation of assets. For the rating agencies, they emphasize greater transparency, specification of the risk factors that go into their rating methodology, and so on.

an increase in such costs inhibits the credit rating agency from doing a thorough investigation. Clearly, both the originator and the credit rating agency tend to gain by imputing a small value for C and announce higher ratings. This major source of problems with securitization and ratings indicate appropriate regulation.

Two approaches to regulation have been generally conceptualized.[27] First, the originators and the SPVs may be expected to follow detailed quantitative restrictions.[28] Second, an independent agency may incur some costs and evaluate the quality of receivables and credit ratings on its own. The existence of such an agency can be expected to impose an additional cost εr^2 on the originator since he will be forced to behave honorably. The choice of r will now be

$$r = p/2(c+\varepsilon)$$

Since the variance of investor earnings are

$$V(g_{\mathrm{i}}) = q^2\sigma^2,$$

[27] Filson and Morales (2005) utilized a somewhat different argument, in a very different context, to arrive at a similar conclusion. Suppose the originator is expected to make a deposit D prior to securitization. The SPV can use this signal to estimate the probability θ with which he would be able to collect the receivables. The SPV then agrees to pay a consideration pr to the originator with a probability θ and zero otherwise (i.e., he will not accept securitization). The expected net profit to the originator is

$$N = pr\theta - D$$

It may now be surmised that the originator would be willing to make a larger deposit the larger the value of θ. Let this be denoted by

$$D = d\theta^2$$

The originator can be expected to maximize N. The corresponding

$$\theta = pr/2d \text{ and}$$
$$D = p^2r^2/4d$$

That is, if the originator agrees to make a deposit D, the corresponding value of θ can be inferred. The originator will not accept this D if the value of θ is lower. That is, by choosing a suitable D, securitization can be limited to desired levels of probability of default.

[28] The prudential norms for the banking sector, as in the case of Basel norms, is a case in point. It was noted that a bank may hold the requisite reserves with the central bank while the quality of its loans is deteriorating. Similarly, a deposit proportional to the amount of receivables in a securitized tranche may provide some relief to the investors of the PTCs in case they cannot be collected. However, it cannot prevent the originator from securitizing more risky assets. IIF (2008) contains a detailed discussion of the precautions that need to be exercised by the originators, SPVs, investors, rating agencies, and the regulators. For the originators, the emphasis is on risk management, stress analysis that takes into consideration the risk in its other assets, and valuation of assets. For the rating agencies, they emphasize greater transparency, specification of the risk factors that go into their rating methodology, and so on.

the choice of ε which minimizes V is given by

$$(c+\varepsilon)\lambda\sigma^2 = A$$

where A is a constant. Greater regulatory vigilance becomes important only when $\lambda\sigma^2$ is low. For, the propensity to offer a more than justified credit rating by declaring a lower than actual volatility of the pools being securitized should be curbed.

Somewhat similar regulation of the SPVs may be conceptualized since, in general, the true sale of receivables to the SPV removes the originator from the risks. That is, risk taking and spreading are primarily in the interest of the SPV.

These results reinforce the following observation of IIF (2008). "Resolution of liquidity issues of current market stress will depend on sound internal risk management decisions by firms; (and) principles based regulation following on outcomes rather than quantitative requirements."

10.6 Efficiency of Securitization

Throughout this study, the total variance experienced by the SPV and the investors has been taken as the only guideline for determining the volatility of a securitized transaction. A few conditions for the emergence of volatility could then be traced.

Observe that the amount pr is collected by issuing many units of PTCs. The price at which each of them can be issued and the number necessary to raise the requisite investment may vary. Such variations need not depend exclusively on σ^2. Instead, the more general market for all such PTCs would be relevant. In such a context, the variability of the price of a certificate and/or the number of certificates becomes relevant. A more inclusive specification is necessary to examine this aspect. Further investigation is warranted.

The assumption that the SPV and the investors will choose an efficient contract needs to be looked into. It is possible that they tend to be selfish and end up using a Nash equilibrium. Errors of judgment of this nature may also contribute to greater volatility.

The framework of the principal agent model is a natural choice in such contracting situations. However, the possibility that some other method yields better insights cannot be ruled out. In particular, volatility may have a macroeconomic interpretation in the sense that the volatility in any one financial instrument may spread to others. Such issues would be worth exploring in greater detail.

Regulatory agencies may try to control the choices of the originator, SPV, and/or credit rating agency. However, it is evident from the above analysis that the initial expectation regarding the ability of credit rating agencies to curb the risk enhancing and risk spreading behavior does not generally materialize. It appears that a deposit with an agency designated by the regulator, commensurate with the volume of receivables being securitized and their intrinsic risk, will be the only effective ex ante control to reduce investor risk. However, unexpected events may still have devastating effects on the functioning of structured financial instruments. More detailed and intrusive regulatory measures will be difficult to design and even more cumbersome to implement. However, precautionary ex ante regulation may turn out to be superior to regulatory action after a securitized transaction results in unexpected and significant losses.

References

Adelson M (2007) The role of credit rating agencies in the structured finance market. Available at http://www.house.gov/apps/list/hearing/financesvcss_dem/adelson.pdf

Caprio G, Domirguc-Knut A, Kane EJ (2008) The 2007 meltdown in structured securitization. World Bank Res Obs 25:125–155

Filson D, Morales R (2005) Equity links and information acquisition in biotechnology alliances. J Econ Behav Organ 59:1–28

Hull J, Predescu M, White A (2004) The relationship between credit default swap spreads, bond yields and credit rating announcements. J Bank Financ 28:2789–2811

Institute of International Finance (2008) Final report of the IIF Committee on best practices: principles of conduct and best practice recommendations. Available at IIF_Final_report_of_the_Committee_on_Market_Best_Practices[1].pdf

Rao TVSR (2011) Securitization, ratings and regulatory policy. Int J Trade Glob Market 4:133–151

Chapter 11
Foreign Institutional Investors

Abstract The finances provided by foreign institutional investors (FII) can be viewed as one of the catalysts that can contribute to capital formation and economic progress. Such finances may also result in stock market gains unrelated to the underlying real economy fundamentals. In either case, there will be some gains to domestic investors. However, there are risks involved in attracting such financial flows. For, depending upon the economic conditions in their own country or opportunities as they arise elsewhere, the FII may withdraw prematurely. Gains to domestic investors will then be reduced. Regulatory regimes have the role of maximizing the share of benefits to domestic investors in the process of risk sharing. The present study conceptualizes this process in a modified principal agent model. Firstly, it will be shown that regulatory diligence and the maximum share of benefits to domestic investors depend on the degree of difficulty and costs involved in making regulatory adjustments in response to the perceived risks and risk aversion of domestic investors. Secondly, we modify the results taking into account the costs of absorbing the investments into the domestic productive system. It can be shown that a greater degree of regulatory diligence will be necessary to make sure that the expected share increase is commensurate with these costs. Thirdly, the effect of FII investments being withdrawn earlier than expected can be shown to depend on the speed with which the domestic economy can convert the financial gains to real returns. In particular, domestic investors may agree to a lower maximum share if the rate of absorption is high. Fourthly, the regulators allowing investments of FII may be sequential. That is, they may allow a low level of investment to begin with and increase the volumes only when the propensity to withdraw is not damaging to the domestic economy. This aspect will also be examined. Fifthly, we investigate the risk-spreading nature of these investments even when risks are shared within an efficient regulatory regime. Surely, all the practical details of implementing the regulatory measures cannot be fully incorporated in the present framework. Similarly, not all aspects of the distinction between purely financial (capital gains-related) returns and real returns can be captured. More work along these lines is warranted.

Based on content from "Foreign Institutional Investors, Risk Sharing and Regulatory Diligence", in O.P. Gupta and K. Gupta (eds.) first published in the edited volume *Indian Capital Markets: Emerging Issues* (Hyderabad: ICFAI University Press), 2010, pp. 3–22. Content reproduced here with permission from ICFAI University Press.

T.V.S.R. Rao, *Risk Sharing, Risk Spreading and Efficient Regulation*,
DOI 10.1007/978-81-322-2562-1_11

11.1 The Background

Opportunities as well as crises have a peculiar character. They are rather unpredictable. However, they should always be anticipated and managed efficiently to ensure the best possible results. As Biyani (2007, p. 27) put it, "(t)here is always a confluence of events for every entrepreneur. At that point the entrepreneur decides to go ahead of his time with the belief that the economy will catch up. He follows a process of hypothetical development envisioning the future." It is always possible that there is an error of judgment. However, individual initiative and entrepreneurial activity is crucial to every development process.

Some consequences of such individual initiatives impinge exclusively on the entrepreneur. Economic policy, which operates from a macro-perspective, need not involve itself in such a situation. However, some consequences affect the society at large. None of the entrepreneurs will acknowledge his role in such events and they will not, in any case, agree to remedy the consequences on their own. Individual action may not be sufficient either. Macroeconomic policy may be adequate if the event has a short-run effect. However, over the long haul, the attempt should be to ensure that such events do not disrupt the economic fundamentals. Regulatory diligence is warranted in such contexts.

Too much regulation stifles entrepreneurial activity. Hence, most economies tend to allow private initiative in searching for opportunities and taking advantage of them. The general approach is to interfere only when such activity results in a macrolevel crisis. This reactionary approach, as an ex post measure, proved disruptive as the various financial disasters of recent origin testify.

Note that even these macroeconomic consequences have their origin in the microlevel decisions of the innovators. This signals lack of due diligence on their part. As Friedman (2008) noted, "there is a fine line between risk taking and recklessness. Risk taking drives innovation; recklessness drives over a cliff. In recent years, we had way too much of the latter. We are paying a huge price for that, and we need a correction." This point of view suggests that the necessary action should be at the microlevel.

Global and liberalized economies experience both external and domestic influences. They have to manage both of them. In the international context, the following factors are at work: a decrease in demand, economic conditions closer to their home that entice foreign institutional investors (FII) to withdraw the finances provided by them, domestic financial institutions making bad investments in subprime assets originated abroad, lack of foreign exchange inflows to balance current account deficit, and so on. In all these situations, macroeconomic policy has a short-run effect. Microlevel regulatory measures are the only definitive long-run solution. These measures are also proactive instead of being solely reactionary as in the context of macroeconomic policy.

The present study attempts to examine the investments of foreign institutional investors from a long-run regulatory perspective. To begin with, it will be acknowledged that foreign institutional investors and the finances they provide can be viewed as one of the catalysts that can contribute to capital formation and economic progress. Such finances may also result in stock market gains unrelated to the underlying real economy fundamentals. In either case, there will be some gains to domestic investors. However, there are risks involved in attracting such financial flows. For, depending upon the economic conditions in their own country or opportunities as they arise elsewhere, the FIIs may withdraw prematurely. Gains to domestic investors will then be reduced.

Regulatory regimes have the role of maximizing the share of benefits to domestic investors in the process of risk sharing. In particular, due diligence may require the regulators to insist that the FIIs should (a) not indulge in short selling and similar purely speculative activities, (b) make the investment for a certain well-defined time horizon, (c) give at least a 3-month notice if they choose to withdraw, and/or (d) agree to conversion at the exchange rate that prevails at the time of exit. Similarly, the regulator may insist that the share of FII investment in the equity of domestic companies should not exceed a limit that minimizes their disruptive potential (i.e., emphasizing ownership affecting management rights alone will not be adequate). Due diligence prescribed by a regulator may take any of these forms or may add to these as the anticipated situation warrants. The present study conceptualizes this process in a modified principal agent framework. In Sect. 11.2, it will be shown that regulatory diligence and the maximum share of benefits to domestic investors depend on the degree of difficulty and costs involved in making regulatory adjustments in response to the perceived risks and risk aversion of domestic investors. In Sect. 11.3, we modify the results taking into account the costs of absorbing the investments into the domestic productive system. It can be shown that a greater degree of regulatory diligence will be necessary to make sure that the expected share increase is commensurate with these costs. The effect of FII investments being withdrawn earlier than expected can be shown to depend on the speed with which the domestic economy can convert the financial gains to real returns. In particular, domestic investors may agree to a lower maximum share if the rate of absorption is high. This is the theme of Sect. 11.4. Section 11.5 examines the possibility that the regulators allow investments of FII to be sequential. That is, they may allow a low level of investment to begin with and increase the volumes only when the propensity to withdraw is not damaging to the domestic economy. In Sect. 11.6, we investigate the risk-spreading nature of these investments even when risks are shared within an efficient regulatory regime. In particular, it will be shown that an efficient regulatory regime will minimize the risk spreading inherent in FII investments though it cannot completely eliminate it. In other words, an efficient real asset creation that absorbs the advantage of having FII financing and a regulatory regime that is sensitive to the risk aversion of the domestic investors will have the salutary effect of maximizing the benefits to domestic investors while minimizing the risk that such investments tend to bring about. Surely, all the practical details of implementing the regulatory measures cannot be fully incorporated in the present framework. Similarly, not all aspects of the distinction between purely financial (capital gains-related) returns and real returns can be captured. More work along these lines is warranted. Some of these issues will be highlighted in the concluding section.

11.2 Modeling FII

It is generally expected that FII investments can be used to finance domestic economic activity for T units of time and generate an additional income Y per unit of time. The gains to domestic investors may be from the increased dividends if there is an improvement in the real economic activity or profits. It may be, on the other hand, capital gains in the stock market. In either case, domestic investors estimate that they will receive a fraction p of the gains so generated and that the rest will accrue to the FIIs. This sharing holds even if capital gains are considered. However, due to the economic conditions in their own country or due to the emergence of better prospects elsewhere, FIIs may pull out while y units of expected income are yet to be realized or t units of time ahead of the expected T. y may be random with actual $y_a = y + u$ with $E(u)$ = expected value of $u = 0$ and $V(u)$ = variance of $u = \sigma^2$.

However, note that, if the domestic firms used FII finances to create productive capacity and/or to utilize existing capital stock more efficiently, it is possible that a fraction $p(y+u)$ can still be recovered after FIIs pull out. This is what domestic firms expect as their share if FIIs stayed on. Suppose domestic firms utilized FII investments to generate productive capacity. These finances may then be locked up. If the FIIs decide to withdraw suddenly, domestic firms may not have the liquidity to repay and/or sustain the real economic fundamentals at the new level. The RBI may provide adequate credit to shore up this much of economic activity rather than allow the stock market to collapse for they will try to sustain the fundamentals in the real economy.

FIIs view their decision to withdraw from the following perspective. If they retrieve the finances prematurely, they will lose at least $(1-p)(y+u)$ for this is what they will get if they do not withdraw. Clearly, their decision to withdraw implies that they expect to receive at least this amount from the alternative use they envisage.

Now, the FIIs incur some cost when they withdraw their investment. One aspect of this cost is the transaction cost of entry and exit. The second arises due to the lock up in physical resources. The third relates to the volume of investment withdrawn. The fourth dimension concerns the reduction in stock prices. It is reasonable to argue that the costs of withdrawing prematurely will be higher the greater the remaining life of the investment. It is generally $y^2/2\delta$ where δ is the efficiency with which the authorities regulate these financial flows. Note that a high δ means unambiguous information regarding the conditions for entry and exit and repatriation of returns from FII investments. Consequently, there is much more surety and a reduction in the costs of conducting transactions. If δ is low, the FIIs are not sure that they can withdraw if and when they wish. Under these conditions, they will find it more expensive to withdraw the finances from the market.

It can therefore be inferred that

$$\begin{aligned} g_i &= \text{gain to the domestic economy} \\ &= p(y+u) \end{aligned}$$

Normally, it can be surmised that the domestic investors are risk averse to the possibility that FII investments are hot money. The value of g_a to the domestic economy can then be written as

$$v_i = py - \lambda p^2 \sigma^2$$

where λ is the degree of risk aversion.

In its turn, the gain to the FIIs will be

$$g_f = (1-p)(y+u) - y^2/2\delta$$

We expect the FIIs to be risk neutral for, after all, they chose to invest in order to derive greater returns and are prepared to withdraw if the situation warrants that action. Consequently, the value of g_f to the FIIs is

$$v_f = (1-p)y - y^2/2\delta$$

FIIs know that withdrawing prematurely will mean a loss to the domestic economy.

In general, allowing FII flows will depend on how the domestic economy can utilize the finances and how much of the income generated they can capture. The domestic investors can be expected to choose

$$p = y/2\lambda\sigma^2$$

for, clearly, the choice of y is the prerogative of the FIIs.

It can be expected that FIIs will take into consideration the behavior of the investors in the host country and its policies toward FIIs, and regulatory diligence in particular, in their decision making. Hence, the FIIs will try to maximize

$$\begin{aligned} N &= v_i + v_f \\ &= y - y^2/4\lambda\sigma^2 - y^2/2\delta \end{aligned}$$

since the participation constraint of domestic investors must be kept in perspective. Their basic choice is y. This will therefore be

$$y = 2\delta\lambda\sigma^2/(\delta + 2\lambda\sigma^2) \text{ and}$$
$$p = \delta/(\delta + 2\lambda\sigma^2)$$

Clearly, ceteris paribus, an improvement in regulatory diligence increases the chances of minimizing the effects of FIIs withdrawing investments. However, as $\lambda\sigma^2$ tends to ∞, regulatory diligence cannot fully shield risk-averse domestic recipients of FII investment. Some amounts will be withdrawn and the domestic corporate firms cannot recover losses resulting from such action.

In actual practice, a fairly large number of FIIs deal with several corporate entities. The risk aversion of these entities will perforce be different. Hence, from a pragmatic viewpoint, the regulators will choose a single value of δ and allow the FII vs. corporate combination to self-select. The experiences with respect to y and p will still be specific to each firm depending on the extent to which regulatory diligence can shield the risks. The design of an optimal regulatory regime should therefore take the center stage.

In general, it would be realistic to expect regulators to pay a great deal of attention to the probability of FIIs withdrawing investments if the domestic corporate firms are highly risk averse. That is,

$$\mathrm{d}\delta/\mathrm{d}\lambda\sigma^2 > 0$$

In particular, the major purpose of regulation would be to ensure that the maximum possible share of the potential losses is recovered. In other words, regulators choose δ to maximize p as $\lambda\sigma^2$ varies. Note that

$$\mathrm{d}p/\mathrm{d}\lambda\sigma^2 = 2\delta(\eta - 1)/(\delta + 2\lambda\sigma^2)^2$$

where η is the elasticity of δ with respect to $\lambda\sigma^2$. This expression will be zero if $\eta = 1$. This is how the regulator can choose the efficient degree of diligence for it signals perfect correction for every $\lambda\sigma^2$. This is the best remedial action that can be expected if FII withdrawing investments is a distinct possibility. The efficient choice of δ is

$$\delta = C\lambda\sigma^2$$

and the amount of retrieval p that can be expected will be

$$p = C/(C + 2)$$

where C reflects the degree of difficulty that the regulator experiences while making the necessary adaptations given the risk aversion of domestic corporate firms. The value of p is the maximum that can be expected because the regulator exhibited perfect diligence.

Three aspects of this choice are noteworthy. First, suppose a firm exhibits a higher degree of risk aversion. It finds regulatory action insufficient and is likely to lose in case FIIs withdraw. Second, suppose $\eta < 1$. That is, the regulator is less than cautious in accommodating risk aversion. The regulator will not be able to make sure that domestic firms can minimize the losses of FIIs withdrawing investments. Consider the possibility of regulatory over reaction. Let

$$\delta = C^*\lambda\sigma^2$$

where $C^* > C$. In such a case

$$\mathrm{d}p/\mathrm{d}\lambda\sigma^2 = 2C^*(\eta - 1)/(C^* + 2)^2\,\lambda\sigma^2$$

That is, the overconfident corporate firm may not make adequate adjustments to its use of FII investments and experience less than satisfactory loss recovery if investments were withdrawn. Third, observe that when the regulatory diligence is efficient, p will be independent of $\lambda\sigma^2$. It will enable firms to make adequate adjustments in their use of investments to a point where their risk aversion has no more effect on the recovery when FIIs withdraw. It also suggests that the degree of regulatory diligence will be low in countries with low risk aversion and they will be prone to inflict losses on their domestic firms.

In sum, it can be concluded that regulatory diligence and the maximum share of benefits to domestic investors depend on the degree of difficulty and costs involved in making regulatory adjustments in response to the perceived risks and risk aversion of domestic investors.

11.3 Costs of Absorbing FII Investments

As noted in the previous section, domestic investors do experience some costs in the use of FII investments. First, there will be some costs in complying with regulatory requirements. Second, if they use these investments to augment productive activity, there will be costs of repayment if there is a sudden need to repay. Third, the awareness of the domestic firms concerning the risks of FII s withdrawing may induce them to exercise some diligence without necessarily depending on regulatory agencies to bail them out under all conceivable circumstances. This too has its cost implications.

The existence of regulatory activity may therefore impose some costs on domestic firms though it has a salutatory effect. In this section, we modify the results of the previous section taking into account these costs of absorbing the new investments into the domestic productive system.

The intensity of the regulatory mechanism and the additional expenditure for the firms depends on the anticipated loss due to FIIs withdrawing prematurely. Hence, these costs to domestic firms can be approximated by ky^2 where k depends on the nature of economic activity that is financed. The value function of the domestic investors then becomes

$$v_i = py - \lambda p^2\sigma^2 - ky^2$$

Hence, as before, the efficient choice of p will be

$$p = \delta / \left[\delta + 2\lambda\sigma^2 (1 + 2k\delta)\right]$$

The a priori expectation would be that when domestic firms agree to this cost, the regulator would be encouraged to perform better and ensure that p will increase. But this effect will be tempered by the increase in costs. Hence, the firms expect only a smaller amount of recovery. Stated differently, a firm that undertakes actions in conformity with the regulatory mechanism feels more assured of protection against losses if FIIs withdraw and consequently even a smaller share of recovery will be satisfactory to them. In general, the advantage consists of the reduction in the expected loss due to FIIs withdrawing their investment from domestic firms.

We should enter one caveat. The advantages of regulatory diligence should eventually be evaluated against the costs implicit in such enterprise. See, for example, Jullien et al. (1999). The results of this study will be satisfactory only under the assumption that benefits of regulation outweigh the costs for, in the contrary case, there will be no justification for regulation at all.

The pertinent question for analysis is the effect of compliance of firms, as reflected in the expenditure ky^2, on the extent of efficient regulatory activity. Consider, to begin with, the optimal choice of δ. As before, it can be verified that

$$\mathrm{d}p/\mathrm{d}\lambda\sigma^2 = 2\delta(\eta - 1 - 2k\delta)/\left[\delta + 2\lambda\sigma^2(1+2k\delta)\right]^2$$

Hence, the maximum value of p is achieved when

$$\eta = 1 + 2k\delta$$

With the consequent implication that the efficient δ is

$$\delta = C\lambda\sigma^2/\left(1 - 2kC\lambda\sigma^2\right),$$

the resulting p would still be

$$p = C/(C+2)$$

For all practical purposes, an increase in the costs incurred by domestic firms (i.e., their own efforts to counteract their risk aversion) will induce regulators to be more agile. It can effectively remove the negative effect on p and restore it to the value obtained in the previous section.

It may be argued that the costs incurred by the domestic firms will enable the regulator to calibrate the caution they exercise. The firms, who are aware of this, may be more careful in the use of the FII financial resources as k increases. We have the possibility that

$\mathrm{d}\delta/\mathrm{d}k > 0$. Then, it can be verified that

$$\mathrm{d}p/\mathrm{d}k = 2\delta\lambda\sigma^2\left[2(\eta-1)k + \eta\right]/k\left[\delta + 2\lambda\sigma^2(1+2k\delta)\right]^2$$

Clearly, p will increase with k if and only if

$$2k/(2k+1) < \eta$$

In sum, the increase in p is a result of the caution exercised by the firms in response to their risk aversion. The result does not depend on regulatory diligence per se.

Generally the regulatory agency may insist that the firm spends kp^2 if they expect to receive any regulatory caution. In other words, the regulator suggests that his actions alone will not be adequate to ensure a higher p. The firms should exhibit complementary diligence. Stated in this fashion, the expenditure of the firms may be independent of the expected loss per se. The efficient choice of p will then be

$$p = \delta / \left[\delta - 2\left(k + \lambda\sigma^2 \right) \right]$$

A finer point of the analysis may now be reported. It is possible to define an optimal value of k in the case under consideration for the firms can maximize v_i by choosing

$$k = \left(\lambda\sigma^2 \right)^{1/2}$$

With this choice in perspective, it can be shown that

$$y = 4\delta \left(\lambda\sigma^2 \right)^{1/2} / \left[\delta + 4\left(\lambda\sigma^2 \right)^{1/2} \right]$$

so that

$$p = \delta / \left[\delta + 4\left(\lambda\sigma^2 \right)^{1/2} \right]$$

Hence, the optimal level of recovery will be higher, compared to the base case, if $k>2$. High risk aversion can be adequately compensated by the firms exercising caution in all such cases.

The regulators should therefore expect domestic firms to exercise due diligence to complement regulatory mechanisms. The necessity for regulatory action can be reduced considerably if domestic firms exercise appropriate caution.

11.4 Rate of Absorption

It was assumed so far that domestic firms expect to utilize FII investments to produce Y units of output for T units of time. However, as the previous section indicates, domestic firms may have the ability to produce $Y^* > Y$ when they recognize that FIIs may withdraw well before the expected time. Such firms may surmise that the FIIs will withdraw t units of time ahead of the expected T. Under such conditions, regulatory diligence may enable the firms to restore ptY of output. Postulating the usual randomness associated with the fulfillment of this promise, the gains to the firms will be

$$g_i = p\left(tY + u \right)$$

Correspondingly, the value becomes

$$v_i = ptY - \lambda p^2\sigma^2$$

Assume, as before, that the firms choose p. The choice will be

$$p = tY/2\lambda\sigma^2$$

The basic difference in the present context is the cost to the FIIs at the time they withdraw. It can be expected that it will be $t^2Y^{*2}/2\delta$ because the intensive use of their finances may make it much more difficult to withdraw. Hence, the gain to the FII investors is

$$g_f = (1-p)(tY+u) - t^2Y^{*2}/2\delta \text{ and}$$
$$v_f = (1-p)tY - t^2Y^{*2}/2\delta$$

The net gain from the contract then becomes

$$N = tY - \lambda p^2\sigma^2 - t^2Y^{*2}/2\delta$$

FIIs can be expected to choose t to maximize N. Such a choice is given by

$$t = 2\delta\lambda\sigma^2Y/\left(\delta Y^2 + 2\lambda\sigma^2Y^{*2}\right)$$

Hence, it follows that

$$p = \delta/\left(\delta + 2\lambda\sigma^2x^2\right)$$

where

$$x = \text{intensity of use}$$
$$= Y^*/Y$$

Clearly, this choice reduces to the result obtained earlier if $x=1$.

As before, note that p is maximized when $\eta=1$. The maximum p possible under regulatory diligence is

$$p = C/\left(C + 2x^2\right)$$

The issue that needs to be considered is about the choice of x by domestic firms. It can be readily shown that only $x=1$ can maximize N. The FII may, instead, maximize their expected gains. Note that

$$v_f = 2Cx^2\lambda\sigma^2/\left(C + 2x^2\right)^2$$

The optimal choice of x is therefore

$$x = (C/2)^{1/2}$$

Regulatory intervention will be meaningful if and only if $C > 2$.

Hence, in general, the effect of FII investments being withdrawn earlier than expected will depend on the speed with which domestic firms can convert the financial gains to real returns. In particular, domestic investors may agree to a lower maximum share if the rate of absorption is high.

11.5 Sequential Entry

Regulatory agencies monitor the performance of the FIIs on a regular basis. They can use the information regarding their performance to allow a greater flow of FII investments if past performance is satisfactory. They will also accept greater risks given the assurance that the chance of failure is not as large as originally anticipated. It would be useful to examine this aspect of regulatory diligence.

Suppose the domestic firms initially expect the FIIs to withdraw while y units of expected output are yet to materialize. In actual practice, investments may not be withdrawn as expected. The domestic firms and regulators may then accept greater risk and allow FII investments that may be withdrawn while $y^* > y$ of output has yet to materialize. As before, it will be postulated that only a fraction of y^* can be recovered if investments are withdrawn. Let the additional gain to the domestic firms be

$$g = q(y^* + u)$$

where q is the fraction of recovery under the new dispensation. The intrinsic nature of the FII investments does not change in any fundamental way just because more cautious sequential entry is conceptualized. Hence, the random variable u is the same as before. It can also be surmised that the risk aversion of domestic firms does not change materially. Consequently, the value of the additional entry to domestic firms will be

$$v_i = qy^* - \lambda\sigma^2 q^2$$

The optimal choice of q will then be

$$q = y^*/2\lambda\sigma^2$$

Consider the gains to the FIIs. The costs they experience will change to $(y^* - y)^2/2\delta$. Hence, the additional gain to FII investors is

$$g_f = (1-q)(y^* + u) - (y^* - y)^2/2\delta$$

Consequently, the value of investments to the FIIs will be

$$v_{\mathrm{f}} = (1-q)\,y^* - (y^* - y)^2 / 2\delta$$

As before, the net value addition from these additional finances is

$$N = y^* - y^{*2}/4\lambda\sigma^2 - (y^* - y)^2 / 2\delta$$

Hence, maximization yields

$$y^* = 2\lambda\sigma^2(\delta + y)/(\delta + 2\lambda\sigma^2) \text{ and}$$
$$q = (\delta + y)/(\delta + 2\lambda\sigma^2)$$

Clearly, the recovery fraction with sequential entry is higher. Fundamentally, domestic investors, who accept greater risks than earlier, need to be compensated. It is also possible that, with the experience in absorbing FII investments, domestic firms can use FII flows more productively and thereby expect that they can recover a greater fraction of the expected losses even if FIIs withdraw prematurely. In all likelihood, regulatory diligence will also increase and have a salutary effect.

We now examine the possibility that regulatory agencies conceptualize both y and y^* a priori though they will reveal y^* only when the situation warrants it. It is of course plausible that domestic investors have no reason to think about y^* initially. Hence, the choices of the domestic firms will be

$$y = 2p\lambda\sigma^2 \quad \text{and} \quad y^* = 2q\lambda\sigma^2$$

The basic difference is in the cost structure of FIIs. If both stages of sequential entry do materialize, they must reckon with the prospect of withdrawing investment even when y^* units of returns can still be generated. Hence, one component of the cost is $y^{*2}/2\delta$. However, they must anticipate an additional cost $(y-y^*)^2/2\delta$ because the regulatory mechanisms will be more stringent initially and they would have made adjustments anticipating this action on the part of the regulators. Hence, the net value of the contract will be

$$N = y + y^* - \lambda\sigma^2 p^2 - \lambda\sigma^2 q^2 - y^{*2}/2\delta - (y - y^*)^2 / 2\delta$$

It can then be verified that

$$y = 2\delta\lambda\sigma^2/(\delta + 2\lambda\sigma^2), \quad p = \delta/(\delta + 2\lambda\sigma^2),$$
$$y^* = 2\delta\lambda\sigma^2(\delta + 4\lambda\sigma^2)/(\delta + 2\lambda\sigma^2)^2 > y, \text{ and}$$
$$q = \delta(\delta + 4\lambda\sigma^2)/(\delta + 2\lambda\sigma^2)^2 > p$$

There is always a possibility that the regulatory agencies tend to be optimistic to begin with and create stringent measures only when failure is recorded. That is, $y^* < y$ and $q < p$ cannot be ruled out. The costs to the FII, at the second sequential stage, may then be $(y + y^*)^2/2\delta$. Hence, this possibility can be easily verified.

One word of caution is in order. As of now, there is no well-defined economic theory concerning the cost functions postulated above. Perhaps a rich variety of regulatory practices can be visualized if alternative specifications are adopted.

11.6 Risk Spreading

We will now argue that risk sharing only spreads risks among the parties and that it cannot assure us that the overall risks are reduced. In other words, risk-sharing contractual agreements may indeed encourage dealing in more risky transactions. It should therefore be expected that many risky FII investments reach the market even under the regulatory regimes that we have been considering.

Return to the basic model of section 2. Given the optimal values of p and y, it can be shown that

$$v_{\mathrm{i}} = \lambda\sigma^2\delta^2 / \left(\delta + 2\lambda\sigma^2\right)^2$$

We will now investigate the propensity of domestic firms to encourage the introduction of more risky FII investments. This can be inferred if v_{i} increases with $\lambda\sigma^2$. In fact, it can be verified that

$$\partial v_{\mathrm{i}} / \partial\lambda\sigma^2 = \delta^2\left(\delta - 2\lambda\sigma^2\right) / \left(\delta + 2\lambda\sigma^2\right)^3 > 0$$

if and only if $\delta > 2\lambda\sigma^2$. Hence, it can be concluded that domestic firms gain from FII entry if $\lambda\sigma^2$ is low and/or the regulatory agencies are more vigilant. In either case, it cannot be denied that domestic firms have an incentive to accept more risky FII investments.

How do FIIs react? Note that

$$\partial y / \partial\lambda\sigma^2 = 2\delta^2 / \left(\delta + 2\lambda\sigma^2\right)^2 > 0$$

That is, FIIs tend to choose high-risk investments. Further, observe that

$$\partial v_{\mathrm{f}} / \partial\lambda\sigma^2 = 4\delta^2\lambda\sigma^2 / \left(\delta + 2\lambda\sigma^2\right)^3 > 0$$

Hence, the FIIs gain by choosing higher risk. It can be concluded that commercial interests of both the FIIs and domestic firms tend to attract hot money.

Will efficient regulation reduce volatility and risk? To examine this in the context of the model of section 2, observe that

$$V(v_i) = p^2\sigma^2$$
$$V(v_f) = (1-p)^2\sigma^2$$

where V denotes variance. Hence, the extent of volatility in FII transactions will be

$$V = \left[p^2 + (1-p)^2\right]\sigma^2$$

Efficient regulation may necessitate minimizing V by choosing δ. Consider the case where σ^2 is taken to be given exogenously. Then,

$$\partial V / \partial\lambda\sigma^2 = 2(2p-1)\sigma^2 \partial p/\partial\lambda\sigma^2 = 0$$

necessitates that p should be minimized. As noted in section 2, this implies

$$\delta = C\lambda\sigma^2$$

and the corresponding p achievable is

$$p = C/(C+2)$$

Hence, the resulting variance can be written as

$$V = \sigma^2\left(C^2+4\right)/(C+2)^2$$

This will be minimum if and only if $C=2$. In any given practical context, this will be satisfied only accidentally. In other words, in general, the minimum conceivable volatility is unattainable. The other point to note is that commercial interests of both the parties may induce them to choose a higher σ^2 and thereby increase the volatility.

Suppose, now, that the regulators prefer to screen the nature of FII investments further. That is, they may choose δ to place limits on σ^2 as well. Minimizing V with respect to σ^2, and keeping in perspective that p is a function of δ and σ^2, suggests that the choice of δ should now be such that $\partial p/\partial\lambda\sigma^2 < 0$. In general, there will be more stringent regulation. However, this will reduce the maximum p achievable. The trade-off is therefore evident. If the regulator targets as low volatility as possible while allowing domestic firms to achieve the largest possible returns, there is no guarantee that the volatility is minimized. On the other hand, if the regulators try to achieve the least volatility, they will reduce FII flows and possible returns to domestic firms.

11.7 Timing of Withdrawal

Starting from the premise that, from a long-run perspective, microlevel regulatory action is necessary to prevent the kind of macrolevel financial disasters that we witnessed in recent times, this study sought to model regulatory mechanisms to counter the ill effects of FIIs withdrawing their finances prematurely. We acknowledged that the absence of regulation, or inadequate regulation, generally makes the impact of FII investments more volatile. However, the volatility may be reduced to some extent if domestic firms can develop physical capital and/or production capacity with the use of FII investments. Our approach was to argue that domestic firms will be forced to incur greater costs while they make such attempts. We demonstrated that domestic investors may agree to lower maximum share of returns if the rate of absorption is high. Even if this is acknowledged, regulatory diligence is necessary to ensure that the impact of FIIs withdrawing their finances is minimal. It was shown that efficient regulation depends on the costs of neutralizing the risk aversion of domestic firms.

We demonstrated that domestic firms tend to improve the rate of absorption of FII investments if they expect FIIs to withdraw their investments well before the expected time. Such intensive use may signal to the FII investors that there will be an increase in the costs of their withdrawing early. This tends to hasten the process of withdrawing finances even if regulatory mechanisms are efficient. Targeting maximum returns to domestic firms and investors may not be the most desirable goal of regulation.

Regulatory institutions have the option of allowing sequential entry. Regulatory diligence suggests that low risk investments would be allowed initially. More risky investments will be allowed only if the ground-level experiences suggest that the ill effects of FII investments being withdrawn are not as extensive as originally contemplated. However, we also demonstrated the possibility that domestic firms, as well as FII investors, would prefer lower regulatory barriers at the outset. This is in their best commercial interest. They would reconcile to more stringent action only if there is an unacceptable level of investors withdrawing finances. From an analytical viewpoint, the difficulty is in fixing the trade-off a priori while defining efficient regulatory diligence.

It was then demonstrated that efficient regulatory measures may yet be inadequate to curb risk taking tendencies. In particular, regulation can only find mechanisms to absorb given risks while maximizing the returns to domestic firms. If the regulators try to choose desirable levels of risk along with measures to curb risk spreading, their choices would result in reducing the gains to domestic firms. The trade-off is clear. However, it is not very easy to analytically specify the desirable level of trade-off.

Several aspects of the problem could not be examined. First, the effect of regulation depends on how and how much of FII investments can be absorbed by domestic firms. This was not explicitly dealt with. Instead, we acknowledged the effects of regulation on the costs that FIIs incur when they withdraw their investments prematurely. A more direct approach will probably yield useful insights into the efficient choice of regulatory mechanisms. Second, the domestic economic system that attempts to absorb FII investments into its productive system must have financial resources on hand to cushion the unexpected reduction in FII investments. We did not explicitly deal with this aspect of regulatory diligence. Third, analogous to our attempt to make efficient regulatory mechanisms a function of the inherent randomness, they may depend on the volume of FII flows and a number of other policy-related measures. There is no clear economic theory which accounts for the costs and/or advantages of such measures. To this extent, the results of the present study are only symptomatic. More detailed analysis is in order. Fourth, regulatory policies may have an effect on the volume of FII investments. This was not taken up explicitly. In general, when this aspect is incorporated, we expect a trade-off between an increase in the losses due to FIIs withdrawing finances and the productive use of additional financial resources. We do not wish to speculate on the regulatory changes that this trade-off necessitates. Fifth, FII investments may be associated with purely speculative capital gains on the stock market. In such a case, FIIs withdrawing finances may also add to the losses of the domestic investors through capital gains. In particular, the arbitrage mechanism may not operate as expected. Will these losses have a very different nature compared to the conceptualization in the present study? We do not rule this out. A more extensive analysis is warranted.

References

Biyani K (2007) It happened in India. Rupa & Co, New Delhi

Friedman TL (2008) If Larry and Sergy asked for a loan. Deccan Chronicle, October 27, 2008

Jullien B, Salanie B, Salanie F (1999) Should more risk averse agents exert more effort? Geneva Pap Risk Insur Theory 24:19–28

Chapter 12
Financial Crisis and Regulatory Policy

Abstract The recent financial crisis generated a great deal of debate about the necessity for, and the quantum of, bailouts. There is also a wide-ranging acknowledgment that prudential regulation is necessary to minimize the frequency and intensity of such systemic failures in the future. However, the existing analytical and policy studies tend to deal with these two aspects in isolation. By way of contrast, this study sets up an analytical framework to endogenously determine the requisite regulatory practices and bailout instruments to overcome the liquidity problems and the associated solvency problem on a long-term basis. Such efficient choices have been structured to resolve the trade-off between growth and stability by maximizing the welfare of all the parties. Prior knowledge that a well-defined bailout policy operates if they adhere to clearly specified regulatory norms signals to the financial institutions that keeping risks within bounds will be in the overall interests of all concerned.

12.1 Nature of Crisis

The recent financial crisis has two essential dimensions. The first aspect is a liquidity problem reflecting the inability of financial institutions (FIs) to continue lending to business since they could not recover past loans that they granted. The second problem is that cumulative losses, or purely unforeseen exogenous economic forces, resulted in the erosion of the market value of their assets. It resulted in increasing their inability to finance even legitimate and fundamentally sound investments. This is generally the solvency problem.

Three types of ripple effects have been observed in some countries. First, some FIs hold titles to the tainted receivables primarily because they erroneously expected

This chapter is derived in part from an article published in *Macroeconomics and Finance in Developing Market Economies*, 2010, © Taylor and Francis, available online: http://tandfonline.com, DOI: 10.1080/17520843.2010.498131

T.V.S.R. Rao, *Risk Sharing, Risk Spreading and Efficient Regulation*,
DOI 10.1007/978-81-322-2562-1_12

higher returns from them. They have to address the resultant liquidity problem.[1] Second, some reduction in liquidity is due to foreign institutional investors (FIIs) withdrawing their dollar investments given the liquidity problems in their countries. The resultant reduction in liquidity must be made up to sustain the economic activity in such contexts. Third, some emerging economies have been dependent on incomes derived from outsourcing activities of developed economies. The financial crisis had the effect of reducing these activities and the associated financial flows. Bailouts as well as regulatory prescriptions should bring these sources into their fold.

Three strands of thought relating to the genesis of the financial crisis have been recorded. The first strand pertains to the nature of financial intermediation. Two different aspects of this have been highlighted. First, there has been a significant widening and deepening of the financial system. The banking system is fairly well organized. However, the activities of other financial intermediaries are not well structured. Structured finance and securitization in particular created a milieu that has not been amenable to organized liquidity and asset creation. Second, the expansion of the financial system resulted in significant interrelatedness of the different segments of the financial system. Consequently, the crisis tends to be magnified even if there is very little risk in any one activity per se. See, for instance, Acemoglu (2009). No one financial institution or economic sector has the ability to conceptualize any correction when the crisis spreads. Note, further, that some microlevel decisions of financial institutions have consequences for the society at large. None of the entrepreneurs will acknowledge his role and cannot remedy the consequences even if they do. The second strand refers to the way financial intermediation takes place in practice. Mendoza (2008) suggests that the operation of the collateral constraint is the primary mechanism

[1] Securitization is at the apex of this problem. The activities of credit rating agencies that support their activity have also come under scrutiny. The riskiness of the securitized pool, in itself, is not the major cause of the recent financial crisis. Instead, a reduction in the overall economic activity resulted in the inability to pay back loans. Similarly, Hull et al. (2004) suggested that credit rating agencies cannot anticipate external exigencies that bring down the value of securitized assets. They can only react to them by downgrades when information is available. Even if such arguments are circumscribed, it will be difficult to eliminate securitization and/or credit ratings since they are well entrenched. This may suggest that bailouts are justified. However, there is hardly any support to conceptualize bailouts. Whalen (2009, p. 3) offered the most compelling reason for this. As he put it, "the crucial quality of the derivative mindset that enabled the multiplication of risk that now threatens the entire global market place (is that) the principal purpose was speculation rather than investment." Instead, a significant restructuring in the use of these instruments is under way. IIF (2008) put the argument succinctly. "Resolution of liquidity issues of current market stress will depend on sound internal risk management decisions by firms; principles based regulation focusing on outcomes rather than quantitative requirements; and ongoing attention by the central banking community to liquidity in an internationally integrated, market based system." A representative sample of the analytical debates consists of Congleton (2009) and Eichengreen (2009). Note that regulatory practices should keep three dimensions in perspective. First, in general, the SPVs do not have the financial structure or stability to absorb risks. It is therefore necessary to define the obligations of the originator more precisely and inclusively. See also Acemoglu (2009). Second, observe that securitization is a complex, individual, requirement-centered instrument. As such, no single measure of risk may be adequate from a regulatory perspective. Third, we do not as yet have a credible framework of the desirable characteristics of a robust securitization model. Perhaps, dimensions, other than risk characteristics, need attention. This study will not pursue this aspect any further.

because an excessive expansion almost always precedes a financial crisis. The constraint operates through two credit channels. First, when the collateral constraint binds, there will be an endogenous financing premium that affects one-period debt, working capital loans, and the return on equity because there will be an increase in the effective cost of borrowing. Second, when the collateral constraint binds, agents liquidate capital in order to meet margin calls. The sale of assets reduces capital and further tightens the constraint, setting off a spiraling collapse of asset prices and a simultaneous decline in production and factor demands. The third strand deals with the psychology of individuals. Two different aspects have been highlighted. First, there has been an acknowledgment that the entrepreneurial function of risk taking is an important driver of economic growth. But uncontrolled individual greed and myopia have led to serious and rather frequent disturbances of the economic system. When confronted with frequent systemic failures in unregulated markets, individuals tend to be myopic and feel that taking great risks is the only way of achieving success when the economic environment is favorable. However, it is important to recognize that private individuals tend to become highly risk averse when they experience repeated failure and they alone have to bear the adverse effects of their risk taking propensities. The cycles of success and instability tend to be more acute due to such myopic attitudes. Second, in earlier studies, pertaining to the foreign exchange crisis in the mid-1990s, Sachs et al. (1996) and Chang and Velasco (1999) observed the following. A bank or an FI offers loans to many individual firms. If they reveal their types, i.e., the risk involved in the activities for which they borrow, the FIs can intermediate efficiently. But they may not do so. This adverse selection problem is at the apex of the probability of default that the FIs experience. Gorton (2008) holds a similar viewpoint even in the context of the current financial crisis. These forces contributed to the recent financial crisis.

In the context of recent events, a rather fast and deep spread of the crisis was discernible. As a result, some quick fix solutions had to be conceptualized and implemented. Since all the major countries affected by the subprime crisis are otherwise economically resilient, the immediate problem has been one of providing adequate liquidity to sustain the economic activity.[2] The other issue is clearly to protect the assets that lost their value temporarily and restore them when these economies bounce back.[3] Bailouts addressed both these requirements. Most of the details relate to effects of a short-term nature.[4] They tend to have a short-term effect of moving the

[2]This may be looked upon as having two dimensions. First, it should be possible to utilize the existing capital stock in various sectors to generate production. This may, in itself, generate adequate income and demand for goods and services. Second, consumer credit and demand for goods and services may have been affected due to the liquidity crisis. Reviving the demand side will also be necessary. In this context, a bailout, an increase in liquidity per se, or lower interest rates may not have the desired effect. The flight to capital, or the lookout for more promising assets for investment purposes, necessitates fiscal action to revive economic activity before bailouts can succeed. See, for instance, Kriegel (2009). This aspect will not be considered in the present study.

[3]The tainted assets are generally held by a trust which exercises a put option once the value of assets improves. The government then recovers its bailout amount. See, for instance, Poole (2008).

[4]The efficacy of the ad hoc nature of the bailouts has been in doubt. First, Palma (2009), among others, argued that bailing out all the losses in a hurry to restore liquidity creates an incentive to remain careless. Second, the FIs do not reveal their true types when they accept a certain bailout.

system out of the crisis. However, if the recent bailout responses are any indication, these ex post policies will be too late and too little. As an ex post measure, this reactionary approach proved inadequate as the various financial disasters of recent origin testify. There is also a fairly general agreement that temporary bailouts cannot be a basis for systemic regulatory change that is necessary to restore the stability of the system on a long-run basis. One such acknowledgment is that of Todorova (2009). Despite the fact that the crises have been frequent and severe long-term regulatory action has not been attempted, even bailouts did not have a systemic structure.

For some odd reason, there is a stubborn adherence to the argument that individuals and markets are mature and responsible decision makers and that they can self-regulate the system toward stable and high growth. This viewpoint persists despite the experience of repeated failure and instability.[5] Acemoglu (2009) has three pertinent observations. First, it must be recognized that market monitoring is not sufficient against systemic opportunism. Second, strictly speaking, even free markets are not totally unregulated. In particular, some institutional mechanism (call it regulator if you wish) must be in place to make sure that markets function efficiently. Third, it is necessary to have an efficient theory of regulation, of both firms and financial institutions, so that the desired balance between growth and stability is attained.

Hence, it may be inferred that microlevel as well as systemic regulatory measures are the only definitive long-run solution. Such regulatory policy is necessary to make sure that self-seeking decisions of the financial institutions do not disrupt economic fundamentals.[6] Such regulatory practices should also ensure that the FIs will take the desired risks by providing an adequate mechanism to compensate them in case of failure that is not under their control. This is the structure of a bailout. It should, therefore, be understood that both bailouts and regulation will have to be defined endogenously

Improvements in social welfare resulting from such bailouts tend to be small because there will be no fundamental change in the decisions of the FIs. They argue that a private insurance mechanism may have better information content. Third, Kriegel (2009) pointed out that banks did not want to lend the extra liquidity because, at low interest rates, the administrative costs of extending loans have been prohibitive. The central banks paying interest on the deposits that banks hold with them only aggravated the problem. On the other hand, banks could not lend because borrowers did not have the necessary collateral. Further, a Keynesian type of liquidity trap is operating in the sense that borrowers did not find many investment opportunities to use the excess credit available. Given this milieu, he argues that monetary policy is ineffective. He, therefore, suggests that fiscal action to increase aggregate demand will have a superior impact by improving the demand for credit and activating the financial system at large.

[5] It must be noted that even the recent G20 summit advocated restructuring global financial institutions in the hope that, once they are in place, the FIs will make wise decisions.

[6] The typical approach to regulation has been advocating the following. The FIs will take great risks if there is no regulation. They may succeed in maintaining systemic stability. Such stable epochs tend to underestimate the inherent moral hazard associated with financial intermediation and minimize the role of the regulator. But excessive risk taking leads to a crisis once the liquidity constraint is binding. See, for instance, Mendoza (2008). The greater the cost of a crisis, the greater will be the call for regulation. It is then essential to specify a proper information system and minimum prudential regulation. On the other hand, strict regulation that succeeds in preventing crises may stifle private entrepreneurial initiative to a point where there is little risk in the system. However, note that the efficient design of regulation is generally considered to be independent of bailout policy.

keeping a desired trade-off in perspective.[7] Maximizing social welfare, which factors in the disadvantages of failure, is one way of specifying this level of trade-off.

For all practical purposes, this is the basic departure from existing studies. It offers one way of defining acceptable risks and the extent to which restructuring activity can be justified without significantly curtailing the entrepreneurial urge to take risk and sustain economic growth.

The rest of the study is organized as follows. Section 12.2 details a principal agent model in which bailouts and regulation can be defined endogenously. A simple bailout policy, based on the perceived degree of difficulty of the FIs in exercising due diligence and maximizing social welfare, offers the FIs an opportunity to select appropriate lending policies. The efficacy of capital adequacy norms has also been considered. It was shown that such a policy is more efficient if the FIs are not adequately diligent or the regulators can resolve information asymmetry and systemic risk more successfully. Section 12.3 extends the framework to long-term lending policies and solvency problems. The additional problem in this context is the possibility that greater than efficient amounts of loans that may be deemed consistent with their asset structure may be granted to accelerate the growth in the system. A simple modification of the bailout and regulatory mechanisms can be shown to limit the volatility so generated. Section 12.4 deals with the flow of foreign institutional investments. The most important result in this context is the possibility that it may be more efficient from a regulatory perspective to offer limited bailouts initially and extend them if they can limit the volatility of the system. In particular, it can be shown that the more diligent FIs may gain from this policy. In the final analysis, it must be noted that these policies reduce the growth to some extent while stabilizing the system. However, they will leave enough leverage with the entrepreneurs to take risks consistent with the overall objective of maximizing social welfare. Section 12.5 then dwells on some extensions of the results and their practical importance.

12.2 Basic Structure[8]

The analysis in this section begins with financing over a short interval of time and for assets that can be liquidated quickly.[9]

[7] Some authors, notably Borio (2009), Davis and Karim (2009), and Farhi and Tirole (2009), advocate this approach. The World Bank has been consistently taking the position that the problems of adverse selection can be avoided altogether if the larger corporate firms know that it would be much more difficult for them to get any bailouts and that penalties for misdeeds are hefty. See, for example, Ratnovski (2009).

[8] Information asymmetry and agency problems tend to limit the risks that investors will be willing to bear. In such a situation, too much control leads to greater risk aversion and hence tends to be counterproductive. Instead, bailouts that signal the regulator's willingness to share the risks will be more efficient. However, these studies do not contain any of the details specified in this section.

[9] Most of the analysis of this study pertains to bailout of the financial sector alone. Many authors have been suggesting that other sectors should not be bailed out. Financial institutions are catalysts on which all real sectors depend. Since they borrow for a short time horizon and lend for a longer

Consider the case of FIs providing loans L. Assume that the FIs provide loans to every possible activity, justifiable by economic fundamentals or purely speculative. Postulate that they charge an interest rate r. The institutions however recognize that not all borrowers are trustworthy. Some of them are bound to renege on loan repayment. Let the actual losses of the FIs be y_a. If the loans are fully recovered, the loss will be $-L(1+r)$. On the other hand, if none of the loans can be recovered, the loss will be L. Hence, y_a can be considered to be a random variable on the support $-L(1+r)$ to L. Denote the expected value of y_a by y and rewrite

$$y_a = y + u$$

where

u is a random variable with
$E(u)$ = expected value of $u = 0$ and
$V(u)$ = variance of $u = \sigma^2$

Any realization of $y_a > 0$ signals a liquidity problem.

The sources of randomness can be specified as follows. First, given the propensity to prefer larger size and growth, every one of the FIs may extend loans without proper caution. This increases the risk of defaults. Second, the interdependence of the financial system is such that there may be systemic risk quite independent of risks created by individual FIs. For, only if every FI keeps its risks within bounds can systemic risk be limited. But there can be free riding leading to violations by one or more FIs. It leads to substantial system risks. In this case, individual FIs will also not have the capacity to moderate system risks. Third, the risk may have its origin outside the financial system. For instance, there may be a sudden reduction in the value of assets of FIs due to recession. Similarly, it may be induced by foreign institutional investors withdrawing their investments.

It is obvious that FIs can exercise due diligence to a certain extent. However, the FIs, by themselves, will not be in a position to moderate risks when they take on systemic proportions. In such a situation, regulatory action will be called for.[10]

---

term, the confidence of the depositors that they can recover their money is crucial. The significant interrelationships between financial institutions and the real sector in the process of intermediation are the compelling reason for providing them bailouts in the context of a financial crisis. The real sectors should not be bailed out simply because their failure is a result of the financial crisis and not its cause. In effect, the real sectors can be expected to bounce back if the financial markets can be restored to their normal functioning. From a political economy perspective, the objection is basically that taxpayer's money should not be utilized to bail out the well-to-do sectors that made enough profits while the economic environment was favorable. In general, bailout of the IT sector and other service activities like airlines has not been favored. Refer to Palma (2009). However, there is a wide-ranging debate about the desirability of extending bailouts to nonfinancial activities. The following analytical perspective applies equally efficiently in both these cases.

[10] Some observers suggest that the original borrowers should get the bailout and, as a corollary, bear the cost of administering the bailout for, after all, equity demands that the assets they acquired with the loan should belong to them. This may be justified if their default is purely accidental because of exogenous economic conditions. The case of bailouts for housing loan defaults in the

The actual loss y_a determines the necessary quantum of bailout. Let the bailout[11] offer be

$$B = py_a$$

The choice of p should indicate the tolerance limits of the society regarding system instability and provide incentives to induce the FIs to make their decisions in such a way that systemic risks can be kept within bounds. The efficient choice of p is less than unity. For, if $p=1$ and the FIs know that the entire loss will be covered, they will not have any incentive to exercise requisite diligence in the choice of loans that they extend. p cannot be zero either for, in that case, FIs need to be excessively cautious and reduce loans to even deserving economic activity. A choice of p such that $0<p<1$ can be expected to reduce risky loans to some extent while preserving the innovativeness of the FIs in encouraging the growth of economic activity.[12] The ex ante announcement about the availability of such bailouts may create the impression that the FIs will be encouraged to take runaway risks.[13] But there is a countervailing mechanism in this formulation.

Observe that y_a may be negative. That is, the FIs are in a position to recover the loans and continue in business. The regulator is then expecting them to make a deposit. This is akin to an insurance mechanism. Bailout amounts can be obtained from this pool when the need arises. The banking sector has similar capital adequacy norms in place. Brunnermeier et al. (2009) and la Torre and Ize (2009) also advocated such countercyclical prudential requirements for the non-banking financial sector. This may improve the stability of the financial system even if it reduces growth marginally. When this arrangement is in place, the gain to the FIs is

$$g_f = p(y+u)$$

USA has been dealt with in this manner for an attempt was made to restructure mortgages by reducing interest rates and reducing EMI by extending the duration of loans.

[11] Note that the bailout may be in the form of credit created by actions of the central bank. It need not be in the form of a fiscal policy action from budgetary resources of the government. The efficiency of one of these routes against the other is also an important issue for the choice may not depend only on considerations of liquidity and solvency. Larger macroeconomic issues like recessionary trends and demand-side management may prevail.

[12] Bailouts cause moral hazard problems reflected in lower levels of effort. But they also provide incentives to reveal the risk types and mitigate adverse selection problems created by information asymmetry. The present study attempts to define acceptable risk endogenously in such a way as to maximize the net benefit to the society.

[13] Actually the managerial compensation mechanisms have been of this nature for, while they receive bonuses in good times, they are not penalized for erroneous decisions. McAfee and McMillan (1991) argued that asking them to make an initial deposit is an efficient mechanism against such opportunism.

The FIs may, in their efforts to preserve their reputation, exercise due diligence in extending loans, be averse to seeking bailouts if they can avoid them, and view such bailouts negatively. Hence, the value of g_{f} to the FIs can be represented by

$$v_{\mathrm{f}} = py - \lambda p^2\sigma^2; \quad \lambda > 0$$

That is, λ is a representation of their degree of risk aversion.[14]

Consider the choice of the FIs. They know that there will be some failure irrespective of their a priori screening of borrowers. Hence, they will be more concerned about recovery rather than the quantum of loans. Stated differently, an FI, who suspects that some loans cannot be recovered, will agree to provide a greater volume of loans and to borrowers whose credit worthiness cannot be ascertained readily, only if p is high. In general, the FIs will choose p to maximize v_{f}. Consequently, the efficient choice of p is

$$p = y/2\lambda\sigma^2$$

The gains to the regulator may now be considered. He acknowledges that the reduction in liquidity will be y_{a} if a default is experienced. Offering a bailout B may entice the FIs to continue lending and accept some loss. Hence, the gain to the regulator will be $(1-p)y_{\mathrm{a}}$. However, the regulator experiences some administrative costs. Similarly, there are opportunity costs of not being in a position to use the bailout amount in other productive uses. Let such costs be $y^2/2\delta$. Two aspects of this specification are pertinent. First, the regulator feels that the costs increase more than proportionately with the propensity of the FIs to take risks. Second, in this specification, δ represents the efficiency with which FIs were recovering loans in the past. The regulator expects lower costs of administering bailouts if the FIs have been more vigilant in the past. The gain to the regulator may then be written as

$$g_{\mathrm{r}} = (1-p)(y+u) - y^2/2\delta$$

In general, the regulators will be risk neutral since they are dealing with many transactions. The value of g_{f} to them will be

$$v_{\mathrm{r}} = (1-p)y - y^2/2\delta$$

---

[14] Another possibility presents itself from an analytical perspective. Confronted with frequent crises and the need to administer bailouts, the regulator may be relatively more risk averse. By way of contrast, the FIs may consider the a priori bailout mechanism in place to be a sufficient license for them to take more risks. That is, in comparison, they appear risk neutral. Identically, the same results can be developed for this variant of the principal agent model.

Observe that the regulators will not be interested in maximizing the value of their own gains. Instead, they will consider net gains to the society. That is, they tend to maximize[15]

$$
\begin{aligned}
N &= v_f + v_r \\
&= y - y^2/2\delta - \lambda p^2\sigma^2
\end{aligned}
$$

However, they must take the participatory constraint of the FIs into account since they are autonomous with respect to their decisions. The regulators will try to limit the quantum and quality of loans that the FIs offer. Substituting

$$p = y/2\lambda\sigma^2$$

and maximizing N with respect to y results in

$$
\begin{aligned}
y &= 2\delta\lambda\sigma^2/\left(\delta + 2\lambda\sigma^2\right) \text{ and} \\
p &= \delta/\left(\delta + 2\lambda\sigma^2\right)
\end{aligned}
$$

Observe that, ceteris paribus, p is lower if $\lambda\sigma^2$ is high.[16] Note further that p tends to 1 as δ tends to ∞. That is, if the FIs exercise utmost diligence while extending loans, they cannot be blamed if a default occurs. It must be purely due to circumstances beyond their control. They will then claim and receive their entire loss in the form of a bailout.[17]

In actual practice, there is an impression that the regulator fixes the quantum of bailout and the FIs exercise preference with respect to the type of loans they negotiate (thereby indicating a preference for y). The choices described in the foregoing model are ex ante. The above observation refers to ex post implementation. More pertinently, the FIs may infer the tolerance of the regulator and the society with respect to defaults from the bailouts offered to them. The analytical distinction will not be an impediment to this practical reality.

For the sake of analytical completeness, consider the case where the regulator claims that the loan default is entirely due to the negligence of the FIs. The regulator may then make the FIs bear the cost of extending the bailouts The gain to the FIs will now be

---

[15] Note that highly inefficient FIs make the costs of bailouts excessive to a point where $y^2/2\delta > y$. Bailouts cannot be justified under these conditions. From an analytical viewpoint, the model described here will be applicable only if $N > 0$.

[16] It will be presently argued that, under certain conditions, higher bailouts can be justified when $\lambda\sigma^2$ increases.

[17] In a more general model, there is a possibility that multiple equilibria exist. Some of them may represent a low-level trap, some may be unstable, and yet others are high growth indicators. In the short run, small increases in liquidity cannot move the system out of the low-level equilibrium trap.

$$g_f = p(y+u) - y^2/2\delta \text{ and}$$
$$v_f = py - y^2/2\delta - \lambda p^2\sigma^2$$

Under this dispensation, the FIs may be more inclined to be diligent and limit the extent of losses represented by y. They will then choose

$$y = p\delta$$

The net value of the contract is the same as before and therefore the choice of p is invariant. That is,

$$p = \delta / (\delta + 2\lambda\sigma^2)$$

The regulator continues to offer the same bailout. However, the expected loss due to default, in equilibrium, will now be

$$y = \delta^2 / (\delta + 2\lambda\sigma^2)$$

This mechanism can be deemed to be more efficient if y can be reduced. That is, if

$$\delta < 2\lambda\sigma^2$$

The regulators will resort to this approach if they have a priori information about low efficiency levels of the FIs.

Another result is important. It starts with an acknowledgment that the FIs will exercise due diligence to counteract their risk aversion as well as the costs that the regulator may impose on them otherwise.[18] This is generally the implication of the claim that the FIs and markets are mature and that they can make efficient decisions to keep systemic instability within bounds. The extent to which they can make the adjustment depends on the externally determined risk σ^2 as well as the costs of monitoring that the borrowers impose on them in their efforts to resolve the information asymmetry. Indeed, if the FIs can convince the regulator that due diligence is exercised, they can claim a bailout to cover their entire losses ($p=1$). Alternatively, if they can convince the regulator that such costs are abnormally high, they may yet manage to get full bailout if their lending scheme is socially desirable. From an analytical point of view, it should be expected that the FIs choose $\delta = \delta(\lambda\sigma^2)$. In general, it can be surmised that

[18] The regulator is dealing with many FIs. Their efficiencies with respect to loan recoveries differ. But it would be far more efficient from an administrative viewpoint if the regulator defines one value of p and allows the FIs, who wish to remain in business, to self-select. This argument suggests that the FIs will adjust their δ to an exogenously determined $\lambda\sigma^2$. This can be shown to result in the choice of p independent of $\lambda\sigma^2$. An argument of this nature was advanced in Jullien et al. (1999) in the context of fairly general contractual arrangements.

$$d\delta/d\lambda\sigma^2 > 0$$

That is, the more diligence the FIs will exercise, the greater the perceived risk of default of loans. Assume that $\eta > 0$ is the elasticity of δ with respect to $\lambda\sigma^2$. It can be readily verified that

$$dp/d\lambda\sigma^2 = 2\delta(\eta - 1)/(\delta + 2\lambda\sigma^2)^2$$

This expression will be zero if $\eta = 1$. This indicates that the FIs make a perfect correction in their diligence corresponding to every change in $\lambda\sigma^2$. In general, loan defaults will be only due to conditions that are not under the control of the FIs. Maximum bailout claims are then justifiable. Suppose $\eta < 1$. That is, the FIs are less than cautious while screening loans. They will then accept a lower p thereby acknowledging that their negligence is a part of the reason for the failure. Suppose initially $\eta > 1$. That is, the FIs are exercising more than the minimum necessary diligence. The more careful FIs recognize that the default and the crisis if it occurs, cannot be due to their negligence. They demand greater bailouts. Thus, even under risk sharing arrangements, there must be an increase in bailouts when $\lambda\sigma^2$ increases to a certain level. The ceteris paribus clause, i.e., of δ being determined exogenously, under the risk sharing formulation could not sustain this result.

Observe that the regulator offers the maximum bailout when $\eta = 1$. This corresponds to

$$\delta = C\lambda\sigma^2$$

where C is a representation of the costs, to the FIs, of exercising due diligence when confronted with information asymmetry. Observe that δ is expected to increase with $\lambda\sigma^2$. The present result indicates that δ increases with C as well.[19] Both these are consequences of the assumption that the FIs seek maximum possible bailouts for a given $\lambda\sigma^2$. The resulting choice of p is

$$p = C/(C + 2)$$

As noted earlier, the FIs claim $p = 1$ if it is extremely expensive for them to anticipate failures induced by extraneous conditions beyond their control.

This result can be interpreted differently. Suppose the regulator defines the p that they are willing to accept a priori. Then, the FIs will be compelled to choose C, δ, and $\lambda\sigma^2$ accordingly. This results in a fairly comprehensive regulation of the activities

---

[19] From a practical standpoint, the FIs may take a myopic view and consider the costs of due diligence represented here exceed the expected gains of bailouts in case of distress. The system will be out of control if self-regulation is expected. The necessity for regulatory action will then be reinforced. Essentially, it must be acknowledged that the necessity for regulation is indicated even in the most favorable case that is presented here.

of the FIs. Such bailouts offer a clear signal about the trade-off between risk and growth that the regulators are willing to concede.

To this point in the analysis, it has been assumed that the FIs will voluntarily make the necessary changes in diligence once they know that they must operate within the stipulated regulatory bounds for them to expect any bailout when conditions turn against them.

However, it can be shown that the FIs still gain by offering risky loans. Note that for the choices set out above

$$v_{\mathrm{f}} = C^2 (C-2) \lambda \sigma^2 / (C+2)^2 > 0$$

if and only if $C > 2$. Under these conditions, v_{f} is an increasing function of $\lambda\sigma^2$. Hence, voluntary compliance is inadequate. FIs will continue to take risks. On the positive side, it should be acknowledged that this bailout mechanism does not stifle risk taking propensities of entrepreneurs.

Similarly, it can be verified that

$$N = \lambda \sigma^2 C / (C+2)$$

This is also an increasing function of $\lambda\sigma^2$. The regulators, in their efforts to maximize social welfare, may not moderate $\lambda\sigma^2$. They will only share the risks with the FIs.

Consider the possibility that the regulator imposes capital adequacy norms as well. The most commonly used mechanism is to define a capital adequacy norm proportional to the loans L and, as a consequence, a fraction of y. Assuming that ky represents the prudential norm imposed on the FIs, it follows that[20]

$$g_{\mathrm{f}} = p(y+u) - ky$$

so that

$$v_{\mathrm{f}} = (p-k) y - \lambda p^2 \sigma^2$$

Similarly, N should be modified as

$$N = (1-k) y - y^2 / 2\delta - \lambda p^2 \sigma^2$$

Once again, taking the participatory constraint into account, it can be shown that

[20] If the FI is a bank, this is clearly analogous to the Basel II norms. The basic difference is that it is made proportional to loans instead of deposits that they receive. Rao (2009) argued that, if the capital adequacy norm is pivoted to deposits, the banks may adhere to it and yet provide many risky loans. Hence, even in that context, capital adequacy must be defined as a proportion of loans. In the context of FIs, there is no lender of last resort. They can, however, be asked to keep such reserves with themselves.

$$y = 2(1-k)\delta\lambda\sigma^2/(\delta + 2\lambda\sigma^2) \text{ and}$$
$$p = \delta(1-k)/(\delta + 2\lambda\sigma^2)$$

It may be then argued that the regulator will try to maximize the net value N while choosing k. In other words, they will choose $k = k(\lambda\sigma^2)$. This results in the optimum choice given by

$$(1-k)^2 = (\delta + 2\lambda\sigma^2)/A\lambda\sigma^2$$

where A represents the degree of difficulty experienced by the regulator in ascertaining the risks involved in the loans that the FIs extend. This is essentially a result of the information asymmetry that they experience. Observe that, as the information asymmetry increases and the value of A accordingly, the regulator expects the FI to keep a larger amount of prudential deposit.

Note that, as before, the FIs will choose $\delta = \delta(\lambda\sigma^2)$ to maximize p. Since this results in
$\delta = C\lambda\sigma^2$, we have

$$(1-k)^2 = (C+2)/A$$

Once again, as C increases, the regulator will feel that the FIs do not exercise due diligence. Hence, they are forced to set a higher prudential norm.

The efficient choice of the bailout will now be

$$p = C/[A(C+2)]^{1/2}$$

p decreases with an increase in A and increases with C.[21] Since $\lambda p^2\sigma^2$ is the essential systemic risk in the model, it follows that risks are reduced if A is high and/or C is low. Further, the imposition of the capital adequacy norm reduces volatility in the financial transactions only if $A > (C+2)$. Higher degrees of information asymmetry tend to make adherence to capital adequacy norms superior to depending on voluntary compliance by the FIs.

It can be shown that while the N achieved voluntarily is

$$N = \lambda\sigma^2 C/(C+2)$$

that under the capital adequacy norm is

$$N = \lambda\sigma^2 C/A$$

[21] Acharya (2009), in particular, argued that a systemic specification of k and p would be superior to leaving them as functions of δ and $\lambda\sigma^2$ for capital adequacy requirements based on each FI's risk fail to mitigate aggregate risk-shifting incentives and accentuate systemic risks. The arguments pertaining to macroprudential norms are similar in spirit.

Hence, if $A>(C+2)$, the net value to the society decreases. Clearly, there is a trade-off between reducing risks and attaining higher values of social welfare. The resolution of the trade-off is at the apex of choosing appropriate regulatory norms and bailouts.

Capital adequacy imposition is superior if the regulator can resolve information asymmetry more economically compared to the FIs exercising due diligence on their own volition. This may not materialize if the instability is purely a result of the decisions of individual FIs. However, the occurrence of systemic risks suggests that individual FIs may not be in a position to assess the risk or react to it. To that extent, action by a regulator may render A smaller than C. This reinforces the argument that defining p and seeking implicit control of risks is necessary and provides an efficient incentive mechanism.

In the final analysis, an FI may ignore all these regulatory bounds and indulge in excessive risk taking. The basic reason may be that their managers consider the bonuses they get for good performance as the only important aspect for they are not likely to be taken to task if they fail. Even if they do not get to attract golden parachutes when they have to leave, they cannot be forced to accept any fiduciary responsibility for the losses they inflict on their lenders (depositors) and borrowers. Asking firms to keep reserves in proportion to perks they offer to the management or insisting that their salaries be reduced does not seem to be practically implementable.

12.3 Solvency Issues

Consider the context in which the FIs offer long-term loans to finance the purchase of fixed assets. Clearly, the FIs will be the owners of these assets until the loans are paid off. Let the FIs expect to receive L per unit of time over T years at the end of which they transfer ownership. Assume that the borrowers default at time t or while y units of repayment is still due. It may so happen that the asset has lost its value in the meantime and the FIs are not in a position to recover the loans by selling the asset. For all practical purposes, the reduction in the value of the assets of the FIs indicates a solvency crisis. They are not in a position to continue their business of providing liquidity to the system. When confronted with a crisis of this nature, it is always optimal to commit to a bailout policy that protects investments against inefficient liquidation. In such a context, the bailout will consist of the regulator taking possession of the tainted assets and offering liquidity so that the FIs continue in business. Normally, the financial system, including the banking sector, will be reluctant to hold these assets. Hence, a fiscal bailout through the government budget becomes a necessity. This will be taken up with the hope that the fiscal action will revive the economy reeling under the recession, the assets will regain their value, and the government can recover the amounts that it offers as a bailout.

The genesis of the problem can be identified as follows. The FIs originally expected an equilibrium in which they can recover L per unit of time over T years. However, in a competitive environment, where short-term growth is emphasized and rewarded, they tend to myopically scale up activities and expect to recover L^* per unit of time. Loans, like mortgages for housing, have been offered without prudential cross-check on collateral. This risk resulted in under-recovery, an excess supply that could not be sustained on the basis of economic fundamentals, and a cumulative reduction in the value of assets.[22] The FIs that held these tainted assets experienced a reduction in the market value of assets that far exceeded losses at any point of time. The under-recovery, as well as the erosion of their asset base, is essentially a characterization of the solvency problem that led to their inability to extend more loans and sustain the economic activity that they initiated.[23]

Postulate that the solvency crisis may arise t units of time ahead of the expected T. The bailout[24] offered may then be ptL $0<p<1$ can be justified on the basis of the argument in Sect. 12.2.[25] In a very basic sense, the behavior of the FIs, i.e., extending more loans callously, does not alter the repaying capacity of the consumers. The randomness u invoked earlier persists. The gain to the FIs will then be

$$g_{\mathrm{f}} = p\left(tL + u\right)$$

Correspondingly, the value of bailouts to the FIs can be written as

$$v_{\mathrm{f}} = ptL - \lambda p^2\sigma^2$$

Assume, as before, that the FIs choose p. Their choice will be

$$p = tL/2\lambda\sigma^2$$

---

[22] The assets of an FI may consist of assets other than those for which they extended loans. They may take the form of land and buildings, equity of other firms, and so on. Morris and Shin (2008) argued that there should be some regulation regarding the composition of assets, their financing, and the loans offered on a given asset base. Rao (Rao 2009, 2010) contains a more general analysis in a somewhat different analytical framework. It is possible to extend the efficient bailout and regulation argument of this section further.

[23] Diamond and Rajan (2009) argued that the economic downturn may have deeper effects than the solvency crisis in itself. In that case, restoring the assets to the FIs will not be adequate to pull the economy out of the low-level equilibrium. Improving the aggregate demand becomes a necessity.

[24] In parallel to the liquidity crisis, situation bailouts reduce the cost of capital to the borrower and entice him to make larger investments than are socially desirable. This viewpoint cannot be sustained if achieving a higher growth rate through acceptable risk taking is considered desirable.

[25] Bailouts will be conditioned by the remaining value of assets. This was the reason for not bailing out Lehman Brothers. Second, it is generally recognized that the financial system per se will not buy these assets. Fiscal action through the government budget is indicated. Third, one of the adverse effects of a bailout is that asset restructuring, which is the only long-term solution, gets delayed. A bankruptcy filing, as in the Lehman Brothers case, is the more efficient option. These arguments are now commonplace. However, notice that the endogenous determination of bailout, as specified here, overcomes many of these problems.

The basic difference, from the viewpoint of the regulator, is that they are forced to bailout a larger value of failed assets. It can be expected that their costs will be $t^2L^{*2}/2\delta$. Hence, the gains, from the regulator's perspective, are

$$g_r = (1-p)(tL+u) - t^2L^{*2}/2\delta \text{ and}$$
$$v_r = (1-p)tL - t^2L^{*2}/2\delta$$

The net value of bailouts, to the system, is therefore

$$N = tL - \lambda p^2\sigma^2 - t^2L^{*2}/2\delta$$

The only choice for the regulator is t. Maximizing N, such a choice is given by

$$t = 2\delta\lambda\sigma^2 L/\left(\delta L^2 + 2\lambda\sigma^2 L^{*2}\right)$$

Hence, it follows that

$$y = tL = 2\delta\lambda\sigma^2/\left(\delta + 2\lambda\sigma^2 x^2\right)$$

where

$$x = \text{a measure of the over indulgence of the FIs}$$
$$= L^*/L$$

Consequently, the efficient choice of p is

$$p = \delta/\left(\delta + 2\lambda\sigma^2 x^2\right)$$

Assume, now, that risk-averse FIs may yet make attempts to exercise due diligence voluntarily once the bailout mechanism is in place for their failure to comply with prudential regulation may not entitle them to any bailouts. It can be verified that the maximum bailout offer will be

$$p = C/\left(C + 2x^2\right) \text{ and}$$
$$\delta = C\lambda\sigma^2$$

The issue that still needs attention is the choice of x. Assume that the regulator chooses x to maximize N. It can be shown that only $x = 1$ can maximize N. On the other hand, if the regulator maximizes v_r, the efficient choice of x will be

$$x = (C/2)^{1/2}$$

Since, by definition, $x > 1$, this approach applies to only those cases where $C > 2$.

The economic logic underlying this derivation is as follows. Suppose the FIs are risk averse. Assume, further, that they find it relatively very expensive to exercise due diligence. They will then be prone to increase x and derive benefits as soon as possible. This is the disadvantage with their short-term growth-oriented behavior. Anticipating this behavior, the regulator chooses x and reduces p accordingly.

Will the more diligent FIs lose due this choice of the regulator? Comparing the values of v_f for $x = 1$ with those when $2x^2 = C$, the diligent FI will gain if and only if

$$1/4 < C^2/(C+2)^2$$

That is,

$$3C^2 - 4C - 4 > 0$$

is necessary. This holds if $C > 2$. Hence, the more diligent FI will prefer the limited bailout policy.[26]

12.4 Foreign Institutional Investors[27]

There is a fairly general acknowledgment that foreign institutional investors and the finances they provide can be viewed as one of the catalysts that contribute to capital formation and economic progress. Such finances may also result in stock market gains unrelated to the underlying real economy fundamentals. In either case, there will be some gains to domestic investors. However, there are risks in attracting such financial flows. For, depending upon the economic conditions in their own countries or opportunities as they arise elsewhere, the FIIs may withdraw their deposits prematurely. This creates economic distress. Some bailouts may be necessary to protect the system against such consequences.

---

[26]This analysis therefore suggests that the regulator may adopt another strategy. To begin with, they may offer a low, or limited, bailout. The FIs may also be informed a priori that they will be offered larger bailouts and allowed to take more risks provided they can convince the regulator that they exhibit the expected diligence. Reduction in the initial bailout and preference for extended bailouts also suggest a risk sharing arrangement for the FIs may reduce the caution exercised if the original bailout is high. Anticipating this, the regulator may decide to ascertain the risk type of the FIs by offering a lower bailout and extending it to the more diligent among them as reflected in their choices.

[27]Yeyati et al. (2008) considered the effect of FII flows on a developing market in the context of the financial crisis. They also explored the efficacy of regulatory mechanisms to moderate both the short-term and long-run deleterious effects of such finances.

To systematize the analysis, assume that FII investments can generally be used to finance domestic economic activity for T units of time and generate an additional income Y per unit of time.[28] However, the FIIs may pull out while y units of income is yet to be realized or t units of time ahead of T. The actual loss, y_a, may be random so that

$$y_a = y + u$$

with $E(u) = 0$ and $V(u) = \sigma^2$

Assume that the government regulator offers a bailout $p(y+u)$. The gain to the domestic economy will be

$$g_e = p(y+u)$$

Normally, it can be surmised that the domestic investors are risk averse to the possibility that FII investments are hot money. The value of g_e can then be written as

$$v_e = py - \lambda\sigma^2 p^2$$

The regulators view their decision from the following perspective. Providing the bailout may yet induce domestic investors to continue the ongoing economic activity even if FIIs withdraw. Hence, the gain to the society will be

$$g_s = (1-p)(y+u) - y^2/2\delta$$

where δ is the efficiency with which the authorities can regulate the FII flows. Hence, the net value of the bailout policy to the society is

$$N = y - y^2/2\delta - \lambda\sigma^2 p^2$$

With obvious adjustments, it can be shown that every one of the results reported in Sects. 12.2 and 12.3 holds in this context as well.

The following additional result is important in the present context. Note that regulatory agencies can monitor the performance of the FIIs on a regular basis. They can use the information pertaining to the performance to allow a greater flow of FII investments if past performance is satisfactory. They will accept greater risks if there is an assurance that the chance of failure is not as large as originally anticipated.

Suppose the regulator initially expects the FIIs to withdraw while y units of expected output are yet to materialize. In actual practice, investments may not be

[28] In Rao (2009), the same model was utilized with an emphasis on regulatory policy alone.

withdrawn as expected. The regulators may then accept greater risk and allow bailouts even if investments are withdrawn while $y^* > y$ units of output have yet to materialize. As before, assume that the bailout is $q(y^* + u)$ where q is expected to be greater than p. Consequently, the value of the additional flow of FII finances to the economy will be

$$v_e = qy - \lambda\sigma^2 q^2$$

The optimal choice of q will then be

$$q = y^* / 2\lambda\sigma^2$$

Consider the gain to the regulator. The perceived cost of the bailout policy to them will be $(y^* - y)^2 / 2\delta$ for they reckon that only risks beyond y^* would necessitate any policy action. Hence, the additional gain to the regulator is

$$g_r = (1-q)(y^* + u) - (y^* - y)^2 / 2\delta$$

Consequently, the associated value will be

$$v_r = (1-q)y^* - (y^* - y)^2 / 2\delta$$

Maximizing the net value, it can be verified that

$$y^* = 2\lambda\sigma^2 (\delta + y) / (\delta + 2\lambda\sigma^2) \text{ and}$$

$$q = (\delta + y) / (\delta + 2\lambda\sigma^2)$$

The possibility that the regulatory agencies conceptualize both y and y^* a priori, though they reveal y^* only when the situation warrants it, may now be considered. The domestic firms that attract FII investments do not have any reason to think about y^* initially. Hence, their choice will still be the same as before. The basic difference is in the cost structure of the regulators. For, if both stages of sequential entry do materialize, they must reckon with the prospect of investments being withdrawn even when y^* units of returns can still be generated. Hence, one component of cost is $y^{*2}/2\delta$. However, they must anticipate an additional cost $(y^* - y)^2 / 2\delta$ because the regulatory mechanism will be more stringent initially and they would have made adjustments anticipating this. Hence, the value of the contract will be

$$N = y + y^* - \lambda\sigma^2 p^2 - \lambda\sigma^2 q^2 - y^{*2} / 2\delta - (y^* - y)^2 / 2\delta$$

The optimal choices will then be

$$y = 2\delta\lambda\sigma^2/\left(\delta + 2\lambda\sigma^2\right), \; p = \delta/\left(\delta + 2\lambda\sigma^2\right),$$
$$y^* = 2\delta\lambda\sigma^2\left(\delta + 4\lambda\sigma^2\right)/\left(\delta + 2\lambda\sigma^2\right)^2 > y, \text{ and}$$
$$q = \delta\left(\delta + 4\lambda\sigma^2\right)/\left(\delta + 2\lambda\sigma^2\right) > p$$

There is always a possibility that the regulatory agencies tend to be optimistic to begin with and create stringent measures only when failure is recorded. That is, $y^* < y$ and $q < p$ cannot be ruled out. The costs to the regulator, at the second sequential stage, may then be $\left(y + y^*\right)^2/2\delta$. This possibility can be easily accommodated in the above analysis.

Will efficient regulation and bailouts reduce volatility and risk? Observe that

$$V\left(g_e\right) = p^2\sigma^2$$
$$V\left(g_r\right) = \left(1 - p\right)^2\sigma^2$$

where V denotes variance. Hence, the extent of volatility in FII transactions will be

$$V = \left[p^2 + \left(1 - p\right)^2\right]\sigma^2$$

Efficient regulation may necessitate minimizing V by choosing δ. Consider the case where σ^2 is given exogenously. Then,

$$\partial V/\partial\lambda\sigma^2 = 2\left(2p - 1\right)\sigma^2 \mathrm{d}p/\mathrm{d}\lambda\sigma^2 = 0$$

implies that p should be maximized. This results in

$$\delta = C\lambda\sigma^2$$

and the corresponding p achievable is

$$p = C/\left(C + 2\right)$$

Hence, the resulting variance can be written as

$$V = \left(C^2 + 4\right)\sigma^2/\left(C + 2\right)^2$$

This will be minimum if and only if $C = 2$. This will be satisfied only accidentally in any practical context. In other words, the minimum conceivable volatility is unattainable. The regulatory policy outlined here does have enough allowance for risk taking and entrepreneurship.

In Rao (2010), a variety of other regulatory options have been examined in the same theoretical framework. In particular, it was suggested that due diligence may require the regulators to insist from the FIIs that they should (a) not indulge in short selling and similar purely speculative activities, (b) make the investment for a certain well-defined time horizon, (c) give a minimum notice if they choose to withdraw prematurely, and/or (d) agree to conversion at the exchange rate that prevails at the time of exit. Similarly, the regulator may insist that the share of FII investment in the equity of domestic companies should not exceed a limit that minimizes their disruptive potential. Needless to say, the breadth and intensity of regulation depend on the perceived optimal risk vs. growth trade-off.

12.5 Stability vs. Growth[29]

Risk taking and entrepreneurship have always been acknowledged as the foundations for economic progress. Private initiative is deemed desirable to encourage risk taking and foster growth. It is generally surmised that individuals and markets are sufficiently mature to balance their urge to grow with the necessity for system stability. However, a return has been offered to the FIs when they are successful while there have been no penalties for excessive risk taking even when systemic failure occurs. Against this backdrop, the psychology of individuals has been to take too many risks and emphasize quick moneymaking and growth. The maturity of individuals and markets has been, at best, a red herring.

These myopic attitudes have been perpetuated by short-term policy choices to bail out such failed institutions. There is no incentive on the part of the FIs to modify their behavior.

Deep systemic crises, like the recent financial chaos, seem to lead to a call for some regulatory mechanisms to reduce volatility in the system. Such regulation may restrict the FIs from taking excessive risks. However, some risks will remain. Hence, there is no assurance that a crisis, even if it is at a somewhat moderate level, will not occur again.

---

[29] A little reflection, based on microeconomic theory, suggests the following. First, firms sell products knowing fully well that they may fail. They offer a warranty to lure the consumer into taking the risk while buying the product. This is akin to a bailout. It also puts a limit on the opportunistic behavior of the firm and curbs its tendencies to pass on lemons. Second, while issuing an insurance policy to a customer, the insurance company knows that it is taking a risk. The customer, who pays a premium to obtain the coverage, can be induced to reveal his type and exercise diligence. These are examples which have a structure similar to the regulation and bailouts considered in this study. Individuals in almost all economies have no hesitation in accepting warranties and insurance because they are private decisions. The resistance to institutionalizing bailouts and regulation is purely ideological. No rational economic logic can deny their necessity or efficiency.

This study has shown that the regulatory mechanism that attempts to leave enough opportunities for risk taking initiatives has seeds of inherent instability. Hence, it is necessary to devise a bailout mechanism alongside the regulatory procedures endogenously to maximize social welfare. In particular, when the regulator is willing to allow certain risks, he should also be willing to support the FIs in case of failure.

Such a bailout mechanism will signal to the FIs that they need to restrict risks to acceptable limits for their own stability. They will then take only measured risks. This may imply a reduced rate of growth but will ensure greater system stability. This is the basic contribution of the present study.

However, it was demonstrated that the benefits to the financial institutions and social welfare will increase with risk taking initiatives of individuals. This occurs irrespective of the level of regulation conceptualized. Hence, the fundamental choice of the trade-off between stability and growth cannot be endogenized on purely theoretical grounds.

The principal agent framework is quite rich. Several alternative behavioral assumptions and parameter configurations can be examined. However, it should be clear that the case most favorable to self-regulation was presented in this study. Some regulatory oversight turns out to be efficient even in this case once the crisis is due to systemic risk. It can also accommodate a variety of regulatory and bailout options and examine their consequences for systemic risk and economic growth. Rao (2009, 2010) examined a variety of options and their consequences for stability and growth. Regulation, in varying degrees, can be justified in almost all configurations of such a framework. The propensity of individual societies to choose the trade-off between growth and stability will eventually determine the nature of bailouts and regulatory policy.

It should, however, be clear that sporadic regulatory tinkering when a crisis occurs or ad hoc short-term bailout measures cannot be considered as efficient responses to the frequent, widening, and deepening financial crises. Individuals have been too fickle and opportunistic that it is not possible to depend on their psychology to restore sanity.

References

Acemoglu D (2009) The crisis of 2008: structural lessons for and from economics. Available at http://econ-www.mit.edu/files/3703

Acharya VV (2009) A theory of systemic risk and design of prudential bank regulation. J Financ Stab 5:224–255

Borio C (2009) The macroprudential approach to regulation and supervision. Available at http://www.voxell.org/index.php?q=node/3445

Brunnermeier M, Crockett A, Goodhart C, Persaud A, Shin HS (2009) The fundamental principles of financial regulation. Center for Economic and Policy Research Press, Geneva

Chang R, Velasco A (1999) Liquidity crises in emerging markets: theory and policy. NBER Macroecon Annu 14:11–58

Congleton RD (2009) On the political economy of the financial crisis and bailout of 2008. Public Choice 140:287–317
Davis EP, Karim D (2009) Macroprudential regulation- the missing policy pillar. Available at http://euroframe.org/fileadmin/user_upload/…/EUROF09_Davis.pdf
Diamond DW, Rajan RG (2009) The credit crisis: conjectures about causes and remedies. Am Econ Rev 99:606–610
Eichengreen B (2009) Origins and regulatory consequences of the subprime crisis. In: Balleisen E, Moss D (eds) Government and markets: towards a new theory of regulation. Cambridge University Press, Cambridge
Farhi E, Tirole J (2009) Collective moral hazard, maturity mismatch and systemic bailouts. Am Econ Rev 102:60–93
Friedman TL (2008) If Larry and Sergy asked for a loan. Deccan Chronicle, October 27, 2008
Gorton GB (2008) The panic of 2007, NBER working paper 14358. Available at http://www.nber.org/papers/w14358
Hull J, Predescu M, White A (2004) The relationship between credit default swap spreads, bond yields, and credit rating announcements. J Bank Financ 28:2789–2811
Institute of International Finance (2008) Final report of the IIF Committee on market best practices: principles of conduct and best practice recommendations. Available at IIF_Final_Report_of_the_Committee_on_Market_Best_Practices[1].pdf
Jullien B, Salanie B, Salanie F (1999) Should more risk averse agents exert more effort? Geneva Pap Risk Insur Theory 24:19–28
Kriegel J (2009) Why don't the bailouts work? Design of a new financial system versus a return to normalcy. Camb J Econ 33:653–663
la Torre A, Ize A (2009) Regulatory reform: integrating paradigms. Available at www.cb.cityu.edu.hk/research/apec/ace/…/ACE%20Program.pdf
McAfee RP, McMillan J (1991) Optimal contracts for teams. Int Econ Rev 32:561–577
Mendoza EG (2008) Sudden stops, financial crises and leverage: a fisherian deflation of Tobin's Q. NBER working paper 14444. Available at http://www.nber.org/papers/14444
Morris S, Shin HS (2008) Financial regulation in a system context. Brook Pap Econ Act 2:229–274
Palma JG (2009) The revenge of the market on rentiers. Why neo-liberal reports of the end of history turned out to be premature. Camb J Econ 33:829–869
Poole W (2008) Market bailouts and the "fed put", Federal Reserve Bank of St. Louis. Review 90:65–73
Rao TVSR (2009) Financial crises and regulatory diligence. Indian Econ J 57:3–25
Rao TVSR (2010) Foreign institutional investors, risk sharing and regulatory diligence. In Gupta OP, Gupta KP (eds.) Indian capital market: emerging issues. Hyderabad: ICFAI University Press
Ratnovski L (2009) Bank liquidity regulation and lender of last resort. J Financ Intermed 18:541–558
Sachs J, Tornello A, Velasco A (1996) Financial crises in emerging markets: the lesson from 1995. Brookings papers on economic activity, pp 147–198
Todorova Z (2009) What makes a bailout acceptable? J Econ Issues 43:319–326
Whalen RC (2009) Rebuilding the U.S. banking system: back to basics in financial markets and institutions. Available at http://ssrn.com/abstract=1428966
Yeyati EL, Schmukler SL, Horen NV (2008) Crises, capital controls, and financial integration. World Bank Policy Research working paper 4770

Chapter 13
Estimating the Parameters

Abstract The estimation of principal agent models is a subset of inverse optimal problems. As of now, there is no consistent method of estimating all its parameters. In general, some proxies for the parameters have been utilized to test plausible economic implications of such models. This study develops a method of estimation for all the parameters using a very limited time series data for one contracting pair. Progress toward empirical reality, based on stylized facts, has been achieved by iteratively modifying the theoretical models and econometric methods. One of these results provides a theoretical justification for the econometric tools utilized in practice as well. However, a fundamental modification of the underlying assumptions is necessary. Given the emphasis on contracts in economic exchange, it is necessary to develop the methods further. The study also outlines some of the pertinent issues.

13.1 Estimation Issues

Contracts are a major mechanism for conducting transactions.[1] They occur more often than market relations even in what is generally considered as a predominantly market-oriented economy. The basic justification for the choice of contracts to conduct transactions was set out in Coase (1937, 1960). Fundamentally, contracts can facilitate greater specialization and division of labor. Consequently, costs of contracting are lower relative to those incurred in conducting transactions on the market. Specificity of the agent in repeated exchange over time also facilitates reduction in transaction costs. This is the crux of the transaction cost argument. On the downside, every contract necessarily generates an agency relationship. Information asymmetry is at the apex of this relationship. Some adverse selection and moral hazard are bound to occur. Agency costs capture the effect of this problem quite naturally.[2]

[1] The recent book by Bolton and Dewatripont (2005) contains details of contract design. However, they did not deal with any econometric issues.

[2] Jensen and Meckling (1976), Barney and Ouchi (1986, pp. 208–210), and Milgrom and Roberts (1990) represent the most influential specifications of agency costs. On the other hand, Williamson (1988) contains a succinct exposition of the distinctions between transaction costs and agency costs.

T.V.S.R. Rao, *Risk Sharing, Risk Spreading and Efficient Regulation*,
DOI 10.1007/978-81-322-2562-1_13

The primary concern of contract theory[3] is in devising mechanisms to minimize this contractual hazard while preserving the advantages alluded to by Coase. The principal agent models essentially contain a formal characterization of this aspect. However, both the principals as well as the agents can have very different objectives depending on the contracting context. This is also true with respect to the instruments available to them. Consequently, a rather rich theoretical literature has been built under the rubric of principal agent models.

Seminal theoretical developments are at least 30 years old and can be traced to Mirrlees (1974) and Holmstrom (1979).[4] However, empirical and econometric work lagged far behind mainly due to the unavailability of data. Nevertheless, the specification and resolution of econometric problems has been a continuing process.

Generally, as Datta and Radner (1994, p. 483) observed, "a notable feature of many real life principal agent contracts is that they specify simple compensation rules, i.e., they identify only a small set of contingencies on which a reward is conditioned." Basically, such a choice is a result of three types of costs of implementing contracts: costs of communicating with the agents; costs of obtaining information about output, profit, etc.; and the costs of computation (and the convenience of the principals) while implementing complex payment schemes stipulated in the contract. See, for instance, Ferrall and Shearer (1999). The most common contract in many practical contexts is a fixed upfront payment plus a share of output.

Given this empirical reality, the linear quadratic models provide the most satisfactory theoretical basis. Perhaps the most influential work has been Kawasaki and McMillan (1987) (KM hereafter). Many recent developments of the state of econometric practices and empirical evidence, based on this and related models, have been surveyed in Masten and Saussier (2002) and Chiappori and Salanie (2003). Significant work is still in progress. However, as of today, many econometric problems remain unresolved.

Availability of data has also been a constraint. Masten and Saussier (2002, p. 289) pointed out the following. "As the number of provisions (objectives of the principals and agents as well as the instruments available to them) analyzed increases, the number of explanatory variables and the size of the data set needed for statistical identification multiplies. Often, sufficient numbers of observations to analyze more than two or three provisions at a time simply do not exist." Further, as Aggarwal (2007, p. 476) reiterated recently, "most of the theoretically (defined) variables are either not observed or only partially observed. Given this problem, the empirical methodology used most often is to regress control choice on a range of

[3] Note that vertical integration and circumventing the market lead to contracts within the firm. The labor market literature predominantly deals with this. Contracts with agents outside the firm, e.g., subcontractors, franchisees, etc., are equally dominant. The first set of studies is closer to the transaction cost argument of Coase while the latter is more concerned about agency costs. They also differ with respect to the duration of contracts. The present study concentrates mostly on the second type of contracts. The reader may refer to Masten and Saussier (2002) for a review of econometric studies dealing with the choice of market versus contracts.

[4] Though somewhat dated, the early exposition by Rees (1985a, b) contains very useful insights about the principal agent models.

proxies relating to the characteristics of the contracting parties (and other variables conditioning the environment in which the contracts are defined and implemented)." This gives rise to the question about how such econometric practices can be justified on the basis of economic theory.

In practice, the choice of contract parameters and their quantitative determination has been conditioned by two other features. First, starting with the work of Yun (1999, p. 105) and Okamuro (2001, p. 377), it was noted that the principals may actually incur some costs in their efforts to choose the most efficient agent and/or monitor them appropriately. This endogeneity problem has also been highlighted in Ackerberg and Botticini (2002) and Chiappori and Salanie (2003). Second, Masten and Saussier (2002, p. 283) suggested that "the more uncertain the environment and the harder it is to accommodate changing circumstances within the contract, the more likely it will be that parties will sacrifice the precision and ease of implementation of definite contract terms for more cumbersome but flexible 'relational' contract terms that define performance obligations less precisely or establish procedures for negotiating adjustments in the terms of trade within the contract." Both these features create formidable econometric problems.

The present study outlines the most basic difficulties in the state of econometric methods based on the simple version of the principal agent models originated by KM. We also offer a more satisfactory method of estimating all the parameters of such models and several more realistic versions of it. It should be noted that meaningful changes to econometric techniques require that we must modify the models and their economic content first. Suitable econometric techniques, to incorporate greater degrees of practical reality and complexity, can be conceptualized only in an interactive fashion.

In a nutshell, these are the issues around which an attempt will be made to develop econometric estimates of the parameters of principal agent models.

The rest of the study is organized as follows. Section 13.2 presents a brief overview of two basic versions of the principal agent model. The linear quadratic model of KM was used as a benchmark since empirically observed contracts do have such a simple structure. In Sect. 13.3, we provide an outline of the current econometric practices in attempts to test such models and their limitations. In particular, it will be noted that all the parameters have not been estimated and that using proxies for some parameters has not been justified on the basis of economic theory. Section 13.4 offers a fundamentally new approach to the estimation of all the parameters. Time series data regarding the revenue and profit of the agent is shown to be adequate to achieve this. This is a significant advantage because data pertaining to the profit for the principal, from any one contract, will be difficult to disentangle from his consolidated profit and loss account. As noted earlier, some contracts contain fixed upfront payment as well. We outline reasons for this choice and provide a method of estimation of the underlying parameters. We also develop conditions under which the use of exogenous variables, or proxies, in a regression framework can be justified. The unexpected result is that the time series pertaining to the profit of the agent is no longer essential to identify all the parameters of the model. Section 13.5 then deals with two important extensions. First, we explore the possibility that the principal offers technical and other forms of assistance to the agent to improve his skills, reduce the randomness in revenue, and/or mitigate moral hazard. Second, we consider the case where the principal fixes some contract parameters without reference to the characteristics of the agent and endogenizes the choice of agents. Such contractual contexts may involve several heterogeneous agents simultaneously. It will be shown that the estimation procedures suggested in this study can be extended to such cases as well. The conclusion in Sect. 13.6 highlights some important theoretical issues as well as the necessary modifications to econometric techniques. In the final analysis, it must be recognized that several important issues remain unresolved though some useful progress has been achieved.

13.2 Basic Approach

Consider the context of a firm, e.g., an automobile assembly plant, which subcontracts the production of various parts. Here, conventionally, the subcontractor is the agent and the automobile assembler is the principal. Assume that the contract is for an output y. For simplicity, it will be assumed that y is revenue as well. The agent spends an amount $y^2/2\delta$ while planning production. In this formulation, δ is the efficiency of the agent. The actual output achieved, say y_a, depends on the agent's actions and/or external production conditions that the agent cannot control. Hence, it can be postulated that

$$y_a = y + u$$

where u is a random variable[5] with expected value $E(u) = 0$ and variance $V(u) = \sigma^2$.

The basic form of the contract is a payment $p(y+u)$ to the agent. That is, he is made to share the risk. A larger p provides him greater motivation to do better. The profit of the agent is then written as

$$\pi_a = p(y+u) - y^2/2\delta$$

Normally, the agent is expected to be risk averse. That is, his valuation of π_a will be

$$v_a = py - y^2/2\delta - \lambda p^2\sigma^2$$

where λ is a measure of his degree of risk aversion.

[5] Strictly speaking, there will be two types of randomness. First, there will be fluctuations in external market conditions. Neither the principal nor the agent can do much to neutralize this effect. Second, there can be moral hazard on the part of the agent. This may be quite unpredictable ex ante. A part of this randomness can be controlled if the principal exercises necessary control. In much of what follows, u contains the effect of randomness of both types. Unfortunately, neither the economic theory underlying the principal agent models nor the econometric methods have been able to deal with these two types of randomness separately.

The agent's first priority is not about what fraction of output he should be paid. Instead, if he increases y, he must incur a larger cost. But, he is not sure about the y_a that can be recovered. Consequently, the agent would be more worried about how much y he can realize.[6]

Such a choice of y is clearly[7]

$$y = p\delta$$

Consider the return to the principal next. It is given by

$$\pi_p = (1-p)(y+u)$$

In the simplest version of the model, it is assumed that the principal need not incur any costs. Further, the firm will be dealing with many such contracts. Hence, it can balance the losses in any one transaction against gains from another. It can be surmised that the firm will be risk neutral. Hence, the value to the principal is

$$v_p = (1-p)y$$

Note that, for all practical purposes, $y^2/2\delta + \lambda p^2\sigma^2$ is the cost, to the principal, of entrusting production to the agent. The principal reckons that the costs would be higher if he produces y on his own. It is this transaction cost argument that prompts him to assign the production to the agent in the first place.

---

[6] For the sake of analytical curiosity, consider the case where the agent chooses both y and p. This results in

$$y = p\delta$$

and

$$p = y/2\lambda\sigma^2$$

These two equations can be satisfied simultaneously if and only if

$$\delta = 2\lambda\sigma^2$$

It may not be realistic to expect this a priori in any practical contracting situation. It is also unrealistic to believe that the principal does not keep any controls under his discretion for this is the only way he can safeguard his interest.

[7] In this formulation, u may be purely exogenous. In such a case, an agent that is made to share risk feels that he is being punished for something he did not do. There is then a possibility that he will reduce y if σ^2 increases. This was noted in Borenstein et al. (2007). Alternatively, Baker (2006) suggested the following. The agent may use more resources and incur greater costs, given his risk aversion, in order to be sure that he may deliver the promised output. This can also give rise to the possibility that y depends on λ and/or σ^2. However, note that in this formulation, it is independent of σ^2 ex ante given p. Ex post p will depend on σ^2 and hence the observed y is not independent of σ^2. By way of contrast, based on some experimental evidence, Sloof and van Pragg (2008) noted that y does not depend on σ^2 even ex post. It is difficult to replicate this result in principal agent models of this vintage.

Hence, from the perspective of the firm, the net value of the contract is

$$N = v_a + v_p$$

Surely, the firm must take the incentive constraint of the agent into account. Hence, it follows that

$$N = p\delta - p^2\delta/2 - \lambda p^2\sigma^2$$

Note that the output and revenue generated are beyond the control of the firm since it does not wish to interfere directly in the production activities of the agent. Consequently, the only choice available to it is p. Maximizing N with respect to p, it follows that[8]

$$p = \delta/\left(\delta + 2\lambda\sigma^2\right)$$

This is the basic structure of the KM model.

The following alternative arrangement between the principal and the agent is quite plausible in many contracts:

(a) An automobile manufacturer may subcontract specialized parts. He may then specify the quantity he wants from the agent, the quality and technological standards that must be maintained, and consequently the cost that the agent should expect to incur. Many other subcontracts, e.g., for shoes, ready-made garments, etc., belong to this category.
(b) Usually the physician treating a patient defines the nature of treatment and the costs to the patient. In other words, the agent here cannot choose y. He may, at best, choose a doctor who claims an efficient amount of value of the treatment to the patient. See, for example, Hernandez (2003).
(c) Consider a firm that offers a warranty for the durable good it sells to a consumer. To begin with, the firm expects the product to fail occasionally. This will result in a loss y to the consumer on an average. The actual losses will, however, be y_a. The firm tries to share the risk by offering $p(y+u)$ of the loss that the consumer experiences. However, the carelessness of the consumer (moral hazard) may be one source of the loss. To keep this under control, the firm usually prescribes maintenance schedules and their costs. The consumer cannot choose

---

[8] Sloof and van Praag (2008) and Aggarwal (2007) pointed out that the choice of p need not depend on δ and/or $\lambda\sigma^2$. A similar argument can be found in Nichols (1983) and Svejnar and Smith (1984). The implications of such choices in franchise contracts have been explored in Lafontaine (1992) and Kaufman and Lafontaine (1994). However, it is rather difficult to develop satisfactory economic theory to justify such a choice by the principal in principal agent models of any vintage. Sharma and Rao (2007) reported one such attempt. Some aspects of this and other implications for econometric estimation will be considered in Sect. 13.5.

y. As in the previous context, he may, at the most, purchase the durable from the firm which leaves the largest share of welfare to him.[9]

(d) Hernandez (2003) also pointed out that when the market uncertainty is high, the principal may find it advantageous to fix y and specify the cost at which it should be produced. In a sense, he is selecting an agent who has the desired efficiency represented by δ.

The possibility that the agent may not be in a position to generate the entire expected y is at the apex of the likely default that the firm envisages. It would therefore be logical to expect the principal to make the choice with respect to output y given a value of p. Correspondingly, the agent must make an investment $y^2/2\delta$ prescribed by the principal. Hence, the agent would be more concerned about recovering his costs whatever the market conditions may be. This depends crucially on the choice of p.

Clearly, these contexts imply that the agent chooses p and the principal defines y. For, now, the agent would like to have control over the recovery of his investment by choosing p. Reconsider the maximization of

$$v_a = py - y^2/2\delta - \lambda p^2\sigma^2$$

This results in

$$p = y/2\lambda\sigma^2$$

Similarly, the N can now be written as

$$\begin{aligned} N &= y - y^2/2\delta - \lambda p^2\sigma^2 \\ &= y - y^2/2\delta - y^2/4\lambda\sigma^2 \end{aligned}$$

Maximization with respect to y yields

$$y = 2\delta\lambda\sigma^2/\left(\delta + 2\lambda\sigma^2\right)$$

But, as before, the ex post p would still be

$$p = \delta/\left(\delta + 2\lambda\sigma^2\right)$$

This variant of model 1 may be superior in such contracting contexts.

For the sake of completeness, note that some contracting contexts have a slightly different structure. Consider the context of an innovator who has a new patented idea that can be commercialized. However, it is generally impractical and expensive

---

[9] In actual practice, it may appear that the firm is fixing the warranty. The consumer can then choose to buy or reject a product. When he does buy, he has the choice of the quantity purchased. This was the spirit of the KM model specification.

for him to pursue the innovation through the many stages of the commercialization process starting from scientific knowledge to the wealth generating end product. The innovator therefore transfers the innovation to a firm that specializes in translating knowledge to commercially viable technology and a marketable product. The innovator, however, acknowledges that his work may not result in the expected output post commercialization. The firm is subjected to some risk and hence the innovator agrees to share the realized output or revenue.

Let the return to the innovator be

$$\pi_{\mathrm{a}} = p(y+u)$$

As before, u may be purely exogenous or it may be a result of the firm's actions. The innovator exhibits risk aversion because he has the alternative of pursuing commercialization on his own. Hence, the value of π_{a} to him is

$$v_{\mathrm{a}} = py - \lambda p^2\sigma^2$$

In a basic sense, the risk aversion is a manifestation of the lack of resource base (inability) and/or unwillingness to bear the entire risk. When the innovator transfers the rights of use of his discovery to the firm, he has no control on output y. Instead, he would be interested in making sure that he receives a proper share of the value generated from its use. That is, the author chooses p to maximize v_{a}. This optimization results in

$$p = y/2\lambda\sigma^2$$

In its turn, the firm receives a profit

$$\pi_{\mathrm{p}} = (1-p)(y+u) - y^2/2\delta$$

As before, since the firm can diversify its risks by undertaking commercialization of many such innovations, it will be risk neutral. Hence, the net value to the firm is

$$v_p = (1-p)y - y^2/2\delta$$

The first priority of the firm is not about how much it wishes to pay the innovator since it should be in a position to realize y in the first instance. Hence, it can be expected that it would be more worried about the choice of y.

It can also be claimed that its entire profit generation is dependent on the existence of the innovator. Hence, it must take the value to the innovator into account in its decision process. Consequently, it can be expected that the firm maximizes

$$N = y - y^2/2\delta - \lambda p^2\sigma^2$$

keeping the incentive constraint of the innovator in perspective. This choice results in

$$y = 2\delta\lambda\sigma^2 / \left(\delta + 2\lambda\sigma^2\right)$$

as one would expect.

For all practical purposes, these are the two variants around which much of the econometric work revolves. In the analysis that follows, these will be designated as models 1 and 2, respectively.

13.3 Econometric Problem: The KM Approach

To begin with, we outline the basic approach adopted by KM and related studies.[10] This enables us to specify the econometric issues clearly before searching for more satisfactory and/or efficient methods.

Consider the time series data that would be available with respect to all contracts of a given firm. Usually, this consists of the observed output y_a and the profits of the agent from each contract, viz., π_a. Estimation of the necessary parameters of the models necessitates the assumption that the null hypothesis i.e., that the data is indeed generated by the optimization process implied by the principal agent model, is valid. They begin estimation by observing that

$$V\left(y_a\right) = \text{variance of } y_a = \sigma^2$$

Hence, this can be used to estimate σ^2. Secondly, note that

$$V\left(\pi_a\right) = s^2 = p^2\sigma^2$$

as implied by the specification of the principal agent model. Consequently, they propose to estimate p as

$$p = s / \sigma$$

The other two parameters of interest are λ and δ. KM then observe that

$$v_a = E\left(\pi_a\right) - \lambda s^2$$

so that we can write

$$\pi_a = \text{constant} + \lambda s^2 + \varepsilon$$

[10] Prominent studies include Asanuma (1989), Asanuma and Kikutani (1992), Yun (1999), and Okamuro (2001). Their studies differ mostly with respect to the proxies used. The econometric methodology is essentially the same. Related studies also include Allen and Lueck (1999), Gonzales-Diaz et al. (2000), Brickley (2002), Aggarwal (2007), Haubrich (1994), and Hernandez (2003).

where ε is a random variable. Now, suppose the data is for a panel of several firms over some years for each of them. Then, π_a and s^2 can be computed as averages for each firm over time. A cross-section regression will then estimate λ. Note that λ need not be the same across all firms. However, even a random coefficient regression approach has not been utilized.[11]

KM then test the hypothesis that their principal agent model is a true theoretical explanation of the observed data. To achieve this, they start with the equation

$$p = \delta / \left(\delta + 2\lambda\sigma^2\right)$$

Hence, it follows that

$$\ln\left[\left\{(1/p) - 1\right\}/2\sigma^2\right] = \ln\lambda - \ln\delta$$

where ln is the natural logarithm. The general approach adopted is to identify proxies for λ and δ and estimate a cross-section regression

$$\ln\left[\left\{(1/p) - 1\right\}/2\sigma^2\right] = a_0 + a_1 \ln x_1 + a_2 \ln x_2$$

where x_1 and x_2 are the proxies chosen. Statistical significance of a_1, a_2, and a high R^2 are then interpreted as a test of the validity of their model.[12]

There are many difficulties with this method of approach to estimation. First, there is no clear definition of the parameters that need to be estimated. In particular, the specification of the KM model postulates that p, δ, λ, and σ^2 will be unobservable parameters. Hence, all of them must be estimated using the same data set. As Masten and Saussier (2002, p. 289) observed, "given that contract provisions will have been chosen simultaneously and are likely to interact with one another … in subtle and unexpected ways … empirical contracting studies should, ideally, estimate the full set of contract provisions simultaneously."[13] This has not been attempted so far. Second, the data set that can be made available is never fully specified. Suppose a time series of only one firm is available. According to the KM approach, only p and σ^2 can be estimated. Third, using panel data to estimate λ by regression assumes that λ is the same for all the firms. This is rarely satisfied in any data set. Hence, they make an ad hoc specification of other intervening variables. Clearly, this is not satisfactory. Fourth, the observable data is generally the actual output or sales revenue and the realized profit from the firm's profit and loss account. Kawasaki and McMillan utilized this information to estimate p. Do they not contain any information

[11] To the extent that I could understand these papers, it is quite clear that they did not really make any attempt to estimate δ from the observed data.

[12] Almost all subsequent empirical work on the principal agent models utilizes proxies. These studies did offer various useful insights into the economic mechanisms underlying such contracts. However, the estimation process rarely follows from the theoretical model specification.

[13] Ferrall and Shearer (1999) also voiced a similar concern.

about other parameters? They did not explore this aspect at all. Fifth, suppose we make an attempt to use the specification

$$\pi_a = py - y^2/2\delta + pu$$

to estimate p and δ. We need information about y. This is not available. Instead, the above equation can be written as

$$\pi_a = py_a - y_a^2/2\delta + u_a$$

where $u_a = \left(u^2 + 2y_a u\right)/2\delta\varepsilon$

Estimation may then be possible. However, this leaves λ undetermined. Sixth, the reader may also easily verify that a maximum likelihood method to estimate all the parameters fails[14] if the data available is only with respect to y_a and π_a.

In general, despite many interesting economic inferences reported in the estimation of principal agent models, there is an uneasy feeling that the econometric methods that form the basis of their inferences are most unreliable. The pertinent question would be that of estimating all the parameters using a single firm time series. Other extensions will be meaningful after this basic task is accomplished.

13.4 Proposed Method

Assume that the data available is a time series for the same principal firm contracting with the same agent. More specifically, let the available data consist of:

(a) y_a, the actual or realized output or revenue
(b) π_a, the profit of the agent

The parameters that must be estimated from this data set are p, σ^2, δ, and λ. Recall that p will be exactly determined if δ, λ, and σ^2 are known. However, it is

---

[14] Note that

$$\begin{aligned} y_a &= p\delta + u \\ &= \delta^2/\left(\delta + 2\lambda\sigma^2\right) + u \end{aligned}$$

Assume that u is normally distributed. Write the likelihood function. Since u is almost never identically zero, the first-order conditions with respect to δ and λ cannot be solved to obtain the corresponding estimators. Similarly, we may write

$$\pi_a\left(\delta + 2\lambda\sigma^2\right)/\delta = \delta^2/2\left(\delta + 2\lambda\sigma^2\right) + u$$

Once again, it is very easy to show that the first-order conditions for the maximization of the likelihood function cannot be solved for δ and λ.

listed as a parameter to be estimated because it is unlikely that any data on this will be available.

Two important observations should be kept in perspective before proceeding further. First, note that if δ, λ, and σ^2 are fixed over time, as the model postulates, the data for any one firm should have the same values of y and π_a. However, the observed data regarding y_a and π_a do vary over time. The exogenously determined randomness is the only source of these variations. All the estimates that we can develop essentially reflect the effect of this randomness instead of any other systematic economic behavior. Second, note that y_a is known. If p can be estimated from π_a, then we also know $(1-p)\,(y+u)$. Hence, π_p does not contain any additional information about the parameters. Similarly, $E(\pi_a) = py - y^2/2\delta$ does not contain any useful information for p and δ must always be chosen to satisfy this equation.[15]

With this background in perspective, estimation can proceed as follows:

(a) Since $y_a = y + u$, y can be estimated from $E(y_a)$. From an operational point of view, this will be the sample average.
(b) Similarly, σ^2 can be estimated from $V(y_a)$.
(c) Note that $\pi_a = p(y+u) - y^2/2\delta$
Hence,

$$V(\pi_a) = p^2\sigma^2 = s^2$$

Therefore, as in KM, p can be estimated as[16]

$$p = s/\sigma$$

(d) Observe that $y = p\delta$ given the incentive constraint of the agent. Hence, it is possible to estimate δ as

$$\delta = y/p$$

(e) Recall that $p = \delta/\left(\delta + 2\lambda\sigma^2\right)$. Hence, λ can be estimated as[17]

---

[15] Strictly speaking, this is valid only when the data generation process corresponds to the optimization implicit in the KM formulation of the principal agent model. In practice, this may not be true. In such a case, an χ^2 test based on the deviations of π_a from its estimated value can be utilized to test the validity of the model.

[16] Okamuro (2001, p. 364) pointed out that this is not a good estimate. Suppose $\pi_a = .1(y+u)$. That is, profit is about 10 % of the sales revenue. Then, it follows that $V(\pi_a) = s^2 = .01\,\sigma^2$. Consequently, $p = .1$. This indicates that there is some risk absorption. However, the following scenario is plausible. Suppose output and cost increase by α percent. Let the price of output remain invariant. Then, profit will also increase by α percent. But, clearly, there is no risk absorption. It is much more important to model systematic fluctuations in demand to get a reliable estimator of p. In other words, as Masten and Saussier (2002, p. 284) pointed out, risk sharing is not the major determinant of output sharing contract choice.

[17] Estimation of λ crucially depends on the choice of p as recorded in the basic model. This can be contested on two counts. First, suppose σ^2 is very high. A risk-averse agent may ask for an even

$$\lambda = \delta\left[(1/p)-1\right]/2\sigma^2$$

This simple approach, utilizing the data pertaining to y_a and π_a, can therefore retrieve all the parameters of the model.

In the context of model 2, it can be readily verified that the estimators will be

$$E(y_a) = y,$$
$$V(y_a) = \sigma^2,$$
$$p = s/\sigma,$$
$$\lambda = y/2p\sigma^2, \quad \text{and}$$
$$\delta = \left[(1/p)-1\right]/2\lambda\sigma^2$$

Hence, all the parameters of these models are identifiable However, the most important drawback of this method is that standard tests of significance will not be available.[18]

As noted earlier, almost all empirical work on the principal agent models utilizes exogenously determined proxies and estimates p as a function of these variables. The central question that should be addressed is how can the model be modified to account for this and what will be the implications for the method of estimating σ^2, δ, and λ?

One approach to the problem starts with the following observation. The actual output or revenue that can be generated by the actions of the agent does not depend only on the randomness determined by external market conditions or the moral hazard inherent in the actions of the agent. Instead, it also depends on systematic market trends, the ability of the agent to absorb the new technology designs, and so on that the principal expects him to use. Perhaps, the principal takes the expected values of these variables into account while determining y. However, the variation

higher fixed upfront payment and a lower p compared to what the model signals. Similarly, when σ^2 is fairly low, he may be emboldened to take the risk. He may then accept a higher p and a lower upfront payment. That is, there may be incongruence between the observed data and the predictions of the model at both extremes of market uncertainty. Second, the principals may have a tendency to underpay agents by substantial amounts for the principal may suspect that the agent is not revealing correct information on three counts. (a) The agent may reveal a lower probability of success hoping that a low output target will be set. (b) The agent may be more risk averse than what he is willing to reveal. (c) The agent exaggerates his level of skill in contract negotiations. Further, the principal, not being fully aware of how δ and λ contribute to his profit, may prefer to reduce p. This possibility implies that the estimated value of δ may be an underestimate and that of λ an overestimate. It is necessary to free the model from its excessive dependence on σ^2 as the key to the entire decision process. Borenstein et al. (2007) also voiced similar concerns.

[18]Two other studies, viz., Dubois and Vukina (2004) and Paarsch and Shearer (2000), utilize the method of moments in a somewhat different manner. Their methods are not useful in the present context because the error u in y_a and the error pu in π_a are strictly correlated and the variance covariance matrix of errors is singular.

of these external factors, around their expected values, is unlikely to be captured while determining y. In other words, the actual output

$$y_a = y + ax + u$$

where $x = X - E(X)$ with X denoting an exogenous variable and
u = random error similar to the original formulation.

Consider model 1. The expressions for v_a and v_p will now contain ax linearly and independent of y. Hence, none of the decisions will be affected. That is, p cannot be a linear function of x. The only difference is in the estimation of σ^2 based on the regression

$$y_a = y + ax + u$$

Note that this regression offers an estimator of the additional parameter in the model as well. However, the model cannot provide a justification for the observed econometric practices.

Assume, on the other hand, that the agent may choose p and the principal chooses y. This possibility was indicated earlier even in the context of model 1. In this case, maximizing v_a with respect to p results in

$$p = (y + ax)/2\lambda\sigma^2$$

and the choice of y that maximizes N is given by

$$y = \delta(2\lambda\sigma^2 - ax)/(\delta + 2\lambda\sigma^2)$$

Simple rearrangement yields[19]

$$p = (\delta + ax)/(\delta + 2\lambda\sigma^2)$$

It is now obvious that running a regression[20]

$$p = a_0 + a_1 x + \varepsilon$$

[19]Observe that the p so defined is not a constant independent of x. Instead, it is somewhat similar to a bonus (or incentive) scheme.

[20]This approach to the estimation problem requires data on p. But this is not available. However, it is clear that $p\lambda$ is estimable. Hence, this can be used in the regression without loss of any other information.

will be justified.[21] Clearly, the u, which represents randomness in market conditions specific to the products transacted under the contract, can be expected to be independent of ε.

It is now important to note that δ and λ can also be estimated with the available information for $\delta = aa_0/a_1$ and

$$\lambda = a(1-a_0)/2a_1\sigma^2$$

Standard tests of significance can also be conceptualized since a, a_0, a_1, and σ^2 are all estimators in the usual sense. See, for instance, Rao (1965, section 6a.2, especially p. 322).

Three important inferences emerge from this analysis. First, all the parameters of the model can be estimated by using the information contained in y_a and x. It was not necessary to resort to the observations regarding π_a. The economic rationale underlying this result is not easy to disentangle. Second, the appropriate proxies for the x variables are not those representing δ and λ. Instead, they should represent variables that can capture systematic productivity and market demand related influences. Third, model 1, with the choice of y left to the agent, cannot justify using the proxy regressions that predominate the empirical literature. Though no independent proof for p being the agent's choice is available, the success of the regression approaches suggests that this is the dominant form in the principal agent model.

For all practical purposes, this is a far superior approach to the estimation of all the parameters of the principal agent model.[22]

In actual practice, contract provisions involve an upfront payment to the agent in addition to the share in output.[23] We must address three questions in this context: (a) What are the proximate reasons for the efficiency of such a choice? (b) How can the principal agent model be restructured to account for this? (c) Can econometric techniques estimate the fixed payment as well?

[21] Note that the random variable ε introduced here is in no way related to the ε in the KM estimation of λ. Further, it can be argued that the y_a and p equations constitute a pair of seemingly uncorrelated regressions. This is a matter of detail and not fundamental to the issue of identification being considered here.

[22] The practical difficulty is the following. Much of the empirical literature suggests that the principal's choice of p will not be a function of δ, λ, or any other exogenous variation of x over time for any contract for a specific product type. The variations in p would only be over a cross section of different products handled by the same principal and/or agents. Even empirical studies utilizing panel data could not come to grips with this issue so far. Consequently, there is a great deal of ambiguity about the appropriate economic model and the corresponding econometric methods of estimation. Given the paucity of data, the best empirical studies should depend on panel data. Economic theory must be developed with this constraint in perspective. For example, the x variables may refer to contracts for different products instead of a time series for the same product. The estimation of δ, λ, and σ^2 should be modified accordingly.

[23] Ferrall and Shearer (1999) pointed out that the payment to the agent may take the form fixed upfront fees $+p(y_a - y_{min})$ where the share is only a bonus when the realized output exceeds a stipulated minimum. The nature of the analytical details does not change materially even if this version is pursued.

At the outset, note that the value of the contract to the agent is[24]
$v_a = p^2\delta/2 - \lambda p^2\sigma^2 \geq 0$ if and only if $\delta \geq 2\lambda\sigma^2$

The agent will not accept the share contract if this condition is not satisfied. In general, the principal has to make an upfront payment if the agent has a reservation level m of value and the parameters δ, λ, and σ^2 cannot guarantee that a share contract will be adequate.[25] It should also be obvious that a similar requirement will arise if the agent has to incur some fixed costs in the execution of contracts. The context in which the agent needs a minimum profit for survival (usually called a liquidity constraint) may also give rise to such contractual choices.[26]

To formalize the analysis, assume that $v_a \geq m$ (a constant) must be satisfied for all values of δ. Since the efficient choice of p tends to zero as δ tends to zero, the minimum upfront payment should be m. The payment to the agent is therefore $m + p(y + u)$. This does not affect the choices of p and y.

Turn to the estimation problem. The parameters δ, λ, σ^2, and p can be estimated as before. We also know that

$$E(\pi_a) = m + p^2\delta/2$$

Hence, m can be estimated from this equation. In general, the basic econometric method is not affected materially.

The versions of the principal agent models analyzed up to this point postulated that the principal need not incur any costs for efficient execution of the contract. This will not be true if the principal must deal with many agents simultaneously:

(a) The principal must incur some costs of coordination. See, for example, Ahmedjian and Oxley (2006).
(b) An automobile assembler has to assemble many parts procured from outside agents to generate the marketable product. As Ahmedjian and Oxley (2006) noted, this entails costs to the principal.

---

[24] The following argument can also be structured by assuming that the agent has a desired minimum level of profit. In that case, we require

$$E(\pi_a) = p^2\delta/2 \geq m$$

It cannot be stated in terms of πa per se since it contains a random realization pu.

[25] Suppose the contract fixes a y and σ^2 increases ex post. The agent may renege. An upfront payment may then have the ability to elicit better compliance and loyalty over time in long-term contracts. A similar argument holds even for ex post changes in y given $\sigma 2$. For all practical purposes, the reason for reneging will be the nonfulfillment of minimum returns. Hence, there is no new information in this argument.

[26] Chiappori and Salanie (2003) acknowledged two other contingencies. (a) The agent may not have sufficient initial wealth to withstand the uncertainties due to minimum income requirements for survival. (b) The agent, who is very likely to face a liquidity constraint even in his efforts to raise finances needed to incur the cost $y^2/2\delta$, has to depend on the principal to provide an upfront payment. These details will not alter the basic structure of the problem.

(c) Almost all franchises depend on their brand name to attract the market. As such, the franchiser is obliged to share some costs to ensure that the brand name is not eroded. The principal incurs these costs even when the franchisee can be expected to maintain the requisite efficiency in the execution of the contract.

For analytical purposes, it is necessary to appreciate the nature of these costs and its relation to the output of the agents. The following details are pertinent:

(a) In a franchise contract, the principal generally checks for compliance with quality standards and so on. This will take very much the same effort whatever the y may be. But it depends on the number of outlets that the franchiser accepts.
(b) Consider the context of a biotechnology firm coordinating the work of many scientists in its efforts to scale up plants to produce a marketable product. The ultimate level of output is rarely relevant for cost determination. Instead, it increases with their number. Usually such costs are incurred while resolving scientific disagreements, ego clashes, and so on.
(c) In the context of subcontracting, the principal need not control the actual production y of any agent. Rather, he has to allocate the total output among agents, ensure that they are the right choice, etc. Coordination costs are a function of the number of agents.
(d) In the context of retailers or marketing agents, the firm simply chooses them, allocates marketing effort, and allows them to deliver the output. Hence, to the principal, the costs of coordination depend only on their number and not the output chosen by any one of them.

In general, these coordination efforts are subject to diminishing returns. However, two exceptions may arise:

(a) As the number of scientists working with the firm increases, there is a better chance of synthesizing a marketable product. A large number may also enable the firm to acquire greater monopoly power by blocking rival firms from developing the same or a competitive product. Danzon et al (2005) noted that this may create a tendency to contract with a larger number than optimal.
(b) Bigger agents, who produce larger quantities of output, are likely to be more efficient and do not require as much supervision and control from the principal. Costs may in fact decrease with the size of the output.

The following model outlines the basic approach but it cannot reflect all these dimensions of reality.

Let n be the number of agents that the principal agrees to work with. Fundamentally, the costs of coordination can be represented by cn^2. With all other notations as before, the output of any one agent can be written as

$$y = p\delta$$

The profit for the principal now becomes

$$\pi_p = n(1-p)(y+u) - cn^2$$

Hence, the net value of the contract is

$$N = np\delta - np^2\delta/2 - \lambda np^2\sigma^2 - cn^2$$

The principal now chooses n and p. It can be readily verified that the optimal choices are

$$p = \delta/\left(\delta + 2\lambda\sigma^2\right) \text{ and}$$
$$n = p\delta/4c$$

The data on such contracts will generally reveal the number n. Hence, it is possible to estimate c along with the other parameters.

However, the following limitations should be kept in perspective:

(a) The n derived here is the maximum. Suppose c is relatively small and the number of franchisees that the principal is willing to take is large. However, the number of franchisees who would be willing to enter the contract may be much smaller. The ex post number of agents is then due to constraints on the agent. However, the analysis implies that the principal is willing to accept agents without any limit.
(b) The estimated c, given the ex post n, is the maximum likely coordination cost. It will almost always be an overestimate. This suggests that maximization by the principal and/or the agents, without fully specifying all the constraints on their decisions, is a bad assumption.
(c) In actual practice, the principal may set up one uniform p for all the agents, without reference to the δ and λ of specific agents, and accept all the agents who find the contract agreeable. The theoretical specification of such models remains elusive.

13.5 Some Extensions

Many contracting contexts require the principal to incur some costs though they are not coordination related as in the previous section. The following examples are symptomatic:

(a) Chisholm (1997) and Mortimer (2000) examined the context of producers of music CDs, DVDs, etc. In general, they distribute these products through retailers. The retailers have a tendency to stock more than expected demand for this is the only way to avoid the loss due to the inability to supply if demand were to arise. Invariably, the producer takes back unsold items at no cost to the retailer. The principals incur some costs as a result of this practice.

(b) Consider the case of a landlord taking a tenant. If payments to the agent are based entirely on the output from the land, the tenant may not make enough investments to preserve the quality of the land. To avoid the tenant returning fallow land, the landlord makes some investment in soil conservation measures.

(c) In the context of technology transfer, an MNC may feel that the agent to whom they entrust production may lack the soft skills necessary to absorb the technology and perform efficiently. Transfer of informal knowledge implies a cost to the principal. Related issues have been examined, among others, in Rao and Sharma (2006) and Sharma and Rao (2006, 2007).

(d) Ferrall and Shearer (1999) and Margiotta and Miller (2000) refer to the implementation costs incurred by the principal. In particular, they identified costs of ensuring that the planned output is realized and the costs of verifying the actual output so that the contract can be implemented. The principal may offer only a fixed upfront payment to the agent if these costs are fairly high.

(e) Moral hazard on the part of the agent may be more pervasive than represented in (d) above. The principal must incur costs in preventing this. Such costs received attention in Allen and Lucek (1999), Ahmedjian and Oxley (2006), and Rao and Sharma (2006).

The costs incurred by the principal may affect the actions of the agent in several ways:

(a) A reduction in moral hazard may manifest itself in the form of a reduction in σ^2. This was the line of argument in Rao and Sharma (2006) and Sharma and Rao (2006, 2007).

(b) Resende-Filho and Buhr (2008) contend that such costs will force the agent to be more efficient. That is, they reduce the costs that he incurs in delivering output y.

(c) The principal may fix a p (constant) for all the agents he deals with. This may be the only practical solution in franchise contracts. The principal will then be compelled to share costs to leave some ex ante rents to the agents who self-select. This theme can be found in Kaufman and Lafontaine (1994) and Aggarwal (2007). In general, these specifications have been characterized under the banner of double-sided moral hazard.

The basic principal agent model may now be modified as follows. The fundamental addition is the cost ky^2 of the principal. Correspondingly, the major change is in the nature of p. It now becomes

$$p = \delta / \left(\delta + \lambda\sigma^2 + 2k\delta^2\right)$$

assuming that σ^2, δ, and/or λ remain unaltered. From the viewpoint of econometric estimation, the changes are with respect to λ and k. To begin with, it must be noted that the information contained in y_a and π_a will not be adequate to estimate k. Instead, we must rely on π_p. Invoking this information, k can be estimated as

$$k = \left[(1-p)p\delta - E(\pi_p)\right]/p^2\delta^2$$

The estimated p will then provide us the estimate of λ as

$$\mathbf{1} = \left[\delta\{(1/p)-1\} - 2k\sigma^2\right]/2\sigma^2$$

This method enables us to retrieve all the parameters of the model. The case where the agent chooses p can be solved in an analogous manner.

Suppose, now, that ky^2 reduces σ^2 to σ^2/k. This is tantamount to assuming that the expenditure by the principal reduces moral hazard. Fundamentally, the principal can choose an optimal k. It can be shown that such a k is given by

$$k = \lambda^{1/2}\sigma/\delta$$

and, correspondingly,

$$p = 1/\left(1 + 4\lambda^{1/2}\sigma\right)$$

All the parameters of the model are estimable given y_a and π_a since k is no longer an independent choice. π_p will no longer be necessary.

The possibility that the principals choose δ and λ, or, more generally, the agents, has been a recurring theme in principal agent models. This is usually designated as the endogeneity issue. It appears in at least three distinct forms:

(a) Ex ante, i.e., before conceptualizing a contract, the principal can usually choose one among many agents that are available. For example, a firm, such as Maruti Udyog Limited, can choose from several tire companies for its vehicles. As Hernandez (2003) suggested, a patient may choose from a number of hospitals and/or physicians that offer the necessary treatment. Similar situations have been described in Ackerberg and Botticini (2002) and Dubois and Vukina (2004). There are many contexts of this nature in practice. The choice may be limited in repeated contracting over time as the principal gains experience.

(b) The principal may specify some minimum contract requirements, receive bids from various agents, and select the one who may deliver the necessary output efficiently. Auctions and tenders are of this nature.

(c) In franchise contracts, the principal spells out the contract terms he is willing to offer. Usually this involves a specification of the sharing of costs, returns, and the extent of monitoring and control. Only those agents, who feel that they can earn ex ante rents under the contractual terms offered by the principal, will then come forward. In a sense, the agents self-select themselves. Normally, the franchisor accepts many franchisees and there is no limit on the number suggesting any maximization. See, for instance, Kaufman and Lafontaine (1994) and Chiappori and Salanie (2003).

The most difficult problem, from the standpoint of economic theory, is the one where the principal fixes *p* a priori and screens the agents on that basis. The following model has been developed with this in perspective. Consider the case of a principal who fixes *p** a priori. He may not fix *y* and/or *k* ex ante in a similar fashion for the size of the franchise outlet and the assistance that the agent may need for maintaining expected quality can only be determined after choosing the agent. Assume that, as a part of the contract, output *y* is chosen. The important feature that needs attention is the cost ky^2 that the principal accepts as a part of the contract. Fundamentally, this reduces the variance $V(y_a)$ to σ^2/k. Consequently, the agent's valuation of his profit is

$$v_a = p^* y - y^2/2\delta - \lambda p^{*2}\sigma^2/k$$

The agent chooses

$$y = p^*\delta$$

Analogously, the net value of the contract is

$$N = y - y^2/2\delta - \lambda p^{*2}\sigma^2/k - ky^2$$

The optimal choice of *k* for the principal becomes

$$k = \lambda^{1/2}\sigma/\delta$$

The maximized value of v_a will now be

$$v_a = p^{*2}\left(\delta/2 - k\delta^2\right)$$

The principal may choose a δ that maximizes v_a. It results in

$$\delta = 1/4k$$

Substitution in v_a yields

$$v_a = p^{*2}/16k$$

The economic justification for these choices of the principal is now evident. Suppose the principal wishes to leave a maximum *m* to its agents. He will choose *p** and *k* such that

$$p^{*2} = 16\text{km}$$

Clearly, there will be several agents, whose minimum expectations are below m, who would agree to the contract. Some of them will be less efficient while others are more efficient. The more efficient among them do not need much assistance from the principal.

More specifically, consider any one agent. He is aware of his δ and λ. The principal fixes p^* a priori. Hence, the agent knows that the principal will choose

$$k = 1/\delta$$

Hence, he can estimate the maximum m he can achieve in the contract. Clearly, it is given by

$$m = p^{*2}/16k$$

The agent also knows that the acceptable value of σ^2 is

$$\sigma^2 = 1/16\lambda$$

The agent will agree to the contract if he estimates that this combination of m and σ^2 is acceptable to him.[27]

Can the principal conceptualize maximization with respect to p^*? Suppose, in the spirit of the development of the principal agent model, he wishes to maximize N. It can be readily verified that given the optimal choices specified so far

$$N = \delta\left(p^* - p^{*2}\right)$$

Hence, he should choose $p^* = .5$. The alternative available to him will be to selfishly maximize his expected profit. It can be shown that

$$E\left(\pi_{\mathrm{p}}\right) = .25\delta\left(4p^* - 5p^{*2}\right)$$

Hence, the corresponding optimal choice will be $p^* = .4$.

Recall that δ, λ, and m vary with the agent. Similarly, the σ^2 acceptable to the agent depends on λ. In his turn, the principal then accepts a specific value of k. Consequently, there is no other parameter in the model on the basis of which p^* may be determined. This explains the two values obtained above.[28]

---

[27] An impression is usually created that ex ante rents will increase with δ. Hence, the δ defined is the minimum. All agents with larger δ earn ex ante rents. This is the implication in Kaufman and Lafontaine (1994) and Chisholm (1997). To the extent that I am aware of it, no principal agent model specification can sustain this result.

[28] Observe that this analysis assumed that only one agent is involved. Since the optimization does not depend on δ, it can be claimed that the result is fairly general. Otherwise, the rest of the analysis should be interpreted as valid only for any arbitrarily chosen p^*. The other drawback is that the model cannot specify the number of agents that the principal would prefer to deal with. Coordination

Consider the econometric estimation of the parameters of this model. As before, for each agent taken in isolation,

$$E(y_a) = y$$
$$V(y_a) = \sigma^2/k$$

The parameter δ can be estimated from the equation

$$\delta = y/p^*$$

The constraint

$$k\delta = 1/4$$

provides an estimate of k.

σ^2 may now be estimated as

$$\sigma^2 = kV(y_a)$$

Similarly, m can be identified as

$$m = \delta p^{*2}/4$$

An estimate of λ can be obtained from

$$\lambda\sigma^2 = 1/16$$

Note that, in this specification, δ and λ are the values at which m is attained. All these parameters are agent specific.[29]

---

problems and the associated diminishing returns, if they are pertinent, have yet to be appropriately incorporated.

[29] Suppose the principal is specifying a p^* without reference to any maximization. Then,

$$V(\pi_a) = p^{*2}\sigma^2/k$$

so that

$$p^{*2} = V(\pi_a)/V(y_a)$$

If the null hypothesis about the validity of the model is justified, this estimate of p^* should be the same for all the agents. Perhaps the variation over the sample, if any, can be utilized as a test of the principal fixing p^* a priori. However, if the null hypothesis is not valid empirically, there is no way of estimating p^* for all the agents.

13.6 Issues to Consider

The estimation problem considered in this study is a member of a wider class designated as inverse optimal problems. In general, these problems cannot be integrated into a unified structure. As such, different classes of these problems have been considered discretely.

The most important finding is that even limited time series information, about the output (revenue) and profit of the agent, will be adequate to estimate all the parameters of the model. It was also shown that the econometric practices currently in vogue would be valid only under very limited assumptions.

The attempt made here, however, represents the tip of an iceberg. In practice, there are many unresolved theoretical issues and lack of appropriate econometric techniques. The principal agent models, if considered logically in an econometric framework, as yet leave several questions unanswered.

From the viewpoint of econometric techniques, the following observations are pertinent:

(a) In the basic version of the model 1, we do need the information contained in π_a to get an estimate of all the parameters. However, with a $y_a = y + ax + u$ specification, the data regarding π_a is not necessary. Nevertheless, we do not have any economic justification for this result.

(b) The broader question is what if more information is available (in comparison to the minimum necessary)? Does this create an identification problem? Should the method of estimation change? There are no clear answers to these questions.

(c) There is another issue that remains unresolved. Suppose

$$y_a = y + ax + u + v$$

where u is externally imposed error and v is endogenous randomness due to the behavior of the agent. Clearly, there is a possibility that

$$V(u) = \sigma^2 \quad \text{and} \quad V(v) = \sigma_v^2$$

It has not been possible to specify a method of estimating the two variances.

(d) Okamuro (2001, p. 377) argued that the principal may, at least in some cases, try to offer a larger share p to induce lower risk aversion from the agent. Conversely, as Chiappori and Salanie (2003) observed, when the principal observes that the agent is highly risk averse, he may induce him to accept the risk by offering a larger p. This is contrary to the basic inference of the principal agent models. The results developed in Sect. 13.5 suggest that this may be justified in one case. Suppose the principal increases k. As a result, $\lambda\sigma^2$ decreases sufficiently so as to make $(\lambda\sigma^2 + k\delta^2)$ smaller. In such a situation, we will observe an increase in p as $\lambda\sigma^2$ increases. However, note that the estimated parameter values will reflect this reality if the data exhibits this property.

(e) Several authors, including Baker (2006), Paarsch and Shearer (2000), and Chiappori and Salanie (2003), contend that an agent, who realizes that the payment py_a to him does not depend on the cost he incurs, may indeed inflate costs. The true values of δ and λ are rarely revealed truthfully. Hence, the estimated values tend to be inaccurate. Clearly, this will depend on the efficacy of the output sharing and monitoring by the principal. The models generally assume that these mechanisms are efficient in eliciting truthful revelation.

(f) Borenstein et al. (2007) suggested that the principal may not actually implement the optimal values of p indicated by the principal agent model for he may not be confident of the sharing mechanism being adequate to elicit truthful revelation from the agent. Estimates based on the optimality assumption may not be reliable under such conditions.

The pertinent issues in economic theory can now be detailed:

(a) The costs incurred by the principal as well as the agent contain several components. However, throughout the analysis, they are represented by one single cost function. At least in some realistic applications, it would be useful to estimate each component separately so as to assist design of efficient mechanisms. As of now, this appears a very difficult task both for economic theory as well as econometric method.

(b) All along, it was assumed that the costs incurred by the agents and the principals depend on the planned level of output. However, there may be some ex post flexibility as the randomness unfolds for ordering some components may be postponed, some items can be inventoried for future use, and so on. The principal agent models could not come to grips with this aspect so far.

(c) Some authors have been skeptical about the optimization assumptions of the principal agent models. There are two aspects of this problem. First, when δ is low and/or $\lambda\sigma^2$ is high, the net value addition from the contract is low. The principals and/or agents may not be willing if the net returns to them fall below a threshold. Further, the principal may find it more expensive to monitor such agents in relation to the net value they contribute. Second, when the principal is dealing with many agents, there will be diminishing returns to effort. In addition, the agents may have to approach the principal for the contract rather than the other way around. This is natural in franchise contracts. In such contexts, the principal adds agents when he feels that the net value addition will be satisfactory.

(d) Referring to the case where p^* is fixed a priori by the principal, it would be natural to argue that the choice will vary depending on the product contracted. Hence, there will be some market-related, or other product-specific, characteristic that should be included in the model. Such efforts have not been reported so far.

It would be fair to say that at this stage we cannot speculate about the nature of econometric tools that will adequately resolve the many problems that analysis of contracts presents.

References

Ackerberg DA, Botticini M (2002) Endogenous matching and the empirical determinants of contract form. J Polit Econ 110:564–591

Aggarwal RM (2007) Role of risk sharing and transaction costs in contract choice: theory and evidence from groundwater contracts. J Econ Behav Organ 63:475–496

Ahmadjian C, Oxley J (2006) Using hostages to support exchange: dependence balancing and partial equity stakes in Japanese automotive supplier relationships. J Law Econ Organ 22:213–233

Allen DW, Lueck D (1999) The role of risk in contract choice. J Law Econ Organ 15:704–736

Asanuma B (1989) Manufacturer supplier relationship in Japan and the concept of relation specific skills. J Jpn Int Econ 3:1–30

Asanuma B, Kikutani T (1992) Risk absorption in Japanese subcontracting: a microeconometric study of the automobile industry. J Jpn Int Econ 6:1–29

Baker R (2006) Risk aversion in maintenance: overmaintenance and the principal agent problem. IMA J Manag Math 17:99–113

Barney JB, Ouchi WG (1986) Organizational economics. Jossey Bass Publishers, SanFransisco

Bolton P, Dewatripont M (2005) Contract theory. MIT Press, Cambridge

Borenstein S, Busse M, Kellogg R (2007) Principal agent incentives, excess caution, and market inefficiency: evidence from utility regulation. NBER working paper 13679. Available at www.nber.org/papers/w13679

Brickley JA (2002) Royalty rates and upfront fees in share contracts: evidence from franchising. J Law Econ Organ 18:511–535

Chiappori PA, Salanie B (2003) Testing contract theory: a survey of some recent work. In: Dewatripont M, Hansen LP, Turnovsky SJ (eds) Advances in economics and econometrics-theory and applications. Cambridge University Press, New York

Chisholm DC (1997) Profit sharing versus fixed payment contracts: evidence from the motion picture industry. J Law Econ Organ 13:169–201

Coase R (1937) The nature of the firm. Economica 4:386–405

Coase R (1960) The problem of social cost. J Law Econ 3:1–44

Danzon PM, Nicholson S, Pereira NS (2005) Productivity in pharmaceutical biotechnology R&D: the role of experience and alliances. J Health Econ 24:317–339

Datta PK, Radner R (1994) Optimal principal agent contracts for a class of incentive schemes: a characterization and the rate of approach to efficiency. Econ Theory 4:483–503

Dubois P, Vukina T (2004) Grower risk aversion and the cost of moral hazard in livestock production contracts. Am J Agric Econ 86:835–841

Ferrall C, Shearer R (1999) Incentives and transaction costs within the firm: estimating an agency model using payroll records. Rev Econ Stud 66:309–338

Gonzales-Diaz M, Arrunada B, Fernadez A (2000) Causes of subcontracting: evidence from panel data on construction firms. J Econ Behav Organ 42:167–187

Haubrich JG (1994) Risk aversion, performance pay and the principal agent problem. J Polit Econ 102:258–276

Hernandez MV (2003) Structural estimation of a principal agent model: moral hazard in medical insurance. Rand J Econ 34:670–693

Holmstrom B (1979) Moral hazard and observability. Bell J Econ 10:74–91

Jensen MC, Meckling WH (1976) Theory of the firm: managerial behavior, agency costs, and ownership structure. J Financ Econ 3:305–360

Kaufman P, Lafontaine F (1994) Costs and control: the source of economic rents for McDonald's franchises. J Law Econ 37:417–453

Kawasaki S, McMillan J (1987) The design of contracts: evidence from Japanese subcontracting. J Jpn Int Econ 3:1–30

Lafontaine F (1992) Agency theory and franchising: some empirical results. Rand J Econ 23:263–283

Margiotta MM, Miller RA (2000) Managerial compensation and the cost of moral hazard. Int Econ Rev 41:669–719
Masten SE, Saussier S (2002) Econometrics of contracts: an assessment of developments in the empirical literature on contracting. In: Brousseau E, Glachant JM (eds) The economics of contracts. Cambridge University Press, Cambridge
Milgrom P, Roberts J (1990) Bargaining costs, influence costs, and the organization of economic activity. Cambridge University Press, Cambridge
Mirrlees J (1974) Notes on welfare economics, information, and uncertainty. In: Balch M, McFadden D, Wu S (eds) Essays in economic behavior under uncertainty. North Holland, Amsterdam
Mortimer JH (2000) The effects of revenue sharing contracts on welfare in vertically separated markets: evidence from the video rental industry. Available at www.econ.ucla.edu/placement/2000/files/Holland.pdf
Nichols S (1983) Agency contracts, institutional mode, and the transition to foreign direct investment by British manufacturing multinationals before 1939. J Econ Hist 43:675–686
Okamuro H (2001) Risk sharing in supplier relationship: New evidence from the Japanese automotive industry. J Econ Behav Organ 45:361–381
Paarsch H, Shearer B (2000) Piece rates, fixed wages and incentive effects: statistical evidence from payroll records. Int Econ Rev 41:59–92
Rao CR (1965) Linear statistical inference and its applications. Wiley, New York
Rao TVSR, Sharma R (2006) Equity participation in international joint ventures. Decision 33:1–20
Rees R (1985a) The theory of principal and agent: Part 1. Bull Econ Res 37:3–26
Rees R (1985b) The theory of principal and agent: Part 2. Bull Econ Res 37:75–95
Resende-Filho MA, Buhr BL (2008) A principal agent model for evaluating the economic value of a tractability system: a case study with injection site lesion control in feed cattle. Am J Agric Econ 90:1091–1102
Sharma R, Rao TVSR (2006) Information asymmetry in international joint ventures. Indian Econ J 54:7–20
Sharma R, Rao TVSR (2007) Technology transfer in international joint ventures. Indian J Econ 87:663–678
Sloof R, van Pragg CM (2008) Performance measurement, expectancy, and agency theory: an experimental study. J Econ Behav Organ 67:794–809
Svejnar J, Smith SC (1984) The economics of joint ventures in less developed countries. Q J Econ 99:149–167
Williamson OE (1988) Corporate finance and corporate governance. J Financ 43:567–591
Yun M (1999) Subcontracting relations in the Korean automotive industry: risk sharing and technological capability. Int J Ind Organ 17:81–108

Chapter 14
Conclusion

Abstract This chapter assembles, in a summary fashion, the different sources of exogenous and endogenous randomness encountered in the various contractual contexts examined in the earlier chapters. These risks are essentially due to the attitudes of firms seeking larger market share in imperfect product markets, reducing the quality of products, attempting to make up the imperfection through warranties and insurance, and expanding their financial base through a variety of financial institutions and complex financial products. Attempts to cushion some risks eventually had the effect of increasing the overall risks in the system. Risk sharing activities generally tend to generate greater risk spreading as well. Such risk spreading through contracts has become so endemic that the efficiency of contracts relative to the market mechanism has been undermined. Contracts tend to be more fragile than markets whose inefficiencies they were expected to mitigate. Self-regulatory action by the contracting parties turned out to be inefficient. Regulatory action tends to offer short-term measures to overcome systemic instability in the hope that mature individuals in the contract will behave honorably and bring the system back to a stable equilibrium. However, it appears highly unlikely that the cost minimization originally envisaged can be achieved.

14.1 Sources of Risks

The provision of formal knowledge (blueprints or disclosure at patent stage) will be sufficient for an entrepreneur to scale up plants to an industrial level (e.g., the use of fermentation processes in chemical technology) in the context of several production processes. However, innovation and entrepreneurship invariably involve risks. Some risks are intrinsic to the nature of activity. For instance, when the technology is relatively new, it may be necessary to provide the innovator the informal knowledge in its use. There will be inefficiency and risks if it is absent or inadequate. Some occasions are conceivable where the expected output cannot be realized. It is also possible that production cannot pass regulatory standards (for instance, in the case of pharmaceuticals) or fail at the stage of field trials (in the context of agricultural crops). A variety of such risks are exogenous to the functioning of the enterprise.

T.V.S.R. Rao, *Risk Sharing, Risk Spreading and Efficient Regulation*,
DOI 10.1007/978-81-322-2562-1_14

Stated in a broader context, exogenous randomness has its origins in information asymmetry. First, a principal (say, a landlord) has a number of agents (tenants) he can choose from initially. He is not aware of their commitment, caliber, and/or willingness to adhere to the requirements specified by the principals. Only repeated contracting experience eliminates some of this asymmetry. Second, with respect to the manufacturing sector, the agents face some risks due to patents when the principal who owns the patents does not reveal all the information necessary to "work the patent." Third, an international firm when entering a foreign country cannot have complete information about the available workforce, management culture, and/or the nature of government policies (in particular with respect to taxation, foreign institutional investors, and other financial arrangements). Risk of premature termination and loss of investments loom large. Fourth, a consumer may feel that the firm is not providing information about the quality of products, cost of production, and the commitment to maintain durable goods. On the flip side, the firm may feel that consumers do not have the habits and experience to use products as stipulated and thereby inflict losses to the principal. This is expected in the case of warranties and insurance generally. Such risks are systemic and not specific to any one contracting party. The studies in this book examined these and other sources of exogenous randomness.

Almost as an axiom, one single entrepreneur cannot manage all the affairs of a firm. This may be due to lack of skills to undertake production and/or his inability to market the product. The innovator then agrees to include several other individuals in the activity. The situation is similar if he does not have the finances or can attract them only at a high cost. Thus the advantages of increasing size through collaboration are evident. However, this process generates new problems. The entrepreneur may make a wrong choice of one or more agents (adverse selection). Similarly, one or more agents may renege (free ride on the efforts of others) after the agreement is reached. They may do so even when they are not satisfied with the returns they receive. There will be an inefficient reduction in output and/or an increase in cost (moral hazard). Hence, a large organization has its downside.

Many other possibilities of endogenous randomness have been considered. First, a principal delegates production of most manufactured goods to a large number of agents through subcontracting. Investment requirements, monitoring and control mechanisms, and so on may be specific to subcontractors. Similarly, the principal may find it more efficient to develop system-wide advertising rather than delegate the activity to individual agents. Second, an agent (subcontractor or a franchisee) may undertake reverse engineering and undercut the principal over time. This is probably valid in most international joint ventures. Third, an agent is almost never sure that a foreign firm (the principal) will offer the latest products or technologies. It is more likely that they will pass on obsolete products thereby undercutting the agent. In general, it is quite difficult to anticipate the multitude of factors that account for endogenous randomness.

It is often acknowledged that though some self-seeking individuals reduce the performance of the organization, others tend to complement each other's expertise cooperatively, be more diligent, and commit to the performance of the organization by internalizing its goals. They tend to neutralize the slack or even do better. That is, collaboration of several individuals may reduce the risk. Clearly, with an increase in its size, the firm will experience some advantages of consolidation as well as some increases in costs purely due to the psychological traits of its members. Basically, the difficulties in predicting the outcome are either due to conditions not related to individuals within the firm (exogenous randomness) or due to individual idiosyncrasies of the agents (endogenous randomness).

A much larger variety of risks generated by decisions within the enterprise have been detailed in several chapters of the study. Of particular importance are the attitudes of firms seeking larger market shares in imperfect product markets, reducing the quality of products, and attempting to make up the imperfection through warranties and insurance, and expanding their financial base through a variety of financial institutions and complex financial products (including securitization and derivatives and foreign institutional investors). In other words, attempts to cushion some risks eventually had the effects of making the overall risks in the system larger. Similar tendencies are discernible even in the context of attitudes of consumers of products and services. When a firm provides a warranty on its products, it expects them to use the products in ways specified by them. However, they have no definite way of ascertaining whether a product failed due to a production defect or due to negligent handling by the consumer. Consider the context of accident and health insurance. Individuals (including hospitals and doctors) tend to be careless and increase systemic risks given the knowledge that their mistakes can be passed on to the insurers. In general, risk-sharing attempts resulted in an augmentation of the sources and magnitude of risk. Many details about how risks originate and their magnitude gets to be determined have been elaborated in several chapters of the book.

14.2 Risk Sharing

An increase in the size of an organization generally provides an opportunity to utilize different talents and expertise efficiently and hope that they will internalize the goals of the organization and perform cooperatively. As Coase, and others following him, emphasized, there is an expectation that costs can be reduced. Similarly, cooperative effort can be expected to consolidate risks and effectively reduce their overall impact.

However, discontent and dissonance cannot be ruled out since individuals tend to be selfish and not necessarily work toward a common goal. As a result, some risks are generated in the operation of the contract. In other words, some endogenous randomness can be expected to materialize alongside the systemic risk in the form of exogenous randomness.

When an organization anticipates exogenous randomness, no one individual in the contract may be in a position to bear it. However, an increase in its size provides an organization with the opportunity of sharing risk and rendering it viable. Consider the incidence of exogenous risk. Return to the basic KM model of Sect. 1.2.

The total risk in the transaction can be represented by $V(u)=\sigma^2$. Out of this, the agent, who incurs the entire variable cost, absorbs $p^2\sigma^2$ of risk while the principal bears $(1-p)^2\sigma^2$ of it. In general, $p^2+(1-p)^2<1$. The principal and the agent themselves do not bear the entire risk. Consequently, a portion of the systemic risk (at most $\sigma^2/2$) must be borne by the consumers of the product arising out of the transaction.

Observe that, for the efficient choice of p, the value to the agent is positive only if $\delta>2\lambda\sigma^2$. It was suggested earlier that the principal will contract with only those agents who satisfy this efficiency requirement. Alternatively, recognizing the risk and the inability of the agent to bear it, the principal may agree to share a part of the cost even if he does not monitor and/or control the performance of the agent. It may be noted that the value of p changes to $\delta/(\delta+2s\lambda\sigma^2)$ if the principal agrees to share a fraction $(1-s)$ of the cost. Clearly, the agent's share of output, and consequently his share of risk, increases. Similarly, the share of the risk for the consumer increases whenever $\delta>2s\lambda\sigma^2$. The analysis of equity sharing in international joint ventures will be similar.

Another possibility suggests itself. The scientist providing the knowledge may be expected to share the risk by becoming an agent even if he does not bear any cost of production. It can be readily verified that the risk sharing will be the same as the case with the agent bearing the entire cost. Generally, when confronted with exogenous randomness, these are the mechanisms for diffusing the risk though its overall magnitude cannot be reduced.

The following variation of risk sharing appears in the context of movie distributors and firms selling music CDs. Generally, neither the producers nor the distributors know the market risks a priori. The distributors may not agree to bear the risk if the expected market does not materialize. It is also not possible to make them share the risk. Instead, the producers retrieve the unsold items and bear the entire risk. Risk aversion manifests itself in the form of unwillingness to forego sales if and when the demand arises.

Consider endogenous randomness next. The three alternatives examined above will still be valid. In addition, the principals may make an attempt to decrease it by monitoring and control or providing incentives to the agents to perform better. This may take the form of sharing a part of the costs, increasing the share of output offered to the agent, and several other mechanisms considered throughout the study. Such mechanisms can be generally expected to result in an integrity effect, an incentive effect, and a control effect. Consider the possibility that the endogenous randomness is exclusively due to the actions of the agent. The principal may decide to incur an additional cost ky^2 to monitor the activities of the agent. The fraction of y accruing to the agent reduces to $p=\delta/(\delta+2\lambda\sigma^2+2k\delta^2)$. Hence, the principal bears a higher share of the risk. This method increases costs and reduces the output of the enterprise. Consider the possibility that risk sharing and/or monitoring and control reduces σ^2. A more efficient agent, such that $\delta>2\lambda\sigma^2$, will be expected to bear the brunt of a higher share of risk.

To this point, in the analysis, it is assumed that the principal and/or the agent can finance the variable costs on their own. In practice, they will depend on a variety of financial institutions to undertake the activity. Part of the reason is of course the necessity to share the risks. However, the introduction of several financial instruments augments the risks involved. Analogous to the above analysis, it can be shown that the contracting parties share some risks while making the ultimate consumers accept their share. There is no assurance that the total risks will not increase. Risk pooling occurs alongside increased systemic risk and the corresponding sharing among the contracting parties.

Note that the contractual context did not so far acknowledge the inevitability of fixed investments and the associated fixed costs. The most important feature of fixed investments is that they can be recovered only when the contracts operate over the life of such assets. The possibility of premature termination and the inability to recover a part of the investment must be acknowledged. The principals may then consider three alternative arrangements. First, reduce p commensurate with expected losses due to termination by the agent. Second, if the principal is likely to initiate it, they may increase p. The choice of either of these alternatives is contingent on the accumulated goodwill in the execution of the contract. Third, the principal may ask the agent to share the fixed costs so as to elicit his commitment over the life of the assets. Fourth, in case the termination occurs unexpectedly, they will have to find the means of recovering the remaining value of the assets. However, it is difficult to ascertain whether the specification of randomness adopted so far is adequate or some new dimensions must be incorporated. This may necessitate moving into uncharted territory.

In general, the tendency of consumers to accept and share larger risks increases with the availability of warranties, insurance, and other financial institutions sharing risks. The specific mechanisms utilized to reduce endogenous randomness will however vary depending on the situation under consideration. It is also clear that risk-sharing arrangements may increase or spread risks. For, reverting to the simplest case detailed above, it can be verified that the net value of the transactions increases if $\delta > 2\lambda\sigma^2$. That is, more efficient agents tend to prefer higher risks. This tendency to spread risks will be reviewed in detail in the next section.

14.3 Risk Spreading

Risk spreading generally denotes either an increase in the variance associated with the randomness or the possibility that it will be borne by a larger number of agents and/or financial institutions that share the costs and returns from the transaction. In particular, each individual in an organization may prefer to increase the overall risk in the organization assuming that his own contribution to risk or his share of losses will be much smaller compared to what it would have been if he is operating alone. The expected loss of reputation of an individual whose inefficiency can be identified will be similar. Further, everyone in an organization is motivated to take more risk while expanding activity with the knowledge that he can pass on at least a part of the risks to others. This will be the case especially when the losses created by a free rider may be compensated by others who are more committed to organizational goals. Thus risk-sharing tendencies may augment risks and spread them. Large organizations take more risk and spread them.

Observe that self-interest seeking of principals may indeed suggest this. Consider the simple contract in Sect. 1.2. The value of the contract to the principal increases with σ^2 whenever $\delta > 2\lambda\sigma^2$. This condition will be satisfied whenever the agent derives a positive value from the contract. Implementing such risky projects increases the overall value of the contract as well.

Suppose an inventor has a large number of good ideas and implementable projects. Within their constraints of competence to develop these projects as well as their liquidity constraints, they tend to keep the development of the more promising projects to themselves. Limits of secrecy may in fact motivate them to do so. Once they are convinced of their brand name as their projects get recognized, they will pass on less promising and high-risk projects to others and expect them to share risks. A similar result can be expected when more financial institutions come forward and provide increasing liquidity. Inefficient products spread risks through contracting. The MNCs passing on obsolete and risky technologies and products through joint ventures can be considered to be of the same genre.

The returns to the principal tend to improve if he can entice some agents to share variable costs. In the context of subcontracting and franchises, spreading the burden of fixed investments and associated costs has been observed as well. The process tends to be accelerated both when established organizations wish to expand while preserving their brand name as well as contexts in which the principals anticipate premature termination due to the obsolescence of the products. More often, given the ease with which agents can finance variable costs, risks spread faster if the fixed cost requirements are low. Note, for example, that small service firms get to be started with much fanfare but close due to bankruptcy equally as fast. Such a phenomenon arises due to information asymmetry in markets characterized as monopolistic competition. Consider the case of the producers of movies and music CDs. They are not sure about the market demand a priori. They tend to claim a larger share of their fixed costs from the distributors and retrieve the items left unsold. On occasions, the producers repay only a part of the deposits they collect as a share of fixed costs.

The expansion of trade has concomitant implications for the financial institutions. A high demand for finances, exceeding the credit-generating limits of conventional sources like banks, financial institutions, and the stock market, resulted in novel methods of finance like mutual funds, securitization, complex derivatives, and so on. To enable the special purpose vehicles (usually trusts) to collect receivables, they have been accorded the rights of true sale. They will issue pass-through certificates to investors against such risky collateral. Mortgage-based assets of long duration are a case in point. In general, the conventional response to liquidity problems is to create more financial instruments to cushion risks. However, they appear to spread more risks rather than to reduce them. For, banks and other financial institutions have limited ability to consolidate risks. The risk-spreading nature of greedy individuals who utilize their services may sometimes be such that the losses cannot be recovered. The emergence of nonperforming assets of banks is a case in point. Similar is the context of losses of mutual funds, financial institutions, and the stock market. Credit rating agencies are generally created with the expectation that they can curb, or at least limit, such tendencies. However, they are induced to offer higher ratings with a view to increasing the finances obtained by the originator and consequently their own. The tendency to spread risks has become endemic with very few signs of containing them to acceptable levels.

Expanding activity with the associated possibility of spreading risks through the system manifested itself in the form of low quality of products in the context of products and services as well. Risk-spreading tendencies have become so endemic that even consumers of products and services indulge in such activities. Consider the context of warranties on products and insurance. Individuals tend to be careless and increase systemic risks given the knowledge that their mistakes can be passed on to the producers who offer warranties on durable consumer goods.

Regulatory agencies that offer bailouts in cases of failure do not seem to have the power or willingness to reverse the trend. Instead, they appear to support risk spreading. For, it is taken for granted that they have to compensate losses due to excessive risk taking in the interest of dynamic stability of the larger system.

On the whole, risk spreading through contracts has become so endemic that the efficiency of contracts as a mechanism to conduct transactions has been undermined. Contracts may be more fragile than markets whose inefficiencies they were expected to mitigate.

14.4 Efficient Regulation

The notion of an efficient contract is not as yet in a steady state. Several necessary conditions have been stipulated at one time or the other. First, initially it was conceptualized to mean a mechanism to conduct transactions that will save on costs, for a given level of output, in comparison to what can be achieved by utilizing the market. Second, the shift of emphasis to risk sharing as the basis of contractual efficiency was conceptualized to maximize the net value to all parties in the transaction after accounting for their individual objectives. That is, it has been suggested that a contract will be efficient only if the contracting parties will not deviate from the net value maximizing requirements. In other words, the stability of a contract depends on the inbuilt incentives, monitoring, and commitment of the parties. Third, there is a possibility that either the principals or the agents do not find the contract terms or their implementation satisfactory. This tends to render the system inefficient. Hence, a contract is efficient only if the contract terms can, in effect, be implemented. Fourth, given the contract terms, some principals may not be willing to supply the volume of services demanded. Conversely, some agents may not have the ability to accept the contract terms. The preventive maintenance conditions of a warranty contract and contractual stipulations of health insurance are examples of this nature. Fundamentally, such a situation suggests that the principals and/or the agents are not in a position to recover either variable and/or fixed costs given efficient arrangements. Similarly, some contracts are designed to cover many principals and/or agents and they will be deemed efficient only when their coverage is satisfactory. Fifth, it has been recognized that the principals in a contract will be prone to spread risks while they share them with all the parties in the transaction. However, increases in risks must be within bounds. The system (either a specific contract or several interrelated contracts) will be under strain at some stage when the risks reach catastrophic proportions. Note that principals target high growth rates that imply higher systemic risks. That is, the greed of individuals may drive the system to its brink. The financial crisis of the recent past is testimony to the greed of individuals who feel that they can pass on their losses to others. It is therefore suggested that contracts and risk spreading remain efficient only so long as they do not render the macrolevel system unstable. That is, contracts (and transactions in general) should be limited to what the macrolevel system can bear. On the whole, the process of specifying efficient contracts has been placing much greater attention on sharing risks while neglecting cost reduction originally envisaged. If anything, the possibility of efficient cost reduction is at best a red herring in contemporary transactions.

Several sources and consequences of inefficiency have been identified. First, since there is a difference, perhaps significantly large, between the costs of conducting a transaction utilizing the markets versus contracts, there will always be tendencies on the part of individuals in a contract to inflate costs. This indicates the possibility of the operation of contracts being inefficient. On occasions, the talents of an individual may be such that he can switch between transactions with ease. This tends to lower his commitment to any one of them thereby increasing his bargaining power and the associated costs. Second, similarly, there can be disagreements between the principals and the agents with respect to the risks in the level of activity chosen, the sharing of gains not being commensurate with the risks involved, and so on. A reduction in the commitment will then be evident. Third, the agents generally reveal a low risk aversion at the contracting stage to attract a higher share of output. In general, they may consider this as a bonding signal to the principal and suggest lower opportunity costs than they will deliver when the contract is executed. Similarly, the principals may announce lower levels of monitoring to convince the agent that his freedom of action will not be curtailed. The actual cost of monitoring may be much higher ex post. Fourth, in warranty and insurance contracts and in joint ventures with MNCs (essentially with respect to technological commitments of foreign firms and regulatory standards of the recipient government), the initial contract terms may indicate lower risks compared to those that materialize in the execution of contracts. It can therefore be suggested that inefficiency of contracts is discernible whenever the costs increase, output is reduced (perhaps due to disagreements in sharing gains), or there is an increase in the level of implied risks. As noted earlier, some inefficiencies may be due to exogenous randomness and others are purely endogenous to the operation of contracts. Similarly, some inefficiencies affect only the parties in the specific contract while others will have macroeconomic systemic consequences.

Confronted with a variety of inefficiencies, the parties to the contracts may initiate self-regulatory action. First, some exogenous randomness and the associated systemic risks, like the incidence of an epidemic, can be controlled if the agents are diligent and insure themselves. Second, the principals can define policies with respect to shares of investment, equity and output sharing fractions, and so on in such a way that the least efficient agents do not gain. The resulting self-selection process by agents minimizes risks. Third, when confronted with high variable and/or fixed cost, the agent may suggest that the stipulated contract terms do not compensate him adequately. The principal may then offer a two-part tariff or a minimum bills contract to cover the fixed cost of the agent. Fourth, some firms may choose collaboration with foreign firms, foreign direct investment, and foreign institutional investors based on past experience with the quality of products and technology and their commitment to continue investments over a long enough time. Such self-regulatory measures can mitigate the incidence of inefficiency. Regulatory activity by the contracting parties may be either ex ante or ex post when infringement is recorded. The principals can be expected to evaluate the promised gains and risks so that expected losses, when they occur, can be kept within the limits that the system can bear. Given the value attributed to individual freedom of action, they will consider this option only if their ability to pass on risks is restricted. The significant increases in the nonperforming assets of banks and consistently poor performance of mutual funds do not suggest the possibility of correction at this level. Similarly, none of the agents is the ultimate bearer of systemic risks. Hence, it would appear that restraint at the level of agents will not be forthcoming without coercion from outside. There is then a necessity for regulatory action to overcome the likely disaster that leads to systemic consequences which the contracting parties cannot control.

Government regulation is necessary in two situations. First, it may be necessary to set up an environment in which contracts will be efficient. In particular, the environment should be defined so that the overall systemic risks can be contained within limits. Some maximum ex ante measure of risks and the possibility of their accurate measurement would facilitate defining and enforcing such constraints. One example of this nature will be the specification of quality of products or the level of service in health care. This may be referred to as enabling regulation. Its main purpose would be to prevent the creation of excessive risk. Second, there are many contracts in which interrelated transactions and the risks that may be generated cannot be ascertained ex ante. They will manifest themselves in contract execution and they can be recognized only ex post. Regulation to reduce such risks will perforce be defined and enforced ex post. Enabling regulation will cover most contracts, whereas ex post regulation emphasizes control to return the system to stability. Similarly, ex post regulatory measures may target soft options like output so that the consequences can be observed over a relatively short time. On the other hand, ex ante regulation will involve hard options that take a longer time to materialize but will have a lasting effect. Note, further, that some infringements affect only the parties in the contract while others have system-wide ramifications. The former class of contracts can generally be dealt with through enabling regulation though some ex post control in case of noncompliance will be warranted. The latter class is far more difficult to anticipate so that preventive regulation can be specified. Perforce, they require corrective action ex post.

Several types of ex ante regulation have been observed. First, suppose an agency, or a regulator, suspects that firms will not limit risks of financial instruments like IPOs (initial public offerings). The creation and efficient functioning of credit rating agencies who endorse such instruments may be deemed adequate. However, their own self-interest generally vitiates such faith placed on them. Second, to prevent the emergence and growth of nonperforming assets of banks, the system stipulated that they should hold with a designated central bank a proportion of their deposits. This is expected to protect the depositors but it does not prevent banks from lending to borrowers that cannot repay. Perhaps the deposit should be made proportional to the loans instead. Third, to prevent the flight of hot money in the form of foreign institutional investors, there may be a regulation stipulating that a proportion of such remittances must be held in reserve with a regulator until a stipulated minimum time. Fourth, interest rates and other conditions for the grant of loans may be defined so that projects that will have risks in excess of some specified maximum can be discouraged. Fifth, consider the setting up of an insurance company. Several dimensions may necessitate regulation. (a) They require a certain minimum investment to be in a position to service their likely liability. (b) They should also invest their deposits in instruments that promise returns commensurate with their estimated liabilities. (c) Similarly, the regulator may restrict entry of new firms if there is a possibility that the system cannot sustain such spreading of risks. (d) The process of granting and setting up an insurance company may result in large premiums that some potential insurers (who require the service) cannot afford. Some regulatory action may be necessary to accommodate such social welfare requirements. In general, each contracting situation has its own internal logic and the ex ante measures will depend on them.

Ex post regulation is of two types. First, consider the possibility that the conflict is between specific agents and a principal. For instance, a firm may refuse to honor a warranty on the grounds that the consumer did not exercise due diligence in the use of the product as stipulated at the time of purchase. Clearly, the regulatory response can take the form of recourse to courts. Second, in response to observed systemic losses, the regulators prefer to maintain their faith in individual initiative to restore stability of the activity over the long run and offer bailouts to normalize the system in the short run. However, note that systemic instability cannot be contained within acceptable limits when this regulatory response becomes endemic and the contracting parties take it for granted that the necessary bailouts will be forthcoming. Even in the context of ex post regulation, the possibilities are many and no set logic or method of regulation has emerged.

14.5 Future Action

To make efficient regulation operational, i.e., to allow only those activities whose risks are within bounds and their costs are commensurate with gains and so on, has been a challenging task. This is reinforced by the large variety of contexts that necessitate regulation. Hence, a fairly disaggregate level of regulatory action is all that can be conceptualized. Similarly, contracts may be preferred to markets since there is less control and a lower probability of extensive disaggregate level of efficient regulation emerging in the near future. This, in itself, makes the regulatory task very daunting. Further, the tendency of individuals to credit themselves with gains when they materialize but attribute losses to the macroeconomic system and expect regulatory corrective action has been endemic. Discrediting the government for the risks and losses that individuals managed to spread has become the order of the day. It would be fair to suggest that the hypothesized gains through contracts have been difficult to achieve. A return to the market mechanism to replace contracts is unlikely given that they have been endemic to the system. At some stage, the limitations of regulatory action to correct repeated systemic failures may offer the best hope for the emergence of the most efficient self-regulatory mechanisms. An empirical evaluation of the relative efficiency of contracts versus the market mechanism is fraught with many conceptual problems so that the process is yet to begin on a desirable scale.

MIX
Papier aus verantwortungsvollen Quellen
Paper from responsible sources
FSC® C105338

If you have any concerns about our products,
you can contact us on
ProductSafety@springernature.com

In case Publisher is established outside the EU,
the EU authorized representative is:
Springer Nature Customer Service Center GmbH
Europaplatz 3, 69115 Heidelberg, Germany

Printed by Libri Plureos GmbH
in Hamburg, Germany